Matching Contributions for Pensions

Matching Contributions for Pensions

A REVIEW OF INTERNATIONAL EXPERIENCE

Edited by

*Richard Hinz, Robert Holzmann, David Tuesta, and
Noriyuki Takayama*

THE WORLD BANK
Washington, D.C.

ISBN (paper): 978-0-8213-9492-2
eISBN (electronic): 978-0-8213-9493-9
DOI: 10.1596/978-0-8213-9492-2

Cover photos: World Bank; *cover design:* Naylor Design

Library of Congress Cataloging-in-Publication Data has been requested.

Contents

Tables

Foreword

Establishing robust, equitable, and effective social protection is essential to reducing poverty and boosting prosperity at all levels of development. The demographic transition that has already transformed most high-income societies will exert similar and growing pressures on others, reinforcing the role of pensions and savings for old age as a central pillar of social protection systems.

Despite this increasing imperative, achieving full coverage and adequate benefits within a financially sustainable pension system remains a difficult challenge for nearly every country. Some that had previously been able to provide generous benefits to earlier generations now face difficult reductions for future retirees and will need to establish supplementary elements of their systems to maintain adequate income for the elderly. Others must find ways to bring the dynamic and rapidly changing workforce of a global competitive economy into their systems to maintain the promise of security in old age.

After decades of reform and innovation ranging from individual mandates to creative forms of tax incentives, coverage of pension systems often remains at less than half of the economically active population—in part because the incentives for contributing to pension savings are often obscure or irrelevant to those who need this protection the most: young and low-income individuals with irregular earnings and little attachment to the formal labor force. Traditional forms of tax incentives have little relevance to those not paying income taxes, and participation mandates are difficult to enforce in the informal sector.

One possible solution that has emerged in recent years that offers the potential to overcome this challenge is the provision of contribution matches to provide an immediate and powerful incentive for participation in pension saving systems. Originating in several high-income settings there are now a number of innovations and substantial experience in low-income countries in using this design to stimulate coverage and savings. This experience now provides a rich opportunity for learning, not just from the longer experience of a few high-income countries but also the more meaningful South-South learning across developing countries.

This volume, which reviews the experience with matching pension contributions across the range of countries that have used the design, makes an initial, but critically important investment in this learning process. The description and analysis of this experience—which is the product of partnership and collaboration across many public and private institutions—provide an invaluable early assessment of the design to inform policy makers and practitioners as well as serve as a model for the kind of cooperation that will be required to address this difficult challenge. At the World Bank, we look forward to being part of this learning process of how to best provide old-age security for all.

Arup Banerji
Director for Social Protection and Labor
The World Bank

Acknowledgments

This publication is the result of extensive collaboration of a diverse group of individuals and institutions. The project originates with an effort to develop new research and policy analysis focused on the challenge of closing the coverage gap, under the leadership of Robert Holzmann in his previous role as Director of Social Protection and Labor at the World Bank and Professor Noriyuki Takayama as Head of the Project on Intergenerational Equity (PIE) of the Research Institute on Policies for Pension and Aging (RIPPA). This effort identified matching contributions as a promising method of extending pension coverage that was increasingly being used by developing countries, leading to a subsequent conference focusing on the use of matching contributions held in June of 2011 at the World Bank.

The conference and this resulting publication were organized and managed by Richard Hinz of the Social Protection Team of the World Bank's Human Development Network (HDNSP), with financial support from the World Bank, PIE/RIPPA through a Grant-in-Aid for Specially Promoted Research from the Japan Society for the Promotion of Science, and the Spanish Bank BBVA. The project would not have been possible without the support of HDNSP's management team during this period, including Arup Banerji, Bassam Ramadan, and Anush Bezhanyan. David Tuesta, Eduardo Fuentes, Enrique Summers, Miguel Angel Caballero, and Patricio Urrutia from BBVA have been instrumental in supporting the effort.

The conference and publication involved contributions from many individuals. In addition to the authors of the chapters, these include participants at the conference who provided lively discussion and insights that focused and refined the issues and presentations. Especially valuable in this process have been Sylvester Schieber, Rafael Rofman, and Gonzalo Reyes, who provided peer review comments on the first draft of the publication. Barbara Karni provided invaluable work in editing the draft chapters, as did Nita Congress in the final copyediting, layout, and design of the book. The timely advice and support of Paola Scalabrin of the World Bank has been essential in completing the publication process. As always, none of this would have been possible without the tireless efforts of the administrative support staff at the World Bank in managing all of the logistics for the conference and publication, notably Amira Nikolas, Francine Pagsibigan, Merced Doroteo, and Sandra Friedman.

Contributors

NEVIN ADAMS is Director of Education and External Relations at the nonpartisan Employee Benefit Research Institute (EBRI), and Co-Director of EBRI's Center for Research on Retirement Income. Prior to joining EBRI in November 2011, he was Global Editor-in-Chief of *PLANSPONSOR* magazine and its web counterpart PLANSPONSOR.com. He is a veteran of the retirement sector, having served in a series of senior management positions in both the defined benefit and defined contribution plan fields at Wachovia Bank and Northern Trust Corporation. He holds B.S. and J.D. degrees from DePaul University in Chicago.

PAULA BENAVIDES is Head of the Research and Actuarial Studies Department of the Budget Office within Chile's Ministry of Finance. Previously, she served as an Economist within the Budget Office's Department of Research, and researched the structural balance of the public sector. In 2006, she was appointed to lead a team providing technical support for the preparation of the law creating Chile's new pension system reform. She holds a master's degree in economics and a commercial engineering degree from the Catholic University of Chile.

AXEL BÖRSCH-SUPAN is Director of the Max Planck Institute for Social Law and Social Policy in Munich, leading the Munich Center for the Economics of Aging (MEA). Previously, he was a Professor of macroeconomics and economic policy at the University of Mannheim, and an Assistant Professor of public policy at Harvard University. He is a member of the German National Academy of Sciences Leopoldina and the Berlin-Brandenburg Academy of Sciences, and a Research Associate at the National Bureau of Economic Research in Cambridge, Massachusetts. He is member of the Council of Advisors to the German Economics Ministry and has co-chaired the German Pension Reform Commission. He has a Ph.D. in economics from the Massachusetts Institute of Technology.

LUIS CARRANZA is Head of the Economics Department at the Universidad San Martín. Previously, he served as Minister of Finance of the government of Peru. He has also served as Peru's Deputy Minister of Finance and as a Board Member of the Central Bank of Peru, and as Chief Economist for Latin America and Emerging Markets in BBVA, among other positions. He holds a Ph.D. in economics from the University of Minnesota.

JIE CHENG is an Assistant Professor at the Institute of Population and Labor Economics, the Chinese Academy of Social Sciences. His research interests include social security, migration and rural development, poverty alleviation, and income distribution. He received his Ph.D. in agricultural economics from the China Agriculture University in 2009.

MICHELA COPPOLA is Head of the Macroeconomic Implications of an Aging Society Research Unit at the Munich Center for the Economics of Aging (MEA). Her research focuses on the analysis of the effects of population aging and pension reforms on saving behavior and on asset choices. She has been with the center since 2007, when it was known as the Mannheim Research Institute. She has degrees in economics from the University of Rome Tor Vergata and the Munich Graduate School of Economics at the Ludwig Maximilian Universität.

ANTOINE DELARUE is an Actuary and Economist, Founder and Managing Director of the consulting firm SERVAC, which specializes in pension scheme design and social transfer engineering. In France, his audits of compulsory pension schemes often led to significant reforms or mergers, linked with the development of new analytical concepts and tools to monitor these. Since 1996, he has developed overseas activities on social insurance issues in numerous developing countries in Eastern Europe, Central Asia, Africa, and Central America. He currently focuses on designing and implementing schemes that extend social coverage. He previously served in the French planning authority, then in the social security administration at a senior governmental level. He graduated from the École Polytechnique in Paris and holds a Ph.D. in applied economics from Stanford University.

MARK C. DORFMAN is a Senior Economist with the Pensions Team in the Social Protection Department of the World Bank where he works on pensions, social security, and contractual savings reform. He has prepared multiple reports on the Chinese pension system, beginning in 1999 when he worked in the World Bank's East Asia and Pacific Region. During his 24 years with the Bank, he has worked on different areas of pension and financial market reform in Latin America and the Caribbean, Sub-Saharan Africa, and East Asia and the Pacific. He holds an MBA in finance from the Wharton School.

RICHARD HINZ is a Pension Policy Adviser for the Social Protection Team of the Human Development Network at the World Bank. Since he joined the Bank in 2003, his work has been focused on the reform of social security systems and the development, regulation, and supervision of funded pension arrangements—subjects on which he has authored and edited a number of articles and publications. Prior to this, he was the Director of the Office of Policy and Research at what is now the Employee Benefits Security Administration of the U.S. Department of Labor, where he managed the economic research and legislative analysis for the agency responsible for regulation and supervision of employer-sponsored pension and health insurance programs in the United States.

ROBERT HOLZMANN holds the chair of Old Age Financial Protection at the University of Malaya (Malaysia) and is a Research Fellow of the Institute for the Study of Labor (IZA) in Bonn and of the CESifo Group Munich. He also serves as a Consultant on financial literacy and education, pensions, labor market, and migration issues. From 1997 to 2011, he held various positions at the World Bank, including Director for Social Protection and Labor. Before joining the Bank, he was a Professor in Germany and Austria, and a Senior Economist at the International Monetary Fund and the Organisation for Economic Co-operation and Development. He has published 33 books and over 150 articles on social, fiscal, and financial policy issues.

BRIGITTE C. MADRIAN is the Aetna Professor of Public Policy and Corporate Management at the Harvard Kennedy School and a Research Associate and Co-Director of the Household Finance working group at the National Bureau of Economic Research. Her research focuses on household saving and investment behavior and has twice been awarded the TIAA-CREF Paul A. Samuelson Award for Scholarly Research on Lifelong Financial Security. She received her Ph.D. in economics from the Massachusetts Institute of Technology.

ÁNGEL MELGUIZO is a Lead Specialist in pensions in the Labor Markets and Social Security Unit at the Inter-American Development Bank (IDB). Before joining the IDB, he worked as an Economist at the Americas Desk of the Organisation for Economic Co-operation and Development's Development Center, contributing to its regional flagship publication *Latin American Economic Outlook*. Previously, he was a Senior Adviser at the Economic Bureau of the Spanish Prime Minister, and a principal economist at the BBVA Financial Group, specializing in research on pension reform in Latin America, fiscal policy, and long-term economic growth. His research interests include Latin America, development, fiscal policy, social security, and pensions. He holds a Ph.D. in public economics and a B.A. in economics from Complutense University of Madrid.

HYUNGPYO MOON is a senior research fellow of the Korea Development Institute (KDI). He joined the KDI in 1989 and served as Director of the department of fiscal policy and social development, and as Managing Director of the Economic Information and Education Center of the KDI. He is also a former Visiting Scholar of the University of California at Berkeley and Assistant Secretary of the Health and Welfare Division in the Office of the President of the Republic of Korea. He has written on numerous socio-economic issues, including tax and fiscal policy, social welfare policy, population aging, and pension systems in Korea. His recent publications include *A Comprehensive Study on Constructing an Old-Age Income Security System in Korea (2007–2008)* and *Socio-Economic Impacts of Population Ageing and Policy Issues (2004–2006)*. He earned a Ph.D. in economics from the University of Pennsylvania in 1989.

PHILIP O'KEEFE is Lead Economist and Human Development Sector Coordinator for China and Mongolia in the East Asia and Pacific Region of the World Bank. He has worked on social protection, labor market, and social services in Eastern Europe and Central Asia, India and Nepal, and the Pacific Islands. Prior to joining the World Bank in 1993, he was University Lecturer in international economic law at the University of Warwick, U.K.

MIKE ORSZAG is Head of Research for Towers Watson, the actuarial and human resources consulting firm. He is also a founding editor of the *Journal of Pension Economics and Finance* (Cambridge University Press) and a co-editor of the *Oxford Handbook of Pensions and Retirement Income*. He holds a Ph.D. in economics from the University of Michigan and an A.B. from Princeton University. He is a member of a number of scientific advisory boards including the Boston College Center for Retirement Research and the Kiel Institute of the World Economy.

ROBERT PALACIOS is Pension Team Leader in the Social Protection Unit of the World Bank. Between 1992 and 1994, he was a member of the team that produced the Bank's influential volume on international pension systems, *Averting the Old Age Crisis: Policies to Protect the Old and Promote Growth*. Since 1995, he has divided his time between operational work and research in more than two dozen countries, most recently focusing on South Asia. His publications include articles and books on old-age poverty, health insurance, and a wide range of pension policy issues.

WILL PRICE is a World Bank Senior Financial Sector Specialist. He focuses on improving pension system design, regulation, supervision, and outcomes, working with client countries and on regional and global issues. He was Head of Policy at the U.K. Pensions Regulator and Vice-Chair of the International Organisation of Pension Supervisors Technical Committee. At the U.K. Finance Ministry, he was Private Secretary to the Chancellor, Head of Assets, Savings and Wealth and worked on development there and at the Department for International Development (DFID). He has degrees in economics from Oxford University and University College London and is a member of the Royal Economic Society and Chartered Institute of Insurance.

GEOFF RASHBROOKE is a Fellow of the Institute of Actuaries. His work experience includes five years as New Zealand Government Actuary and five years as a Principal Policy Analyst with the New Zealand Department of Social Development. He is currently an honorary Research Associate with the Institute of Governance and Policy Studies of Victoria University of Wellington, and a committee member of the Pensions, Benefits and Social Security section of the International Association of Actuaries. He also provides actuarial services to assist ongoing reform of the Fiji National Provident Fund.

ANETTE REIL-HELD studied economics at the Universität Mannheim. As part of an interdisciplinary research network, the Sonderforschungsbereich 504, she undertook research into the relationship between private transfers, saving behavior, and the public pension system. In 2002 she earned her Ph.D. at Universität Mannheim. She managed what is now the Munich Center for the Economics of Aging's (MEA's) research unit on Old-Age Provision and Social Policy between 2002 and 2008 and was Chief Operating Officer until 2008. Her main research interests are saving behavior and social policy.

DALLAS SALISBURY is president and CEO of the Employee Benefit Research Institute (EBRI). He is a Fellow of the National Academy of Human Resources. He currently serves as an appointee of President Obama on the Pension Benefit Guaranty Corporation

(PBGC) Advisory Committee (having served in the late 1980s as an appointee of President George H. W. Bush) and an appointee of the Comptroller General of the United States to his Board of Advisors. Mr. Salisbury has written and lectured extensively on economic security topics. He holds a B.A. from the University of Washington and an M.P.A. from the Maxwell School of Citizenship and Public Affairs.

RENUKA SANE is a Research Economist with the Finance Research Group at the Indira Gandhi Institute of Development Research, Mumbai. Her research interests include pension economics, household finance, financial intermediation, and public policy. She has a Ph.D. in economics from the University of New South Wales, Sydney, Australia.

NORIYUKI TAKAYAMA is Distinguished Scholar at the Research Institute for Policies on Pension and Aging (RIPPA) and JRI Pension Research Chair Professor at Hitotsubashi University. He holds a Ph.D. from the University of Tokyo. He is Director General and Chief Executive Officer of a Research Project on Intergenerational Equity (PIE). His articles have been published in *Econometrica* and *American Economic Review*. His publications include *Taste of Pie: Searching for Better Pension Provisions in Developed Countries*, *Closing the Coverage Gap: Role of Social Pensions and Other Retirement Income Transfers*, and *Priority Challenges in Pension Administration*. He is the author of a Japanese book, *Saving and Wealth Formation*, which was awarded the 1996 Nikkei Prize for the best book on economic issues.

DAVID TUESTA is Chief Economist of the Pension Unit of BBVA Research. He previously held the position of Global Trends Chief Economist and Chief Economist of Peru with BBVA Research. He has also worked for the Ministry of Finance of Peru as Chief Economist at the National Tax Authority, and was a Board Member of the Peruvian National Energy Regulatory Authority and an Economist for Apoyo Consulting. His research is mainly focused on public finance, fiscal decentralization, pensions, and banking.

JACK VANDERHEI is the Research Director of the Employee Benefit Research Institute (EBRI). He is also the Director of both the EBRI Defined Contribution and Participant Behavior Research Program and the EBRI Retirement Security Research Program and the Co-Director of the EBRI Center for Research on Retirement Income. He has worked on more than 150 research publications devoted to employee benefits and insurance. His major areas of research focus on the financial aspects of private retirement plans. He received his B.B.A. and M.B.A. from the University of Wisconsin–Madison and his M.A. and Ph.D. from the Wharton School of the University of Pennsylvania.

HERMANN VON GERSDORFF is Vice Chair of the Budget Office within Chile's Ministry of Finance. He previously worked for the World Bank in Washington, D.C., Zagreb, and Buenos Aires as Manager and Economist for Social Protection, Finance and Private Sector Development for Europe and Central Asia and Latin America. With the United Nations Economic Commission for Latin America and the Caribbean, he served in Mexico as an Economist in the Industrial Department. He was a Professor of project evaluation at the Instituto Tecnológico Autónomo de México, and a Professor in price theory at both the Universidad de Chile and the Universidad del Norte, Chile. He was a Program Officer with the United Nations Industrial Development Organization in Venezuela. He holds degrees from the University of Chicago and the University of Cologne.

DEWEN WANG is a Social Protection Economist for China and Mongolia in the East Asia and Pacific Region of the World Bank in Beijing. His work focuses on China's social insurance and social assistance programs, labor market dynamics, demographic transition, and population aging. He was a Professor and Division Chief of the Institute of Population and Labor Economics, Chinese Academy of Social Sciences, before he joined the World Bank Social Protection team.

EDWARD WHITEHOUSE is Head of Pension Policy Analysis in the Social Policy Division of the Organisation for Economic Co-operation and Development (OECD). He is lead author of the OECD flagship report on retirement income systems, *Pensions at a Glance*, whose fourth edition was published in March 2011, and a range of publications including the first three chapters of *OECD Pensions Outlook 2012* and the joint World Bank–OECD report *Pensions Panorama: Retirement-Income Systems in 53 Countries*, published in November 2006. He has worked on pension reform in a number of countries with the World Bank and the OECD. Previously, he was a lead writer and social affairs correspondent for the *Financial Times* and worked at the Institute for Fiscal Studies in London.

MITCHELL WIENER is a Pension Actuary with more than 35 years of domestic and international experience. He is currently the World Bank's Social Protection leader in the Indonesia country office and one of the Bank's pension leaders in the East Asia and Pacific region. He has extensive international experience, primarily in Southeast Asia and Eastern Europe. His focus has been on the reform of national social security systems, introduction of mandatory and voluntary private pension systems, improvement of pension and insurance regulation, and development of the local actuarial profession. He has worked on pension issues in Thailand in various capacities for the past 10 years.

Abbreviations

BEP	Beneficios Económicos Periódicos (Periodic Economic Benefits) (Colombia)
CODA	cash or deferred arrangement
EBRI	Employment Benefit Research Institute
EGTRRA	Economic Growth and Tax Relief Reconciliation Act (United States)
EPF	Employee Pension Fund (Japan)
EPFO	Employee Provident Fund Organization (India)
ERISA	Employee Retirement Income Security Act (United States)
FGPM	Fondo de Garantía de Pensión Mínima (Minimum Pension Guarantee Fund) (Colombia)
FPS	Ficha de Protección Social (Social Protection Index) (Chile)
FSP	Fondo de Solidaridad Pensional (Pension Solidarity Fund) (Colombia)
GDP	gross domestic product
ICI	Investment Company Institute
IDA	individual development account
IMSS	Instituto Mexicano de Seguridad Social (Mexican Social Security Institute)
INPS	Instituto Nacional de Previdência Social (National Institute of Social Protection) (Cape Verde)
IRA	individual retirement account
IRS	Internal Revenue Service (United States)
ISSSTE	Instituto de Seguridad Social y Servicios Sociales de los Trabajadores del Estado (Institute for Civil Servant Social Insurance and Services) (Mexico)
KGFS	Kshetriya Grameen Financial Services
KNH	Kosei Nenkin Hoken (Japan)
MAROP	Mecanismo de Ahorro para el Retiro Oportunidades (Mechanism for Saving for Retirement Opportunities) (Mexico)
MDC	matching defined contribution
MHRSS	Ministry of Human Resources and Social Security (China)
MOCA	Ministry of Civil Affairs (China)
MYPES	micro- and small enterprises (*micro y pequeñas empresas*)
NHCE	non–highly compensated employee
NPS	New Pension Scheme (India)
NRPS	National Rural Pension Scheme (China)

NSF	National Savings Fund (Thailand)
OECD	Organisation for Economic Co-operation and Development
PAYE	pay as you earn (New Zealand)
PENSIONISSTE	National Pension Fund for Civil Servants (Mexico)
RAIS	Individual Savings System with Solidarity (Régimen de Ahorro Individual con Solidaridad) (Colombia)
RAP	retirement allowance plan (Japan)
RPM	Régimen de Prima Media (Average Premium System) (Colombia)
RPPS	Rural Pension Pilot Scheme (China)
SEJ	Subsidio al Empleo Joven (Youth Employment Subsidy) (Chile)
SPTJ	Subsidio Previsional a los Trabajadores Jóvenes (Social Security Subsidy for Young Workers) (Chile)
TQPP	Tax-Qualified Pension Plan (Japan)
URPS	Urban Resident Pension Scheme (China)
UTAP	Union Tunisienne de l'Agriculture et de la Pêche (Tunisian Union of Agriculture and Fishing) (Tunisia)

All dollar amounts are U.S. dollars unless otherwise indicated.

PART I

Introduction and Conceptual Issues

CHAPTER 1

Early Lessons from Country Experience with Matching Contribution Schemes

Robert Holzmann, Richard Hinz, and David Tuesta

Matching defined contribution schemes are gaining popularity in both rich and poor countries as a promising means to reduce gaps in the participation in formal pension systems. Matching contributions by employers, the government, or both to defined contribution schemes are used alone or jointly with other interventions to motivate participation in pension schemes. Although it remains far too early to develop firm conclusions or policy guidance, this chapter provides an overview of the currently available evidence that is presented in this volume and offers preliminary observations about the potential use of this design. This experience, mostly derived from higher-income countries that is now being supplemented with some early experience from other settings, suggests that matching is moderately effective in increasing program participation but not generally measurably effective in raising contributions and thus benefit levels. Other interventions—which are increasingly guided by lessons from behavioral economics and finance—may prove to be more effective and typically cost much less, which may help explain some of the differences in outcomes across countries. It is not yet clear how transferrable the experience in higher-income environments will be to other settings; considerable further evaluation is needed before any firm conclusions can be reached.

Addressing the Coverage Gap

Achieving broad pension coverage and adequate levels of income protection in old age remains an elusive goal for nearly every country. In general, coverage has advanced with development and growth in income, and there is a strong relationship between the level of per capita income and participation in formal pension systems. However, there are considerable differences among countries at similar levels of development in pension coverage and in the way in which participation in pension systems has evolved in different settings. The differences in experiences and outcomes indicate that context, the design of the system, and the path of its development play a central role in the dynamics of pension coverage and benefit levels.

In the vast majority of countries, less than half the working population is currently covered by a formal pension scheme. In low-income and developing countries, the number of working-age adults participating in a pension scheme is very often less than 1 in

---

This chapter was presented at review meetings and seminars in Madrid and Washington, D.C., and has profited from written comments by internal and external reviewers, in particular by Will Price, Rafael Rofman, and Sylvester Schieber. The authors are grateful for the comments and suggestions received but are ultimately responsible for any gaps or errors. The views expressed are their own and do not necessarily reflect those of the institutions with which they are affiliated.

10. Many middle-income countries have seen coverage rates decline in recent decades despite the expansion of coverage mandates and efforts to reform their systems to establish stronger individual incentives (Rofman and Oliveri 2012). In higher-income countries, coverage levels under mandated schemes remain high, but fiscal pressures caused by the generous benefits provided to early cohorts and exacerbated by rapidly falling fertility rates are now imposing the need for reductions in future benefit levels. Such reductions will require a substantial increase in supplementary retirement savings if income replacement rates are to be maintained.

All of these factors have brought the imperative for the extension of coverage to the forefront of the pension policy debate. An earlier World Bank publication investigated the role of social pensions and other transfers to increase retirement income support across countries of different development levels (Holzmann, Robalino, and Takayama 2009). This volume extends the consideration of how to provide adequate income to elderly populations by focusing on the potential role of matching contributions to induce broader participation in pensions and other retirement saving to help close the coverage and adequacy gap.

THE POTENTIAL PROMISE OF MATCHING CONTRIBUTION SYSTEMS

An approach that has been adopted in a growing number of high-income countries is the provision of matching contributions. These contributions provide more tangible incentives for individuals to participate in pension funds than the more traditional approach of mandating participation and providing preferential tax treatment, especially for low-income groups and individuals who may not participate in the formal labor force and therefore receive no advantage from tax-based incentives.

In principle, matching contributions may be provided for public programs or by the sponsors of private occupational plans and could be associated with either defined contribution or defined benefit systems. In practice, there are numerous cases of both public and private schemes utilizing the design; however, nearly all current examples are associated with various types of individual retirement savings accounts. This volume, which reviews experience to date and seeks to derive some initial observations and policy lessons, focuses on what is here termed matching defined contribution (MDC) schemes.

In all of these systems, the matching design feature has the common goal of increasing system participation and saving levels. Four characteristics are common to MDC schemes examined here: individual accounts, defined contribution, direct contribution from sponsor to complement individual contributions, and prefunding of benefits. The prevalence of defined contribution systems is likely a reflection of two factors. First, although in theory it is possible to incorporate a contribution match in a defined benefit system, the linkages between the match and the benefit received are complex and less transparent. More importantly, the populations these arrangements are seeking to reach, especially lower-income groups or those in developing countries, may have irregular earning patterns over their life cycle or be predominantly engaged in the informal sector. The systems reviewed vary considerably in the structure and level of the matching contribution. Although the majority of schemes provide ex ante matches, some provide ex post matches.

The use of individual accounts with defined contributions as the underlying structure provides direct linkages between density and level of contributions to align individual incentives and provides transparency in the value of benefits. Directly matching contributions provides an immediate and easily understandable value proposition to prospective entrants to the system. Funding of the accumulated contributions and returns with financial institutions should offer credibility, portability, and appropriate returns. The expected saving incentives created by MDCs are an alternative or complement to other potential incentives such as preferential tax treatment and the presentation of choices in a way intended to influence behavior (what Thaler and Sunstein have termed "nudging"), as well as efforts to create a more conducive old-age saving environment such as financial education and straightforward advocacy. MDC schemes are also attractive because they define and constrain future fiscal exposure. They should increase coverage but not encourage informality. If individuals are sufficiently incentivized by the match, the accumulated amounts at retirement may reduce or even eliminate the need for basic benefits. Inducing funded supplemental coverage will facilitate reductions in mandated public systems for higher-income groups. Ideally, coverage should increase and the level of labor informality decrease at lower fiscal costs than expanding noncontributory systems or subsidizing earnings-based defined benefit programs.

POLICY QUESTIONS

Addressing the coverage gap raises a range of interrelated policy questions that vary by setting. In low- and middle-income countries, the primary challenge is to expand pension coverage beyond civil servants and the small proportion of the workforce employed in the formal sector. When much of the labor force has no fixed employer, or is self-employed, the traditional method of expanding coverage through wage-based mandated contributions is not a viable option. In these countries, establishing pension systems with incentives for participation that are attractive to low-income and young people with no prior experience with social insurance and saving systems imposes enormous challenges. These groups nearly always struggle to meet short-term needs and require liquidity in any savings that they are able to accrue in order to manage a variety of risks. Effective solutions must not impose disincentives for participation in the formal sector through high payroll tax contributions or create adverse redistribution through tax-based subsidies that provide value only to the highest-income groups.

In other middle-income settings, the challenge is to maintain the coverage rates achieved in earlier decades in the face of increasing informality of the workforce due to transitions from centrally planned economies or changes in labor patterns resulting from economic development and competition in a global economy. In middle-income and most higher-income countries, the imperative is also to establish retirement income and saving systems that are able to supplement the diminished capacity of earlier earnings-based public systems in order to provide adequate income replacement for future cohorts. The social policy concern is accentuated by low, stagnating, and at times falling coverage of old-age pensions and other social programs—a stark contrast with expectations that emerging economies would follow the same path as the current high-income economies, achieving coverage expansion in step with income growth.

When initially confronted with this coverage challenge, policy makers believed that reforms designed to establish better links between contributions and benefits in mandated and earnings-related schemes, often by creating individual and funded accounts, would overcome these problems. To date, limited success has been achieved, however, and in some cases coverage has declined following such reforms.

Closely related to these social policy issues are broader economic concerns over the high and often rising level of informality. This growth is perceived as hampering economic development because workers in the informal sector are considered less prone to learn, innovate, and use productivity-enhancing technologies. Applying basic coverage options—such as universal or means-test benefits for the elderly—to take care of informal sector workers may prove counterproductive, because such options reduce the incentive to become formal while increasing the pressure on formal sector workers to become informal as their tax burden increases. A number of recent studies indicate that this may be happening in countries across Latin America (see, for example, Aterido, Hallward-Driemeier, and Pagés 2011; Levy 2008; and Ribe, Robalino, and Walker 2012) although at present the empirical evidence remains tentative.

In all settings, fiscal concerns arise from the cost of coverage expansion through noncontributory basic schemes, the need to control the fiscal costs of traditional national earnings-based defined benefit systems, and the effects of sustained informality on productivity and public revenues.

All three issues are potentially linked in a downward spiral in which (1) coverage concerns lead to the introduction or strengthening of basic provisions, which (2) constrain employment and increase informality, (3) increasing pressure to leave the formal sector, (4) worsening the fiscal position of the public pension scheme, (5) leading to benefit cuts, which in turn increase the need for better basic benefits.

Against this background, policy options in low- and middle-income countries are limited and largely untested. The most obvious and direct approach is to establish stronger incentives for participation in formal pension and saving schemes. The key challenge is to develop a design that will motivate lower-income groups—which require powerful, immediate, and readily understood incentives to overcome their inherent consumption preference and liquidity constraints—to direct their limited resources to retirement income. Such a system must also be attractive to informal sector workers, many of whom may be of moderate or even higher-income levels, while not increasing the incentives for workers to leave the formal sector.

PURPOSE AND ORGANIZATION OF THIS VOLUME

Several high-income countries, most notably Germany, New Zealand, and the United States, have adopted the MDC design to complement benefit levels under public schemes. Other countries, including Japan and the United Kingdom, have recently initiated MDC schemes to raise savings earmarked for retirement income. This has fostered interest in the design in a variety of other settings. Emerging economies in Asia (China, India, Thailand) and Latin America (Chile, Colombia, Mexico, Peru) have implemented or are considering implementing MDC-based schemes to encourage participation in voluntary and sometimes mandated schemes by individuals who would otherwise have no coverage at all. Such matching incentives may not in principle be restricted to defined contribution schemes, but examples of their use in defined benefit systems are rare (only the case of a new system in Republic of Korea is included in this volume) but worthwhile to review.

Despite the growing experience, there is little consolidated knowledge to provide evidence-based policy guidance about the role and limits of MDCs for expanding retirement savings, about best practice in the design and implementation of MDC programs, or about the interaction of MDC policies with other interventions such as financial literacy as complementary (or substitute) approaches. Nearly all of the experience with these arrangements and associated research has come from higher-income countries. Applicability to the vastly different circumstances in middle-income and developing countries remains uncertain.

Against the backdrop of pilots in emerging and developed economies, the Social Protection Unit of the World Bank's Human Development Network, in cooperation with the Research Institute for Policies on Pension and Aging (RIPPA) of Japan, organized a conference in June 2011 to provide a forum for sharing information and analyzing experience from around the world with this emerging design. The Spanish Bank BBVA, which manages pension funds in a number of Latin American countries, participated in the conference and subsequently joined with the World Bank and RIPPA to provide the resources to supplement and organize the material presented at the conference and produce this publication.

This volume—based on the presentations at the conference—provides overviews and analyses intended to inform the ongoing design and use of MDC schemes. The publication thus presents a first stocktaking of country experiences and some limited observations about the potential role and effectiveness of the design that can be derived from experience to date. It is not an effort to formulate or articulate a World Bank policy position or to provide any specific direction to countries considering the design. The evidence is far too limited to support such an effort, and as noted above, there is insufficient evidence to assess the transferability of the more extensive experience from higher-income countries to other settings. Not considered at the conference and in the volume are similar matching design approaches to increased coverage under health care or other social insurance programs. There is, however, considerable value in consolidating the knowledge that can be gleaned from the wide range of experiments with the design, considering what lessons are beginning to emerge and how these can inform future initiatives and a research agenda; these issues are summarized in this introductory chapter.

The book contains four parts. Part I provides an overview of the more general issues and experience in expanding supplementary pension coverage in Organisation for Economic Co-operation and Development (OECD) countries to establish a broader framework of the challenges of coverage expansion. Part II reviews experience with MDCs in high-income countries. Part III describes early efforts in lower- and middle-income settings. Part IV provides an overview of lessons from the emerging field of behavioral economics and reviews key issues in the enabling environment and the main parameters likely to be relevant in establishing an MDC in a developing country context.

The remainder of this introductory chapter is organized as follows. The next section offers a conceptual framework for the objectives, intervention, mechanisms, and modalities of MDCs. The following sections provide country examples, extract some tentative lessons from their experience, and draw preliminary policy conclusions.

Objectives, Interventions, Mechanisms, and Modalities

Assessing the effectiveness of a policy intervention starts with consideration of the objectives, a clear understanding of how the core elements of the intervention are defined, and how it expects to achieve the desired outcomes. Such a "theory of change" is critical to assess the effectiveness of any intervention and is at the core of monitoring and evaluation efforts.[1]

SETTING OBJECTIVES

Policy discussions in countries that have or are planning to introduce MDC systems suggest three primary objectives: expanding pension coverage, reducing informality, and increasing fiscal efficiency. Considering these requires some degree of conjecture as countries are rarely explicit about the objectives of a policy intervention and even less specific regarding how to measure outcomes. Furthermore, the political discussion is often overloaded with secondary objectives driven by group interests or political imperatives.

Expanding Coverage

The increase in basic or supplementary benefit coverage is probably the primary objective in most countries that have or are planning to introduce MDC-type pension systems. This objective is particularly relevant for low- and middle-income countries, where most people are not afforded even basic coverage for old-age income and health care.

Supplementary coverage is additional coverage for people who participate in mandated systems (as workers or beneficiaries) but whose benefit levels are considered inadequate. Providing such coverage is particularly relevant in high-income countries, where the large majority of the population is covered under earnings-related schemes or everyone is covered under universal schemes that only partially replace their income in old age.

One measure of the success of the basic benefit coverage is the number of people who receive a benefit at or above a minimum level (typically the poverty line). For supplementary benefits, success in coverage expansion may be measured by the number of people whose benefits rise above a threshold of a specified percentage or amount. In this case, however, the benefit increase may be caused by shifts in savings from unsubsidized to subsidized forms without an increase in net wealth.

Obviously, the success of the program rarely depends entirely on the financial incentives provided but will also be affected by government and operational capacities in addition to other factors.

Reducing Informality

Reducing the incentives to participate in the informal sector (that is, evading the costs of participating in mandated social insurance schemes) is another important objective of an MDC system, particularly in middle-income countries. This objective may be conceptualized as establishing conditions that will encourage individuals to make contributions and acquire rights for the first time or contribute more to an MDC scheme. Success can be measured in terms of the number of registered participants as well as by changes in the contribution density of participants. MDCs should also not create incentives to reduce the level of pension savings by those already contributing.

In developing countries, mandated participation in pension systems is often conditional on the number of employees in a firm; workers in firms below a certain size may be exempt from mandatory contributions. In other instances, workers may not be able to contribute because the firm is not formally registered or licensed. In such cases, an MDC alone may not be the appropriate intervention.

Increasing Fiscal Efficiency

MDCs create fiscal costs—either directly, through the matching contributions by governments, or indirectly, through preferential tax treatment of individuals or their employers. A simple measure of success would be the increase in the coverage rate or adequacy target per currency unit of public expenditure for matching and/or foregone tax revenue resulting from the increased savings that is excluded from taxation.

Another fiscal element that is often explicitly part of the design of an MDC scheme is the cost saving through reduced transfers to the elderly in the form of universal or means-tested benefits. These kinds of ex post transfers may include the costs for minimum benefits in an earnings-related scheme. Very optimistically, one could imagine a take-up of low-level matching contributions that largely eliminates the need for these transfers, with the saved fiscal costs well exceeding the new fiscal costs of the matching payments. Very pessimistically, one could imagine that MDCs merely shift savings from unsubsidized to subsidized forms—or, even worse, that most people substitute public funds for individual savings, with take-up concentrated largely in the upper-income strata.

Other Objectives

In a system with progressive income tax rates, favorable tax treatment of pension contribution disproportionately favors people with higher incomes. By providing a subsidy that is directly proportional to the contribution, an MDC scheme may not suffer from this shortcoming unless, again, the take-up is concentrated among high-income earners.

MDCs may also be linked with the objective of facilitating the transition to a fully or partially funded system by inducing individual contributions to support a funded or capitalized reserve from which benefits will be paid.

DEFINING THE INTERVENTION: CORE ELEMENTS OF MATCHING DEFINED CONTRIBUTION SCHEMES

The following features define an MDC scheme:

- **Individual account.** Accounting records should be maintained to clearly distinguish individual contribution and retirement saving outcomes.
- **Defined contributions.** Benefits are solely based on the accrued value of contributions and earnings on accumulated assets.
- **Sponsor.** Employers, the government, or other sponsoring entities make direct financial contributions to encourage individuals' participation.
- **Own contributions.** Regular and own contributions by individuals are expected, although sometimes after an initial "kick-start" contribution.

- **Funding.** In principle, schemes can be funded or unfunded (using a derived crediting rate and notional accounts). In practice, there are no examples of matching being incorporated into unfunded retirement savings schemes.
- **Mandatory or voluntary.** Mandatory schemes typically focus on extension of coverage. Voluntary schemes are typically employer based or designed to supplement other systems with broad coverage but relatively low benefit levels.

Other known design elements of MDCs are complementary and potentially substitutive to matching. As with matching, these intend to encourage the participation of individuals in retirement saving programs. The main examples include the following:

- Tax preferences for contributions and/or benefits under a comprehensive income tax approach that aims to eliminate distortions of taxation on savings and move toward a consumption-type structure (exempting contributions and interest from taxation but taxing the disbursement, or taxing contributions but leaving interest earnings and disbursement tax free)
- Nudging or choice architecture (Thaler and Sunstein 2009) to motivate individuals to participate in savings plans; specific mechanisms include automatic enrollment, default contribution levels, investment options, and thresholds for matching levels
- Financial education and related interventions to create the enabling environment for individuals to learn about the importance of planning and retirement saving and offer them support to acquire the requisite skills, attitudes, and behaviors.

ENVISAGED MECHANISM: THE THEORY OF CHANGE

Identifying the mechanism through which outcomes will be achieved begins with an analysis of the problems to be solved and the rationale for government intervention. Public interventions are traditionally undertaken for two key reasons: to correct market failures and to redistribute income. Market failures are often linked to asymmetric information, which leads to poorly functioning (or nonexistent) markets. Government interventions are intended to substitute for or improve market outcomes. Redistribution is undertaken to correct perceived failures in the way markets generate and distribute income. To these motivations for public intervention, a third has been added in recent years: to correct the behavioral limitations of individuals. A fourth reason may be to correct government failure itself—by, for example, redesigning social insurance programs that do not achieve sufficient coverage due to poor design or implementation.

Individuals may rationally evade government social insurance programs for a variety of reasons, including the high costs associated with participation in the formal sector, liquidity preferences, the poor fit between a program and individual preferences, and lack of trust. These factors can be conceptualized as increasing the discount rate individuals apply to pension schemes. An MDC scheme seeks to increase the internal rate of return of a pension scheme in order to increase participation, contributions, or both.

Individuals may fail to employ market-based social risk management instruments to address long-term contingencies, such as old age, for a variety of reasons, including the absence of appropriate instruments, the inability to plan ahead, and the existence of more immediate shocks for which risk management instruments are not available. In the absence of an additional external motivation, these factors may make it rational for some people to focus on the short rather than the long term. Under such circumstances, matching may actually distort rational individual decisions and divert resources from, say, human capital accumulation to retirement saving.

Whether contributions grow as a result of the provision of a match is a priori undetermined. A saving subsidy in the form of a match potentially creates both a substitution effect (which makes current consumption more expensive and hence increases current saving) and an income effect (which increases the demand for current and future consumption and hence decreases current saving). MDC interventions with multitier structures have even more complicated effects on individuals, which depend on the position of the individual before and after the introduction of or change to the intervention. Some configurations are predicted to clearly encourage or discourage saving; the effect of others is indeterminate. The predictions are broadly borne out in the country lessons discussed in the chapters.

DESIGN AND ADMINISTRATIVE MODALITIES

The main design features of MDC schemes include the following:

- **Matching rates** typically range from 25 percent to 100 percent but can reach 300 percent and more. For supplementary MDCs offered by employers, there may be complex structures with lower match rates for higher contribution levels or no match for a first tier before a declining match applies. For basic matches offered by governments, flat-rate and multitiered matching contributions (which address informal sector workers, for whom earnings cannot be easily established) are more typical.

- **Thresholds and ceilings** on the contribution base (linked to a multiple of average income) or overall limits on matched amounts direct subsidies to lower-income groups and limit fiscal costs.

- **Eligibility conditions** for matching include very specific characteristics of the beneficiary (income level, age, family status, number and age of children, employment status, company size, level of formality) to focus the match on a target population.

- **Matching contributions** provide an ex ante transfer linked with ex post transfer (minimum pension) that is conditional on a required amount of prior contributions (length or level) by the beneficiary or family members.

- **Withdrawals** can be made to purchase a first home or to buffer periods of unemployment or other contingencies.

- In addition to the match, consumption-type **tax treatment** is provided for savings, subject only to income tax at time of receipt (similar to other pension savings plans).

- **Payout modalities** include lump sums, phased withdrawals, mandated immediate or deferred annuitization, and annuitization defaults (for example, minimum annuity levels, deferred annuities).

Administrative modalities include the following:

- Contribution collection by employer, financial institution, social security institution, or local "aggregators" (nongovernmental organizations or others that collect payments from contributors)
- Recordkeeping and client communication by financial institution or regional or national social security fund
- Asset management by pension/health funds, specialized asset manager, or regional or national social security institution
- Benefit disbursement by financial institution or regional or national social security institution.

Country Examples

MDC schemes reflect diverse policy objectives at different stages of the pension system development. Common features can be organized by the main coverage extension scenarios:

- Supplementing universal (basic or means-tested) benefits
- Supplementing low or reduced earnings-related benefits
- Expanding coverage within the mandated social insurance scheme
- Expanding coverage outside the mandated social insurance scheme (universal approach)
- Expanding coverage outside the mandated social insurance scheme (sector- or group- specific approach).

This section illustrates these coverage objectives with country examples detailed in later chapters in this volume to distill lessons and to raise policy and research questions.

SUPPLEMENTING UNIVERSAL (BASIC OR MEANS-TESTED) BENEFITS

Two countries have sought to use MDC schemes to supplement universal benefits or limit mandated provisions: New Zealand (which introduced such a plan in 2007) and the United Kingdom (which had intended to introduce such a plan in 2010 but canceled the program following the election of a new government).

New Zealand is one of the few countries with an old-age program in which everyone receives a pension (this type of program is known as a *demogrant*). Every resident of New Zealand age 65 and older who has lived in the country for at least 10 years receives a flat-rate pension based on a certain percentage of the average wage. Provision for old age above this basic and taxable benefit was left to voluntary savings, creating issues of adequacy of retirement income.

After discussions and a defeated referendum on introducing mandated earnings-related benefits to eventually replace the demogrant, the government introduced an MDC-type scheme, the design of which was, to a significant degree, informed by the emerging field of behavioral economics; this design is both complex and comprehensive.

The KiwiSaver program, described in chapter 5, utilizes several tiers of matching-type incentives. It provides a flat contribution (known as a kick-start) on the opening of an account, a tax credit (actually a pure subsidy) for contributions, and mandates matching contributions by employers (2 percent of payroll, to increase to 3 percent by 2013). Employees can choose to contribute 2 percent, 4 percent, or 8 percent of their earnings. It combines these subsidies with an auto-enrollment feature in which new employees are automatically enrolled in the system but afforded the ability to opt out after a specified period. It allows preretirement withdrawals for several purposes, most notably the purchase of a first home.

The United Kingdom has had a Beveridge-inspired basic pension scheme with flat-rate contributions and benefits since the 1940s. The country has a long history of trying to improve saving outcomes of all types—from short term (precautionary) saving to very long-term pension and retirement income saving—in order to complement basic pension plan provisions. The Saving Gateway program, described in chapter 6, planned to use matching contributions to increase the savings of people with low incomes. Programs— tested through limited-scale pilot efforts in 2002–04 and 2005–07—experimented with different matching rates, contribution limits, eligibility rules, and recruitment mechanisms.

In 2008, the Labour government then in power decided to roll out Saving Gateway nationally to up to 8 million people, or 20 percent of the population between the ages of 16 and 65. In May 2010, the newly elected Conservative–Liberal Democrat coalition government canceled the scheme as part of its broader program of fiscal retrenchment. However, with the National Employment Savings Trust (NEST), the U.K. government is aiming to increase coverage of the privately funded pension system from 2012 by using auto-enrollment together with matching as another example of nudging behavior. A minimum contribution requirement is gradually being introduced, ultimately reaching 4 percent of wages by individuals, 3 percent from employers and 1 percent from the government in tax relief. Employees and employers are free to contribute more, and some employers will match higher contributions. Auto-enrollment is being used because such employer matching has been in existence for many years, and many employees did not join schemes even when very generous matches were offered by employers.[2]

SUPPLEMENTING LOW OR REDUCED EARNINGS-RELATED BENEFITS

A number of MDC schemes are related to low levels of income replacement or reforms that reduced the generosity of public earnings-related schemes, primarily in high-income OECD countries. There are wide variations in design and operation across countries.

A number of high-income countries have introduced compensatory supplementary and funded pensions with more modest amounts of direct fiscal support through flat-rate and similar subsidies (beyond consumption-type tax treatment). To provide some background on the overall issue of providing supplementary coverage, chapter 2 reviews the experience among OECD member countries with policies that encourage private pension saving.

The 401(k) plans used in the United States (named after a section of the tax code that authorized the particular type of tax-preferred saving arrangement), examined in chapter 3, are probably the most important and most investigated MDC scheme in the world. These plans emerged in the early 1980s as part of the employer-sponsored pension system that supplements the relatively low (on average, less than 40 percent) income replacement rates of the mandatory public social security system. These were part of the transition in voluntary employer pension coverage from defined benefit to defined contribution plans. The underlying arrangement enables workers to determine the level of pre-tax contributions (technically known as salary deferrals) to a defined contribution plan. To ensure that the value of this tax preference did not disproportionately favor individuals with higher incomes (who not only had a greater ability to save but who, because of the progressive income tax system, obtained a larger value from the tax deferral), rules were established that limited the amount higher-income workers could contribute; this amount is linked to the overall average share of income deferred by all participants. This rule led employers to create a wide range of matching contribution designs to induce higher contributions from low- and average-income workers to enable the higher-paid to take full advantage of potential tax preferences. The widespread use of 401(k) plans and the diversity of matching arrangements have been the subject of extensive study and are the source of much of the knowledge about the behavioral effects of various matching designs that are discussed in chapter 15.

In 2001, Germany introduced another important variant of the supplemental arrangement that is known as the Riester pension (in recognition of the former minister of labor and social security who was a main proponent of the initiative) after having imposed a significant prospective reduction in the value of public pension system benefits. The Riester pension plans that were introduced in stages from 2002 to 2008 involve a means-tested match of contributions from the government, an additional per child subsidy, a tax preference on contributions up to a maximum level, and an associated (largely annuitized) payout plan. The development of and experience with this system is discussed in chapter 4. This MDC scheme is heavily subsidized by the budget and at times substitutes for corporate pensions. After a slow start and several design changes, including simplifications, in 2005, Riester pension plans took off very quickly. Saving incentives have been effective in reaching households with children; they have been somewhat less successful in attracting low-income earners.

In more recent years, Japan has, like the United States, sought to expand its occupational pension system to include defined contribution plans as it attempts to address dramatic demographic changes that will constrain the public social security system and thereby relieve some of the pressures on traditional corporate defined benefit plans. The Japanese pension system and the new defined contribution plans are discussed in chapter 7. In an interesting variation, matching was introduced in 2011 with a design in which the employee is permitted to match the employer's contribution to the defined contribution plan—reversing the typical arrangement. Thus far, however, there is no evidence that this design will meet with any more success than other defined contribution plans, which have had only very limited acceptance, thus indicating the importance of context and incentives in matching arrangements.

EXPANDING COVERAGE WITHIN THE MANDATED SOCIAL INSURANCE SCHEME

Social insurance schemes in middle-income countries have difficulty expanding coverage to low-income groups. Some vulnerable groups, such as youth, are difficult to reach, but their early integration into a social insurance scheme is important for later behavior. Everywhere in the world, self-employed workers exhibit low participation and contribution efforts, particularly in rural areas.

A number of countries are attempting to encourage participation by groups that are difficult to integrate by offering matching incentives within the mandated social insurance scheme. The match is financed by the budget or through redistributed contributions.

Korea's social insurance pension scheme, discussed in chapter 8, was established in 1988 and made universal in 1999. It covers all working-age (age 18–60) adults who make or are exempted from making contributions. Contribution delinquency remains an issue, creating concerns for future pension adequacy. To strengthen participation of farmers and fishers, the government has, since 1995, when the national pension extended its compulsory coverage to all rural residents, offered contribution subsidies of 50 percent of the total contribution (with a cap). This subsidy is scheduled to end in 2013. Although the Korean pension scheme is of the defined benefit type and does not squarely fall into the MDC definition, it offers one of the few matching schemes in middle-/high-income countries that have been evaluated. As the subsidy does not apply to other self-employed groups beyond farmers and fishers, it offers a natural experiment for testing its effectiveness. It is found to have had a moderate effect in increasing participation in the system by individuals who would otherwise be expected to evade making contributions.

In Colombia—which is examined along with Mexico and Peru in chapter 10—at least three MDC schemes have been established to encourage voluntary contributions. Two are already in operation, one as part of the funded individual account system and one as part of the alternative unfunded defined benefit scheme. Individuals must choose between the two schemes. In both cases, the match provides minimum income guarantees for retirees and is financed by contribution income.

Mexico has had at least two matching-type schemes in operation since the mandated individual account pension scheme was established in the late 1990s. The first scheme targets low-wage workers by providing a flat-rate "social contribution" to all participants below an income ceiling (introduced in 2009) equal to 5.5 percent of the presumed minimum wage for each day of work. A second scheme, for civil servants, was introduced with the 2007 reform that moved their pensions toward a funded defined contribution scheme. The match—a government match of Mex\$3.25 for each Mex\$1 of employee contribution, with a ceiling of 2.0 percent of the contribution base for the employee and 6.5 percent for the employer—should increase contributions.

Peru's MDC scheme, originally legislated in 2008, was designed to promote coverage for workers in small and microenterprises while enhancing competitiveness and encouraging participation in the formal labor market. The matching component of this law, the Welfare Pension System (Sistema de Pensiones Sociales), has recently been included in the 2012 reform of the private pension system. This scheme is focused only on microenterprise employees (those working in firms with no more than 10 employees) and is mandatory for people under age 40 and earning less than 1.5 times the legal minimum wage. Both the contribution rate and the government matching are to be defined during the year. It is likely that the government will finally implement this scheme.

Chile, examined in chapter 9, introduced two youth employment subsidy schemes, with the objective of promoting formal youth employment through incentives for both the supply of and demand for labor. The schemes' introduction, in 2008, occurred around the time of a major pension reform that introduced ex post subsidies—in particular, guaranteed old-age income through the solidarity pillar of the pension system. The Subsidio Previsional a los Trabajadores Jóvenes (SPTJ) scheme provides an explicit subsidy for social security contributions. A first component (introduced in October 2008) amounts to 50 percent of social security contributions at minimum wage. This, however, is paid to the employer to provide a subsidy for the cost of hiring younger workers while also providing an incentive for contributions to the social security system. A second component (introduced in July 2011) provides a matching payment to the worker of the same amount to subsidize contributions.

EXPANDING COVERAGE OUTSIDE THE MANDATED SOCIAL INSURANCE SCHEME (UNIVERSAL APPROACH)

In most low- and many middle-income countries, the majority of workers work in the informal sector. Integration of the workers into the formal sector pension scheme is unlikely to be realistic in the near term. A few countries, including India and Thailand, do offer voluntary coverage outside the mandated social insurance scheme and provide a government match to induce participation.

In India, discussed in chapter 12, less than 10 percent of the population works in the formal sector—and much of the formal sector employment is in the public sector. To address a looming pension problem in an existing defined benefit system for central government workers, the reform of 2004 introduced a funded defined contribution scheme for new entrants to the civil service and unbundled recordkeeping and asset management. With an administrative structure established through this reform, the New Pension Scheme provided the potential infrastructure for an MDC scheme for all informal sector workers. An effort to expand the system was initiated in 2010, by which an annual matching contribution of Re 1,000 (about $20) was offered for all workers who enroll and pay contributions of Re 1,000–12,000 (about $20 to $225) a year, with no means test applied. To enhance the decision architecture, the scheme uses "aggregators" at the village level to collect contributions and has a simplified account structure with lower fees. The scheme's very recent implementation makes it impossible to draw conclusions about its success. An early look at a small set of data indicates that participation in the scheme may be associated with income and education levels and might be negatively associated with access to alternative sources of retirement savings.

Thailand, discussed in chapter 14, initiated a national MDC scheme for informal sector workers in 2012. Individual deposits can be made at any time, with a minimum deposit of B 50 (about $2). The government match and ceiling are graduated by age, with a 50 percent match for people age 15–30 up to a maximum of B 3,000 (about $100), an 80 percent match for people age 31–50 with a maximum of B 4,800 (about $155), and a 100 percent match for people age 51–60 with a limit of B 6,000 (about $200).

These efforts in India and Thailand trigger many questions that will require further evidence and rigorous evaluation to answer, including the following:

- What is the appropriate matching structure for informal sector workers in low- and middle-income countries? In particular, how important are matching rates compared with contribution ceilings?

- What is the role of matching compared with other participation determinants, such as the decision architecture and potential members' perceptions of the service providers?

- How effective are aggregators and efforts to increase access through "points of presence" (the establishment of a means to make contributions in a village such as a bank or post office) in increasing participation into rural areas?

- What mechanisms encourage continued pension saving efforts beyond increased participation?

EXPANDING COVERAGE OUTSIDE THE MANDATED SOCIAL INSURANCE SCHEME (SECTOR- AND GROUP-SPECIFIC APPROACHES)

In countries with a large informal sector and the desire to increase formal sector participation, a universal voluntary system for informal sector workers may not be the best way to achieve higher levels of pension coverage. A focus on specific groups may be justified, however. Self-employed workers lend themselves to such an approach, as they are difficult to integrate into a formal mandated scheme.

A number of countries have started to move in this direction. China, discussed in chapter 11, started a voluntary MDC pilot for the rural sector in 2009; the program was expanded to the urban sector in 2011, and full national coverage is envisaged by 2013. These voluntary schemes will coexist with the mandated urban pension scheme, which covers about half the urban workforce.

China's introduction of the National Rural Pension Scheme and the Urban Resident Pension Scheme has been one of the most ambitious voluntary pension saving and minimum elderly assistance schemes in a low- or middle-income country. Both schemes have innovative features. They provide a basic pension benefit from age 60 on if a vesting period of 15 years is fulfilled. Individuals select a contribution level of between Y 100–500 ($16–$80) per year. A partial match is then provided by local governments, with a minimum required match of Y 30 ($5), although this may be at a higher level that is locally determined. The rapid expansion of these voluntary schemes that now are reported to cover more than 350 million participants may be linked to the minimum pension benefit, which is offered immediately if conditions are fulfilled. But it also reflects the influence the government has on inducing participation in public social insurance systems as well as a solid advocacy campaign.

Another important challenge in developing countries is reaching independent workers, who offer their labor in often irregular patterns—such as fishers in offering their labor and skills to the owners of boats. Because this employment model does not lend itself to long-term relationships, these kinds of workers cannot make steady contribution payments into a social insurance fund. Their situation calls for innovative new payment and financing solutions adapted to the particular circumstances of the targeted workers that include nudging elements as well as matching-type contributions by contractors. An exploratory study of Cape Verde and Tunisia, presented in chapter 13, offers an outside-of-the-box thought piece on this issue.

These country examples of innovative MDC schemes suggest that coverage can be expanded by moving beyond simple matching design to improving the decision architecture. Linking ex post and ex ante transfers, as China has done, or offering new financing and payment structures, as proposed for Cape Verde and Tunisia, exemplify this approach.

Tentative Lessons from the Experience with Matching Contributions

The country experience and reported results offer a rich, although incomplete (and likely somewhat biased), body of evidence on the use of matching contribution arrangements. Most of the rigorous evaluation of the dynamics and outcomes of matching are focused on participation and contribution effects in 401(k) plans. These address particular groups (generally higher-income employers in a high-income country who are offered the chance to participate in an employer-sponsored plan) and therefore may not be relevant for other countries. These studies do not address some of the key questions for other settings such as impact on informality or overall fiscal effectiveness, as the matching is by employers and any fiscal effects are indirect. Most other country experiences have not (yet) been subject to rigorous evaluation; in many circumstances, there has been no evaluation at all. Consequently, the discussion presented below includes more hypotheses than lessons that have been inspired by empirical results and validated in other countries.

EXPANDING COVERAGE

Participation

There is consistent empirical support across country income levels that matching is effective in increasing participation. The evidence from a few high-income countries (mostly the United States) indicates positive but modest effects of matching on participation, with overall effects increasing participation in the range of 5–10 percent of potential beneficiaries. The associated finding that a 25 percent match of individual contributions is associated with about a 5 percent increase in participation appears to be robust across a range of programs and analysis in the United States. This magnitude is also broadly consistent with results from Korea, where a 50 percent match for farmers and fishers increased the probability of making a pension contribution by 7.4 percent. The presence of a large initial match—a significant element of the KiwiSaver system in New Zealand—elicited enrollment from many people with little or no earnings, including children, providing further evidence of the potential effectiveness of significant matches on at least initial enrollment.

Increase in Retirement Saving

The effect of the match on the saving rate is typically found to be small, and the sign is not always positive or statistically significant. This finding is consistent with the theoretical ambiguity arising from the conflict between substitution and income effects. What seems to emerge consistently is that the structure of the match—the matching rate, thresholds, and caps—does have significant consequences. Consistent across estimates (essentially from the United States and, to a lesser extent, the United Kingdom), the match threshold seems to have a greater impact than the matching rate. Providing a lower match of 25 percent on contributions for a higher level of 10 percent of pay will induce individuals to save more than a higher match of 50 percent for a lower level of 5 percent of pay, although both formulations result in similar costs to the organization providing the match (see chapters 3, 6, and 15). A possible explanation for this result is that matching acts as a signaling device or implicit advice on saving levels. Also notable is the "stickiness" of saving levels, as evidenced by the fact that most people remain at contribution levels that were established as defaults even when the defaults are subsequently reduced.

Increase in Overall Saving/Total Pension Wealth

Comprehensive evidence from the United States on the effect of scheme saving on other saving is mixed, but suggests up to 20–30 percent net increases in saving levels (see chapters 3 and 15). In the United Kingdom (chapter 6), the saving rate increased but the measured net worth of individuals did not change. Evidence from Germany (chapter 4) suggests that matched saving did not squeeze out other saving.

Other Determinants for Participation and Contribution Efforts

The evidence from developed and developing countries strongly suggests that other features of savings programs and related interventions may have a critical—perhaps even a dominant—effect on participation and contribution levels. Most of these features have not yet been subject to the rigorous testing across a range of settings that could begin to distinguish between inherent effects and those associated with a particular set of circumstances, cultural setting, or population group.

- **Automatic enrollment and defaults.** Evidence from the United States, the United Kingdom, and New Zealand suggests that making participation the default option has two to four times the impact of the match. (Of course, an automatic enrollment default option works only under formal employment conditions.) The role of other default schemes on contribution efforts is mixed and at times negative, possibly because of inertia or the low default contribution rate.

- **Simplification of design and access.** Empirical results for the United States and the United Kingdom and lessons from the German Riester pensions suggest that simplified design affects participation and, perhaps, contribution/saving efforts.

- **Social marketing and advocacy.** Retirement saving remains an objective that most will embrace but find difficult to implement. In the United States, employers have found that information sessions and advocacy are a useful adjunct to the incentives of matching contributions. In Germany, take-up of the match increased with greater awareness of the scheme associated with information campaigns. New Zealand has coupled introduction of its system with information and advocacy campaigns which are perceived to have had the expected effect. There is some very preliminary evidence of a positive impact through the introduction of account aggregators in India. Yet rigorous empirical evidence is missing on the effectiveness of information campaigns for short-term participation and long-term contribution efforts.

REDUCING INFORMALITY

Evidence on the effect of MDC schemes on informality is very limited and mixed. There is no empirical evidence that the modest matching schemes in Colombia or Mexico have reduced informality or increased coverage, nor any clear expectation that the soon-to-be-implemented matching scheme in Peru will lead to these outcomes. This is possibly because of the small size of the programs and important distortions in the labor market. Data from national household surveys in these three South American countries show an enormous potential for saving in the informal sectors. The estimate for Korea suggests that the match for farmers and fishers had a modest positive impact on participation in the national pension scheme. The matching programs in Chile to incentivize the participation of young workers in the formal labor market—and hence in the pension scheme—increased participation, but the programs have not yet been subject to rigorous evaluation. The rural pilots in China that started in 2009 reportedly reached 358 million rural workers as of the end of 2011, and full coverage (of some 500 million people) is envisaged in 2013. The pilots increased coverage but, strictly speaking, had no effect on informality. This is likely to be because the target group had very little potential to become formal sector workers to begin with.

A number of countries (including China, India, and Thailand) have established or are planning voluntary matching programs in parallel to formal matched or unmatched schemes. Individuals joining these voluntary programs have no obligations to join the mandated scheme (as they do in Germany and the United States). Not enough evidence is available to determine whether these schemes create disincentives to formalization.

INCREASING FISCAL EFFICIENCY

Assessing the effect of matching schemes on coverage and informality is relatively straightforward, and effectiveness comparisons can be done within or across similar schemes. To measure fiscal efficiency requires the pricing of the intervention and comparison with alternatives or a counterfactual. This analysis is hardly ever done, however, as these schemes are designed and implemented—making consideration of potential fiscal effects more art than science.

In considering the possible fiscal efficiency of matching schemes, two comparisons are proposed: (1) a comparison of the fiscal costs with the additional savings volume created by the match and (2) a comparison of fiscal costs for the match with the costs of alternative interventions such as ex post subsidies. The most useful comparison may depend on the purpose of the intervention. If the objective is to promote supplementary coverage, evaluating the marginal increase in savings seems more relevant. If promoting basic coverage is the objective, the more relevant comparison is with alternative interventions.

Comparison to Additional Savings Created

Comparison of total fiscal costs with MDC savings created can be done on a flow and stock basis. Each requires some heroic assumptions.

- **Comparing the annual contributions by participants to annual fiscal costs.**
  Assuming that all contributions are new saving, fiscal effectiveness requires that
  the ratio of the annual flow of new savings to the annual cost of matches (a fiscal efficiency ratio) be larger than 1 so that the public expenditure and potential
  public dis-saving are at least compensated by additional contribution revenues of
  equal magnitude. Taking account of distortions (for example, through changes in
  general revenue collections) would increase the opportunity costs and therefore
  increase the required fiscal efficiency ratio. Using empirical results of new savings
  created of, say, only a third, fiscal effectiveness would require an efficiency ratio
  greater than 3. For the German Riester pensions, for example, the share of annual
  contributions to direct fiscal costs is slightly above 2 and falling (chapter 4).

- **Comparing the additional national capital stock created with the accumulated fiscal expenditure.** The idea behind this comparison is that on a net basis
  (aggregate new savings less aggregate cost of the subsidy), the match should
  increase the pension wealth of the elderly and the capital stock on which future
  benefits are paid by more than the overall cost of the subsidy. Such a calculation
  would take account of compensating or strengthening effects. Ex ante projections with an appropriate overlapping generations model would offer first indications of effects; for the more relevant ex post evaluation, the data and estimation
  requirements need to be developed.

Comparison to Ex Post Subsidy

Are matching contributions (ex ante subsidies) for voluntary or mandated schemes less
expensive than noncontributory or subsidized benefit levels (ex post subsidies)? Measuring fiscal efficiency requires considering the likely cost and comparing it with alternatives.
Doing so yields the following considerations:

- A demogrant provides everyone with a minimum transfer in old age, regardless
  of individual circumstances. This approach is very effective in distributive terms,
  but not fiscally efficient because the leakages are high as many receiving the benefit do not need it to maintain the level of consumption in old age that such a
  benefit is intended to achieve. The same minimum income support for needy
  elderly can be generated at much lower cost when targeted transfers are provided
  in the form of general social assistance or categorical social pensions (Grosh and
  Leite 2009). Of course, targeting, however well done, will lead to inclusion and
  exclusion errors.

- Compared to both demogrants and targeted ex post benefits, an MDC scheme
  can be constructed that is fiscally more efficient as long as individuals do some
  additional saving and targeting works effectively. If individuals are not induced
  by the match to increase their saving, for whatever reason, then matching leads to
  distributively inferior results. This has implications for the lowest-income groups
  where saving capacity for old age is limited. If individuals do some saving but ex
  ante targeting does not work well, it can lead to either fiscally less efficient outcomes than ex post targeting or distributionally less efficient outcomes or both.

This will depend on the size of the inclusion and exclusion errors and the reaction of individuals to the subsidy provided. Unfortunately, the relevant experience and data are not available to undertake such a comparison.

None of the countries reviewed appears to have established a comprehensive set of outcome measures or undertaken estimates of the fiscal effectiveness of the matching design in relation to alternatives. No studies have been undertaken to provide comparative measures even at the conceptual level of the cost-effectiveness of key parameters. Such a study should be relatively simple at the individual level; however, at the macrolevel, the comparison would have to make a number of heroic assumptions to allow for comparability.

Preliminary Policy Conclusions and Next Steps

Because few MDC schemes have been subjected to a rigorous impact evaluation, policy lessons are by necessity very preliminary. Based on the evidence presented in this volume, a few conclusions and suggestions for future analysis can nevertheless be drawn:

1. Empirical evidence, collected largely from high-income countries, suggests that MDC schemes raise participation in pension systems moderately and have at best modest (and in some instances ambiguous) effects on contribution levels of participating individuals. Both findings are consistent with theoretical predictions. The persistence of any of these effects—and ultimately their influence on lifetime wealth accumulation and the provision of retirement income—will require much longer-term assessment. The net impact of matching on individual wealth and macroeconomic savings levels is empirically even more difficult to assess and subject to conflicting views. The weight of the limited evidence to date for high-income and perhaps some high-middle-income countries is that MDCs will make a helpful but insufficient contribution to solving the challenges of pension coverage, income maintenance, and informality of labor. They may, however, be effective for special groups that are difficult to reach by other means.

2. It is unclear to what extent the results for high-income countries will translate into the context of lower- and middle-income countries. The groups for which there is experience in high-income countries may not be representative of the broader population, nor are they likely to share characteristics and behavior patterns with target populations in low- and middle-income settings, which are likely to be characterized by many more constraints in their everyday life and much larger shocks for which social risk management instruments are not available. As a result, the incentives by MDC programs to enhance retirement savings may translate less well or at least differently. Since few programs of this kind existed until recently in developing economies, and none has been subject to rigorous impact evaluation, not much is yet known about how the experience in other settings will translate; caution is therefore advised.

3. The threshold and other parameters of the match seem to have as much, or even a greater, effect as the overall level of the match on behavior and saving outcomes

in high-income countries. Similar empirical evidence is not yet available for low-and middle-income countries. In view of the many more binding constraints in developing countries, complex matching rates and other parameters may be required to achieve the envisaged outcomes. A key design challenge in these settings will be to balance this with a need for simplicity and transparency. At least equally important for participation and saving effects are interventions directed toward overcoming behavioral and other limitations, in particular through the provision of information and financial education, a choice architecture consistent with the observed inertia in behavior, and social marketing, public service announcements, and other types of advocacy. Key considerations in designing such programs include the following:

- Information about the subsidized scheme and its operation is critical in creating awareness, which seems to be an important factor in changing behavior (in general and for retirement income saving in particular).

- Many (but not all) experts believe that the ability to understand the offered saving products and to apply that knowledge is a critical factor for participation in social risk management programs (whether mandated or voluntary, unsubsidized or matched).

- The setting of defaults and other forms of choice architecture are increasingly recognized as key determinants of outcomes. Policy makers need to take advantage of lessons from behavioral economics about harnessing the power of inertia (in particular through automatic enrollment with limited opt-outs), simplifying administrative processes, and setting parameters.

- Advocacy and education efforts—such as seminars, public service advertising, social marketing, publicly sponsored retirement savings information websites, and entertainment education—may be very important in promoting MDC schemes.

4. Individuals at all income levels evade participation in mandated schemes for a variety of reasons, including ineffective design choices, poor alignment of incentives with the environmental context, and lack of trust in public and financial institutions. Addressing these issues may go a long way toward increasing participation. These efforts should be undertaken before matching schemes are introduced.

5. The effect that pension-related matching incentives may have in changing employment patterns or reducing the level of informality in developing and transition economies remains wholly unknown. Thus far, there is little evidence that these schemes are sufficient to change individual decisions. This remains a difficult issue to effectively evaluate, but one that merits investigation despite the methodological challenges.

6. Examples and a framework are lacking for a comprehensive cost-benefit analysis for MDC designs to compare them with potential alternatives. Rigorous impact evaluation focused on microeconomic assessment is necessary to guide program

design. This needs to be complemented by a more comprehensive welfare analysis, including cost-benefit evaluation of alternative approaches. Such analysis should address areas not covered in the research to date including consideration of the following:

- A pure saving instrument (and pooling risks over time by individuals) or a traditional risk management instrument (pooling risks across individuals) in relation to matching designs
- Differentiation of MDC outcomes in relation to various income groups; theoretical considerations and empirical indications suggest that matching to improve retirement saving is not likely to be effective for the poorest in society, and initial evidence suggests large substitution effects among higher-income groups
- Gender analysis of MDC, addressing differences in labor force participation, longevity, and other factors likely to create different outcomes
- The longer-term role of matching designs and possible development of exit strategies for their use as a transitional device to generate participation as economies meet thresholds where coverage expansions become feasible.

7. Finally, it will be important to consider the possible future role and new designs of MDC schemes under different social policy scenarios, such as the following:

- The marginalization or even the demise of pay-as-you-go earnings-based (Bismarckian) public pensions in countries with a high level of informality
- A further reduction of the mandatory defined contribution pension systems in countries with low informality but also facing demographically driven reductions in the generosity of public earnings-related and basic schemes
- The need for more portability of social benefits and the portability of the subsidy element of MDCs across borders.

Notes

1. All modern monitoring and evaluation books apply a similar logic, although they may use different terminology. For recent highly readable publications on monitoring and evaluation, see Gertler and others (2010); Khandker, Koolwal, and Samad (2009); and Leeuw and Vaessen (2009). Also see the websites of the Massachusetts Institute of Technology's Poverty Action Lab (http://www.povertyactionlab.org/), the World Bank (http://www.worldbank.org/oed/ecd), and the World Bank's Strategic Impact Evaluation Fund (http://go.worldbank.org/X81HJAZSG0).

2. See http://www.direct.gov.uk/en/Pensionsandretirementplanning/Companyandpersonalpensions/WorkplacePensions/DG_200722 for on overview of the government's plans and time schedule.

References

Aterido, Reyes, Mary Hallward-Driemeier, and Carmen Pagés. 2011. "Does Expanding Health Insurance beyond Formal-Sector Workers Encourage Informality? Measuring the Impact of Mexico's Seguro Popular." IZA Discussion Paper 5996, Institute for the Study of Labor, Bonn.

Gertler, Paul J., Sebastian Martinez, Patrick Premand, Laura B. Rawlings, and Christel M. J. Vermeersch. 2010. *Impact Evaluation in Practice.* Washington, DC: World Bank.

Grosh, Margaret, and Phillippe Leite. 2009. "Defining Eligibility for Social Pensions: A View from a Social Assistance Perspective." In *Closing the Coverage Gap: The Role of Social Pensions and Other Retirement Income Transfers*, ed. R. Holzmann, D. A. Robalino, and N. Takayama, 161–86. Washington, DC: World Bank.

Holzmann, R., D. A. Robalino, and N. Takayama. 2009. *Closing the Coverage Gap: The Role of Social Pensions and Other Retirement Income Transfers.* Washington, DC: World Bank.

Khandker, S. R., G. B. Koolwal, and H. Samad. 2009. *Handbook on Quantitative Methods of Program Evaluation.* Washington, DC: World Bank.

Leeuw, F., and J. Vaessen, 2009. *Impact Evaluations and Development: NONIE Guidance on Impact Evaluation.* Washington, DC: World Bank.

Levy, Santiago. 2008. *Good Intentions, Bad Outcomes.* Washington, DC: Brookings Institution.

Ribe, Helena, David Robalino, and Ian Walker. 2012. *From Right to Reality: Incentives, Labor Markets, and the Challenge of Achieving Universal Social Protection in Latin America and the Caribbean.* Latin American Development Forum Series. Washington, DC: World Bank.

Rofman, Rafel, and Maria Laura Oliveri. 2012. "La cobertura de los sistemas previsionales en América Latina: conceptos e indicadores." (English version in preparation.) Series de Documentos de Trabajo sobre Políticas Sociales No. 7, World Bank, Buenos Aires.

Thaler, Richard H., and Cass R. Sunstein. 2009. *Nudge: Improving Decisions about Health, Wealth, and Happiness.* New York: Penguin Books.

CHAPTER 2

Policies to Encourage Private Pension Savings: Evidence from OECD Countries

Edward Whitehouse

Private pensions provide about 20 percent of retirement income on average in Organisation for Economic Co-operation and Development (OECD) countries. They are mandatory or quasi-mandatory in 14 of the 34 OECD countries; in the other 20, an average of almost 30 percent of the working-age population has either a personal pension plan or an employer-provided plan. In most countries, the share of retirement income provided by private pensions has been increasing for at least two decades. The trend is likely to continue, thanks to the introduction of compulsory private pensions and the fact that more private retirement savings are needed to fill the pension gap resulting from lower public benefits in the future. Tax benefits and matching contributions are used to motivate individuals to save for retirement. Other policy options, such as automatic enrollment, should be considered as well, although rigorous evidence beyond a few countries is needed to determine how effective automatic enrollment is in extending coverage of private pensions.

Mandatory pension benefits, especially public pensions, will be much lower for workers entering the labor market today than they were for their parents and grandparents. Voluntary private provision for old age will therefore be necessary to maintain living standards into retirement. Indeed, many of the reforms to public pensions have been predicated on the assumption that voluntary retirement savings will increase.

In some countries, such as Canada, Japan, the United Kingdom, and the United States, voluntary savings have long been necessary. Such savings are a new phenomenon in other countries, such as France and Germany. Moreover, the need to save for old age now encompasses more of the population, including groups such as low earners, who have not traditionally made active retirement saving decisions.

Some data from the Organisation for Economic Co-operation and Development (OECD) suggest that coverage of and contributions to retirement savings plans are adequate. Others imply that there may be substantial gaps. This inconclusive evidence

Andrew Reilly of the Organisation for Economic Co-operation and Development helped prepare this chapter. Participants at the conference on the Potential for Matching Defined Contribution (MDC) Design Features in Pension Systems to Increase Coverage in Low- and Middle-Income Countries, organized by the World Bank and the Research Institute for Policies on Pension and Aging of Japan, provided useful comments. In particular, the author is grateful to Richard Hinz, Robert Holzmann, Robert Palacios, John Piggott, Sylvester Schieber, and Noriyuki Takayama.

suggests no grounds for complacency among policy makers. Fortunately, governments throughout the OECD are designing and implementing policies to encourage private pension saving.

This chapter is organized as follows. It begins by presenting evidence on the growing role of private pensions in providing retirement income in OECD countries. It then looks at the coverage of private pensions, distinguishing between voluntary and mandatory schemes. The third section examines financial incentives for voluntary private pension savings (tax incentives and matched contributions). The fourth section looks at mandating contributions to private pensions and soft compulsion. The last section summarizes the chapter's main findings.

The Growing Role of Private Pensions

Private pensions have been playing a greater role in providing incomes for some time. Between 1990 and 2007, aggregate expenditure on private pension benefits grew 23 percent faster than national income, rising from 1.3 percent to 1.6 percent of gross domestic product (GDP). Over the same period, public pension spending increased 15 percent faster than GDP and accounted for 7.0 percent of GDP in 2007.

The share of private pensions in total benefits in 23 OECD countries grew moderately between 1990 and 2007, from 17.5 percent to 21.5 percent, with only 4 countries registering declines (figure 2.1). In 2007, private pensions provided about half of all benefits in Switzerland (through mandatory private pensions), the Netherlands (through quasi-mandatory schemes), and Canada and the United Kingdom (through widespread voluntary private pension provision). In Iceland, more than 60 percent of pension spending was private (through mandatory private plans). As a share of GDP, the largest private expenditures were in Switzerland (6.0 percent) and the Netherlands (5.2 percent), followed by the United Kingdom and the United States, at about 4.5 percent each.

In addition to the aggregate-level analysis of figure 2.1, it is useful to look at micro-level data. Figure 2.2 shows the pattern of income sources from household survey data. For people over age 65, income comes from three sources: public transfers (mainly public pensions), work (employment and self-employment), and capital (mainly private pension benefits).

In the 27 OECD countries shown, public transfers make up an average of 60 percent of older people's incomes. People over age 65 are most reliant on the state for their incomes in France and Hungary, where 85 percent of their incomes come from public transfers. The state provides at least three-quarters of old-age income in Austria, Belgium, the Czech Republic, Luxembourg, Poland, and the Slovak Republic. At the other end of the spectrum, public transfers represent just 15 percent of average old-age income in Finland (this figure is low, however, because it includes mandatory occupational plans as capital income, whereas the national accounts and OECD *Pensions at a Glance* studies treat these schemes as part of the public sector). The share of old-age income derived from public transfers is also very low in the Republic of Korea, where the public pension scheme was established only in 1988 (and old-age pensions paid only as of 2008). Public transfers also provide less than half of old-age income in Australia, Canada, Japan, the Netherlands, Switzerland,[1] the United Kingdom, and the United States.

FIGURE 2.1 **Expenditure on private pension benefits as percentage of total pension expenditure, in selected OECD countries, 1990 and 2007**

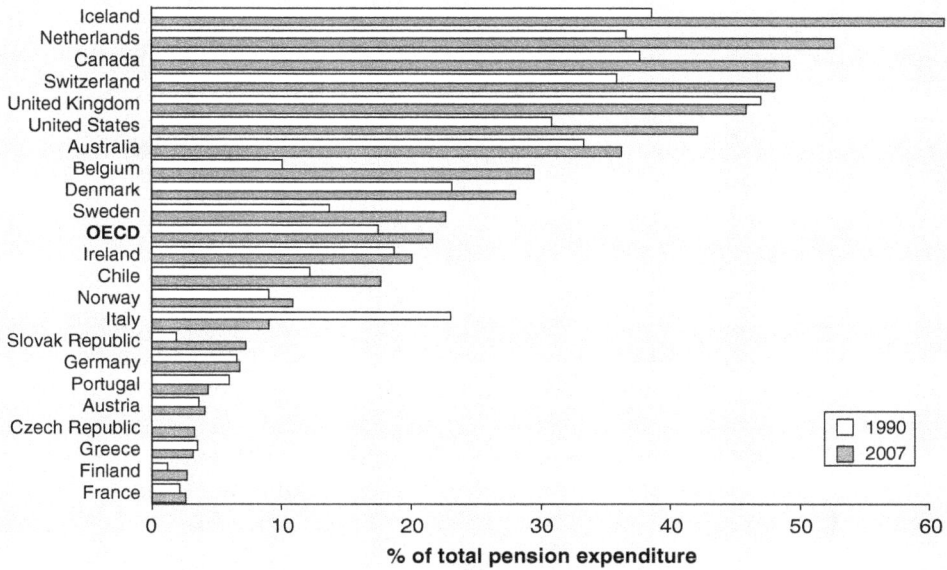

% of total pension expenditure

SOURCE: OECD 2011.

FIGURE 2.2 **Sources of income of people over 65 in selected OECD countries, mid-2000s**

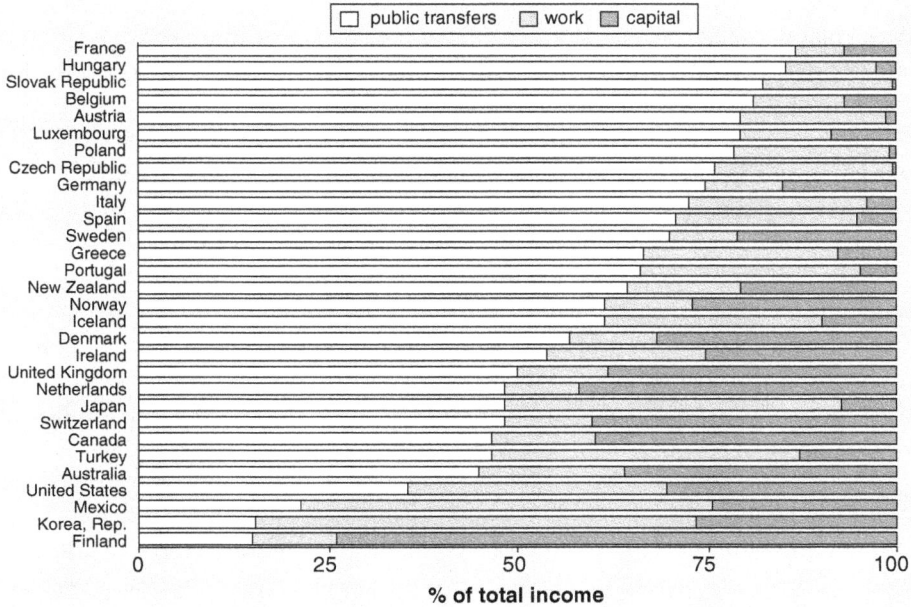

% of total income

SOURCES: OECD 2008, 2009.

In the East Asian OECD countries, employment and self-employment provide a very large proportion of income for people over age 65: 44 percent in Japan and 59 percent in Korea. Income from work accounts for at least a quarter of old-age income in the Czech Republic, Greece, Iceland, Portugal, Spain, and the United States. In some of these countries, the large share of work income probably reflects the fact that many people have not had full contribution histories in the public pension scheme and therefore keep working to fill these gaps. In Iceland and the United States, for example, the retirement age is typically set at 65, but many people continue to work longer, and some choose to delay receiving their pension benefits to increase their value. In contrast, income from work (employment and self-employment) accounts for less than 10 percent of older people's incomes in France, the Netherlands, and Sweden.

Income from capital—mainly in the form of private pensions—is the most important source of old-age income in Australia, Canada, Denmark, the Netherlands, the United Kingdom, and the United States (Finland apart, for the reasons described above). In these countries, capital income accounts for about 30 percent or more of older people's incomes.

Figure 2.2 shows average values. The composition of income varies widely across the income distribution: poorer older people derive their income almost exclusively from public transfers; private pensions and other capital income play a significant part only among richer pensioners (see Disney and Whitehouse 2001, 2003; Förster and Mira d'Ercole 2005). The fact that the role of private pensions and capital in retirement income has been growing may exacerbate growing income inequality in old age.

The analysis of aggregate financial flows from public and private pensions and income distribution data is backward looking, in the sense that it reflects the past design of pension systems. A significant development in many countries around the world has been the introduction of mandatory private pensions. In most cases—in Chile, Estonia, Mexico, Poland, the Slovak Republic, and Sweden—these pensions are a substitute for all or part of public, earnings-related schemes. In Australia, Norway, and Switzerland, compulsory private pensions were added to existing public provision.

Figure 2.3 shows the structure of the projected retirement income package for a worker entering the labor market in 2008. Data are presented for 21 OECD countries where private pensions are either mandatory or voluntary but coverage is high. The horizontal axis shows weighted-average pension wealth, defined as the net present value of the lifetime flow of pension benefits; it is shown as a multiple of economywide average earnings (the weights reflect the national earnings distribution). Iceland, where the total pension is worth 19 times average earnings, shows the largest overall figure. This approach is designed to capture differences in the structure of the pension package with individual earnings. In many countries, lower-income workers will be more reliant on public benefits than richer people.

Countries are ranked in figure 2.3 by the role of public benefits in the overall package, with the largest public share at the top. In the Czech Republic and New Zealand, for example, contributions to voluntary private pensions typically represent a small share of earnings.[2] In Chile, where the formal pension system covers about 60 percent of the workforce, retirees receive more than 80 percent of their income from private pensions.

FIGURE 2.3 **Contribution of public and private components to simulated lifetime benefits in 21 OECD countries, 2008**

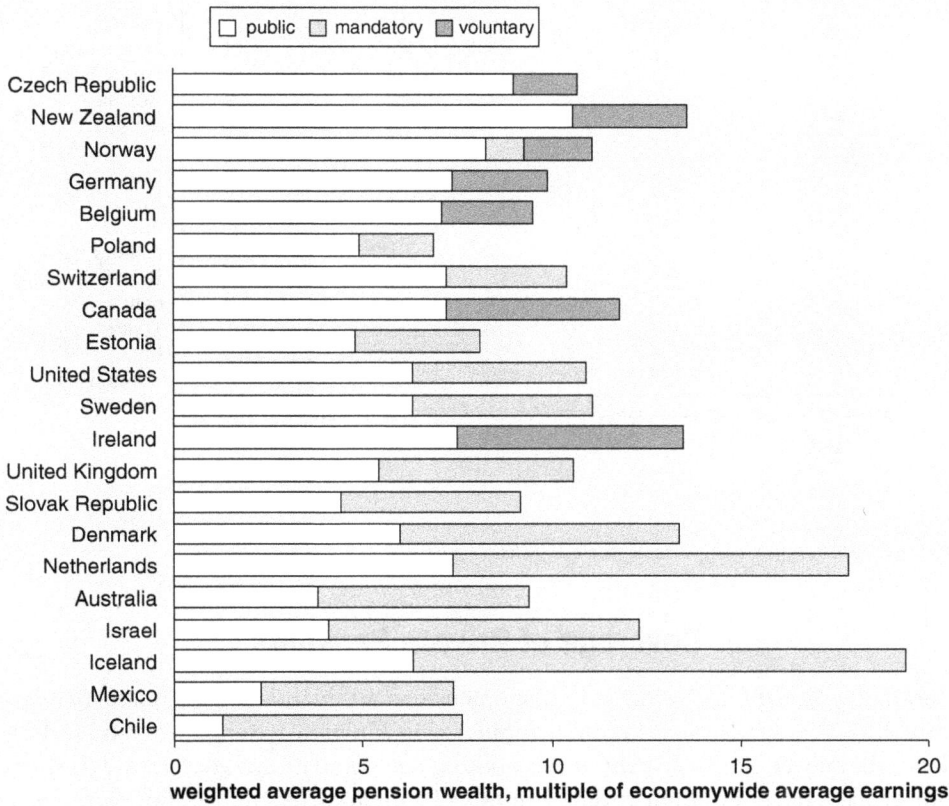

SOURCE: OECD 2011.

In Mexico, where the formal pension system covers less than half the workforce, retirees receive about 70 percent of their income from private pensions.

One of the major drivers of the shift to private pension provision is the reduction in public pension benefits. Figure 2.4 shows the change in overall lifetime pensions (including both public and mandatory private benefits) that resulted from pension reforms adopted since the early 1990s. It compares simulations of pension entitlements for workers spending a full career under the prereform and postreform rules. The average reduction in benefits is 22 percent, with Finland, France, and Sweden cutting benefits by slightly less than this figure and the Slovak Republic and Italy cutting benefits by rather more. In some cases, reductions in benefits have been accompanied by increases in both coverage of and contributions to private pensions. But in many cases, there does not appear to have been a reaction to fill the pension gap.

FIGURE 2.4 **Impact of pension reforms on lifetime retirement income benefits in selected OECD countries**

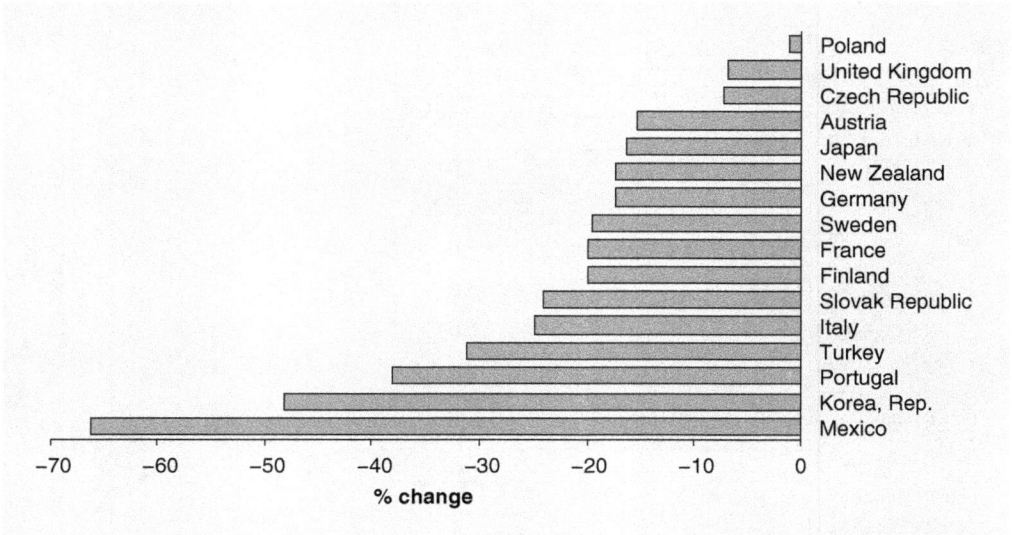

SOURCE: OECD 2009; see Whitehouse and others 2009 for more details.

Coverage of Private Pensions

In 14 of the 34 OECD countries, private pensions are mandatory or quasi-mandatory (figure 2.5). Occupational plans are compulsory in Finland, Iceland, Norway, and Switzerland; they cover 70–80 percent of the working-age population. Quasi-mandatory occupational plans have very high coverage rates in Denmark, the Netherlands, and Sweden, as a result of collective bargaining agreements at the sectoral or national level. Mandatory personal pensions are in place in eight OECD countries

Voluntary schemes can be optional in two senses. For occupational plans, employers are free to choose to establish a plan or not. Once a plan is established, it is possible for employers to make the plan a compulsory part of the employment contract in some cases. In some countries, employees either must be offered a choice as to whether to join (the United Kingdom and the United States, for example) or this is common practice. For personal plans, participation is entirely up to individuals.

Measuring coverage from administrative data can be difficult, because individuals can be members of both occupational and personal voluntary pension plans. Therefore total voluntary pension plan coverage cannot be obtained by summing occupational and personal coverage data.[3]

The coverage of voluntary pension plans (both occupational and personal) exceeds 50 percent in the Czech Republic, Germany, New Zealand, Norway, and the United Kingdom. It is very low in a range of countries at the bottom of the chart, such as Greece, Luxembourg, Mexico, Portugal, and Turkey.

Figure 2.6 examines some of the patterns in private pension coverage. Coverage increases with earnings (figure 2.6a) and is hump-shaped with respect to age (figure 2.6b).

FIGURE 2.5 **Private pension coverage in selected OECD countries, 2009**

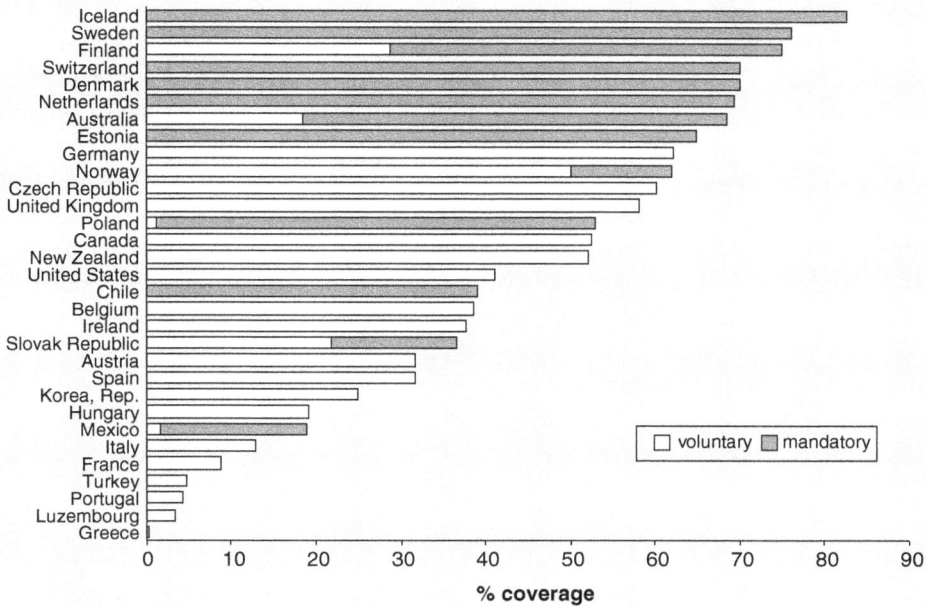

SOURCE: OECD 2011.

NOTE: Data for Australia, Belgium, Canada, and Switzerland are for 2008. Information for Hungary was adjusted to reflect the closure of nearly all mandatory individual accounts.

FIGURE 2.6 **Relationship between private pension coverage and age and earnings in selected countries**

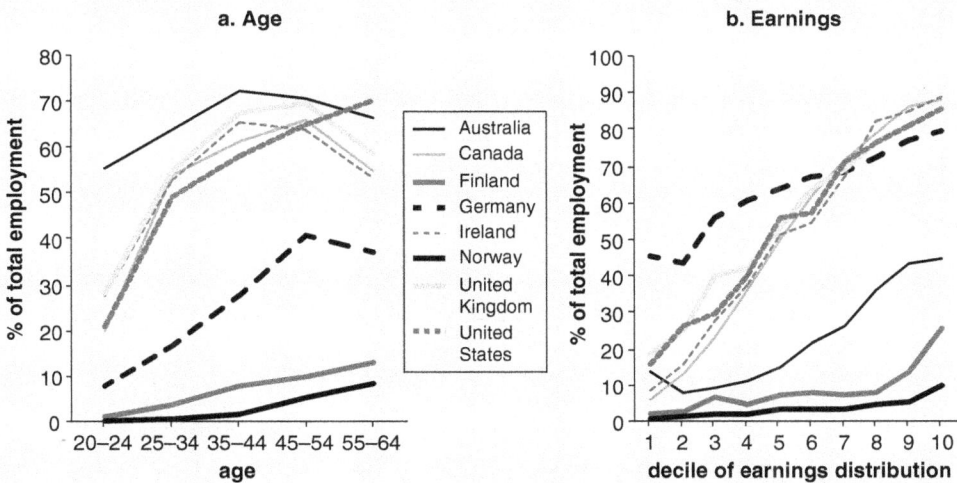

SOURCE: OECD 2011.

In most countries, it peaks at prime working ages (35–44 or 45–54, depending on the country). Exceptions are the United States and the two countries with low overall coverage of voluntary plans (Finland and Norway), where membership continues to increase with age.

The relationship between private pension coverage and both age and earnings is similar in Canada, Ireland, the United Kingdom, and the United States. Germany is a significant outlier in both respects, achieving much higher rates of coverage of younger and lower-income workers than other countries do. One explanation for this phenomenon might be that English-speaking countries have public pension systems that redistribute from high earners to low earners, through basic pension schemes (Canada and Ireland), a redistributive formula in an earnings-related scheme, or both (the United Kingdom). Means-tested benefits are a significant component of retirement incomes, received by a quarter to a third of pensioners in all countries except the United States. As a result, there is a much smaller "pension gap" for low earners than for high earners in these countries: replacement rates for low earners are high relative to richer workers. This is not the case in Germany (see Antolín and Whitehouse 2009 for a more detailed analysis of the pension gap and voluntary retirement savings).

Financial Incentives

A standard policy for encouraging private voluntary retirement saving is the granting of preferential tax treatment to pension plans. The idea is that a higher net rate of return on savings will encourage people to save more. These tax incentives tend to come with conditions, usually governing the duration of saving and restrictions on the way benefits can be withdrawn. It is such conditions that qualify these as "retirement savings."

Matching contributions are another type of financial incentive. The difference between a tax incentive and a matching contribution can be simply a matter of nomenclature: whether government support is labeled a "tax" or a "match" can be irrelevant to the financial flows involved. There can, however, be significant structural differences between the two that affect the financial flows. Tax relief may be provided at individuals' marginal rates. A sizable group of people of working age does not pay income tax and does not generally benefit from tax relief unless it is provided in the form of "nonwasteable" what are sometimes call "refundable" tax credits (that is, relief granted to both nontaxpayers and taxpayers). Similarly, fiscal incentives will tend to benefit people who pay tax at the highest marginal rates more than those paying lower or standard rates.

IMPACT OF FISCAL INCENTIVES

Economic theory is ambiguous regarding the effects of tax incentives for savings on individual behavior, even in a simple world in which the only motivation for saving is to provide for retirement.[4] The various effects include the following:

- Because pensions are typically illiquid, they increase overall savings for households that face binding borrowing constraints (Hubbard and Skinner 1996).
- Tax incentives increase the net rate of return on pensions relative to other kinds of saving. The income effect of the higher return reduces saving; the substitution effect increases saving.

- Pensions are an annuitized form of saving. By providing longevity insurance, they should both increase welfare and reduce saving to protect against an uncertain life span (Hubbard and Judd 1987).

- Pensions may induce earlier retirement, which will increase pension saving (Feldstein 1974).

Do tax incentives increase coverage of private pension plans? The OECD has measured incentives to save in pension schemes by comparing the effective tax rate on pensions with the effective rate applied to benchmark savings (typically the bank deposit rate) (Yoo and de Serres 2004a, 2004b).[5] The scale of tax incentives is calculated as a percentage of contributions, measured in present value terms over a given time horizon. Because the calculation considers revenues foregone from deductible contributions and tax-free investment returns from the nontaxation of accrued income and takes account of revenues collected when benefits are withdrawn, it can be said to be on a net basis. The calculations average over nine age groups with different investment horizons.

The results are shown in figures 2.7 and 2.8. Figure 2.7 separates the tax treatment of pension savings at three stages: when contributions are made, as investment returns accumulate, and when benefits are withdrawn. Relative to benchmark saving, the size of the tax incentive for investing in private pensions varies significantly across countries, ranging from about zero in Mexico and New Zealand to nearly 40 percent of contributions in the Czech Republic. Most countries provide incentives of at least 10 percent of contributions; the average is more than 20 percent.

The incentive is naturally highest in countries that exempt pension contributions from tax and lower in countries, such as Sweden and Italy, that tax investment returns of pension plans. However, given that the net tax cost reflects the generosity of tax treatment of private pension savings relative to alternative nonpension savings vehicles, there is no systematic pattern (figure 2.8). In fact, several countries that exempt private pension contributions and investment returns (Greece, Iceland, Mexico, Poland, Korea, the Netherlands, and the Slovak Republic) also provide generous tax breaks for alternative savings vehicles. Hence, there is only a small incentive to save in the form of pensions relative to benchmarks.

Figure 2.9 explores whether coverage of voluntary private plans is higher in countries with more generous tax incentives. The link between the two is very weak and a possible causality can go both ways. There is a cluster of countries at the left of figure 2.9 with relatively low coverage of private pensions and another group at the right with much higher coverage. But the level of tax incentives is not very different between the two groups: 24 percent in the left-hand cluster and 28 percent in the right-hand cluster. A simple regression shows that coverage increases somewhat with the size of the tax incentive but that the effect is far from significant.

This simple cross-country analysis fails to capture many of the nuances of single-country studies, which are able to address two policy issues:

- Are contributions to a tax-privileged pension plan "new saving," or are they simply diverted from other savings vehicles?

- If additional household saving is motivated by the tax break, does it exceed the revenues foregone from the tax incentive?

FIGURE 2.7 **Tax treatment of investment returns, private pension contributions, and withdrawals in selected OECD countries**

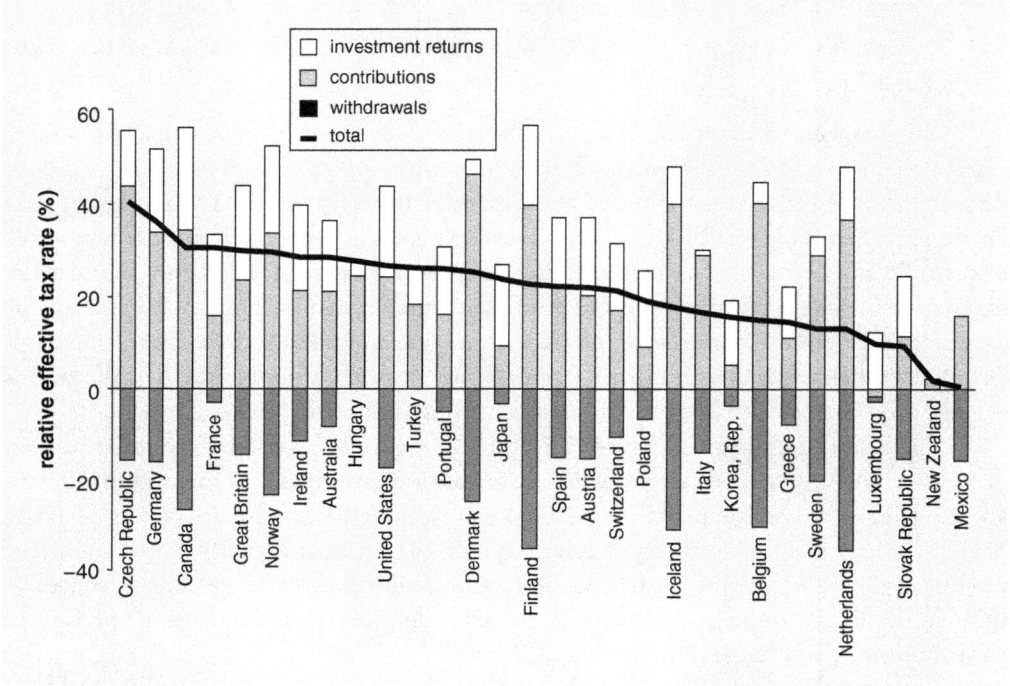

SOURCES: Yoo and de Serres 2004a, 2004b.

FIGURE 2.8 **Tax treatment of benchmark savings and private pensions in selected OECD countries**

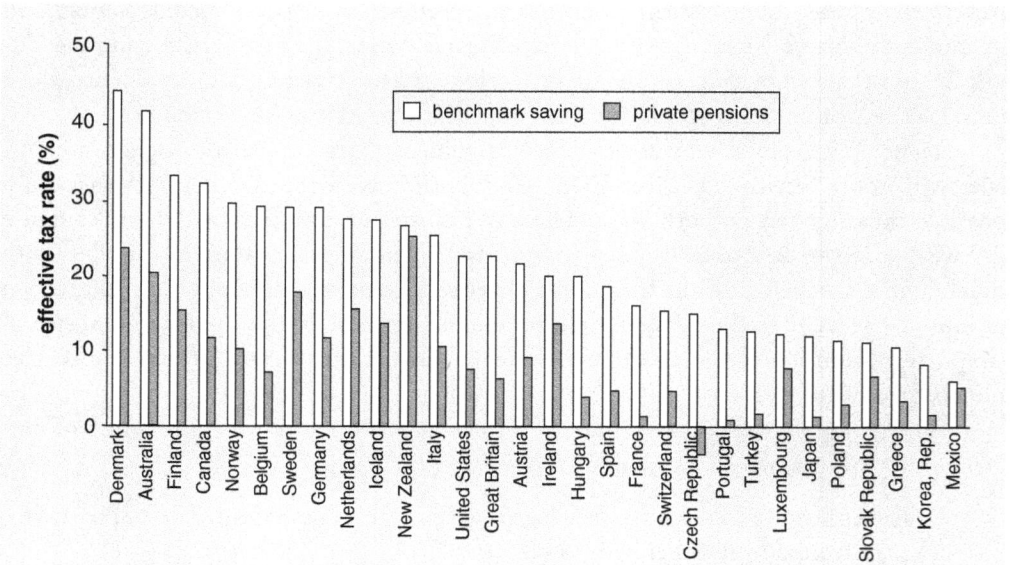

SOURCES: Yoo and de Serres 2004a, 2004b.

FIGURE 2.9 **Correlation between coverage of voluntary private pensions and tax incentives for private pensions relative to benchmark savings**

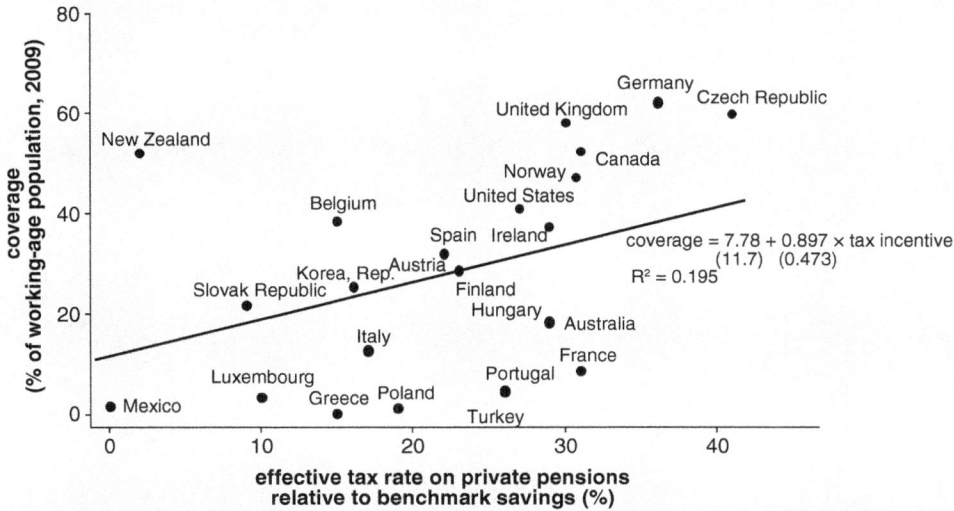

SOURCES: Data on tax incentives are from Yoo and de Serres 2004a, 2004b; data on coverage are from OECD 2009.

The impact of pension plans and tax incentives on savings is the subject of a long-running debate, dating back to the 1960s. Much of the literature concerns the United States, particularly individual retirement accounts (IRAs) and 401(k)s, a type of employer-based defined contribution plan (discussed in detail in chapter 3). Figure 2.10 summarizes the results of these studies.

Some researchers (for example, Poterba, Venti, and Wise on the United States and Venti and Wise 1995 on Canada) find a large, significant effect of tax-favored retirement saving schemes in terms of increasing net saving. Other researchers report little or no net effect, merely diversion of savings from less tax-favored instruments (see, for example, Milligan 2002 on Canada; Attanasio and Banks 1998 and Attanasio, Banks, and Wakefield 2004 on the United Kingdom; and Engen, Gale, and Scholtz 1994, 1996 on the United States).

In principle, it should be possible to gauge the effect of tax incentives on saving by comparing the total savings of individuals who contribute to such schemes with the savings of individuals who do not contribute. But this approach is valid only if eligibility is exogenous to the propensity to save. In practice, higher savings of people participating in tax-favored savings plans could reflect only their greater underlying preference for saving rather than a genuine net increase in overall savings. Different approaches to controlling for heterogeneity in saving preferences (and other unobservable characteristics) are an important factor behind the breadth of the range of empirical results.

Venti and Wise (1990, 1991) compare assets of households with contributors to IRAs with assets of noncontributors, controlling for initial wealth. They conclude that most IRA contributions are new saving. However, two individuals with the same initial

FIGURE 2.10 **Percentage of IRA and 401(k) saving that is new saving**

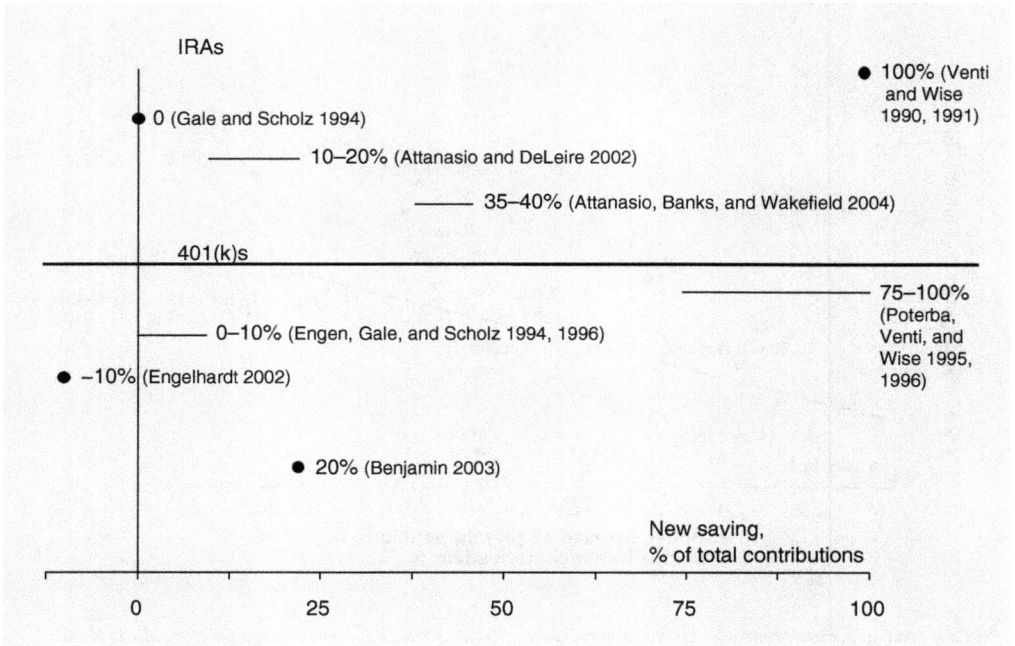

IRAs

● 100% (Venti and Wise 1990, 1991)

● 0 (Gale and Scholz 1994)

———— 10–20% (Attanasio and DeLeire 2002)

———— 35–40% (Attanasio, Banks, and Wakefield 2004)

401(k)s

———————— 75–100% (Poterba, Venti, and Wise 1995, 1996)

———— 0–10% (Engen, Gale, and Scholz 1994, 1996)

● –10% (Engelhardt 2002)

● 20% (Benjamin 2003)

New saving, % of total contributions

0   25   50   75   100

wealth do not necessarily have the same underlying preferences toward saving. Gale and Scholz (1994) allow saving behavior to vary according to whether the individual is an IRA contributor or not, assuming different marginal propensities to save in IRAs and other savings vehicles. They then identify the impact of IRAs on saving by looking at the effect of a change in the IRA contribution limit, distinguishing between contributors who reached and contributors who did not reach the established ceilings. They conclude that a negligible fraction of contributions to IRAs represents new saving. However, their approach does not eliminate the possibility of inferring incorrectly that IRA saving displaces other forms of saving (Bernheim 1999). Moreover, their results are highly sensitive to small changes in the sample chosen for the analysis (by income level) (see Poterba, Venti, and Wise 1996a, 1996b).

Attanasio and DeLeire (2002) exploit the idea that correlations between IRA saving and non-IRA saving can be particularly informative in the case of new contributors. They compare consumption growth in households that recently opened an IRA with growth in households that had already contributed to an IRA. They find that households finance IRA contributions not from a reduction in consumption but rather from existing or planned saving. They estimate that 9–20 percent of total IRA contributions were new saving.

Poterba, Venti, and Wise (1995, 1996a, 1996b) compare the financial assets of households eligible for 401(k)s with the assets of households without access to a 401(k) plan. They find little substitution between saving in 401(k)s and other financial assets. They also find that 401(k) eligibility correlates significantly with financial wealth. They therefore conclude that virtually all contributions to 401(k)s represent new saving.

Engen, Gale, and Scholz (1994, 1996) and others challenge the assumption of exo-geneity of eligibility for a 401(k) that underlies these studies. They argue that employ-ees with greater preference for saving tend to gravitate toward jobs with good retirement provision (see Allen, Clark, and McDermed 1993 and Even and Macpherson 2000 for evidence). Furthermore, employers may use 401(k) programs to attract employees with such tastes (because preference for 401(k) plans may correlate with other desirable charac-teristics, such as loyalty and long-term planning). Alternatively, they may establish 401(k) plans to meet the preferences of existing employees. Engen, Gale, and Scholz conclude that only a negligible part of 401(k) contributions represents new saving.

A second difference between these studies is the range of assets considered. Poterba, Venti, and Wise find an upward shift in the relative financial assets of people eligible for a 401(k), concluding that all contributions are new savings. Engen, Gale, and Scholz include home equity (property value less mortgage) in their measure of assets, arguing that some 401(k) contributions might be financed by equity withdrawal, leaving total net wealth unchanged. By allowing for substitution between real (property) and financial assets, Engen, Gale, and Scholz find a much smaller effect of 401(k) eligibility on total wealth than Poterba, Venti, and Wise find for financial assets alone.

Caveats apply to all of these studies. First, all studies compare the wealth of different groups of workers. But outside factors, such as the roller coaster path of equity markets since the mid-1980s, have a huge impact on wealth at any point in time that is likely to dwarf the behavioral effects of the availability of tax-favored retirement savings plans. Similarly, Engen, Gale, and Scholz's results are affected by changes in housing prices over time. Second, most studies are based on a time series of cross-section data. However, the composition of both eligible workers and plan participants is likely to change over time. For example, coverage of 401(k)s and IRAs expanded over time. If newly covered individ-uals were less motivated savers than early adopters, there would be a spurious downward shift in participants' wealth that would offset some of the behavioral effect of tax-favored retirement savings plans. Third, employers have played a major role in wealth and savings composition with the substitution of 401(k)s for other kinds of retirement income provi-sion (Andrews 1992; Papke 1995, 1999).

The impact of 401(k) on saving probably lies somewhere between the two extreme conclusions of "no new saving" and "all new saving" (Hubbard and Skinner 1996), although a wide range of estimates is plausible. Börsch-Supan (2004) finds that the evi-dence of new saving in European countries is even weaker than it is in the United States.

More recent studies report different results for different kinds of people. Engen and Gale (2000) find that tax incentives for 401(k)s raise savings for low earners and low savers but have little effect on high earners and high savers. Benjamin (2003) finds that 401(k)s are more effective in increasing new saving by people in rented housing and households without IRAs than they are for homeowners and people with IRAs.

FISCAL COST OF TAX INCENTIVES

Tax incentives for pensions necessarily involve a fiscal cost in terms of revenues foregone. These costs have been quantified as "tax expenditures." This expenditure concept of tax preferences, originally put forward by Surrey (1973), has been used in many OECD reports (1984, 1995, 2010) that look at tax breaks for a range of purposes. These reports review national reporting of tax expenditures. They include national calculations of the cost of tax incentives for private pensions.[6]

The literature on tax expenditures provides a number of warnings. Tax expenditures should not be added up (because they interact but the calculations of their value are independent), they should not be compared across countries (because they are calculated relative to different benchmarks), and they should not be compared with direct expenditures. The analysis that follows breaks two of these three rules and so comes with caveats.

Figure 2.11 presents information from the OECD's Social Expenditure Database (SOCX) on tax expenditures for private pensions, which come from national authorities. The bars show the proportion of national income in revenues foregone, a figure that ranges from close to zero in France and Italy to more than 2.5 percent in Australia. The numbers next to the bars show these tax expenditures as a proportion of direct expenditure on public pensions and other benefits for older people. Tax incentives cost an average of 14 percent of direct pension spending; the figure is much higher in Australia (80 percent) and in Canada and Iceland (about 50 percent). The share is also high in Ireland and the United Kingdom, where tax expenditures represent more than 1 percent of national income.

To address their public finance difficulties, many OECD countries are embarking on fiscal consolidation. Some countries have already made changes to private pension taxation in order to reduce the revenues foregone through fiscal incentives. In other countries,

FIGURE 2.11 **Revenues foregone from tax incentives for private pensions in selected OECD countries as a percentage of GDP and a percentage of public expenditure on pensions, 2007**

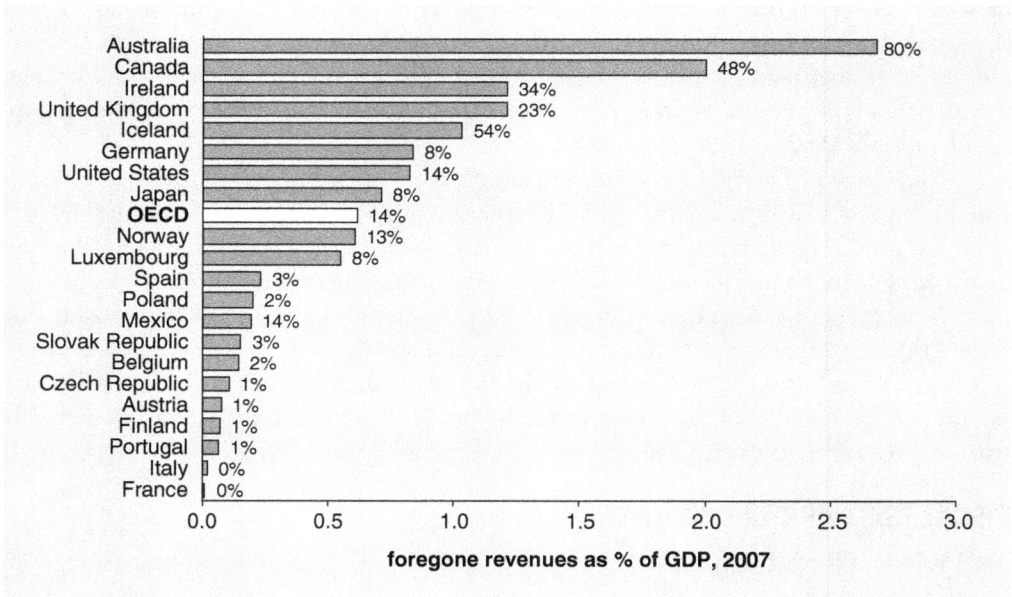

SOURCE: OECD 2011.

NOTE: Percentages noted alongside the bars are the cost of tax incentives in relation to direct pension spending.

there is a lively debate about reform, such as reducing the ceilings on deductible pension contributions in Australia, Ireland, and the United Kingdom. In addition, Ireland is levying an annual tax of 0.6 percent of assets on pension funds for four years. Since its introduction in 2007, New Zealand's KiwiSaver plan (discussed in greater detail in chapter 5) has seen frequent changes in tax treatment, compulsory employer-matched contributions, and government contributions. The most recent changes have been to curtail financial incentives, which are costly, as the government provides 41 percent of the money going into accounts, according to the Retirement Commission (2010). Germany extended the financial incentives for Riester pensions that were due to expire at the end of 2008, but not without debate about their cost. As chapter 4 shows, 37 percent of contributions to these plans have come from state coffers.

Bucking this trend, Chile and Poland have expanded tax relief in recent years. In both cases, voluntary plans had failed to have much of an impact. Tax incentives were strengthened in order to increase take-up.

Mandating Contributions and Using Soft Compulsion

Mandating contributions is an easy way to achieve both high coverage of private pensions and more uniform coverage across ages and incomes (figures 2.5 and 2.6). Two policy approaches to compulsion can be identified.

In countries such as Australia, Iceland, Norway, and Switzerland, voluntary private pensions historically had broad coverage (50 percent or more of employees). Governments made it mandatory for employers to organize and contribute to private pensions on their employees' behalf. The mandatory level of pension provision was below the customary level that prevailed when private pensions were provided voluntarily, however.

A second policy has been to mandate private pension contributions as a substitute for part of the public pension. Chile, Estonia, Hungary, Mexico, Poland, the Slovak Republic, and Sweden have all taken this approach, and the Czech Republic will do so in 2013. In contrast, Hungary recently nationalized its private pension funds, and Poland has partially reversed its reform (OECD 2012).

The main arguments for compulsion are that it protects people from regretting not having saved enough for their retirement when they were younger and protects societies from having to pay for safety net benefits for people who did not provide for their own old age. Implementing this paternalistic approach is simple: it involves choosing a target replacement rate (which may or may not vary with earnings) and then ensuring that people reach that target through either public retirement income provision or mandatory private pension plans.

An important, but unresolved, question is whether compulsion is necessary. Are people myopic? Left to their own devices, will they fail to save enough for retirement?

One way to investigate this question is to exploit historical differences in the degree of mandatory pension provision. Comparing the outcomes for retirement incomes of today's pensioners might show evidence of myopia in countries in which voluntary pension provision has long played a major role.

Figure 2.12 shows how pensioner incomes compared with the incomes of the population as a whole. The data are net incomes, adjusted for household size. There is

FIGURE 2.12 **Pensioners' incomes as a percentage of population income in selected OECD countries, mid-2000s**

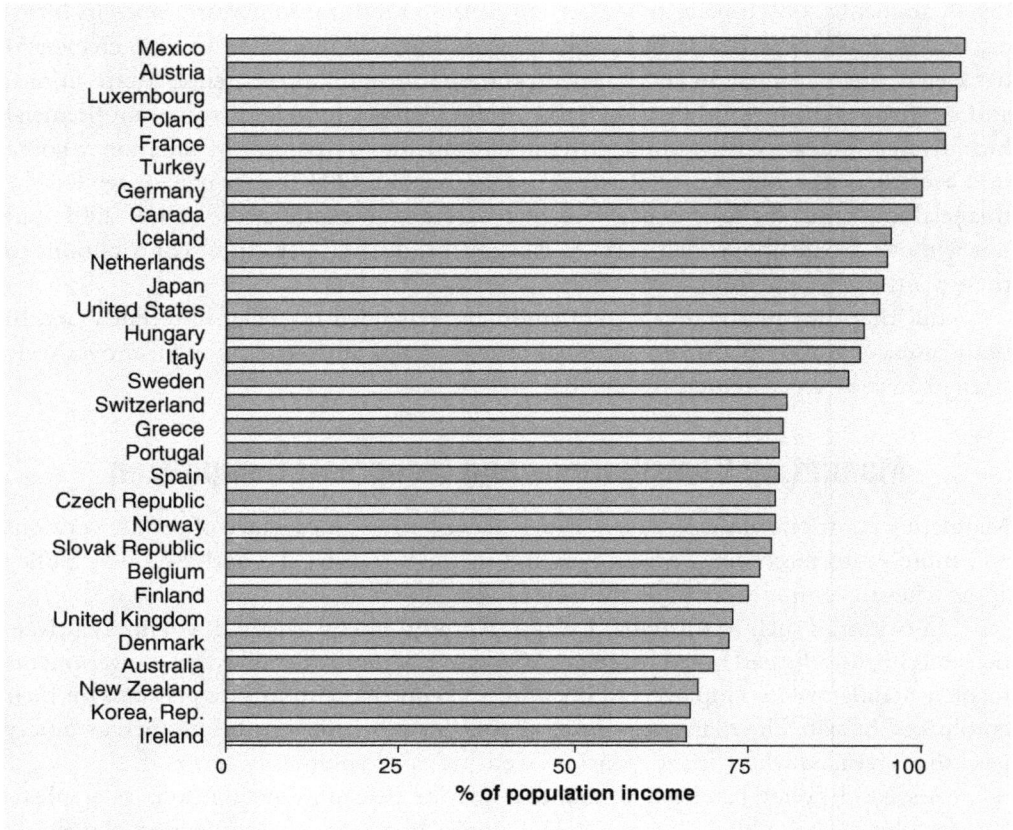

SOURCES: OECD 2008, 2011.

significant bunching of countries with older people's incomes of 75–85 percent of the population average, covering a dozen countries from Hungary to Finland; the OECD average is 82 percent. But there is no link between relative incomes and the type of pension system. Voluntary private pensions play an important role in Canada and the United States, where older people's incomes are relatively high, as well as in Ireland and the United Kingdom, where they are well below average. The OECD (2001) describes this phenomenon as "convergent outcomes, divergent means." These data provide some evidence that the myopia hypothesis does not hold.

Several arguments can be made against compulsion:

- Even if individuals are myopic, it does not mean that greater mandatory pension provision is always a good thing. Mandating retirement saving means choosing a target replacement rate. It is difficult but important to get this rate right, as losses of individual welfare from forcing people to oversave can be as great as losses from myopia and undersaving. Resources diverted to retirement savings, for example, might come at the expense of raising and educating children.

- Formal pension plans are not the only way people can and do save for retirement. People might want to invest in property or their own business. This perfectly rational behavior is not possible with large, mandatory saving through formal pension schemes.

- Mandatory contributions to pensions are often perceived as a tax, which is likely to discourage people from working.

- Providers of voluntary pension arrangements—especially occupational pension schemes—often oppose compulsion because it would crowd out existing plans. There is also the risk that existing provision is leveled down to the amount of the mandate.

In countries such as Denmark, the Netherlands, and Sweden, more than 85 percent of employers offer private pension plans, even though the plans are not mandatory. Coverage of this extent is achieved through industrial relations agreements in different sectors. Employers covered by the agreement must offer a pension plan, and their employees must join it (for this reason, these plans are called "quasi-mandatory" in OECD analyses). Coverage of voluntary pension arrangements in Belgium and Germany has also edged upward in recent years, as a result of the establishment of industrywide pension plans. However, this model is difficult to export to other countries, where labor market and industrial relations structures are less amenable to achieving near-universal coverage of private pensions.

Figure 2.13 compares coverage of voluntary private pensions with the simulated pension entitlements of full-career workers. These entitlements are shown relative to economywide average earnings. Taking a weighted average across the earnings distribution captures the redistributive features of the pension system (which reduce the need for low earners to save for retirement) and the impact of ceilings (which increase the need for high earners to save). The modeling includes all mandatory components of the retirement income system, including compulsory private pensions where appropriate.

The relationship between voluntary private pension coverage and mandatory retirement income provision is negative and statistically significant. Coverage is high in Canada, Germany, the United Kingdom, and the United States, where public pensions are (or will be for today's workers) relatively low. In Greece and Luxembourg, by contrast, public benefits are high: few workers need private pensions as a supplement, and very few have them. Comparing figure 2.13 with the analysis of tax treatment in figure 2.9 shows that the "space" left by the mandatory retirement income system appears to have much more impact on the extent of coverage than do fiscal incentives. Figure 2.13 is consistent with the finding of "convergent outcomes, divergent means" in the discussion of figure 2.12.

Compulsion has disadvantages, especially the risk of forced oversaving for retirement in formal pension plans. But purely voluntary pension provision runs the risk of undersaving. Automatic enrollment offers a third way between compulsion and voluntarism. It is often therefore called "soft compulsion."

The idea is that people have to opt out of saving for retirement rather than opt in. Surveys of financial literacy, such as the OECD's (2005), routinely find that people agree that saving for retirement is important and that they feel they should be planning for old age. Unfortunately, these beliefs often fail to translate into action: inertia and procrastination predominate.[7] An obvious reason for this inertia is that the process of signing up for

FIGURE 2.13 **Coverage of voluntary private pensions compared with tax incentives for private pensions relative to benchmark savings in selected OECD countries**

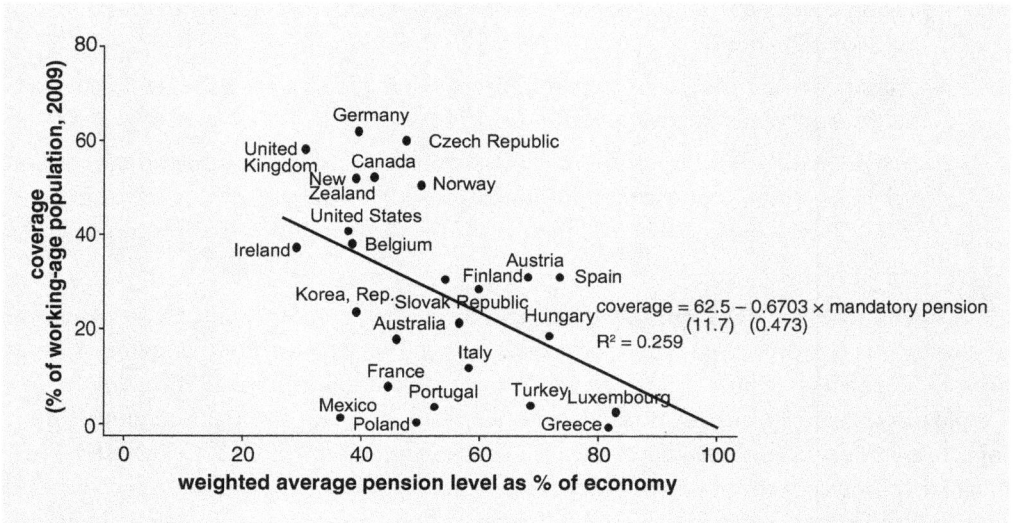

SOURCES: Weighted average pension level data are from OECD 2011; for data on coverage, see figure 2.5 and its notes.

NOTE: The weighted average pension level is the simulated pension relative to economywide average earnings for full-career workers, with the weights reflecting the national earnings distribution.

a pension plan can be long and complex. Indeed, many people say that retirement planning is "more stressful than going to the dentist" (OECD 2005). Automatic enrollment is designed to capture such people and turn them into retirement savers.

Two countries have introduced automatic enrollment (with an opt-out clause) into private pension plans at the national level. The results have been mixed. New Zealand achieved a coverage rate of 43 percent with its KiwiSaver scheme. This figure understates the impact, as people are subject to automatic enrollment only when entering the labor force or when they change jobs (the government has discussed extending this provision to existing employees at some point). About a third of automatic enrollees have chosen to opt out. In Italy, severance pay is automatically paid into an occupational pension plan unless employees explicitly choose to retain severance pay. Although this provision has been in place for people working in companies with 50 employees or more since 2007, only 13 percent of the working-age population is covered by a voluntary pension plan in Italy. The United Kingdom's new automatic enrollment scheme is being rolled out over six years beginning in October 2012.

Other countries have discussed adopting such an approach. The Retirement Security Project in the United States has developed a bipartisan proposal for a national scheme with automatic enrollment (Iwry and John 2007). Both the current and previous governments in Ireland have backed this approach (Department of Social and Family Affairs 2007). Germany has also considered introducing automatic enrollment for the salary conversion (Entgeltumwandlung) (Leinert 2004, 2005). One reason for the prominence of this policy has been the rapid development of the discipline of behavioral economics, which has quickly achieved influence among policy makers.

A number of employer-provided pension plans in the United Kingdom and the United States have long used automatic enrollment to increase coverage among their employees. The evidence from the United States is discussed in detail in chapters 3 and 15.

This chapter therefore discusses some of the evidence from the United Kingdom. According to the Government Actuary (2006), 48 percent of occupational plans automatically enrolled all new employees in 2005, and another 12 percent applied automatic enrollment to some employees. These figures represent a modest increase over 1995, when 43 percent of employees were in plans that automatically enrolled everyone and 7 percent in plans with some automatic enrollment. However, there are some definitional questions about what constitutes automatic enrollment. The Department for Work and Pensions distinguishes four enrollment procedures. The department's survey found that 44 percent used a process of "streamlined joining," which required the employee only to sign a completed form (McKay 2006). Only 19 percent of employees were covered by plans with full automatic enrollment—that is, plans that require an active opt-out. As in the United States, both of these enrollment procedures were more common among larger employers. Traditional opt-in accounted for 19 percent of plans, weighted by the number of members.

Most of the evidence on the effectiveness of automatic enrollment in the United Kingdom is based on case studies of a handful of schemes. Horack and Wood (2005) examine 11 company pension schemes in the United Kingdom that changed their enrollment arrangements. Two firms that introduced automatic enrollment increased coverage (one from 25 percent to 58 percent, the other from 45 percent to 62 percent). The other two firms already had very high coverage rates (86 percent and 88 percent), most likely because the schemes did not require employee contributions. Automatic enrollment increased these shares to 92 percent at one firm and 100 percent at the other.

Hawksworth (2006) reports the most dramatic increase in coverage from automatic enrollment—from 15 percent to 100 percent—in the Building and Civil Engineering scheme. The Government Actuary's survey of occupational plans in the United Kingdom finds coverage of 89 percent in plans that automatically enroll everyone, 73 percent in plans in which some employees are enrolled, and 59 percent in plans without automatic enrollment. The survey carried out for the Department of Work and Pensions finds coverage of 41 percent in traditional opt-in plans and 60 percent in plans with automatic enrollment (McKay 2006). These figures relate to larger employers (firms with more than 20 employees). Among smaller employers, coverage was virtually the same with traditional and automatic enrollment (at 67 percent).

The studies of the United Kingdom and United States suggest an important effect of automatic enrollment on coverage of private pensions. However, it can be difficult to disentangle the impact from other features of the pension plan, such as the scale of the required employee contribution and the amount the employer is willing to contribute.

In New Zealand, for example, coverage of private pensions was relatively low before the KiwiSaver reform: at about 20 percent, it was substantially lower than in other countries with similar pension systems (see figure 2.13). Two-thirds of KiwiSaver members actively chose to sign up, according to the Inland Revenue, with the other third automatically enrolled. About half went directly to a provider to enroll; another 14 percent did so through their employer. These findings suggest that the main factor driving the high level of coverage of the new scheme was the financial incentive, comprising both government contributions and tax relief.

Conclusion

Private pensions provide about 20 percent of retirement income on average in OECD countries. In most countries, this share has been increasing for at least two decades. The trend is likely to continue, thanks to the introduction of compulsory private pensions and the fact that more private retirement savings are needed to fill the pension gap resulting from lower public benefits in the future.

This volume is concerned principally with financial incentives for private pensions. However, these incentives should be seen in the broader context of other policy options, such as automatic enrollment. Both the World Bank and the OECD are exploring the issues of financial literacy and capabilities, along with the types of programs that can improve them. In principle, greater awareness of the need to save for retirement might expand coverage of and increase contribution rates to private pensions; better knowledge of how to save for retirement and facilitation of access to private pension plans, particularly through the workplace, might make it easier to save for retirement. In practice, policy initiatives in this area—such as making it easier for smaller employers to set up occupational plans in the United States and the requirement for employers in the United Kingdom to offer stakeholder pensions—have not led to significant expansions of coverage.

OECD countries have traditionally provided tax relief on pension contributions at individuals' marginal tax rates. This practice has been questioned on a number of grounds. First, estimates suggest that 80 percent of the value of tax relief in Ireland accrues to the richest quintile of the income distribution. Figures for the United Kingdom show that a quarter of the tax expenditure goes to the wealthiest 1.5 percent. Second, tax incentives have not proved effective at expanding coverage among low earners or younger workers. Riester pensions in Germany and KiwiSaver in New Zealand involve government matching and flat-rate contributions. In Germany at least, these mechanisms have been effective in engaging hard-to-reach groups. Both KiwiSaver and the new automatic enrollment scheme in the United Kingdom include compulsory employer matching contributions as an additional financial incentive.

Regarding automatic enrollment, more evidence is needed to determine how effective it is in extending coverage of private pensions. Longer-term data are needed to assess the degree of persistence in pension coverage. For example, over time, workers may overcome their inertia in the opposite direction and realize that opting out is a quick way of increasing current income. Moreover, schemes with automatic enrollment involve sizable subsidies to individual savings. All occupational plans in the United Kingdom and the United States include employer contributions of varying sizes. Care is therefore needed to isolate a "pure" automatic enrollment effect on coverage from the effect of the subsidies.

The automatic enrollment approach to extending coverage of private pensions is likely to spread. Survey evidence suggests that automatic enrollment is much more popular with individuals than compulsion in the United Kingdom (Bunt and others 2006; Hall, Pettigrew, and Harvey 2006). And voters' views are shared by many politicians, who worry that workers will view mandatory contributions to private pensions as an unwelcome tax on their earnings. If soft compulsion fails to deliver a sustained increase in private pension coverage, governments adopting this approach must keep the policy of compulsion in reserve.

Notes

1. Data for Switzerland are not shown, because capital (mainly private pensions) and work incomes are aggregated in the database. Together they account for 52 percent of older people's income on average, with the 48 percent residual coming from public transfers.

2. Figures for the Czech Republic do not take account of the new mandatory defined contribution scheme, which will be introduced in 2013 at the earliest.

3. Using Canada as an example, 34 percent of the working-age population is enrolled in occupational plans, and 35 percent has personal pensions. Overall voluntary pension coverage in Canada is only 53 percent, however, because 48 percent of people with occupational pension plans also have personal plans.

4. This discussion draws on Antolín and Lopez Ponton (2007).

5. An earlier but more comprehensive study of household saving is by the OECD (1994). Whitehouse (1999) presents results pertaining to pensions.

6. Other OECD studies—Yoo and de Serres (2004a, 2004b) and Antolín, de Serres, and de la Maisonneuve (2004)—calculate their own estimates of the revenue effect of the tax treatment of private pensions.

7. See chapter 15 of this volume and the references therein.

References

Allen, S. G., R. L. Clark, and A. A. McDermed. 1993. "Pensions, Bonding, and Lifetime Jobs." *Journal of Human Resources* 28: 463–81.

Andrews, Emily. 1992. "The Growth and Distribution of 401(k) Plans." In *Trends in Pensions 1992,* ed. John Turner and Daniel Beller, 149–76. Washington, DC: U.S. Government Printing Office.

Antolín, P., A. de Serres, and C. de la Maisonneuve. 2004. "Long-Term Budgetary Implications of Tax-Favoured Retirement Saving Plans." Working Paper 393, Organisation for Economic Co-operation and Development, Economics Department, Paris.

Antolín, P., and E. R. Whitehouse. 2009. "Filling the Pension Gap: Coverage and Value of Voluntary Retirement Savings. Social, Employment and Migration Working Paper 9, Organisation for Economic Co-operation and Development, Paris.

Antolín, P., and E. Lopez Ponton. 2007. "The Impact of Tax Incentives on Retirement Savings: A Literature Review." In *OECD/IOPS, Global Private Pension Conference Proceedings.* Paris: Organisation for Economic Co-operation and Development.

Attanasio, O. and J. Banks. 1998. "Trends in Household Saving Don't Justify Tax Incentives to Boost Saving." *Economic Policy* 13 (27): 547–83.

Attanasio, O., J. Banks, and M. Wakefield. 2004. "Effectiveness of Tax Incentives to Boost (Retirement) Saving: Theoretical Motivation and Empirical Evidence." *OECD Economic Studies* 39: 145–72.

Attanasio, O., and T. DeLeire. 2002. "The Effect of Individual Retirement Accounts on House-hold Consumption and National Saving." *Economic Journal* 112: 594–38.

Benjamin, D. J. 2003. "Does 401(k) Eligibility Increase Saving? Evidence from Propensity Score Subclassification." *Journal of Public Economics* 87 (5–6): 1259–90.

Bernheim, B. D. 1999. "Taxation and Saving." NBER Working Paper 7061, National Bureau of Economic Research, Cambridge, MA.

Börsch-Supan, A. 2004. "Mind the Gap: The Effectiveness of Incentives to Boost Retirement Saving in Europe." *OECD Economic Studies* 39: 111–44.

Bunt, K., L. Adams, Z. Koroglu, and E. O'Donnell. 2006. "Pensions and Pension Reform." Research Report 357, Department for Work and Pensions, London.

Department of Social and Family Affairs. 2007. "Green Paper on Pensions." Stationery Office, Dublin.

Disney, R. F., and E. R. Whitehouse. 2001. "Cross-Country Comparisons of Pensioners' Incomes." Research Report 142, Department of Work and Pensions, London.

————. 2003. "The Economic Well-Being of Older People in International Perspective: A Critical Review." In *Economic Outcomes in Later Life*, ed. S. Crystal and D. Shea. *Annual Review of Gerontology and Geriatrics* 22. New York: Springer Publishing.

Engelhardt, G. V. 2002. "Have 401(k)s Raised Household Saving? Evidence from the Health and Retirement Study." Working Paper 2002-023, Department of Economics, Syracuse University, Syracuse, NY.

Engen, E. M., and W. G. Gale. 2000. "The Effects of 401(k) Plans on Household Wealth: Differences Across Earnings Groups." NBER Working Paper 8032, National Bureau of Economic Research, Cambridge, MA.

Engen, E. M., W. G. Gale, and J. K. Scholz. 1994. "Do Saving Incentives Work?" *Brookings Papers on Economic Activity* 1: 85–151.

————. 1996. "The Illusory Effect of Saving Incentives on Saving." *Journal of Economic Perspectives* 10 (4): 113–38.

Even, W. E., and D. A. Macpherson. 2000. "The Changing Distribution of Pension Coverage." *Industrial Relations* 39 (2): 199–227.

Feldstein, M. S. 1974. "Social Security, Induced Retirement and Aggregate Capital Accumulation." *Journal of Political Economy* 82 (5): 905–26.

Förster, M., and M. Mira d'Ercole. 2005. "Income Distribution and Poverty in OECD Countries in the Second Half of the 1990s." Social, Employment and Migration Working Paper 22, Organisation for Economic Co-operation and Development, Paris.

Gale, W. G., and J. K. Scholz. 1994. "IRAs and Household Saving." *American Economic Review* 84 (December): 1233–60.

Government Actuary's Department. 2006. *Occupational Pension Schemes 2005: The Thirteenth Survey by the Government Actuary.* London: Government Actuary's Department.

Hall, S., N. Pettigrew, and P. Harvey. 2006. "Public Attitudes to Personal Accounts: Report of a Qualitative Study." Research Report 370, Department for Work and Pensions, London.

Hawksworth, J. 2006. "Review of Research Relevant to Assessing the Impact of the Proposed National Pension Savings Scheme on Household Savings." Research Report 373, Department for Work and Pensions, London.

Horack, S., and A. Wood. 2005. "An Evaluation of Scheme Joining Techniques in Workplace Pension Schemes with an Employer Contribution." Research Report 292, Department for Work and Pensions, London.

Hubbard, R. G., and K. L. Judd. 1987. "Social Security and Individual Welfare: Precautionary Saving, Borrowing Constraints and the Payroll Tax." *American Economic Review* 77 (4): 630–46.

Hubbard, R. G., and J. S. Skinner. 1996. "Assessing the Effectiveness of Saving Incentives." *Journal of Economic Perspectives* 10 (4): 73–90.

Iwry, J. M., and D. C. John. 2007. "Pursuing Universal Retirement Security through Automatic IRAs." Policy Brief 2007-02, Retirement Security Project, Washington, DC.

Leinert, J. 2004. "Automatische Entgeltumwandlung: Hohe Teilnahmequoten ohne Zwang." *Wirtschaftsdienst* 2004-2.

———. 2005. *Betriebliche Altersvorsorge: Automatik statt Zwang. Warum das opting-out Modell besser ist.* Deutsches Institut für Altersvorsorge, Köln, Germany.

McKay, S. 2006. "Employers' Pension Provision Survey 2005." Research Report 329, Department for Work and Pensions, London.

Milligan, K. 2002. "Tax-Preferred Savings Accounts and Marginal Tax Rates: Evidence on RRSP Participation." *Canadian Journal of Economics/Revue canadienne d'économique* 35 (3): 436.

OECD (Organisation for Economic Co-operation and Development). 1984. *Tax Expenditures: A Review of Issues and Country Practices.* Paris: OECD.

———. 1994. *Taxation and Household Saving.* Paris: OECD.

———. 1995. *Tax Expenditures: Recent Experiences.* Paris: OECD.

———. 2001. *Ageing and Income: Financial Resources and Retirement in Nine OECD Countries.* Paris: OECD.

———. 2005. *Improving Financial Literacy: Analysis of Issues and Policies.* Paris: OECD.

———. 2008. *Growing Unequal? Income Distribution and Poverty in OECD Countries.* Paris: OECD.

———. 2009. *Pensions at a Glance: Retirement-Income Systems in OECD Countries.* Paris: OECD.

———. 2010. *Tax Expenditures in OECD Countries.* Paris: OECD.

———. 2011. *Pensions at a Glance: Retirement-Income Systems in OECD and G20 Countries.* Paris: OECD.

———. 2012. *Pensions Outlook.* Paris: OECD.

Papke, L. E. 1995. "Does 401(k) Introduction Affect Defined Benefit Plans?" *National Tax Association Proceedings*: 173–77.

———. 1999. "Are 401(k) Plans Replacing Other Employer-Provided Pensions? Evidence from Panel Data." *Journal of Human Resources* 34: 346–68.

Poterba, J. M., S. F. Venti, and D. A. Wise. 1994a. "Targeted Retirement Saving and the Net Worth of Elderly Americans." *American Economic Review* 84: 180–85.

———. 1994b. "401(k) Plans and Tax-Deferred Saving." In *Studies in the Economics of Aging*, ed. D. A. Wise. Chicago: University of Chicago Press for the National Bureau of Economic Research.

———. 1995. "Do 401(k) Contributions Crowd Out Other Personal Saving?" *Journal of Public Economics* 58: 1–32.

————. 1996a. "How Retirement Saving Programs Increase Saving." *Journal of Economic Perspectives* 10 (4).

————. 1996b. "Personal Retirement Saving Programs and Asset Accumulation: Reconciling the Evidence." NBER Working Paper 5599, National Bureau of Economic Research, Cambridge, MA.

————. 1998a. "Personal Retirement Saving Programs and Asset Accumulation: Reconciling the Evidence." In *Frontiers in the Economics of Aging*, ed. D. A. Wise. Chicago: University of Chicago Press for the National Bureau of Economic Research.

————. 1998b. "Implications of Rising Personal Retirement Saving." In *Frontiers in the Economics of Aging*, ed. D. A. Wise. Chicago: University of Chicago Press for the National Bureau of Economic Research.

————. 1998c. "Lump-Sum Distributions from Retirement Saving Plans: Receipt and Utilization." In *Inquiries in the Economics of Aging*, ed. D. A. Wise. Chicago: University of Chicago Press for the National Bureau of Economic Research.

————. 2001. "The Transition to Personal Accounts and Increasing Retirement Wealth: Macro and Micro Evidence." NBER Working Paper 8610, National Bureau of Economic Research, Cambridge, MA.

Retirement Commission. 2010. *Review of Retirement-Income Policy*. Wellington: Retirement Commission.

Surrey, S. S. 1973. *Pathways to Tax Reform: The Concept of Tax Expenditures*. Cambridge, MA: Harvard University Press.

Venti, S. F., and D. A. Wise. 1990. "Have IRAs Increased US Saving? Evidence from Consumer Expenditure Surveys." *Quarterly Journal of Economics* 105 (3): 661–98.

————. 1991. "The Saving Effect of Tax-Deferred Retirement Accounts: Evidence from SIPP." In *National Saving and Economic Performance*, ed. B. D. Bernheim and J. B. Shoven. Chicago: University of Chicago Press.

————. 1995. "RRSPs and Saving in Canada." National Bureau of Economic Research, Cambridge, MA.

Whitehouse, E. R. 1999. "The Tax Treatment of Funded Pensions." Pension Reform Primer Series, Social Protection Discussion Paper 9910, World Bank, Washington, DC.

Whitehouse, E. R., A. C. D'Addio, R. Chomik, and A. Reilly. 2009. "Two Decades of Pension Reform: What Has Been Achieved and What Remains to Be Done?" *Geneva Papers on Risk and Insurance* 34: 515–35.

Yoo, K. Y., and A. de Serres. 2004a. "Tax Treatment of Private Pension Savings in OECD Countries." *OECD Economic Studies* 39 (2): 73–110.

————. 2004b. "Tax Treatment of Private Pension Savings in OECD Countries and the Net Tax Cost per Unit of Contribution to Tax-Favoured Schemes." Working Paper 406, Organisation for Economic Co-operation and Development, Economics Department, Paris.

PART II

High-Income Country Experience

CHAPTER 3

Matching Contributions in 401(k) Plans in the United States

Nevin Adams, Dallas Salisbury, and Jack VanDerhei

Matching contributions have long been used in the United States to encourage lower-income workers to participate in defined contribution pension plans at levels necessary to ensure that these programs comply with certain nondiscrimination tests mandated by the Internal Revenue Service, the U.S. tax authority. A review of the literature suggests that for voluntary 401(k) plans, employer matches have a positive impact on plan participation and that automatic enrollment in a matched plan encourages a level of participation that is adequate to produce sufficient retirement income for people with a full savings career in that system. Whether more widespread adoption of automatic enrollment will affect the perceived need for, and level of, the employer match in providing a future with retirement income security remains to be seen.

Defined contribution plans—and matching employer contributions—were fixtures on the U.S. retirement scene well before the advent of 401(k) plans in the early 1980s.[1] Then, as now, matching contributions were used as incentives to encourage participation by less highly compensated workers, as a means of ensuring that these programs—typically defined contribution stock bonus/thrift savings plans—were able to remain in compliance with nondiscrimination tests. These tests, designed to ensure that a disproportionate share of the benefits do not accrue to the more highly paid members of the plan, must be fulfilled in order for the contributions and investment earnings of an employer-sponsored pension plan to receive favorable treatment under U.S. income tax laws (in which contributions and earnings on investments are excluded from the taxable income of the plan's members until they are distributed). These employer contributions, which matched worker contributions in rates specified in plan documents, provided a financial incentive for saving by lower-income workers in the plan at participation and contribution levels that would enable the more highly paid group to make the level of contributions it desired, up to the limit permitted under the tax laws.

Industry studies and other surveys continue to find a high degree of correlation between the level of the employer match and voluntary contributions by employees. Of six plan features listed in the 2005 Retirement Confidence Survey, the feature most cited by respondents who did not participate in their employer's 401(k)–type plan as likely to encourage them to join was a generous employer match of up to 5 percent of salary.[2] Three in 10 respondents reported that they would be much more likely to contribute to their employer's plan if this option were available, and 4 in 10 reported that they would be somewhat more likely to do so. However, an employer match would not persuade all nonparticipants to contribute. The 2006 Retirement Confidence Survey found that

87 percent of employees offered a plan with a match reported participating, compared with 70 percent without a match.

More recently, a 2010 survey by the Principal Financial Group found that the design of the employer match can be a powerful motivator in boosting the amount of money participants put into their 401(k) retirement accounts, even when the employer's total contribution does not change (Principal Financial Group 2010). A survey by Fidelity Investments finds that 92 percent of participants surveyed indicated that one of the main reasons they participate is to take advantage of company contributions (67 percent cited this factor as very important and 25 percent as somewhat important); about a quarter (23 percent) of surveyed workers who were not previously participating said that wanting to take full advantage of the company match was the reason for increasing their contributions when they did join. In contrast, the Principal Financial Well-Being Index for the second quarter of 2010 notes that half of employees participating in the survey report that the deciding factor in determining how much to contribute to the plan was how much they could afford.

The growing interest in, and adoption of, automatic enrollment plan designs—and the decision of a significant minority of employers to suspend their matching contributions in the wake of the 2008 financial crisis—continues to attract interest about the future role of the matching contribution in effective plan design.

This chapter explores the origins and emergence of the 401(k) plan as a dominant retirement savings vehicle in the United States, as well as the evolution and impact of certain design elements, notably the application of an employer matching contribution, in influencing individual saving behaviors. It is organized as follows: the first section explores the origins and development of the 401(k) as a dominant defined contribution plan structure in the United States, as well as the shifting legislative and regulatory environment that attended its rapid growth. The second section outlines the factors affecting the level and timing of matching contributions during the emergence and maturity of the 401(k). The third section examines the research on the link between matching practices and worker responses. The fourth section explores the response of participant-savers to changes in the rate of matching contributions. It also looks at future trends in plan design, notably automatic enrollment, and their impact on the rate and prevalence of matching contributions. The last section summarizes the main findings.

Drivers and Outcomes

Defined contribution plans are retirement plans that specify the level of contributions by both employer and employee and in which the contributions are placed into individual employee accounts. Among the plan types included in this category in the United States are money purchase plans, in which employer contributions are mandatory and are usually stated as a percentage of employee salary; profit-sharing plans, in which total contributions to be distributed are often derived from a portion of company profits; stock bonus plans, which are similar to profit-sharing plans but usually make contributions and benefit payments in the form of company stock; savings and thrift plans, in which employees may contribute a predetermined portion of earnings, all or part of which the employer matches; and employee stock ownership plans (ESOPs), in which the employer contributes a designated amount into a fund that is generally invested primarily in company stock.

The 401(k) is a type of defined contribution plan, generally a subset of what would technically be considered a saving and thrift plan. It did not emerge until several years after the passage of the Employee Retirement Income Security Act (ERISA), the federal legislation that in 1974 codified the rules and reporting structures for employer-sponsored private sector retirement plans in the United States.[3]

EARLY DESIGNS

In pre–401(k) thrift/savings plans, employees could contribute up to 10 percent of their income on an after-tax basis. These employee contributions were treated as the deposit of compensation already received and in the control of the worker and thus subject to income taxation. However, as an incentive to encourage employee participation in these programs, employers were allowed to make a tax-deductible contribution to employee accounts. Whereas employee contributions were made on an after-tax basis, taxation to the individual worker on the value of the employer matching contributions credited to an individual participant's account was (and is) deferred until distribution, as were any resulting investment gains in the individual account. The deferral of tax obligation on these amounts by the individual participant was predicated on deposit to a qualified pension fund held as a trust account, subject to certain restrictions.

A less common plan design at the time was a cash or deferred arrangement (CODA). In such an arrangement, the individual participant was essentially given the choice of receiving a form of cash compensation (generally some kind of year-end bonus payment) or deferring that payment until some future point in time. In legal terms, the employer could either provide a specified amount to the employee in the form of cash or some other taxable benefit, or contribute an amount to a trust or provide an accrual or other benefit to be received (and therefore subject to tax) at some point in the future. The underlying operating principle of taxation deferral is that the employee must decide to defer receipt before he or she has actual receipt, or control, of the compensation (in regulatory parlance, before the taxable benefit is "currently available" to the employee).

These programs allowed eligible employees to either take cash now (generally some kind of annual bonus or profit-sharing payment) or defer compensation by having it deposited into a retirement plan. However, questions arose over time regarding the elective nature of these contributions—namely, whether an employee who has the option to decide whether to take the cash is in "constructive receipt" of the funds and thus liable for current taxation of the contribution.

Through a series of court cases and tax rulings, by the early 1970s, the U.S. tax authority (the Internal Revenue Service [IRS]) had established that a CODA could be part of a profit-sharing plan and that the voluntary employee contributions would be treated as employer contributions for income tax purposes (thereby allowing the associated income tax to be deferred) providing that the following conditions were met:

- The applicable contributions were made by an irrevocable election before the end of the year in which the profits on which they were based were determined.
- Certain nondiscrimination measures were met (at the time, more than half the participants had to be in the lowest-paid two-thirds of all eligible employees).

- The applicable contributions were subject to the same restrictions on withdrawals and distributions as other employer contributions made to the plan.

Over time, a number of employers extended this bonus/profit-sharing structure to allow employees to elect to reduce their normal salary through such deferrals and expanded the salary reduction design to money purchase plans. Not surprisingly, many lower-paid workers chose to take these bonuses in cash, whereas higher-paid workers were inclined to defer the payment and the taxation of the payment (something that was particularly important in a period in which income tax rates were much more steeply progressive). Still, as recently as the early 1970s, fewer than a thousand CODAs were in existence.

Concerned that a disproportionate share of tax benefits from these arrangements was going to higher-paid workers, on December 6, 1972, the IRS issued a proposed regulation that provided that contributions made at the election of an employee "in return for a reduction in his basic or regular compensation or in lieu of an increase in such compensation" would be taxed as if they had been received by the employee. Although the proposed regulation did not specifically reference CODAs involving bonuses or amounts paid in addition to regular compensation, it cast a shadow on their future treatment as well. At the same time, the U.S. Treasury Department, which has a broader policy role in the regulation of pensions than the IRS (which is a bureau of the U.S. Treasury), announced that it would further study these plan designs and determine how they should be treated.

THEN CAME ERISA

Before any regulations were issued, in 1974 ERISA was enacted. This landmark federal law—the result of many years of debate and negotiations in Congress—established minimum standards for pension plans sponsored by private sector employers as well as rules governing the federal income tax effects of transactions associated with employee benefit plans. Included in the legislation was a provision specifically prohibiting the Treasury Department from issuing regulations that would affect the tax treatment of these arrangements before January 1, 1977. This provision was intended to provide Congress with an opportunity to take action on the issue. This deadline was extended twice, once to January 1, 1978 (by the Tax Reform Act of 1976) and a second time to January 1, 1980 (by the Tax Treatment Extension Act of 1978). In July 1978, the IRS withdrew its 1972 proposed regulation.

In the Revenue Act of 1978, Congress finally acted by adding Section 401(k) to the Internal Revenue Code (Raish n.d.). This new section of the tax code, which would eventually lend its name to the 401(k) plan, provided that a profit-sharing or stock bonus plan would not be barred from the favorable tax treatment afforded to qualified pension plans merely because it allowed employees to make a voluntary pretax contribution (as allowed under a qualified CODA). It also set forth the criteria for those arrangements.

Section 408(a)(8), added to the tax code in the same legislation, explicitly provided that contributions made by employees to a qualified trust at an employee's election under a qualified CODA were to be treated as if they were employer contributions and therefore not subject to federal income taxation at the point of contribution. On November 10, 1981, the IRS published proposed regulations under the new 401(k) that provided guidance about how employers could implement these arrangements—an event many practitioners now consider the birth of the 401(k) plan. Within two years, surveys showed that nearly half of all large firms were either offering, or considering offering, a 401(k) plan.

PARTICIPATION BOOSTERS

The Tax Reform Act of 1984 established two mandatory nondiscrimination tests for CODAs, which were applicable to 401(k) plans. Rather than merely complying with the general nondiscrimination tests, these 401(k) programs now also had to pass the muster of a new nondiscrimination test called the "average deferral percentage" test. Passing this test required that the average rate of pretax contributions deferred by non–highly compensated employees (NHCEs; at that time, essentially the lower two-thirds of the workforce eligible to participate in the plan) fall within a narrowly defined range of the average percentage of the deferrals made by the group defined as highly compensated.

Contributions made in excess of those limits could either be returned to highly compensated employees (generally employees who deferred at the highest rates, not always the most highly compensated) and taxed or recharacterized as after-tax contributions to the plan (if the plan permitted such contributions). Alternatively, certain additional contributions (called qualified matching contributions or qualified nonelective contributions) could be made by the employer to effectively increase the deferral levels of NHCEs. These qualified contributions must be immediately 100 percent vested; they can therefore be an expensive solution to bringing the plan into compliance. Additionally, the first method cited above—returning contributions—was viewed as extremely disruptive in employee relations, particularly with a key constituency (the highly compensated). The available correction methods provided a strong incentive for plan sponsors to avoid falling short of the nondiscrimination test standards, reinforcing the emphasis on encouraging participation by NHCEs.

Despite the imposition of these restrictions, the continued popularity of these programs—and their tax-deferral design—had real implications for government revenue flows. In fact, to reduce fiscal pressures, in 1984 the Treasury Department proposed eliminating Section 401(k) from the Internal Revenue Code.

The Tax Reform Act of 1986 brought further restrictive changes to the 401(k), notably a ceiling on allowable pretax contributions of $7,000 per year (adjusted annually based on the consumer price index) and changes to the nondiscrimination test.[4] Changes to the nondiscrimination test included a revised definition of compensation as well as a revised, and generally narrower, definition of highly compensated employee. At the same time, another nondiscrimination test (the average compensation percentage test)—designed to achieve the same objective of limiting differences in matching contributions and after-tax employee contributions—was introduced, putting additional pressure on the amounts that could be contributed by more highly compensated workers.

These new nondiscrimination tests provided a particularly strong incentive for employers to encourage lower-paid workers to contribute as much as possible to the plan. Indeed, targeting a high participation rate among NHCEs was necessary not only to maximize the deferral levels of the higher-paid group but to ensure legal compliance. And while the ability to contribute (and save) pretax provided incentives to the NHCEs, the employer matching contribution already in place in many thrift or savings plans (many of which were to add a 401(k) feature) also acted as a powerful financial contribution incentive. With more stringent standards to meet, interest in boosting the saving behaviors of the NHCEs was higher than ever.[5]

LATER CHANGES

The Small Business Job Protection Act of 1996 was the first law to move back toward encouraging the expansion of 401(k)s by providing design-based "safe harbor" methods for satisfying the nondiscrimination tests applicable to 401(k) plans.[6] These methods basically allowed employers to avoid passing the standard 401(k) nondiscrimination test by either making a 3 percent contribution for all eligible workers or providing a basic match of at least 100 percent on the first 3 percent of pay deferred plus 50 percent on the next 2 percent. The act also repealed the limits imposed under the Internal Revenue Code's Section 415(e), which reduced the amount that could be contributed to defined contribution plans (including 401(k) plans) if the employer also sponsored a defined benefit plan for the same employees and greatly simplified the definition of highly compensated employees.

In 1998, the IRS issued Revenue Ruling 98–30, which gave a stamp of approval for employers to make "negative elections" (that is, automatic enrollment) into 401(k) plans for newly eligible employees. In 2000, the IRS followed up with Revenue Ruling 2000–8, providing additional guidance on negative elections by allowing automatic enrollment in 401(k) plans for already eligible employees who were deferring at a rate less than the automatic enrollment rate.

The Economic Growth and Tax Relief Reconciliation Act of 2001 (EGTRRA) made significant changes to the 401(k) (Facts from EBRI 2005). These changes, subject to the nondiscrimination testing limits, were designed to increase individual savings in these programs. The law dramatically increased elective annual deferral limits (to $11,000 in 2002, rising by $1,000 a year until 2006, when inflation indexing would take over), permitted additional "catch-up" contributions by participants 50 and older (up to $1,000 in 2002, $2,000 in 2003, $3,000 in 2004, and $4,000 in 2005), increased the maximum compensation limit (as a percentage of salary) to $200,000 from $170,000 (with amounts indexed thereafter), and increased the annual defined contribution dollar limit from $35,000 to $40,000 under Section 415(c) and allowed annual indexing thereafter in $1,000 increments. Additionally, the compensation limit in Section 415(c) was increased to 100 percent of compensation, from 25 percent at the time EGTRRA was passed, and the vesting requirements of employer matching contributions were accelerated beginning after 2001 (requiring that they be vested at least as rapidly as three-year cliff vesting or two- to six-year graded vesting).[7]

EGTRRA also laid out the provisions for a Roth 401(k), to be effective in 2006, slated to sunset at the end of 2010 along with the rest of the EGTRRA provisions. Roth contributions are deferred as after-tax dollars (that is, income tax is paid or withheld in the year contributed). Combined with regular 401(k) pretax deferrals in determining the maximum annual deferral, qualified distributions from a designated Roth 401(k) account, including all income, were to be tax free. (A traditional 401(k) account is funded with pretax dollars. In general, tax must be paid when the original contribution and earnings are withdrawn.) All employer matching funds are deposited into the account on a pretax basis, even if all of the employee's contributions are Roth contributions. Employer contributions may be subject to vesting rules set by the plan documents requiring the employee to reach a certain number of years of service before he or she is entitled to keep the matching funds.

Actual implementations of this Roth provision at the plan level were modest, because of the late implementation relative to the other provisions of the law, the relatively brief window of applicability (2006 to the sunset in 2010), the cost of implementing the change, and the potential confusion among participants long accustomed to hearing about the benefits of deferring on a pretax basis.

However, in August 2006, the Pension Protection Act was signed into law, with a major emphasis on fostering retirement saving and 401(k) plan participation. The act provided a safe harbor for automatic enrollment that included a provision allowing for automatic annual increases in deferrals. It also resolved the potential conflict between the practice of automatic enrollment and some state laws prohibiting wage garnishment. Additionally, it made permanent certain provisions of EGTRRA that were set to expire or sunset at the end of 2010, including increased deduction limits, increased rollover options, and a start-up tax credit for small-employer plans.

At the same time, the Roth 401(k) provisions that became effective in 2006 gained new life with the removal of the 2010 sunset. After years of hesitation, by 2011, about 30 percent of employer respondents to the PLANSPONSOR Defined Contribution Survey had adopted a Roth provision, though enrollment by participants remained weak.

The Pension Protection Act's automatic enrollment safe harbor provided fresh vigor to the adoption of the design, even among plan sponsors that, either deliberately or inadvertently, failed to qualify for the full protections of the legislative safe harbor (Adams 2011). A 2008 analysis by the Employment Benefit Research Institute (EBRI) of the provision indicates that, even under the most conservative assumptions for auto-escalation of contributions, switching 401(k) plans to automatic enrollment was seen as likely to have a very significant positive impact on generating additional retirement savings for many workers, especially low-income workers (EBRI 2008).

Overall, the emergence of 401(k) plans brought a new dynamic to defined contribution plans in the United States, enabling workers of all income levels to defer payment of taxes on compensation contributed to these plans. Popular as these programs were to become, their stricter nondiscrimination rules made the participation of NHCEs a critical factor. Employer matches were an important source of encouragement, not only for participation but also for participation at an effective level.

The Level of the Match

Cost was a key factor for employers in determining the level of deferral at which to match, but plan sponsors also wanted to avoid the necessity of having to refund "excess" contribution deferrals to highly compensated workers—contributions exceeding the limits imposed by the average deferral percentage nondiscrimination tests. Many opted to match deferrals of 4–10 percent of pay at various rates (commonly $0.25 or $0.50 on the dollar), with deferrals above those amounts left unmatched.

The new nondiscrimination requirements—and heightened interest in the rates of plan participation of NHCEs—also led to greater interest in employee education about these workplace programs, both to explain the program and to encourage participation. This heightened interest was particularly true in the period following the introduction of the new (and more restrictive) tests of the Tax Reform Act of 1986. Although nondiscrimination testing constraints remain an active concern for many plan sponsors, they have become less of an issue because of subsequent modifications in the test structure, as well as the introduction of new safe harbor plan designs (with minimum employer contribution requirements, which preclude the need for a nondiscrimination test) and the expanding impact of automatic enrollment (which serves to boost participation levels and the deferral averages for NHCEs).

Total contributions to 401(k) plans more than doubled between 1984 and 1987, from $16.3 billion to just over $33.0 billion. The percentage of contributions to defined contribution plans stemming from CODAs also rose, from 42 percent in 1984 to 55 percent in 1987 (Andrews 1992).

Among the early adopters of the 401(k) design were smaller businesses that had either not previously sponsored a plan or in some cases had offered a profit-sharing program. For businesses that had not sponsored a plan, the 401(k) did not require employer contributions (unlike profit-sharing plans, which, by definition, involved the sharing of employer profits). Small businesses were to grow even more enamored of the design after passage of the Tax Reform Act of 1986, which prohibited individuals above certain compensation levels from making pretax contributions to an individual retirement account (IRA) if they were covered by a profit-sharing plan.

According to PLANSPONSOR's 2011 Defined Contribution Survey of plan sponsors, only about 3 in 10 plan sponsors (fewer among larger programs) said that "all or nearly all" participants were deferring enough income to take full advantage of the maximum employer match (Adams 2011). Less than a quarter of the largest programs (401(k) assets in excess of $1 billion) reported that 90 percent or more of their participants were deferring at a level sufficient to receive the full employer match. Among large and mid-size plans, the percentage was even lower (table 3.1). Among the 23 percent of respondents who reported decreasing their workplace plan contribution percentage at some point, 46 percent said they needed extra money; 9 percent reported that the reduction was caused by elimination of the company match.

Although an employer match of 50 percent of employee deferrals up to 6 percent of pay is often presented as the norm, there is actually a great deal of variety in how defined contribution matches are structured. Seventy-seven percent of the defined contribution client base of Vanguard (a large mutual fund company) did, in fact, incorporate the 50 percent of deferral up to 6 percent of pay as a structure, but it applied to only 60 percent of its participant accounts. In contrast, 15 percent of the plans—and 35 percent of participants—operated under a dollar-for-dollar match on the first 3 percent of pay, with 50 percent on the next 2 percent. PLANSPONSOR's 2011 Defined Contribution Survey of nearly 7,000 plan sponsors also reveals an array of options (tables 3.2 and 3.3).

Impact of Matching Contributions on 401(k) Saving

The sensitivity of participation and contributions to plan characteristics—notably the employer matching rate—may play a critical role in retirement saving. It has long been

TABLE 3.1 **Percentage of active participants deferring enough salary to take full advantage of the maximum employer match, by company size**

Participation	Percentage of companies					
	All firms	**Micro**	**Small**	**Midsize**	**Large**	**Mega**
All or nearly all participants (90% or more)	29.2	37.9	25.4	21.1	16.8	22.2
Vast majority (75% or more)	20.6	16.9	21.8	22.3	27.7	27.8
About half	25.6	18.2	28.5	33.1	32.0	38.9
Less than half	24.7	27.0	24.4	23.6	23.5	11.1
Average	65.9	66.7	64.9	64.2	65.0	71.9
Median	74.0	75.0	70.0	70.0	70.0	74.5

SOURCE: PLANSPONSOR's 2011 Defined Contribution Survey.

NOTE: The PLANSPONSOR survey categorized plans as follows: "mega": more than $1 billion; "large": $200 million–$1 billion; midsize: $50 million–$200 million; small: $5 million–$50 million; and "micro": less than $5 million in plan assets.

TABLE 3.2 **Level of match offered by companies offering matching contributions, by company size**

Level of match (as percentage of 6% of salary)	Percentage of companies					
	All firms	**Micro**	**Small**	**Midsize**	**Large**	**Mega**
More than 100	4.2	4.2	4.7	2.7	3.7	5.0
100	6.2	4.3	4.8	8.0	9.9	17.8
51–99	27.3	24.4	25.1	28.9	37.0	42.6
50	30.7	33.7	29.8	28.4	30.3	19.3
Less than 50	31.7	33.4	35.6	31.9	19.1	15.3

SEE table 3.1.

TABLE 3.3 **Type of employer contributions, by company size**

Type of contribution	Percentage of companies					
	All firms	**Micro**	**Small**	**Midsize**	**Large**	**Mega**
Match of participant contribution	66.4	56.4	69.7	78.7	80.4	83.3
Nonelective contribution	14.9	10.8	13.4	21.0	26.9	27.5
Profit-sharing contribution	28.6	26.0	35.0	29.2	22.9	16.4
Other	12.4	12.7	12.2	10.5	12.8	14.5
No contribution	11.0	16.2	7.6	6.6	5.5	5.6

SEE table 3.1.

assumed that matching employer contributions—the allure of "free money" to participants (and would-be participants)—provided a strong financial motivation to contribute to defined contribution plans, notably 401(k)s. Industry surveys have suggested that
employee contribution levels tend to cluster around the matching levels, reinforcing a
cause-and-effect connection.

Historically, providing employer matching contributions to 401(k) plans was seen
as a primary means of increasing the likelihood of passing the nondiscrimination (average deferral percentage) tests (Brady 2007). However, Ippolito (1997) finds an alternative explanation might be more plausible: in essence, employers use the 401(k) match
to attract and retain a workforce with specific characteristics, and matches reward workers with lower discount rates. Mitchell, Utkus, and Yang (2005) posit that employee
demand could offer an alternative explanation, with the result that highly compensated
employees demand more generous tax-deferred employer matches. Both of these arguments view the employer match as a workforce management tool rather than a regulatory response.

EMPIRICAL STUDIES ON THE IMPACT OF MATCHING CONTRIBUTIONS ON PARTICIPATION

Over the past 20 years, empirical studies have analyzed the effect of matching contributions on the probability of participating in 401(k) plans that rely on voluntary enrollment
(see Andrews 1992; Bassett, Fleming, and Rodrigues 1998; Engelhardt and Kumar 2007;
Even and Macpherson 2005; GAO 2007; Kusko, Poterba, and Wilcox 1998; Mitchell,
Utkus, and Yang 2005; Papke 1995; Papke and Poterba 1995; Yakoboski 1994). The
magnitude of the results varies considerably depending on the type of database used, the
methodologies employed, and the assumptions made. However, the consensus is that for
401(k) plans that have not employed automatic enrollment, an employer match has had
a positive impact on plan participation (see chapter 15 for additional discussion of and
experience with these issues).

An important caveat is that most survey data do not contain detailed information
on plan design. In an attempt to mitigate this shortcoming, Mitchell, Utkus, and Young
(2005) use 2001 data on 500 401(k) retirement plans covering nearly 740,000 employees to evaluate how employer matching incentives affect retirement saving levels. Their
analysis includes two notable innovations. First, they evaluate employee saving behavior
separately for highly compensated and non–highly compensated employees at the firm
level. Second, in an attempt to deal with nonlinear 401(k) matching formulas (explained
in more detail below), they bifurcate these formulas into an "incentive element" (the
degree to which the employer matches various increments of employee compensation)
and a "liquidity element" (indicating how much the employee must contribute in order to
receive the entire employer incentive payment).

Their ordinary least squares regression analysis finds that every 10 percent increase
in the match rate raises NHCE participation rates by about 1 percentage point. However,
for this group, the participation incentives (3–6 percent of pay) are statistically insignificant and turn negative for matches above 6 percent of pay. As a consequence, the authors
of this analysis conclude that the incentive effects of employer matching contributions are
small:

The empirical model implies that close to 65 percent of NHCEs at the typical firm would join their 401(k) plan regardless of the presence of a match. Plan participation would be estimated to rise over a narrow range, by 5 to 15 percentage points, responding to a range of match offerings, from a modest ($0.25 per dollar on the first 3 percent of pay) to a very generous match ($1.00 per dollar up to 6 percent of pay). At the modal promised employer match ($0.50 per dollar on 6 percent), over one-quarter of NHECs fails to participate in the 401(k) plan; even with a generous match, more than 20 percent still fail to join (Mitchell, Utkus, and Yang 2005, 16).

Given that the participation percentages for certain groups of eligible participants (especially young and low-income workers) have increased substantially under automatic enrollment, many observers have wondered whether the matching contributions would continue to be associated with higher participation rates under these plans.

Beshears and others (2007) estimate the impact of the employer match on savings plan participation under automatic enrollment in two ways. First, they analyzed a plan sponsor with an automatic enrollment 401(k) plan that replaced its employer match with a nonelective contribution.[8] They find that plan participation rates decreased by at most 5–6 percentage points among new hires after the plan change.

Second, they pooled data for nine firms with automatic enrollment to identify the relationship between participation rates and the match. They find that a 1 percentage point decrease in the maximum potential match was associated with a 1.8–3.8 percentage point decrease in plan participation at six months of eligibility.

Based on these findings, the authors estimate that for a typical employer match (that is, 50 percent match on the first 6 percent of pay), eliminating the match under an automatic enrollment plan could reduce plan participation by 5–11 percentage points.

Dworak-Fisher (2011) uses microdata from the National Compensation Survey to develop a new line of research on the impact of employer matches on 401(k) participation rates. The study finds that for those with the lowest income, employer matches have little or no effect on participation, but automatic enrollment has dramatic effects. Among those in the middle income group, employer matches have substantial effects, which may be larger than the effects of automatic enrollment. However, these results should be interpreted with care, as they are based on microdata from the respondents in 2002–03, and only a small percentage of the plans in the sample (6 percent) were governed by automatic enrollment provisions at that time.

EMPIRICAL STUDIES ON THE IMPACT OF MATCHING CONTRIBUTIONS ON CONTRIBUTION BEHAVIOR IN VOLUNTARY ENROLLMENT 401(K) PLANS

Logically, the notion that an employer match increases the incentive for an employee to contribute to a 401(k) plan appears incontrovertible. The analysis becomes more complex with respect to the level of contributions the employee will make, for two reasons.[9]

First, although a larger match rate provides a greater financial incentive for the employee to contribute (at least within a specified range), employees may have a certain target in mind with respect to the total (employee and employer) contribution that needs to be made each year to satisfy their personal financial planning objectives. For example, if an employee has determined that he or she needs to save a total of 9 percent of compensation, the required employee contribution would be 6 percent if the employer matched

50 percent up to 6 percent of compensation but only 4.5 percent if the employer matched 100 percent up to (at least) 4.5 percent of compensation. Thus, for some employees, a higher match rate may result in a lower employee contribution rate.

Second, empirical analysis that considers only the match rate (as opposed to the match cap or the interaction between the two) may provide unexpected results. For example, if an individual employee's primary concern is to make sure he or she receives the maximum match possible, the employee would be more likely to contribute up to the level of the match cap. In that case, an employer match of 50 percent of the first 6 percent of compensation would likely generate a larger employee contribution rate than one incented by matching 100 percent of the first 3 percent of compensation—even though the maximum total employer match for the worker would be 3 percent of compensation in either case.

These phenomena help explain the results from some of the early empirical work in this area. Using plan data from the Form 5500 filed annually by ERISA-qualified plans with the U.S. government, Papke (1995) finds substantial employee contribution increases when an employer moves from a zero to a small or moderately sized match rate proxy. At higher match rates, however, employee contributions fall. Using a subset of the EBRI/Investment Company Institute (ICI) 401(k) database with salary information, Holden and VanDerhei (2001) perform a regression analysis of the influence of the match rate on participants' contribution rates. They find that participant before-tax contribution rates fell minimally as the employer match rate rose.[10] However, as the match cap chosen by the employer increased, participant contribution rates rose.

Kusko, Poterba, and Wilcox (1998) use employee-level data from the 401(k) plan at a medium-size U.S. manufacturing firm to analyze the participation and contribution decisions of eligible workers.[11] Their analysis suggests that contribution decisions of eligible employees are relatively insensitive to the rate of employer matching on worker contributions and that most employees maintain the same participation status and contribution rate year after year, despite substantial changes in the employer's match rate. Moreover, they find that institutional constraints on contributions, imposed by either the employer or the IRS, are an extremely important influence on contributor behavior.

Yakoboski and VanDerhei (1996) confirm these results in their analysis of participant data from three large 401(k) sponsors. Moreover, they find significant clustering around the match cap, as illustrated below:

- Company A had a maximum pretax contribution of 9 percent of earnings and a match rate of 30 percent for the first 5 percent of earnings. A total of 21 percent of participants contributed 5 percent of pay to the plan, 45 percent contributed 9 percent of pay, and 1 percent contributed up to the allowable maximum for that year under Section 402(g). The average deferral percentage for Company A was 6.7 percent.

- NHCEs at Company B were allowed to contribute a maximum of 15 percent of pretax income, with a 100 percent match on the first 3 percent of earnings. Twenty-one percent contributed 3 percent of pay, 10 percent contributed 15 percent, and 0.1 percent contributed the allowable limit.[12] The average deferral rate was 5.4 percent.

- Highly compensated employees at Company B were allowed to contribute a maximum of 10 percent of pretax income, with a 100 percent match on the first 3 percent of earnings. Fifteen percent contributed 3 percent of pay, 10 percent contributed 10 percent, and 15 percent contributed at the Section 402(g) limit. The average deferral rate was 5.9 percent.

- Company C had a maximum pretax contribution of 16 percent of earnings and a match rate of two-thirds on the first 6 percent of earnings. A total of 30 percent of participants contributed 6 percent of pay to the plan, 7 percent contributed 16 percent of pay, and 12 percent contributed up to the Section 402(g) limit. The average deferral percentage for Company C was 6.3 percent.

Although this analysis is based on the experience of only three plan sponsors, it shows that in addition to individual-specific characteristics (for example, age, wages, and tenure), employee contribution behavior can be influenced to a large extent by plan design variables (the match cap and plan limits for pretax contributions) as well as the maximum legal annual deferral limits.

VanDerhei and Copeland (2001) attempt to deal with these plan design influences on employee contribution behavior by working with a small subset of the EBRI/ ICI 401(k) database, which allowed them to track 137 "pure" matching formulas (that is, formulas without a nonelective contribution).[13] Participants in the database were excluded if they were under age 20 or over 64, had been with the current employer for less than one year, or earned less than $10,000 a year. Applying each of these screens and deleting participants with existing account balances who did not make employee contributions in 1998 left a total of 163,346 participants for analysis.

In previous research, the level of contributions was estimated by assuming that it was a function of demographic variables and some measure of a match rate of the plan. However, this approach fails to account for the fact that some plans have different match rates for different levels of the percentage of compensation contributed. For example, a plan may offer a dollar-for-dollar match for the first 2 percent of compensation contributed and a 50 percent match for the next 3 percent of compensation contributed. In addition, this approach does not clearly distinguish between a plan that matches 50 percent of contributions for the first 4 percent of compensation from plans that match 50 percent of contributions for the first 6 percent of compensation.

As the data used in this research contain plan-specific matching formulas, the actual match rate at each percentage level of contributions is known. Therefore, VanDerhei and Copeland (2001) use an estimation procedure that takes advantage of knowing the differing incentives that an employee eligible to contribute to a 401(k) faces at each percentage of compensation level of contributions.

The parameters of a model for the first increment can be estimated from the entire sample by dividing it into two groups: employees who make the contribution and those who do not. The parameters of a model for the second increment can be estimated by dividing the subsample of employees who make the first incremental contribution into employees who make the next 1 percent of compensation contribution and employees who do not. Successive iterations are estimated until the maximum plan limit of all match formulas is obtained. In this model, the decision of an eligible employee is examined at each level of possible contributions. This strategy captures changes in the incentives of contributing an additional percentage of compensation and controls for whether the participant is allowed to contribute (for example, in some plans a highly compensated employee might be barred from making additional contributions beyond 6 percent of compensation, whereas an NHCE might be allowed to contribute 15 percent of compensation).

Because each percentage of compensation contributed is modeled as a separate decision, an employee either contributes or does not contribute the *i*th percent of compensation. As a binomial variable is the dependent variable in the estimation, a probit regression is used to represent the nature of the dependent variable. The conditional estimation model for an individual to contribute (C) is

$$P(Ci = 1) = ai + b1iMTCHi + b2iAMTCHi + b3iage + b4iage^2 + b5iage^3 +$$
$$b6iwage + b7iwage^2 + b8iwage^3 + b9itenure + b10itenure^2 + b11itenure^3 + ei,$$

where *i* represents the *i*th interval of contributions; *MTCH* and *AMTCH* are the plan match variables; *age*, *wage*, and *tenure* (and their squared and cubed values) are the demographic variables; and *ei* is the error term for each interval regression.

The demographic variables are self-explanatory. The plan match variable, *MTCHi*, is the match rate percentage at each level of contribution. However, this variable was thought to be insufficient to capture the entire incentive of contributing at each interval. For example, a participant facing a match rate of 50 percent for the first 6 percent of compensation might have more incentive to contribute the second percent of compensation than the fifth percent because of the value of additional matches that would be foregone if he or she decides not to contribute at that level. In other words, given that the employee already contributed 4 percent, the decision not to defer the fifth percent of compensation costs the employee the 50 percent match on the fifth percent plus the option to receive a 50 percent match on the sixth percent (a current match of 0.5 and a future match of 0.5). In contrast, the decision not to defer the second percent of compensation, given that an employee already contributed 1 percent, costs the employee the 50 percent match on the second percent plus the option to receive a 50 percent match on the third, fourth, fifth, and sixth percent (a current match of 0.5 and a future match of 0.5 * 4 = 2.0 percent). Therefore, an additional match value variable (*AMTCHi*) was included, representing the option value of the additional match value at a given percentage of contributions.

A series of probit regressions was conducted for each possible level of percentage of compensation contributed in order to estimate the total level of contributions to this model. Each estimation of the percentage of compensation contributed has a different set of results for the differing incentives of contributing that level of compensation. In the first interval, the probability of an eligible employee contributing anything to the plan is estimated. In the second interval, the probability that a participant who contributed 1 percent of compensation contributes a second percent of compensation is estimated; people who do not contribute 1 percent of compensation are not included in the estimation of the second percent of compensation. Under this process, only employees who are faced with the decision to contribute the next percentage are investigated.[14]

Two specifications of this basic model structure were estimated for employees' decisions to contribute to a 401(k) up to 18 percent of compensation. The first specification included only the match rate (*MTCHx*, *x* = 1, 2, ..., 18) immediately facing the employee at each level of compensation without any plan dummies. The second specification added the additional plan match value variable ($AMTCHx$, x = 1, 2, …, 18).

To illustrate this model, VanDerhei and Copeland (2001) compute the probability that a 22-year-old employee with one year of tenure with his or her current employer and wages of $15,000 who already contributed 4 percent of compensation will contribute an additional percent. This value is estimated to be as low as 81 percent if this is the last interval of compensation that is matched by the employer (that is, the additional match is equal to zero). In contrast, the same employee is estimated to have a 90 percent probability of contributing the extra percent of compensation if the option to earn an extra 1 percent of employer match would be forfeited if the employee continued to contribute the maximum percentage of compensation matched. In each of the three intervals illustrated, the model predicts that employees with the lowest estimated probability of contributing the extra percent of compensation when the additional match is set equal to zero (young employees and employees with lower levels of wage and tenure) will be the most sensitive to increases in the additional match level.

Figure 3.1 displays the predicted contributions for stylized participants under typical plan matching formulas. It shows that older participants and participants with higher levels of wage and tenure are expected to make higher employee contributions for a given plan design, and it also allows investigation of how the change in plan design will affect the expected contribution behavior. For example, a change from a 50 percent match on the first 6 percent of compensation to a 75 percent match over the same range results in an expected increase in employee contributions for all of the stylized participants. Figure 3.1 also reveals the ability of the model to predict contributions under a two-tier matching formula (for example, a 75 percent match on the first 2 percent of compensation, decreasing to 50 percent for the next 3 percent of compensation), as well as its ability to model employees participating in a plan with no employer match.

FIGURE 3.1 **Predicted employee contributions for selected persons and plan matching formulas**

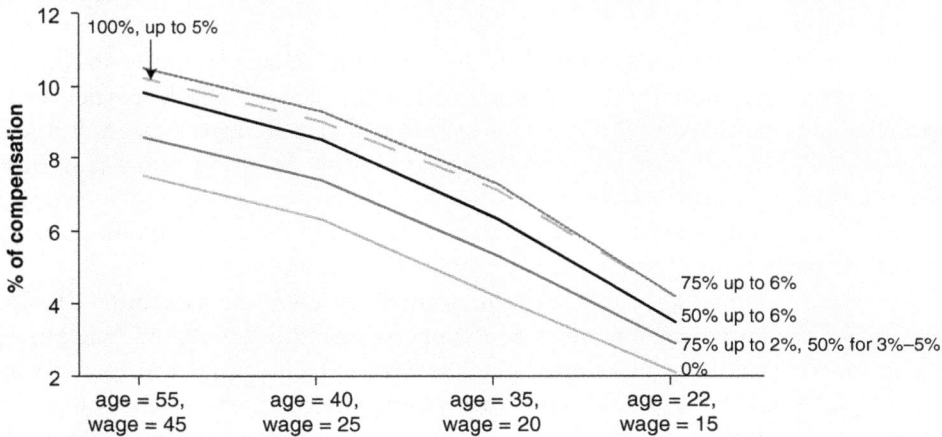

SOURCE: VanDerhei and Copeland 2001.

HOW IMPORTANT IS THE SHIFT FROM VOLUNTARY ENROLLMENT TO AUTOMATIC ENROLLMENT IN 401(K) PLANS?

The previous sections summarized the importance of employer matching contributions on participation and contribution decisions in 401(k) plans. But the real issue, certainly in terms of public policy research, is whether these decisions result in adequate retirement wealth accumulation. It is difficult to accurately simulate these results, given the complex interactions between plan design parameters and the participation, contribution, investment, and cash-out decisions of employees. Fortunately, the EBRI/ICI 401(k) database includes a detailed administrative record of tens of millions of employees from tens of thousands of plans, with longitudinal linkages for both plans and participants going back as far as 1996 in some cases.

In the first simulation publication using these data, Holden and VanDerhei (2002) provide an analysis of workers participating in 401(k) plans with voluntary enrollment. They show that workers participating in these voluntary enrollment 401(k) plans may be able to generate account balances (either retained in the original plan or rolled over to a successor employer plan or an IRA) capable of replacing a significant percentage of their pre-retirement income if they participate in a 401(k) plan their entire working life.

However, if workers are not always eligible to participate in a 401(k) plan, the adequacy of the retirement income generated by these plans drops substantially (Holden and VanDerhei 2002). Several studies simulating the likely retirement income generated under these plans for all (or a significant portion of) the workforce also find evidence that significant numbers of future retirees could reach retirement age with account balances too small (even when combined with expected social security income) to achieve replacement rates within conventionally defined targets (70–85 percent of pre-retirement income); this literature is reviewed in Appendix II of GAO 2007.

Another simulation study (Holden and VanDerhei 2005) demonstrates how valuable automatic enrollment designs would be to savings accumulations of low-income 401(k) contributors. A year after this study was conducted, the Pension Protection Act of 2006 included several advantageous provisions for 401(k) sponsors with a specific type of automatic enrollment design.

VanDerhei (2010) simulates the likely impact of this change on future 401(k) accumulations for a significant portion of workers (not just current 401(k) participants or people eligible to participate) if the switch to automatic enrollment is made. It updates previous EBRI research (VanDerhei and Copeland 2008) by using actual plan design modifications of large plan sponsors to estimate the employer response. The analysis indicates that the adoption of automatic enrollment is likely to have a very significant impact on retirement savings for many workers, especially low-income workers.

For example, under the baseline set of assumptions used, the median 401(k) accumulations for the lowest-income quartile of workers currently age 25–29 (assuming all 401(k) plans were voluntary enrollment plans as typified by the large plan sponsors used in the analysis) would be only 0.08 times final earnings at age 65 (this is largely due to the fact that a sizable percentage of workers—as opposed to participants—were assumed to have zero balances at age 65).

If, however, all 401(k) plans by large plan sponsors are assumed to have automatic enrollment provisions in place, the median 401(k) accumulations for the lowest income quartile jumps to 4.96 times final earnings, assuming that 401(k) participants revert back to the default contribution (3 percent of pay) when they change jobs and participate in a new 401(k) plan. Under the assumption that the participants retain their current contribution level when they change jobs, the median 401(k) accumulations for the lowest income quartile jumps to 5.33 times final earnings.[15] Even among the top 25 percent of these workers (when ranked by 401(k) accumulations as a multiple of final earnings), there are large increases: the multiple under a voluntary enrollment scenario is 2.41 times final earnings whereas automatic enrollment provides multiples of 9.15 or 9.81, depending on the assumptions for employee reversion to default contribution rates upon job change.

IMPACT OF AUTOMATIC ENROLLMENT ON EMPLOYER CONTRIBUTION RATES

Soto and Butrica (2009) conclude that among a sample of large 401(k) plans, match rates are lower among firms with automatic enrollment than among firms without automatic enrollment, after controlling for firm characteristics. There are, however, two major limitations of this analysis. First, the study was based on U.S. Department of Labor Form 5500 data, which do not include specific information on 401(k) match rates. Rather, the authors constructed an estimate of the match rate as being the ratio of employer-to-employee contributions for each 401(k) plan. Second, the authors merged the Form 5500 data with information on automatic enrollment from the Pensions and Investments database of the top 1,000 pension funds, relying on a flag indicating whether plan administrators reported offering automatic enrollment in their plans. However, as this database does not report when the automatic enrollment provision was adopted, there is no way of knowing how long this design was in place.

The results of the regression analysis of this database suggest a negative relationship between automatic enrollment and match rates that is statistically significant at the firm level, according to the authors of the study. In particular, match rates are about 7 percentage points lower among firms with automatic enrollment than among firms without automatic enrollment, after controlling for firm characteristics. The authors acknowledge that although the regressions suggest a relationship between automatic enrollment and match rates, they do not necessarily imply that automatic enrollment causes lower match rates—a crucial qualification that has been ignored in many third-party accounts of their study.

These conclusions conflict with previous EBRI research (VanDerhei 2007), which surveyed defined benefit plan sponsors administered by Mercer Human Resource Consulting to gauge their recent activity and planned modifications to their defined benefit (pension) and defined contribution (401(k)-type) plans. The survey also determined what, if any, increases in employer contributions to defined contribution plans were made in conjunction with reductions to the defined benefit plans.

Although the association between the adoption of automatic enrollment and employer contributions to 401(k) plans was not the focus of the study, it found that one-third of the defined benefit plan sponsors surveyed indicated that they had already increased or planned to increase their employer match to a defined contribution plan and that 20.9 percent indicated that they had already increased or planned to increase their nonmatching employer contributions to a defined contribution plan. There was some overlap between the two groups, but overall, 42.5 percent of the defined benefit plan sponsors surveyed indicated that they had already increased or planned to increase their employer match or nonmatching employer contribution to the defined contribution. This increase in contribution was particularly evident among defined benefit plan sponsors that had closed a defined benefit plan to new hires, frozen their defined benefit plan to all members in the last two years, or planned to do so in the next two years.[16]

The 2007 EBRI study found an extremely high correlation between the adoption of automatic enrollment for a 401(k) plan and the freezing or closing of the defined benefit plan.[17] Among defined benefit plan sponsors that had closed their defined benefit plans in the previous two years, 80.5 percent had either already adopted or were considering adopting automatic enrollment features for their 401(k) plans.[18]

VanDerhei (2010) analyzes in detail plan-specific data on about 1,000 large defined contribution plans for salaried employees from Benefit SpecSelect (a trademark of Hewitt Associates LLC) in 2005 and 2009. A subsample of plan sponsors was created that had adopted automatic enrollment 401(k) plans by 2009 but did not have them in 2005 (the last observation not influenced by the Pension Protection Act of 2006). For each plan, VanDerhei coded the default contribution rate for the automatic enrollment plan in 2009, the match rate contribution formulas for both years,[19] and all nonelective contributions paid to the defined contribution participants by the employer.

Whether plan sponsors were more or less generous after adopting automatic enrollment was evaluated with three metrics:

- The average 2009 first-tier match rate was $0.8778 for each $1 contributed; the average 2005 first-tier match rate was $0.8126 for each $1 contributed. The difference of $0.0652 per $1 contributed suggests that, to the extent that this sample is representative of the universe of large 401(k) sponsors, sponsors adopting automatic enrollment were more generous to the 401(k) participants (when measured by this variable) after automatic enrollment was implemented than before.

- The average effective match rate was 4.32 percent of compensation in 2009 but only 4.00 percent in 2005. The increase of 0.32 percentage points suggests that large 401(k) sponsors adopting automatic enrollment were more generous to the 401(k) participants (when measured by this variable) after the adoption of automatic enrollment than before.[20]

- The average total employer contribution rate (the sum of the effective match rate and the nonelective contribution rate) was 6.35 percent of compensation for 2009 and 5.46 percent in 2005. The increase of 0.89 percentage points suggests that large 401(k) sponsors adopting automatic enrollment were more generous to the 401(k) participants when measured by this variable than before.

This information was then combined with the defined benefit information for the same sponsor in an attempt to analyze whether EBRI's 2007 findings of the association between defined benefit freezing/closing and enhanced 401(k) contributions were corroborated.

The average improvements for all three metrics were much greater for sponsors that had frozen or closed their defined benefit plans than the overall average (table 3.4). For example, the change in the total employer contribution rate for all frozen plans was 1.64 percent of compensation versus 0.89 percent for the overall average. Employers that had closed their defined benefit plans to new employees had an even larger average improvement (2.82 percent of compensation).

The defined benefit plan sponsors that had frozen or closed their plans were then separated into firms that had done so before adopting automatic enrollment and firms that had changed their defined benefit plans between 2005 and 2009. If the hypothesis that the 401(k) improvements were at least partially a result of a simultaneous quid pro quo for the decreased accruals in the defined benefit plan, one would expect that the earlier modifications would be less generous than the modifications that took place at about the time of the conversion to automatic enrollment—exactly what is found for all six comparisons in table 3.4. For example, the average total employer contribution improvement for firms that had frozen their plans before 2005 was 0.69 percent of compensation, compared with 2.45 percent for firms that froze their plans between 2005 and 2009. Similar evidence is found for firms that closed their pension plans to new employees: the average improvement in total employer 401(k) contribution was only 0.56 percent of compensation for firms that closed their plans before 2005, but it was 3.34 percent for firms that closed their plans between 2005 and 2009.

TABLE 3.4 **Changes in employer contribution rates to 401(k) plans that adopted automatic enrollment between 2005 and 2009, by type of modification**
PERCENT

Modification to defined benefit plan	Change in first-tier match rate	Change in effective match rate	Change in total employer contribution rate
Frozen	14.68	0.73	1.64
Before 2005	10.29	0.24	0.69
2005–09	18.40	1.15	2.45
Closed to new employees	15.06	0.58	2.82
Before 2005	5.56	0.22	0.56
2005–09	17.26	0.66	3.34
Total	6.52	0.32	0.89

SOURCE: EBRI analysis of plan-specific data from Benefit SpecSelect (a trademark of Hewitt Associates LLC).

Persistence of Contributions

An important issue in understanding the behavior of workers contributing to 401(k) plans and interpreting the long-term implications is the persistence of behavior when the matching formula is changed. In the wake of the 2008 financial crisis, a number of employers reduced, suspended, or terminated their matching contributions, providing a natural experiment that sheds some light on this issue.[21]

A Towers Watson analysis of 260 companies that made changes to employer match contributions in response to the economic crisis finds that 231 suspended their matches and 29 reduced them (Apte and McFarland 2011). According to the study, most of the companies chose to reinstate their match (75 percent). Of the firms that did so, 74 percent reintroduced the original match amount. Among these plan sponsors, the most frequent match formula before and after the crisis was 50 percent up to 6 percent of salary. For companies on which specific change dates were available, the median duration for match suspensions was 12 months, and most companies reinstated their match after 9–12 months.

Separately, by the middle of 2009, almost 10 percent of defined contribution plans administered by Fidelity suspended or reduced their contribution dollars. By December 2010, 55 percent of those plan sponsors indicated that they planned to reinstate their match within the next 12 months. Fidelity also reported that among larger companies (firms with more than 5,000 employees), 71 percent had reinstated or planned to reinstate their match. More than 60 percent of employers with a plan size of 500–999 employees had already reinstated or indicated they planned to reinstate their match, up from 38 percent just 10 months earlier. Among employers with fewer than 1,000 employees in their plan, the percentage was 46 percent.

In February 2012, an interim report from the IRS of responses from its 401(k) compliance check questionnaire—which polled 1,200 randomly selected plan sponsors via a secure website— revealed that the share of firms that had suspended or discontinued matching contributions in their plans increased from 1 percent in 2006 to 4 percent in 2008, the share that had suspended or discontinued the nonelective contribution in their plans increased from 2 percent in 2006 to 5 percent in 2008, and the share that had reduced nonelective contributions in their plans increased from 1 percent in 2006 to 5 percent in 2008.

Given the impact of employer matching contributions on employee participation and contribution decisions (at least in voluntary enrollment plans) documented above, a common concern with respect to plan sponsors suspending their contributions is the potential impact on employee savings. For example, if an employee were contributing 6 percent of compensation to receive the maximum match from a plan with a 50 percent match on the first 6 percent of compensation, would a suspended match end up decreasing the total contribution for the employee from 9 percent to 6 percent? Or would the reduced incentive drive savings below 6 percent (perhaps to zero)?

In an attempt to provide preliminary evidence with respect to the impact of suspending employer contributions on employee behavior, VanDerhei (2009) analyzed all 401(k) plans in the EBRI/ICI 401(k) database with more than $100,000 in employer contributions in 2007 and none in 2008 (all plans were still active as of year end 2008).[22] The percentage of 401(k) participants continuing to contribute in 2008 after a suspension in employer contributions was analyzed as a function of a match rate proxy.[23]

For all plans with a match rate proxy of less than 50 percent, the percentage of 401(k) participants continuing to contribute in 2008 was at least 86 percent. However, the percentage among participants with more generous match rate proxies decreased substantially. For participants with a match rate proxy of 50–100 percent, only 80 percent of participants continued contributing after the suspension. For participants with match rate proxies of more than 100 percent, the percentage was only 73 percent.

Going Forward

In order to avoid the complications associated with nondiscrimination testing, a growing number of employers have embraced the safe harbor plan design outlined above. Rather than relying on a match incentive, this design requires certain minimum amounts of employer contribution (table 3.5).

Over time, the expanded availability of automatic enrollment may result in reduced reliance on the match as an incentive to participate (table 3.6).

From inception, the additional nondiscrimination tests imposed on the 401(k) design (and their subsequent iterations) have ensured that the benefits of these programs did not skew disproportionately to highly compensated workers by requiring certain minimum participation and contribution levels by NHCEs. Compliance with these rules has required that sponsoring employers be attentive to the participation of NHCEs, in order to preserve the qualification for tax preference, as well as the benefit levels for highly compensated employees. The employer match has long, and consistently, been promoted as a means of offering "free money" to workers who might otherwise have foregone participation or done so at lower contribution levels. More recently, and following their strengthened codification in the Pension Protection Act of 2006, automatic enrollment plan designs have provided an effective means for plan sponsors to encourage or expand participation without necessarily tying participation to a financial incentive.

Automatic enrollment encourages a level of participation that is adequate to produce sufficient retirement income for people with a full savings career in that system. Whether more widespread adoption of automatic enrollment will affect the perceived need for, and level of, the employer match in providing a future with retirement income security remains to be seen.

TABLE 3.5 **Inclusion of safe harbor plans in defined contribution plans, by company size**

Company size	% offering safe harbor plans
Micro	44.6
Small	38.6
Midsize	37.5
Large	41.4
Mega	41.7
Total	41.5

SEE table 3.1.

TABLE 3.6 **Use of automatic enrollment in defined contribution plans, by company size**

Company size	% offering automatic enrollment
Micro	19.9
Small	38.4
Midsize	50.3
Large	50.7
Mega	55.7
Total	33.4

SEE table 3.1.

Conclusion

Matching contributions have played a central role in the emergence of 401(k) plans, the most common type of defined contribution pension savings account in the United States. Employers have used various kinds of matching arrangements to encourage broad-based participation as a means of ensuring that these plans remain in compliance with a complex set of nondiscrimination rules designed to ensure that the value of contributions into these arrangements does not unduly benefit higher-income workers at the sponsoring firms.

Several empirical studies analyze the effect of matching contributions on the probability of participating in 401(k) plans that use voluntary enrollment. The magnitude of the results varies considerably, but generally the employer match has been found to have a positive impact on overall employee participation in 401(k) plans, though not necessarily for all groups of employees.

In a study using the most comprehensive set of administrative data for this topic, Mitchell, Utkus and Yang (2005) conclude that nearly two-thirds of NHCEs at a typical firm would participate regardless of the presence of a match and that the impact of a match is limited to a relatively narrow range of outcomes. More than a quarter of the workers who did not fall within the group defined as highly compensated did not participate in plans that employed the most common matching formulas used in this sampling, and even with a more generous match, more than one in five still did not choose to participate.

The literature on the impact of matching contributions on employee contribution behavior for 401(k) plans with voluntary enrollment is much less developed than that dealing with the participation decision—understandably, given the complexity of the modeling. VanDerhei and Copeland (2001) provide a framework for integrating the impact of the participant's age and wage with plan-specific incentives that look at the incremental match rates and maximum amounts matched in voluntary enrollment designs.

A more recent design evolution is the application of automatic enrollment in these programs. It appears that a significant percentage of workers participating in these arrangements do so at the default contribution rates and adhere to the automatic escalation design parameters established by the plans. A number of employers that have adopted automatic enrollment features for their 401(k) plans have adopted the simplified safe harbor matching provisions of the Pension Protection Act of 2006. Some plan sponsors may be concerned that the increase in participation rate that frequently accompanies automatic enrollment adoption could lead to a sudden increase in matching contribution costs. One way to mitigate a potential increase in employer costs is to decrease the generosity of the employer match provisions of the plan. It is too soon to determine whether employers have done so, especially given the considerable financial turmoil in recent years, which will make it difficult to disentangle the effects of the design from other factors.

A considerable knowledge gap remains with respect to the impact of an employer match on participation in 401(k) plans utilizing automatic enrollment. Based on a sample of nine firms, Beshears and others (2007) estimate that eliminating the match under an automatic enrollment plan would likely reduce plan participation by 5–11 percentage points. Public policy analysts will be keenly interested in seeing whether these results continue to hold as the number of plan sponsors adopting automatic enrollment provisions continues to increase.[24] Ultimately, whether matching contributions are an effective means of closing the retirement income savings gap depends to a large extent on the type of plan design (automatic versus voluntary enrollment) chosen by the plan sponsor and the income level of participants.[25]

Notes

1. In the United States, the legal definition of a defined contribution plan is a plan that provides for an individual account for each participant and provides benefits based solely on the amount contributed to the account, plus or minus income, gains, and expenses and losses allocated to the account.

2. The Retirement Confidence Survey is sponsored by the Employee Benefit Research Institute, the American Savings Education Council, and Mathew Greenwald & Associates.

3. Additional information about these plan designs and their applications can be found in the Employment Benefit Research Institute's Fundamentals of Employee Benefit Programs, available at http://www.ebri.org/publications/books/?fa=fundamentals.

4. The Tax Reform Act of 1986 also changed the law such that, effective for plan years beginning on or after January 1, 1987, contributions under qualified profit-sharing plans no longer needed to be limited to current or accumulated profits of the employer. As a consequence, employers could maintain qualified CODAs as part of profit-sharing plans, regardless of whether they actually had profits.

5. Currently, two nondiscrimination approaches are permitted for the average deferral percentage and average compensation percentage tests. The first is "current year" testing, where current year deferral and contribution percentages are used to compare the percentages of both highly compensated and non–highly compensated employees. The other approach is "prior year" testing, where the deferral and contribution percentages for NHCEs in the prior year are compared with the deferral and contribution percentages of highly compensated employees in the current year. This approach means that the average deferral percentage and average compensation percentage limits for highly compensated employees are known in advance, reducing the chance of a failed test at year end or the need for taxable refunds or other corrective measures. The method used must, however, be specified in the plan document.

6. A safe harbor is a statutory, regulatory, or contractual provision that provides protection, usually from a penalty or liability.

7. Graded vesting schedules provide for a gradual increase in the ownership interest in employer contributions over time. Under a cliff vesting schedule, the worker's ownership (vesting) of the employer contributions generally happens at a single point in time.

8. The original matching contribution (25 percent on the first 4 percent of pay contributed) was replaced with an employer contribution equal to 4 percent of pay plus an annual profit-sharing contribution.

9. The impact of matching contributions on employee contribution behavior has been studied extensively in voluntary enrollment 401(k) plans. Relatively little research has been conducted on automatic enrollment plans. Nessmith, Utkus, and Young (2007) provide evidence that new employees hired under automatic enrollment 401(k) plans have participation rates that are nearly twice those of new employees hired under voluntary enrollment 401(k) plans (86 percent versus 45 percent). However, they show that overall plan contribution rates under automatic enrollment fall, because many new participants who would have voluntarily chosen a higher contribution rate remain at the low default levels. For additional research conducted

on a relatively small sample of 401(k) plans, see Choi, Laibson, and Madrian (2004); Choi and others (2004); and Madrian and Shea (2001).

10. This result is from a regression on a sample of all participants (whether they contributed or not) for whom information on the match rate and level was provided or derived. The regression model included age, tenure, salary, plan loan provision (yes/no), the employer match rate, and employer match level variables to examine their effects on participant before-tax contribution rates.

11. The EBRI/ICI 401(k) database includes detailed records (including demographic information and contribution behavior) on individual participants from more than 60,000 plans. Because of strict confidentiality standards, no information on the individual was included.

12. This limitation affects elective deferrals to Section 401(k) plans and to the federal government's Thrift Savings Plan, among other plans. The limitation under Section 402(g)(1) on the exclusion for elective deferrals in 401(k) plans was $17,000 for 2012.

13. Even for plans without nonelective contributions, several participants had employer contributions that were not equal to the predicted amount based on the plan's matching formulas, the employee's before-tax or after-tax contributions, or both. This apparent discrepancy may reflect the use of different definitions of compensation applied by the individual 401(k) plan for these purposes versus the compensation data provided in the database. The authors attempted to control for this unknown effect by computing the difference between actual and predicted employer contributions (as a percentage of compensation) and excluding any participant with more than a 0.2 percent of compensation differential.

14. If the plan does not allow an employee to defer to the next level of contributions, that employee is not included in the next contribution interval. This feature allows for the examination of only those employees who can actually contribute the next percentage of compensation, based on either a prior choice or plan-specific constraints.

15. Technically, the stochastic simulation model assumes that future 401(k) eligibility is a function of current eligibility.

16. The proportion of defined benefit plan sponsors that indicated that they had already increased or planned to increase their employer match or nonmatching employer contribution to a defined contribution plan ranged from 62 percent (for sponsors that had frozen the defined benefit plan in the previous two years) to 81 percent (for sponsors that intended to close the plan for new members in the next two years).

17. As hypothesized in VanDerhei (2007), some employers that discontinued accruals in the defined benefit plans may want to continue to have a very large percentage of their eligible employees participating each year. As many industry studies have shown, participation rates among eligible young and low-income employees are significantly higher under 401(k) plans with an automatic enrollment feature.

18. Similar levels applied to defined benefit plans that were to be closed or frozen in the next two years.

19. Many plans will use a multitier formula—another reason why using simple averages of employer-to-employee contributions, as Soto and Butrica (2009) do, is problematic.

20. The effective match rate is a measure of the total amount of the employer's contribution via the matching formulas if the employee contributes enough to receive the full match. This measure simultaneously controls for the match rate, the maximum amount matched, and the possibility of a multitiered formula. For example, an employer that matches 100 percent of the first 1 percent of compensation and 50 percent of the next 5 percent would have an effective match of $1 * 1 + (0.5 * 5) = 3.5$ percent of compensation.

21. Some plan sponsors may have turned to their 401(k) plans as a means of freeing up cash flow for their legally required minimum contributions to defined benefit plans. A review by Salisbury and Buser (2009) of 251 plan sponsors that had suspended matching contributions for their 4.4 million workers finds that firms employing half of the workers also maintained an open defined benefit plan. Sixteen percent of workers were with employers that were still obligated to fund a frozen defined benefit plan, whereas 8 percent were with an employer that had both an open and a frozen defined benefit plan that carried funding obligations.

22. More refined analysis is currently under way to link the 2006 and 2007 contributions on a plan-specific basis and filter out midyear suspensions.

23. The proxy was aggregate employer contributions divided by employee contributions for 2007. This measure is only a rough proxy; it will be inaccurate to the extent that nonelective contributions exist for the plan, or employees contribute in excess of the maximum amount needed to obtain the full match. This analysis is currently being refined using year-end 2010 data.

24. Given that such a small percentage of 401(k) sponsors adopted automatic enrollment before passage of the Pension Protection Act of 2006, it is possible that their workforces may not be representative of the broader distributor of all eligible workers.

25. VanDerhei (2010) simulates median accumulation multiples for employees currently age 25–29, who are assumed to have 31–40 years of eligibility throughout their working careers. He projects that the highest income quartile will have sufficient accumulations to purchase a real annuity to replace at least one-third of their final earnings at age 65. The impact of lower participation rates under voluntary enrollment plans becomes more pronounced as income decreases.

References

Adams, Nevin E. 2011. "Points of Hue: PLANSPONSOR's 2011 Annual Defined Contribution Survey." *PLANSPONSOR Magazine* November.

Andrews, Emily. 1992. "The Growth and Distribution of 401(k) Plans." In *Trends in Pensions 1992*, ed. John Turner and Daniel Beller, 149–76. Washington, DC: U.S. Government Printing Office.

Apte, Vishal, and Brendan McFarland. 2011. "A Look at Defined Contribution Match Reinstatements." Towers Watson, *U.S.—Insider* October. www.towerswatson.com/united-states/newsletters/insider/5641.

Bassett, William, Michael Fleming, and Anthony Rodrigues. 1998. "How Workers Use 401(k) Plans: The Participation, Contribution, and Withdrawal Decisions." *National Tax Journal* 51 (2): 263–88.

Beshears, John, James J. Choi, David Laibson, and Brigitte C. Madrian. 2007. "The Impact of Employer Matching on Savings Plan Participation under Automatic Enrollment." NBER Working Paper 13352, National Bureau of Economic Research, Cambridge, MA.

Brady, Peter J. 2007. "Pension Nondiscrimination Rules and the Incentive to Cross Subsidize Employees." *Journal of Pension Economics and Finance* 6: 127–45.

Choi, James J., David Laibson, and Brigitte Madrian. 2004. "Plan Design and 401(k) Savings Outcomes." NBER Working Paper W10486, National Bureau of Economic Research, Cambridge, MA.

Choi, James, David Laibson, Brigitte Madrian, and Andrew Metrick. 2004. "Defined Contributions Pensions: Plan Rules, Participant Decisions, and the Path of Least Resistance." In *Tax Policy and the Economy*, ed. James M. Poterb, 67–113. Cambridge, MA: MIT Press.

Dworak-Fisher, Keenan. 2011. "Encouraging Participation in 401(k) Plans: Reconsidering the Employer Match, Industrial Relations." *Journal of Economy and Society* 50 (4): 713–37.

Engelhardt, Gary, and Anil Kumar. 2007. "Employer Matching and 401(k) Saving: Evidence from the Health and Retirement Study." *Journal of Public Economics* 91 (10): 1920–43.

Even, William E., and David A. Macpherson. 2005. "The Effects of Employer Matching in 401(k) Plans." *Industrial Relations: A Journal of Economy and Society* 44 (3): 525–49.

Facts from EBRI. 2005. "A History of 401(k) Plans: An Update." Employee Benefit Research Institute, Washington, DC. http://www.ebri.org/pdf/publications/facts/0205fact.a.pdf.

GAO (Government Accountability Office). 2007. "Private Pensions: Low Defined Contribution Plan Savings May Pose Challenges to Retirement Security, Especially for Many Low-Income Workers," GAO, Washington, DC.

Holden, Sarah, and Jack VanDerhei. 2001. "Contribution Behavior of 401(k) Plan Participants." EBRI Issue Brief 238, Employee Benefit Research Institute, Washington, DC.

———. 2002. "Can 401(k) Accumulations Generate Significant Income for Future Retirees?" EBRI Issue Brief 251, Employee Benefit Research Institute, Washington, DC.

———. 2005. "The Influence of Automatic Enrollment, Catch-Up, and IRA Contributions on 401(k) Accumulations at Retirement." EBRI Issue Brief 283, Employee Benefit Research Institute, Washington, DC.

Ippolito, Richard A. 1997. *Pension Plans and Employee Performance.*" Chicago: University of Chicago Press.

Kusko, Andrea, James Poterba, and David Wilcox. 1998. "Employee Decisions with Respect to 401(k) Plans." In *Living with Defined Contribution Pensions: Remaking Responsibility for Retirement*, ed. Olivia S. Mitchell and Sylvester Schieber, 69–96. Philadelphia: University of Pennsylvania Press.

Madrian, Brigitte, and Dennis Shea. 2001. "The Power of Suggestion: Inertia in 401(k) Participation and Savings Behavior." *Quarterly Journal of Economics* 116 (4): 1149–87.

Mitchell, Olivia S., Stephen P. Utkus, and Tongxuan Yang. 2005. "Turning Workers into Savers? Incentives, Liquidity, and Choice in 401(k) Plan Design." NBER Working Paper W11726, National Bureau of Economic Research, Cambridge, MA.

Nessmith, William E., Stephen P. Utkus, and Jean A. Young. 2007. "Measuring the Effectiveness of Automatic Enrollment." Vanguard Center for Retirement Research, Malvern, PA.

Papke, Leslie. 1995. "Participation in and Contributions to 401(k) Pension Plans: Evidence from Plan Data." *Journal of Human Resources* 30 (2): 311–25.

Papke, Leslie, and James Poterba. 1995. "Survey Evidence on Employer Match Rates and Employee Saving Behavior in 401(k) Plans." *Economics Letters* 49 (September): 313–17.

Principal Financial Group. 2010. "New Data from the Principal Reveals Power of Employer Match." News Room: News Release Archive, November 30. www.principal.com/about/news/2010/ris-match-stats113010.htm.

Raish, David L. n.d. "Cash or Deferred Arrangements (Portfolio 358)." Bloomberg/BNA. www.bna.com/Cash-Deferred-Arrangements-p7555/.

Salisbury, Dallas, and Elizabeth Buser. 2009. "Many 401(k) Sponsors Suspending Matching Contributions Also Funding Defined Benefit Pension Plans." *EBRI Note* 30 (6), Employee Benefit Research Institute, Washington, DC.

Soto, Mauricio, and Barbara A. Butrica. 2009. "Will Automatic Enrollment Reduce Employer Contributions to 401(k) Plans?" CRR Working Paper 2009–33, Center for Retirement Research at Boston College, Boston.

VanDerhei, Jack. 2007. "Retirement Income Adequacy after PPA and FAS 158: Part One: Plan Sponsors' Reactions." EBRI Issue Brief 307, Employee Benefit Research Institute, Washington, DC.

———. 2009. "Falling Stocks: What Will Happen to Retirees' Incomes? The Worker Perspective." Presentation at the Association for Public Policy and Management Fall Conference, the Economic Crisis of 2008: What Will Happen to Retirees' Incomes?

———. 2010. "The Impact of Automatic Enrollment in 401(k) Plans on Future Retirement Accumulations: A Simulation Study Based on Plan Design Modifications of Large Plan Sponsors." EBRI Issue Brief 341, Employee Benefit Research Institute, Washington, DC.

VanDerhei, Jack, and Craig Copeland. 2001. "A Behavioral Model for Predicting Employee Contributions to 401(k) Plans." *North American Actuarial Journal* 5 (1): 80–94.

———. 2008. "The Impact of PPA on Retirement Income for 401(k) Participants." EBRI Issue Brief 318, Employee Benefit Research Institute, Washington, DC.

Yakoboski, Paul. 1994. "Salary Reduction Plans and Individual Saving for Retirement." EBRI Issue Brief 155, Employee Benefit Research Institute, Washington, DC.

Yakoboski, Paul, and Jack VanDerhei. 1996. "Contribution Rates and Plan Features: An Analysis of Large 401(k) Plan Data." EBRI Issue Brief 174, Employee Benefit Research Institute, Washington, DC.

CHAPTER 4

Riester Pensions in Germany: Design, Dynamics, Targeting Success, and Crowding-In

Axel Börsch-Supan, Michela Coppola, and Anette Reil-Held

Riester pensions are heavily subsidized voluntary private pension schemes designed to fill the emerging pension gap in Germany. After a slow start and several design changes, the plans took off very quickly. Saving incentives have been effective in reaching households with children; they have been somewhat less successful in attracting low-income earners. There is no evidence that the pensions have crowded out other saving: aggregate national saving has increased since their introduction.

Demographic change poses major problems for public pay-as-you-go pension schemes around the world, forcing many to reduce their generosity. In Germany, reductions in benefits took place in several steps, starting in 1992 with the indexation of benefits to net rather than gross earnings and the introduction of semiactuarial adjustments in case of early retirement and extending to the introduction of the "sustainability factor" in 2004, which indexes benefits to the inverse of the system dependency ratio (that is, the ratio of contributors to beneficiaries). It is estimated that in 2040, the average benefits-to-earnings ratio in Germany will be about 18 percentage points lower than in 2010.

These reforms will result in a large and potentially increasing gap in old-age income relative to current benefit levels. Recognizing this, the governments of Germany and many other countries have accompanied public pension reform with efforts to strengthen funded second-pillar (occupational) and third-pillar (private savings) pensions. In order to accelerate the uptake of such private pensions, countries have adopted two competing strategies: making such supplementary pensions mandatory (as the Netherlands and Sweden have done) or heavily subsidizing savings for private pensions, typically by matching contributions, providing tax credits, and/or permitting contributions to supplementary pensions to be excluded when calculating income for tax purposes. Germany has taken the incentive-oriented approach, with its Riester pensions (named after Walter Riester, former secretary of labor and social security), which were legislated as part of the 2001 pension reform.[1]

This research was prepared for a World Bank workshop on matching defined contribution schemes held in Washington, D.C., in June 2010. The authors are grateful for comments by Frank Eich, Richard Hinz, Robert Holzmann, and David Tuesta Cardenas and for financial support by the Research Institute for Policies on Pension and Aging and the German Science Foundation, which generously financed the creation of the SAVE panel data set and research based on these data.

Riester pensions are effectively state-subsidized voluntary individual saving arrangements with an associated (largely annuitized) pay-out plan. They are designed to enable all individuals receiving a public pension or a similar state-provided benefit to fill the emerging pension gap through individual savings to an extent that at least offsets the reduction in public pensions. As low-income households and households with children are assumed to have the greatest difficulty in offsetting these reductions, large tax credits are targeted to these households. A more modest tax deduction for contribution applies to everyone.

This chapter focuses on public acceptance of the Riester pensions and the dynamics of take-up over time. It highlights the distributional and cost aspects: who joined the new pension scheme, how costly is the scheme, who pays for it, and who is likely to be able to fill the emerging pension income gap. The chapter also investigates whether the new private pension plans displace saving for other purposes.

Riester pensions and their matching subsidies were introduced in a step-wise fashion from 2002 through 2008, allowing the effects of subsidies on uptake rates to be identified. Data come from SAVE, a new panel data set on households' saving and asset choices, sociodemographic characteristics, and the psychological determinants of saving and old-age provision behavior. The SAVE data capture the period 2001–10. They offer a unique opportunity to investigate old-age provision based on very recent data with a broad set of explanatory variables.

The issues investigated contribute to the discussion of the impact of retirement saving incentives in various countries. In the United States, Venti and Wise (1990) on one side and Gale and Scholz (1994) on the other sparked a controversial discussion about the efficacy of individual retirement accounts (IRAs) as saving devices (see Skinner and Hubbard 1996 for an early review). Disney, Emmerson, and Wakefield (2001) provide a helpful review tailored to the situation in the United Kingdom. These controversies have accompanied pension reform in almost all developed countries, generating interest in cross-national analyses of retirement saving behavior under different tax and subsidy regimes (see Börsch-Supan 2003, 2004). This chapter adds the recent German experience to this discussion and updates the paper by Börsch-Supan, Reil-Held, and Schunk (2008).

The chapter is structured around the themes of design, cost, and the effectiveness of the new system. The first section describes the key initial design features of Riester pensions in Germany. The second section documents the uptake of Riester pensions between 2001 and 2010 and the design adaptations that contributed to the uptake dynamics. The third section summarizes the costs of the Riester scheme and the changes in retirement saving associated with them. The following three sections address the effectiveness of the scheme. Section 4 provides descriptive statistics on the dynamics of enrollment in Riester pension plans by socioeconomic characteristics. Section 5 reports circumstantial evidence on the macroeconomic impact of Riester pensions, in particular whether they have crowded out other saving. Section 6 shows how the pension income gap is likely to be filled, the ultimate aim of the scheme. The last section provides some concluding observations.

Initial Design of Riester Pensions

Riester pensions are designed to fill the gap that will be created by the scheduled reduction of public pension benefits in response to the pressures of population aging. In order to achieve this goal, the 2001 German Retirement Savings Act (Altersvermögensgesetz) introduced a comprehensive regime of saving incentives for certified pension products that have become known as Riester pensions. These new retirement saving arrangements are eligible for two kinds of subsidies: a match of the participant's contribution and the deduction of all contributions from income for tax purposes. The initial certification regulations and subsidy mechanisms were rather complex. They were significantly simplified in 2005.

CRITERIA FOR "CERTIFIABLE" PRODUCTS

Initially, private pension plans were eligible for subsidies if they fulfilled 11 criteria stipulated by the Certification of Retirement Pension Contracts Act. These criteria included, among others, the following requirements:

- Savers must make regular contributions.
- Providers must guarantee that the nominal investment return in each calendar year be positive.
- Benefits must be disbursed as certain types of lifelong annuities.
- Lump-sum payments at retirement must not exceed 20 percent of the accumulated wealth.
- Administrative and marketing costs must be spread over at least 10 years.
- All providers must be registered with a supervisory board.

Most Riester products were provided by the insurance industry, but banks and investment funds also offered Riester products.

ELIGIBILITY

Not all households are eligible for the subsidies. The eligibility criteria are complex, although the intention was that everyone affected by the reduction in public pension benefits should be eligible for private pension subsidies. The group of eligible beneficiaries includes employees paying mandatory social insurance contributions, recipients of wage compensation benefits (such as unemployment benefits, child-raising benefits, and so forth), self-employed people who are mandatory members of the public pension system, farmers, and tenured civil servants. Spouses of eligible individuals are also entitled to receive subsidies ("indirect entitlements"), provided they enroll in a separate pension plan of their own.

SUBSIDIES

As a result of government budget constraints, the generosity of the subsidy scheme was phased in starting in 2002 and ending in 2008, with a doubling of the applicable parameters in each step (table 4.1). Column 1 shows the percentage of gross earnings that must be contributed to the plan in order to qualify for the full subsidy. The full subsidy (columns 2–4) has three components. The first is a basic subsidy (column 2) that is a match of the participant's own contribution. This basic subsidy is means tested for low- and middle-income households. Individuals eligible for this basic subsidy pay their savings

TABLE 4.1 **Statutory incentives for supplementary pension provision, 2002–08**

Year	Maximum contribution (% of gross earnings) (1)	Basic subsidy (€/year) (2)	Child subsidy (€/year) (3)	Maximum tax deduction (€/year) (4)
2002	1	38	46	525
2004/05	2	76	92	1,050
2006	3	114	138	1,575
2008	4	154	185[a]	2,100

SOURCE: Authors' compilation.

A. The child subsidy is €300 for children born after 2007.

into a certified pension plan; in the initial design, they had to file an application form to receive the subsidy each year. The plan provider receives the matching basic subsidy from the government and credits it to the participant's account as part of the total contribution. The second component is an additional subsidy for each child (column 3). The third component is the tax deductibility of contributions to Riester pension plans, which are treated as special expenses up to a maximum amount (column 4). This amount was fixed in nominal terms at €2,100 from 2008 onward; unless raised over time, this component will eventually be eroded.[2]

The matching contribution subsidy is reduced proportionally if contributions to the Riester plan are lower than the maximum indicated in column 1 of table 4.1. As the subsidy itself is counted as part of that contribution, some mathematical skills were required to compute the exact contribution required to receive the full subsidy—another feature that reduced the transparency of the design. The minimum own contribution depended on the number of children and the year in which the individual had enrolled in the Riester plan.

The complexity of the design made the substantial size of the subsidies less apparent for many people. Low-income participants received a relatively large subsidy, thanks to the matching basic subsidy; higher-income participants accrued additional subsidies from the tax deductions, thanks to the progressive nature of income tax rates. As a result, the profile of subsidies was slightly U-shaped (figure 4.1). Overall, subsidies averaged about 45 percent of contributions, ranging from 24 percent to 90 percent, depending on income and number of children. At the mean earnings (€42,000), the statutory subsidy rate was 39 percent.

OWNER-OCCUPIED HOUSING

Pension savings typically must accumulate until retirement, after which they are disbursed in some type of annuity. The 2001 law permitted withdrawals of €10,000–€50,000 from the accumulated capital, which had to be paid back into the pension plan in monthly installments by the age of 65 (if not, the subsidies received had to be paid back). The law was changed in 2008 to permit withdrawals of up to 100 percent of the accumulated capital to purchase owner-occupied housing without having to pay back the amount

FIGURE 4.1 **Subsidy as percentage of total (own plus government matching) contribution**

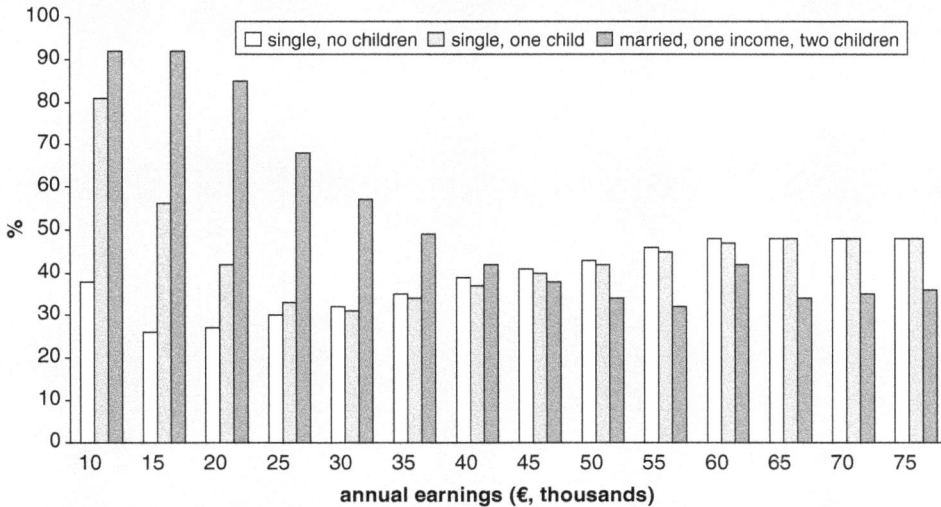

SOURCE: Deutsche Bundesbank 2002.

NOTE: Share of government assistance (direct subsidy/tax advantage) in total savings for supplementary old-age provision.

withdrawn. In addition, loan agreements (*Darlehensverträge*) and building society saving contracts (*Bausparverträge*) can be certified as Riester products receiving the subsidies described above. To date, such housing-related products do not constitute a significant share of Riester products.

Uptake Dynamics and Amended Design

About 1.4 million Riester pension plans were taken up in the first year after the introduction of incentives (figure 4.2).[3] After a period of initial enthusiasm, however, demand for Riester pensions flattened in 2003 and 2004. This lackluster growth and widespread criticism of the complex eligibility and subsidy design led to a simplification of the design in 2005 in an effort to improve acceptance of the new system by households and providers.

The changes introduced in 2005 did not affect the subsidies described in table 4.1 and figure 4.1. They included the following:

1. The application procedure was simplified by replacing it with a one-time permanent subsidy application. Savers eligible for subsidies were allowed to authorize their pension provider to submit a subsidy application on their behalf every year.

2. The number of certification criteria was reduced from 11 to 5.

3. The share of Riester pensions to be annuitized was reduced from 80 percent to 70 percent (that is, 30 percent of the accumulated capital could be received as a lump sum).

FIGURE 4.2 **Development of Riester pensions (million contracts)**

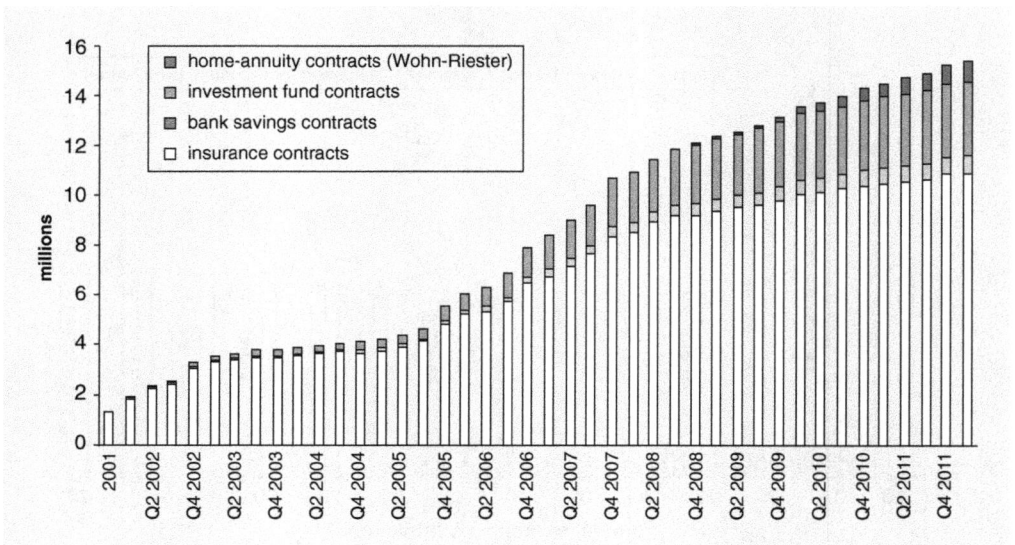

SOURCE: Authors' calculations based on data from quarterly press releases of the Federal Ministry for Labour and Social Affairs (www.bmas.de).
NOTE: Q = quarter.

4. The participant's minimum own contribution was standardized to €60 a year.

5. The transparency of pension saving products and providers was improved. More information on investment options, the structure of the portfolio, and the risk parameters was required. Providers were required to introduce a standardized calculation facilitating comparisons of alternative products.

6. The period over which acquisition and marketing costs could be spread was reduced from 10 to 5 years, making selling Riester pensions more attractive for providers. Although there were no formal limits for such charges, the certification process imposed some soft restrictions on charges that could be interpreted as usurious.

7. These changes were accompanied by a modest government-sponsored public relations campaign. Main advertising efforts, however, were left to providers of Riester products.

Demand for Riester pensions rose significantly in 2005 after these changes came into effect (figure 4.2). About 900,000 new policies were signed in the last quarter of 2005 alone—about four times as many as during all of 2004. This upward trend continued throughout 2008. By the end of 2008, more than 12 million pension plans eligible for subsidy support had been taken up.

After 2008, the rate of increase flattened. This trend may have been the result of three factors: the maximum contribution rate was reached in 2008; some sociodemographic strata may have reached saturation levels; and the financial crisis, which resulted in very low or negative returns, may have discouraged new households from starting a

Riester pension. Although the increase in the number of contracts slowed after 2008, the number of contracts continued to increase, at a linear rate. By the end of 2009, about 40 percent of households potentially eligible for subsidies held at least one Riester plan (Coppola and Gasche 2011).

The dynamic development of the Riester pensions occurred in parallel with the uptake of occupational pensions. In contrast, the uptake of other unsubsidized private retirement saving arrangements was essentially flat (figure 4.3).

FIGURE 4.3 **Coverage by private and occupational pensions, 2003–10**

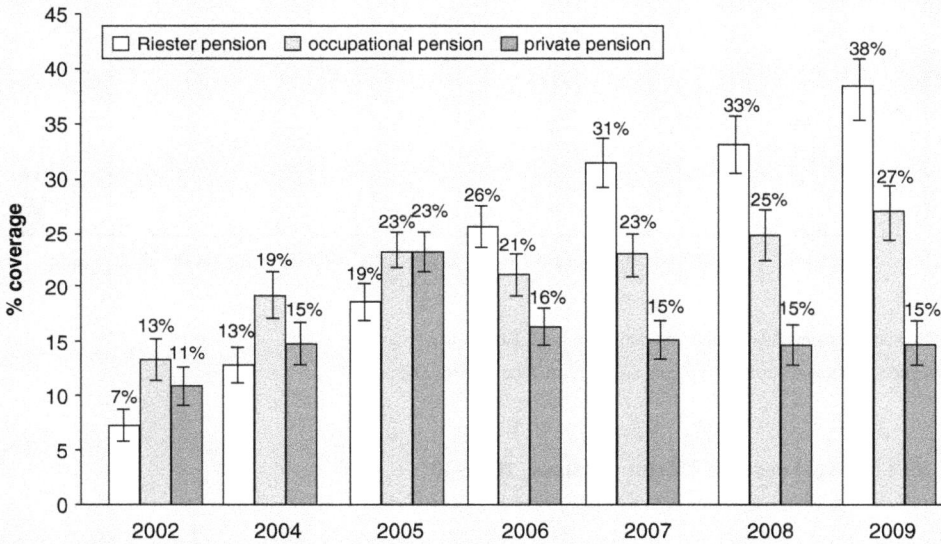

SOURCE: Authors' calculations based on data from the SAVE panel.
NOTE: Brackets show 95 percent confidence intervals. Figures are weighted.

In 2006, Riester pensions overtook occupational pensions as the main instrument for funded pension provision in Germany. Largely as a result of this development, the share of households with no private supplemental pensions decreased from 73 percent in 2001 to about 45 percent in 2009. By 2010, about a quarter of households had at least two saving instruments for their old-age provision (figure 4.4).

Fiscal Costs and Savings

Riester pensions create direct fiscal costs, in the form of the means-tested basic and child subsidies and the foregone tax revenue that results from the exclusion of the allowable contribution levels. In 2010, these costs reached €3.5 billion, about 80 percent of which are attributable to the means-tested direct subsidies (figure 4.5). In comparison, costs for public pension benefits (old-age, disability, and survivor pensions) were €225 billion in 2010.

FIGURE 4.4 **Percentage of households with private and occupational pension instruments, 2003–10**

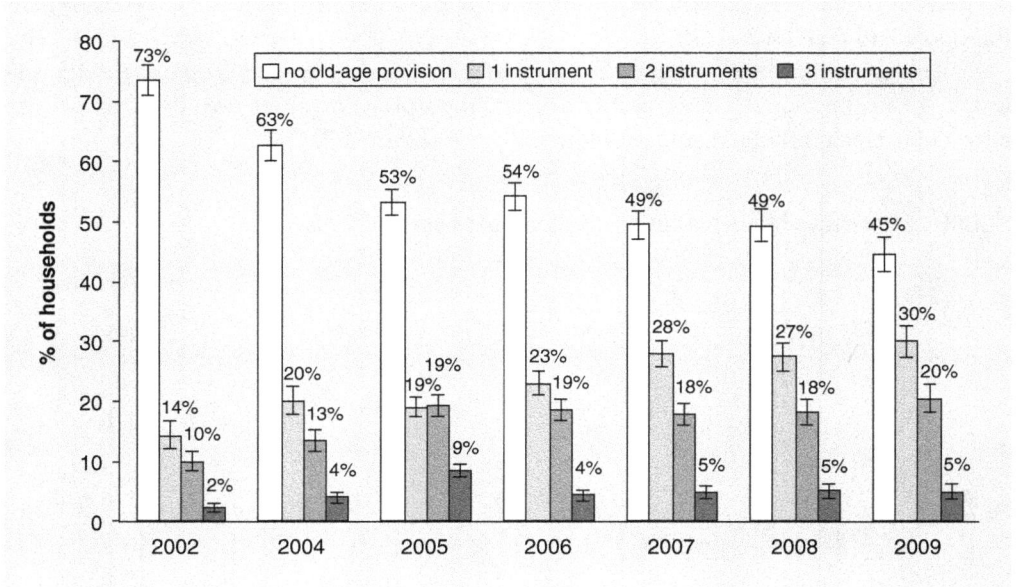

SOURCE: Authors' calculations based on data from the SAVE panel.

NOTE: Brackets show 95 percent confidence intervals. Figures are weighted.

FIGURE 4.5 **Fiscal costs of Riester pensions, 2003–10**

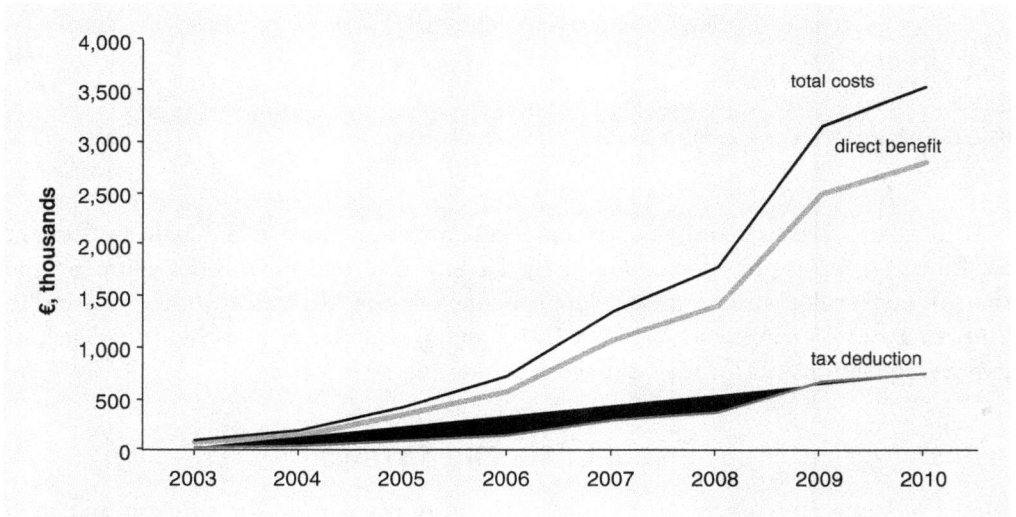

SOURCE: Deutsche Rentenversicherung 2011.

The fiscal costs shown in figure 4.5 are the actual payment of subsidies or foregone income tax revenue resulting from the new system. As Riester subsidies can be claimed up to two years after paying into the account and tax losses typically occur the year after income generation, it is not easy to match induced Riester savings with the subsidies paid out the same year. In addition to a potential mismatch between years are the deeper questions of causality and substitution, which are addressed later in this chapter.

Stolz and Rieckhoff (2008, 2009, 2010, 2011) attempt to matching savings and subsidies (table 4.2). Their calculations, however, include only the direct subsidies, not the tax deductions. Total savings in the accounts are composed of the matching subsidy and contributions by individuals on which the subsidy is calculated. Assuming that these overall savings would not have been made without the incentive of the subsidies, €1 of subsidies (not including the value of the income tax exclusion) induced an additional €2.2 savings for old age. Under these strong assumptions, this figure could be interpreted as a measure of the cost-effectiveness of the subsidy.

TABLE 4.2 **Direct subsidies and associated savings in Riester plans, 2005–08**

Year	Direct subsidies (€, thousands)	Total savings (€, thousands)	Own contribution (€, thousands)	Effectiveness (%)
2005	521,917	1,762,749	1,240,832	2.4
2006	1,134,339	3,635,886	2,501,547	2.2
2007	1,445,688	4,834,565	3,388,877	2.3
2008	2,543,300	7,815,500	5,272,200	2.1

SOURCES: Stolz and Rieckhoff 2008, 2009, 2010, 2011 based on data from the Central Subsidies Agency.

Gerber and Zwick (2010) link data from the Central Subsidies Agency (ZfA) with income tax data in order to include the effects of tax deductions. They compute a broader measure of subsidy rates that can be converted into a similar measure of cost-effectiveness. Because the linkage solves some but creates other time matching problems, the results are not fully comparable with the results shown in table 4.2. The cost-effectiveness measure of €1.9 of new savings for each €1 of subsidies across all households is similar to the €2.2 figure Stolz and Rieckhoff estimate. The estimate is substantially higher for households with children (€2.4) than for childless households (€1.1).

Targeting Success

Another dimension of program effectiveness is the ability of the subsidy to reach the targeted population. Riester pensions were specifically designed to help low-income earners and families with children—two segments of the German population in which saving rates are typically low—build up savings for retirement. The Central Subsidies Agency provides quarterly uptake figures that are associated with a limited number of socioeconomic characteristics. Analyses by Stolz and Rieckhoff (2008, 2011) show that individuals with low labor income, women, families, and employees in the former German Democratic Republic are well represented among subsidy recipients.[4] These data are based on subsidized individuals, not households, however; they do not reveal total household income, only those income components that are subject to means testing.

The analysis of targeting reported here used the SAVE data set (Börsch-Supan and others 2010 provide a detailed description of the data set; Essig 2005 and Schunk 2006 provide additional details). The panel was surveyed in 2001, 2003, and then annually from 2005 through 2010. SAVE provides data at the level of the individual respondent and the respondent's spouse (hereafter referred to as the *household*). In 2006, the total sample size was about 3,500 households. In this chapter, the analysis is restricted to households that have not yet retired.[5] All descriptive statistics are weighted based on the income and age distribution of the German microcensus.[6]

One would expect to find age-related differences, because the replacement rate of the public pension system will slowly decline for future cohorts as a result of the recent reforms. Younger generations are thus more strongly affected than older generations. In addition, younger generations have a longer period over which to accrue the subsidies of the new system, and they are more likely to have dependent children and thus be eligible for the higher level of subsidies. One would therefore expect higher participation rates among younger households than among older ones. This is indeed what figure 4.6 indicates.

UPTAKE AMONG HOUSEHOLDS WITH CHILDREN

Figure 4.7 shows the strong positive relationship between the number of children and the proportion of households with a Riester pension plan. As Riester subsidies increase linearly with the number of children, it is not surprising that there is strong demand for Riester products among parents with more than two children.

About 60 percent of households with two or more children—more than twice as many as among childless households—had a Riester pension plan in 2010. Uptake was strongest among households with more than three children. Figure 4.8 provides significant evidence of the effectiveness of the system in enrolling families with children. This success can be attributed to the large child subsidy, as there was no comparable increase in other private pension instruments.

UPTAKE AMONG LOW-INCOME HOUSEHOLDS

Reaching low-income households has proven to be more difficult than eliciting participation by families with children. The proportion of households holding private pension instruments increases with disposable household income (figure 4.9). This pattern is most apparent for occupational pensions. Only about 19 percent of households in the lowest income bracket have taken up Riester pension plans. In contrast, almost half of households in the top two income brackets report participating in the system.

Given the substantial challenges in reaching low-income groups with any type of retirement savings, it is a measure of some success of the system that low-income households hold more Riester pensions than any other kind of private pension. As a result, Riester pensions are more equally distributed by income than occupational pensions or unsubsidized private pension schemes.

FIGURE 4.6 **Uptake of Riester pensions by age group**

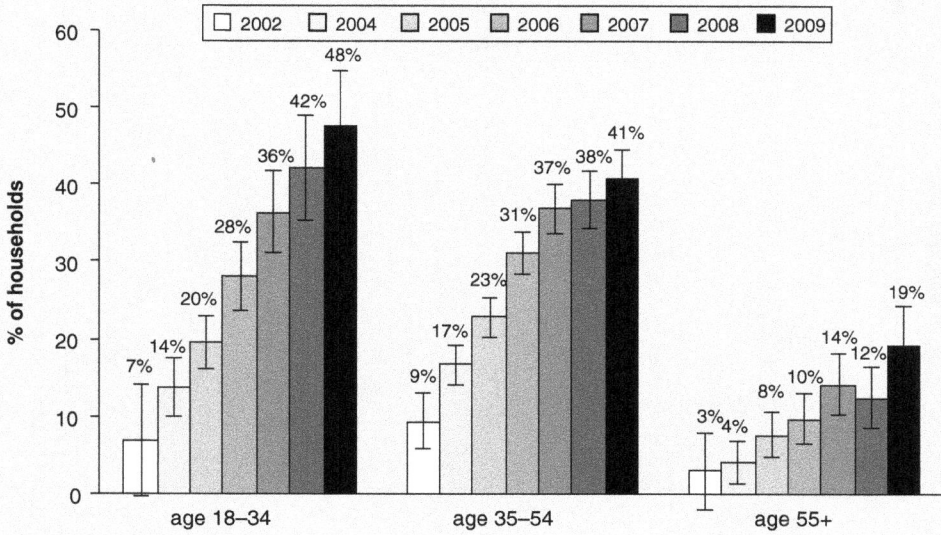

SOURCE: Authors' calculations based on data from the SAVE panel, households eligible for subsidies.

NOTE: Brackets show 95 percent confidence intervals. Figures are weighted.

FIGURE 4.7 **Uptake of Riester pensions by number of children**

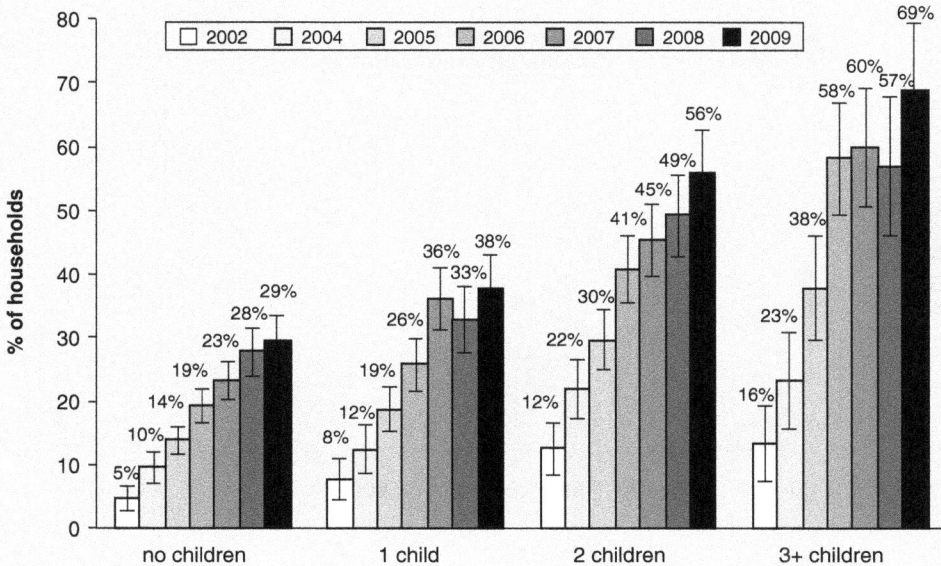

SOURCE: Authors' calculations based on data from the SAVE panel, households eligible for subsidies.

NOTE: Brackets show 95 percent confidence intervals. Figures are weighted.

FIGURE 4.8 **Private pension instruments by number of children in 2009**

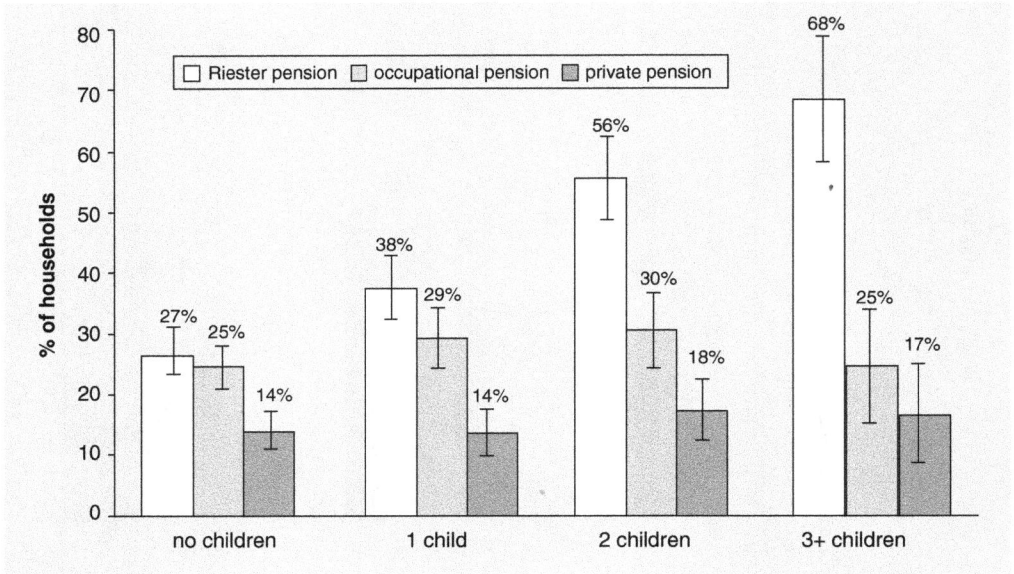

SOURCE: Authors' calculations based on SAVE 2010, households eligible for subsidies.

NOTE: Brackets show 95 percent confidence intervals. Figures are weighted.

FIGURE 4.9 **Private pensions by monthly household disposable income in 2009**

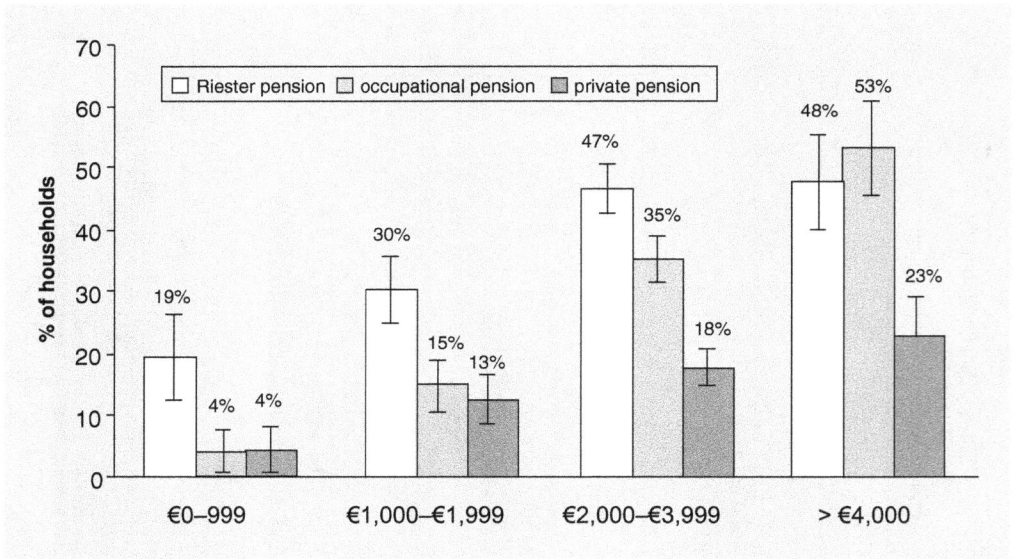

SOURCE: Authors' calculations based on SAVE 2010, households eligible for subsidies.

NOTE: Brackets show 95 percent confidence intervals. Figures are weighted.

Demand for supplemental pensions increased among all income groups since 2002 (figure 4.10). Starting from an already lower initial level, the increase in percentage points is least apparent in the lowest income bracket. This effect is less pronounced when expressed in relative percentage terms. Particularly striking is the impressive growth of occupational pensions and unsubsidized private pension instruments among high-income households.

FIGURE 4.10 **Uptake of Riester pensions by quintiles of monthly household disposable income**

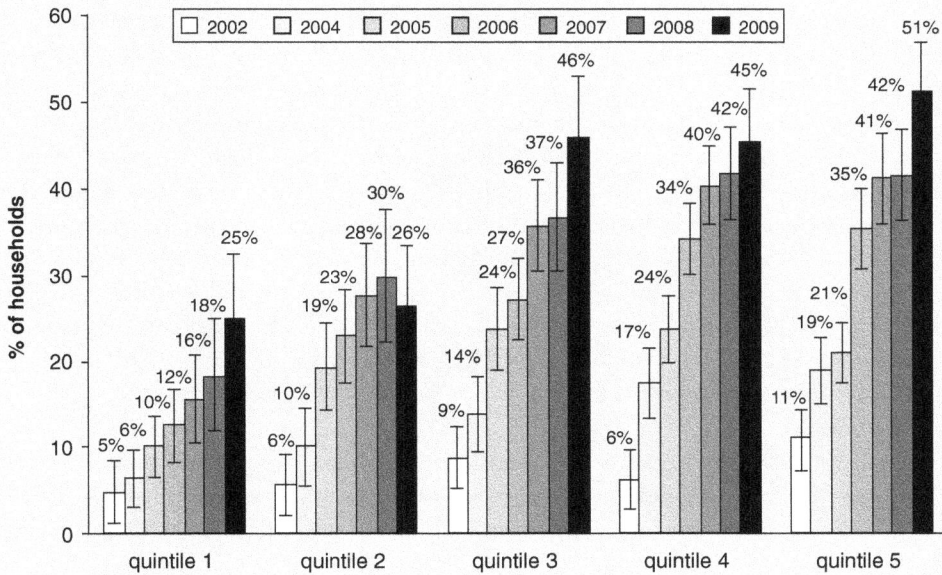

SOURCE: Authors' calculations based on data from the SAVE panel, households eligible for subsidies.

NOTE: Brackets show 95 percent confidence intervals. Figures are weighted.

An important finding from figure 4.10 is the unbroken increase in the share of households with Riester pension plans in the lowest income quintile since 2002. Low-income earners actually had a slightly higher percentage rate of increase in their uptake than the middle of the income distribution. Hence, the jury is still out with regard to how well Riester pensions will end up serving low-income households.

Displacement Effects or Crowding In?

As the earlier discussion of fiscal costs shows, Riester pensions are an expensive government program. The subsidies increase direct government spending and thus potentially reduce aggregate national savings. In addition, the successful uptake of Riester pensions may have simply displaced other saving, in particular saving within other types of private funded pensions. The macroeconomic effect of subsidizing Riester pensions may thus be zero or even negative.

Corneo, Keese, and Schröder (2009, 2010) and Pfarr and Schneider (2010, 2011) provide econometric analyses that cannot refute the hypothesis that subsidizing Riester pensions produces only displacement effects. In all those papers, however, strong implicit assumptions must be made in order to overcome the problem of a missing counterfactual (thanks to the design of the Riester scheme, virtually everyone is eligible, so there is no natural control group). They assume, for example, that having a Riester pension and having other savings are independent decisions.

The causal effect of the subsidies on total saving cannot be unambiguously isolated, as most households are eligible. Cross-sectional analyses are difficult, because ineligible households (for example, certain groups of self-employed workers) have quite different socioeconomic characteristics. Comparisons over time are more credible, although a clean counterfactual is not available. Evidence is thus more circumstantial than causal.

One way to address the issue is to ask households about the extent to which the subsidies stimulated new savings. Coppola and Reil-Held (2010) analyze responses to these types of questions. Responses to questions about changes in behavior may be subjective and contain elements of wishful thinking or ex post justification. Nevertheless, the results shown in figure 4.11 are unambiguous: only a minority of households reports saving less in total since enrolling in a Riester pension plan, and most households report saving more. Particularly striking is the fact that a very large proportion of low-income households indicate that they saved more. The two upper quintiles of income provided similar patterns of responses.

As a less subjective piece of evidence, figure 4.3 shows that the increase in Riester pensions was not accompanied by a decline in the use of other pension instruments: after introduction of Riester pensions, occupational pensions also increased, and unsubsidized pension plans stayed essentially flat between 2004 and 2009. Perhaps most important, the aggregate household saving rate rose, increasing from 9.4 percent of disposable income in 2001 to 11.4 percent in 2010. Moreover, the new pensions did not result in an increase in aggregate dis-saving. Until the financial crisis and its large-scale fiscal stimulus packages, government deficits declined.

Börsch-Supan, Reil-Held, and Schunk (2008) provide an econometric analysis of supplemental pensions, taking account of many socioeconomic variables. They provide evidence on displacement effects through two channels. First, they employ a bivariate regression model in which the decision to take up a subsidized Riester pension plan and the decision to enroll in other unsubsidized private pension plans are modeled simultaneously. A negative correlation between the two equations would indicate displacement. Second, they include competing motives for saving as explanatory variables. A negative coefficient on such variables would also indicate displacement.

Table 4.3 presents selected results of two specifications. Specification A describes disposable income as a set of four quintile indicators. Specification B employs a quadratic function of disposable income. In both specifications, the first dependent variable (columns 1 and 3) indicates whether a household has a Riester pension plan, and the second dependent variable (columns 2 and 4) indicates whether a household has an unsubsidized private pension plan. All variables are as of the end of 2005.

FIGURE 4.11 **Change in total saving after enrolling in a Riester plan**

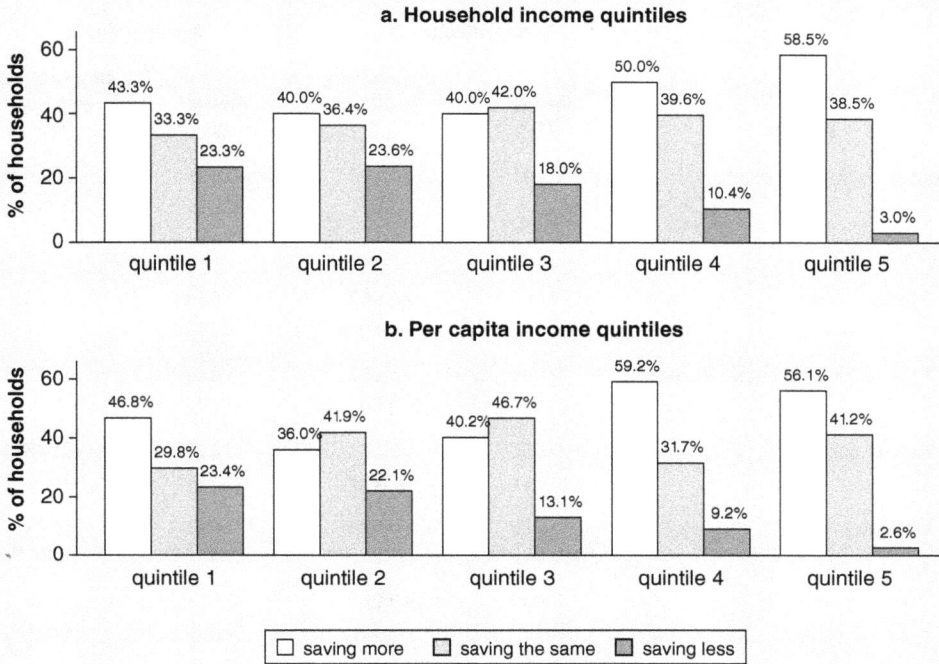

SOURCE: Coppola and Reil-Held 2010, based on SAVE 2008 households with Riester pensions.
NOTE: Data are weighted.

The regressions have a very satisfactory fit (see McFadden R^2 values at the bottom of table 4.3). Moreover, the estimated model exhibits a positive correlation between the two equations, or, more precisely, between the unobservables in the decision to take up a subsidized Riester pension plan and the decision to enroll in unsubsidized private pension plans. Although the correlation is small and not statistically significant, it does not support the hypothesis of crowding out of unsubsidized private pension plans by Riester pensions.

Table 4.3 shows a set of variables in the regression that reflect the importance of different saving motives for respondents. Of interest are three saving motives: acquiring real estate, bequeathing wealth, and pocketing state subsidies. There is evidence pointing to a possible displacement effect between old-age provision and the purchase of real estate. This effect is apparent when looking at households that report a particular interest in saving for the purchase of real estate property. The more important this saving motive is, the less likely respondents are to have taken up a Riester pension plan. A second significantly negative coefficient is attached to the variable indicating the desire to save for a bequest. This result may suggest that the requirement that Riester plans be paid out as annuities acts as a disincentive for households for which making a bequest is an important saving motive.

TABLE 4.3 **Selected determinants of the demand for Riester and other private pension products**
BIVARIATE PROBIT ESTIMATES

	Specification A		Specification B	
Variable	Riester (1)	Other private pensions (2)	Riester (3)	Other private pensions (4)
Intention to buy real estate	0.001	0.143	−0.001	0.147
	(0.01)	(1.67)*	(0.01)	(1.71)*
Saving motives				
Buy real estate	−0.090	−0.057	−0.089	−0.058
	(2.11)*	(1.39)	(2.08)**	(1.43)
Provide for unforeseen events	−0.096	−0.057	−0.086	−0.052
	(1.44)	(0.86)	(1.28)	(0.79)
Pay off debts	−0.055	−0.041	−0.054	−0.043
	(1.24)	(0.99)	(1.22)	(1.03)
Old-age provision	0.229	0.694	0.218	0.691
	(3.06)***	(7.87)***	(2.92)***	(7.86)***
Holiday	0.009	−0.068	0.012	−0.069
	(0.18)	(1.49)	(0.25)	(1.51)
Finance major purchases	0.042	0.039	0.035	0.037
	(0.81)	(0.77)	(0.68)	(0.72)
Finance (grand)child education	−0.038	−0.091	−0.038	−0.094
	(0.81)	(2.02)**	(0.80)	(2.09)**
Inheritance	−0.124	0.090	−0.128	0.090
	(2.32)**	(1.80)*	(2.39)**	(1.80)*
State subsidies	0.264	−0.015	0.269	0.008
	(6.03)***	(0.38)	(6.13)***	(0.20)
Alternative instruments				
Other form of supplementary pension provision (dummy)	0.469 (6.27)***	0.462 (6.56)***	0.466 (6.25)***	0.466 (6.64)***
McFadden R^2	0.137		0.136	
Rho [Chi²(1)]	0.055 [1.32]		0.060 [1.54]	
Number of observations	2,255		2,255	

SOURCE: Börsch-Supan, Reil-Held, and Schunk 2008.

NOTE: Absolute value of the z statistics in parentheses. Regression also includes a large set of socioeconomic control variables. ***$p < 0.01$, **$p < 0.05$, *$p < 0.1$.

In addition to Riester plans and unsubsidized private pension plans, occupational pension plans and whole life insurance products have been very popular as instruments to provide supplemental retirement income (Bundesministerium für Arbeit und Soziales 2006). The coefficient of a variable indicating the presence of such instruments is statistically significant and positive: households already covered by one of these pension types are more likely to have a Riester pension plan. One interpretation of this phenomenon is that households that think ahead and invest in old-age provision at all tend to use several instruments for this purpose. As opposed to saving for real estate acquisition or bequests, this result is consistent with a form of "crowding in" among pension products.

Filling the Pension Gap

The ultimate measure of success is the extent to which Riester pensions fill the pension gap created by the reduction of benefits provided by the pay-as-you-go financed public pension system. Börsch-Supan and Gasche (2010) simulate pension payments from the public system and pension payments from a Riester annuity for a typical employee saving exactly the amounts required to obtain the maximum subsidy according to table 4.1. Figure 4.12 shows the policy-induced decline in public pension benefits and the increasing annuity from Riester savings.

Individuals retiring in 2008 had accumulated very little Riester savings, as the program started only in 2002. Individuals retiring later have a longer time span in which to accumulate Riester savings, until an equilibrium will be reached in about 2047. Although the combined pension benefits will be larger than the current public pension benefits

FIGURE 4.12 **Benefits from public and Riester pensions**

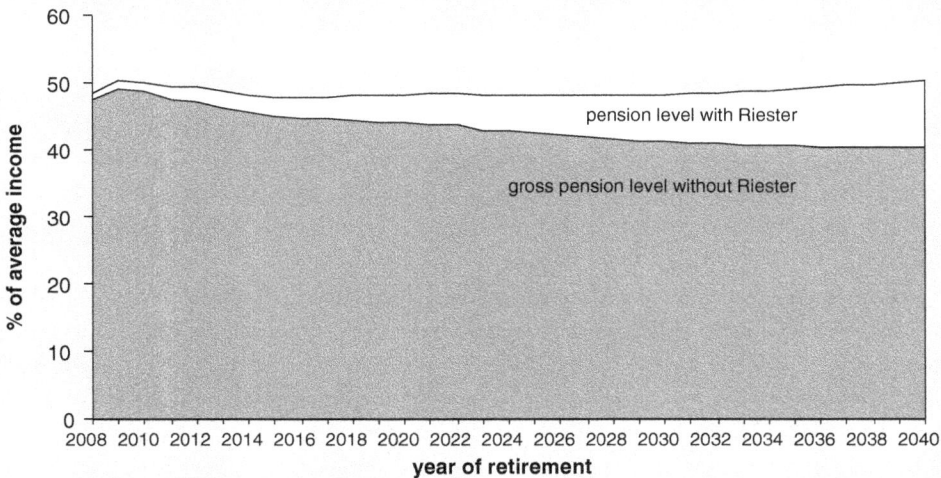

SOURCE: Börsch-Supan and Gasche 2010.

from about 2030 onward, the transitional generation will not be able to fill the pension gap completely (figure 4.13).

FIGURE 4.13 **Filling the pension gap**

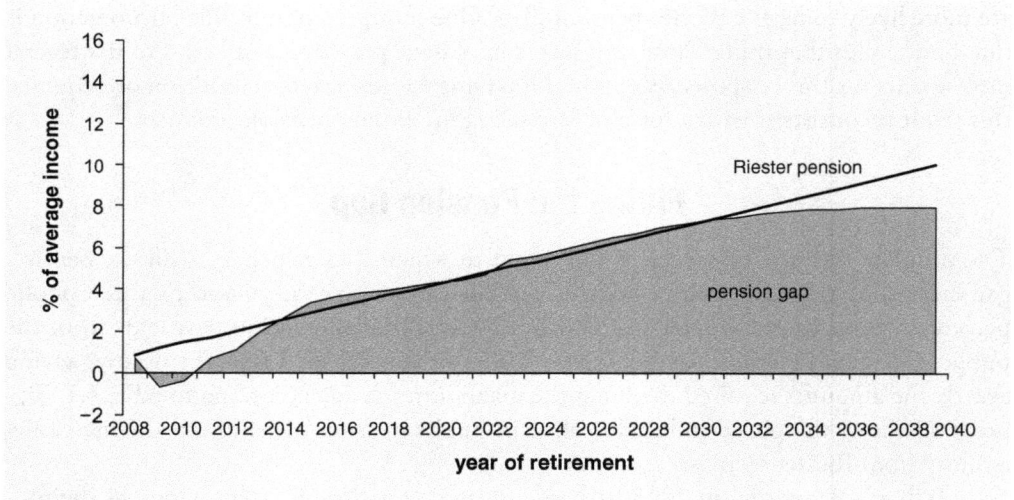

SOURCE: Börsch-Supan and Gasche 2010.

Actual saving for old age may be less than suggested by table 4.1, as uptake is well below 100 percent and individuals may not save the full amount or may interrupt contributions (because of unemployment or other episodes of financial distress, for example). It may also be greater than suggested by table 4.1, as individuals may have other old-age savings plans, such as unsubsidized individual account pension plans or occupational pensions.

Börsch-Supan, Essig, and Wilke (2005) provide a simulation exercise based on actual household data that sheds some light on this issue. They measure current financial wealth and the current financial net saving rate for all households in the SAVE panel. Assuming constant net saving rates and a real return of 2.8 percent, they compute financial wealth at retirement and convert it into a real annuity. This annuity is then compared with the pension gap.

On average, Germans have more than closed the emerging pension gap. More than two-thirds will be able to fill the gap between what they would have received in retirement income under the old and new public systems. The coverage rate for this gap (the Riester annuity divided by the pension gap) is 120 percent for the average household. The distribution, however, is skewed. Predictably, results are very different for people with different socioeconomic characteristics, especially income. Although the median household will be able to compensate for the cuts in public pensions, about 27 percent of the households represented by the SAVE panel will not be able to fill the pension gap.

Conclusions

The most obvious lesson from Germany's experience with Riester pensions is that new forms of subsidized savings need time before they are able to take off. It took more than 10 years in the United States before IRAs were accepted by households in the upper 60 percent of the income distribution (Venti and Wise 1990). In Germany, Riester pension plans exhibited more rapid and dynamic growth. Growth in the first few years was very steep. It then stalled before rebounding after the 2005 legislative changes. Overall, growth rates are much higher than those experienced in the United States. The higher take-up rate may reflect the direct subsidies or the urgency of off-setting the benefit reductions in the wake of the public pension reforms.

There are several explanations for the discontinuous development of Riester pensions. Poor product design probably accounted for the initially lower rates of acceptance. In addition, the learning process regarding the need and way to invest in old-age provision took time, despite heavy advertising. As people learn from their social environment, the pace of this development depends on how widespread such pensions are in the population at large (Ruprecht 2004), generating exponential growth until saturation is reached.

It is not possible to identify whether the dynamic spread of Riester pensions reflects the financial incentives, the availability of information, or marketing efforts by government and providers, mainly insurance companies. However, it is striking that the acceleration in Riester saving kicked in only after substantial simplifications were made to the scheme. Therefore, an important lesson is to avoid complex savings plans, which are not immediately understood by customers. Further simplifications are possible without jeopardizing the aims of the program (see, for example, Westerheide and others 2010).

The target groups of the Riester reform in 2001 were mainly families with children and individuals with low income. Among these groups, parents with more than one child seem to be the group that was most easily reached. The evidence is less compelling for the other target group, low-income households. Although take-up continues to rise, its level is still low, with just 25 percent in the lowest income quintile participating in the system.

A key lesson is that high subsidies alone are not enough to reach low-income households: information and social acceptance appear to be crucial in reaching this group. Coppola and Gasche (2011) find that the level of knowledge about eligibility for Riester subsidies is directly related with household income: households in the bottom quintile of the income distribution have a higher probability to wrongly believe that they are not eligible for the subsidies than households in the upper quintiles.

This insight is strengthened by the regression results of Börsch-Supan, Reil-Held, and Schunk (2008) and Coppola and Reil-Held (2010), which show that holding other characteristics, such as income and family size, constant, households with higher levels of educational attainment are more likely to enroll in Riester pensions than households that have not completed any vocational training. This finding is consistent with the broader experience indicating that knowing future pension replacement levels correlates positively with enrolling in private pension schemes. Another lesson therefore is that information and knowledge about arrangements relating to old-age pension provision are vital to achieving high take-up rates.

Although the SAVE data do not allow for a cleanly designed experiment, they provide circumstantial evidence about possible displacement effects. The results indicate that households that want to purchase residential real estate are significantly less likely to enroll in a Riester pension plan. The clumsy withdrawal rules of the Riester regulations do not provide these households with sufficient liquidity to persuade them to make provision for old age alongside with saving to acquire real estate property. There is also evidence that stated bequest motives displace Riester pension plans, with their strict annuity rules. These findings do not indicate that these restrictions should be removed. On the contrary, they are needed, as Riester pensions were designed to fill the gap in public pension benefits after pension reform, and pay-as-you-go pensions are paid out as life-long annuities.

The desire to purchase property and bequeath assets are saving motives that appear to compete with taking up Riester pensions. Occupational pensions and whole life insurance, however, are complements rather than substitutes for Riester pensions. This finding provides another important lesson. Households that think ahead and invest in old-age provision tend to use several instruments for this purpose. In this sense, there are "crowding in" effects of fostering retirement saving. Although subsidization of Riester pensions is expensive, the net effect (that is, the additional savings created after subtracting subsidies and reductions in other savings vehicles) appears to be positive.

The ultimate measure of success is the extent to which Riester pensions will fill the pension gap created by the reduction in benefits provided by the pay-as-you-go financed public pension system. On average, Germans will be able to more than close the growing pension gap. The distribution is skewed, however. Although the median household will be able to compensate for the cuts in public pensions, about 27 percent of German households will not be able to fill the pension gap.

Riester pensions are not a panacea for the problem of inadequate retirement income; preventing poverty in old age requires different instruments. This new pension instrument can be regarded as a success story for the middle of the income distribution in Germany, however. It has moved about €9.4 billion from consumption or other saving instruments not related to old-age provision into savings earmarked for old age, making the system of retirement income more robust and stable. At the same time, it has reduced pressure on younger generations by permitting lower pay-as-you-go contribution rates than before reform. Whether this change justifies the Riester scheme's tax and subsidy costs of €3.5 billion a year—equal to 1.5 percent of the total pay-as-you-go pension budget—remains a subjective judgment.

Notes

1. In essence, the formerly monolithic German pay-as-you-go system is transiting to a multipillar system of public, occupational, and private pensions. For a detailed description of the pension reform process in Germany, see Börsch-Supan and Wilke (2004).

2. The Commission for the Sustainable Financing of the German Social Security Systems (2003) suggested including an automatic inflation adjustment. Currency values in this chapter are given in euros; €1 = $1.29.

3. For an analysis of the initial phase, see Dünn and Fasshauer (2003).

4. In 2008, 57.1 percent of beneficiaries were women, and 24.4 percent of people receiving subsidies were from states in the former German Democratic Republic. About 9.8 million people received a basic subsidy and 3.7 million people an additional child's subsidy (Stolz and Rieckhoff 2011).

5. The interview is conducted with the individual who best knows the household's finances.

6. As in all surveys that deal with sensitive topics such as household finances, nonresponse to sensitive questions cannot be ignored (see Essig and Winter 2003 and Schunk 2006 for discussion and documentation). To prevent biased inference based on an analysis of complete cases only, researchers applied an iterative multiple imputation procedure to the SAVE data (Schunk 2008). All results reported in this chapter use the fully imputed SAVE data.

References

Börsch-Supan, A. 2004. "Mind the Gap Incentives: The Effectiveness of Incentives to Boost Retirement Savings in Europe." *OECD Economic Studies* 39: 111–44.

Börsch-Supan, A., ed. 2003. *Life-Cycle Savings and Public Policy: A Cross-National Study of Six Countries.* London: Academic Press.

Börsch-Supan, A., M. Coppola, A. Eymann, L. Essig, and D. Schunk. 2010. "The German SAVE Study. Design and Results." MEA Study No. 6, Mannheim Research Institute for the Economics of Aging, University of Mannheim.

Börsch-Supan, A., L. Essig, and C. Wilke. 2005. "Rentenlücken und Lebenserwartung. Wie sich die Deutschen auf den Anstieg vorbereiten." Deutsches Institut für Altersvorsorge, Köln.

Börsch-Supan, A., and M. Gasche. 2010. "Kann die Riester-Rente die Rentenlücke in der gesetzlichen Rente schließen? " Diskussionspapier Mai, Mannheim Research Institute for the Economics of Aging, Mannheim University.

Börsch-Supan, A., A. Reil-Held, and D. Schunk. 2008. "Saving Incentives, Old-Age Provision and Displacement Effects: Evidence from the Recent German Pension Reform." *Journal of Pension Economics and Finance* 7 (3): 259–319.

Börsch-Supan, A. and C. Wilke. 2004. "The German Public Pension System: How It Was, How It Will Be." NBER Working Paper 10525, National Bureau of Economic Research, Cambridge, MA.

Bundesministerium für Arbeit and Soziales. 2006. *Renten- und Alterssicherungsbericht 2005.* Berlin. http://www.bmas.de.

Commission for the Sustainable Financing of the German Social Security System. 2003. "Final Report." German Federal Ministry for Health and Social Affairs, Berlin.

Coppola, M., and M. Gasche. 2011. "Die Riester-Förderung: Das unbekannte Wesen." Diskussionspapier Mai, Mannheim Research Institute for the Economics of Aging, Mannheim University.

Coppola, M., and A. Reil-Held. 2010. "Jenseits staatlicher Alterssicherung: die neue regulierte private Vorsorge in Deutschland." In *Die Alten der Welt. Neue Wege der Alterssicherung im globalen Norden und Süden*, ed. Lutz Leisering. Frankfurt: Campus.

Corneo, G., M. Keese, and C. Schröder. 2009. "The Riester Scheme and Private Savings: An Empirical Analysis Based on the German SOEP." *Schmollers Jahrbuch* 129 (2): 321–32.

———. 2010. "The Effect of Saving Subsidies on Household Saving: Evidence from Germany." Ruhr Economic Paper 170, Ruhr-Universität Bochum, Bochum.

Deutsche Bundesbank. 2002. "Funded Old-Age Provision and the Financial Markets." Monthly Report July: 25–39, Frankfurt.

Deutsche Rentenversicherung. 2011. "Rentenversicherung in Zahlen 2011." Deutsche Rentenversicherung Bund, Berlin.

Disney, R., C. Emmerson, and M. Wakefield. 2001. "Pension Reform and Saving in Britain." *Oxford Review of Economic Policy* 17 (1): 70–94.

Dünn, S., and S. Fasshauer. 2003. "Ein Jahr Riesterrente: Eine Übersicht aus Sicht der gesetzlichen Rentenversicherung. " *Deutsche Rentenversicherung* 1–2.

Essig, L. 2005. "Methodological Aspects of the SAVE Data Set." MEA Discussion Paper 80-05, Mannheim Research Institute for the Economics of Aging, University of Mannheim.

Essig, L., and J. Winter. 2003. "Item Nonresponse to Financial Questions in Household Surveys: An Experimental Study of Interviewer and Mode Effects." MEA Discussion Paper 39-03, Mannheim Research Institute for the Economics of Aging, University of Mannheim.

Gale W. J., and J. K. Scholz. 1994. "IRAs and Household Saving." *American Economic Review* 84: 1233–60.

Gerber, U., and M. Zwick. 2010. "Daten zur kapitalgedeckten Altersvorsorge: Die Riesterrente." *Deutsche Rentenversicherung*, Heft 2/2010, S. 197–207.

Pfarr, C., and U. Schneider. 2010. "Angebotsinduzierung und Mitnahmeeffekt im Rahmen der Riester-Rente: eine empirische Analyse." SOEP Paper on Multidisciplinary Panel Data Research 341, DIW, Berlin.

———. 2011. "Anreizeffekte und Angebotsinduzierung im Rahmen der Riester-Rente: Eine empirische Analyse geschlechts- und sozialisationsbedingter Unterschiede. " *Perspektiven der Wirtschaftspolitik* 12 (1): 27–46.

Ruprecht, W. 2004. "Automatische Entgeltumwandlung in der betrieblichen Altersversorgung: Eine Replik. " *Wirtschaftsdienst* 10: 651–56.

Schunk, D. 2006. "The German SAVE Survey: Documentation and Methodology." MEA Discussion Paper 109-06, Mannheim Research Institute for the Economics of Aging, University of Mannheim.

———. 2008. "A Markov Chain Monte Carlo Algorithm for Multiple Imputation in Large Surveys." *Advances in Statistical Analysis* 92 (1): 101–14.

Skinner, J., and R. G. Hubbard. 1996. "Assessing the Effectiveness of Saving Incentives." *Journal of Economic Perspectives* 10 (4): 73–90.

Stolz, U., and C. Rieckhoff. 2005. 2008. "Förderung der zusätzlichen Altersvorsorge für das Beitragsjahr 2005 durch die ZfA." *RVaktuell* 9/2008.

———. 2009. "Beitragsjahr 2006: Erstmals mehr als eine Milliarde Euro Zulagenförderung durch die ZfA." *RVaktuell* 10/2009.

———. 2010. "Beitragsjahr 2007: Zulagenförderung nochmals um mehr als ein Viertel gestiegen." *RVaktuell* 11/2010.

———. 2011. "Förderung der Riester-Rente für das Beitragsjahr 2008: Mehr als neun Millionen Personen mit Zulagen." *RVaktuell* 12/2011.

Venti, S., and D. Wise. 1990. "Have IRAs Increased U.S. Savings? Evidence from Consumer Expenditure Surveys. " *Quarterly Journal of Economics* 105: 661–98.

Westerheide, P., M. Feigl, L. Jaroszek, J. Leinert, and A. Tiffe. 2010. *Transparenz von privaten Riester- und Basisrentenprodukten*. Abschlussbericht zu Projekt Nr. 7/09, Zentrum für Europäische Wirtschaftsforschung, Mannheim.

CHAPTER 5

New Zealand's Experience with the KiwiSaver Scheme

Geoff Rashbrooke

New Zealand's automatic enrollment KiwiSaver retirement scheme, launched in July 2007, has proven very effective in achieving relatively high levels of participation in supplementary retirement saving. In a relatively short period, participation has been extended to nearly half the population under age 65 and an even larger proportion of the labor force. As a result, New Zealand now has one of the highest rates of coverage for supplementary retirement saving in the world. The level of coverage likely reflects the combination of automatic enrollment and substantial matching incentives. Consistent with the power of defaults and inertia, the proportion of people who opt out after automatic enrollment is relatively low. The fact that many members continued to make contributions at the default rate even after that rate was reduced confirms the stickiness of default parameters and reinforces the importance of the default rate in establishing participation patterns.

New Zealand has had a comprehensive system of public, tax-funded, flat-rate old-age pensions since at least 1938. In addition, until 1989, participation in formal private retirement saving arrangements was encouraged through a number of tax incentives, such as tax-free accrual of investment returns and tax exemptions on contributions, plus some scope for obtaining benefits as lump sums free of tax.[1]

In 1989, all concessions for private retirement saving arrangements were removed, based on the belief that workers could be left to make sensible choices in their individual best interests, without any encouragement from the state beyond light-handed regulation and provision of some education on saving. This stance remains a strong current in the ongoing policy debate in New Zealand.

Coverage of workers in occupational schemes had never been particularly high. It fell markedly after concessional tax treatment was withdrawn (figure 5.1).

As a response to this trend and other concerns about preparation for retirement and saving behavior in general, in the mid-2000s the government commissioned a working party and subsequently an external report. Its results led to the setting up, on July 1, 2007, of an automatic enrollment national retirement saving scheme known as KiwiSaver.

The automatic enrollment ("soft compulsion") feature of KiwiSaver is its key element and an innovation for national retirement schemes worldwide. As a new approach,

This chapter draws heavily on a presentation by Peter Whiteford, of the University of New South Wales, at the World Bank conference, The Potential for Matching Defined Contributions (MDC) Design Features in Pension Systems to Increase Coverage in Low- and Middle-Income Countries, held June 6, 2011. The author thanks Teneti Ririnui, of New Zealand's Department of Inland Revenue, for providing the Excel spreadsheets from the 2011 KiwiSaver evaluation report.

FIGURE 5.1 **Coverage in occupational retirement schemes, 1990–2003**

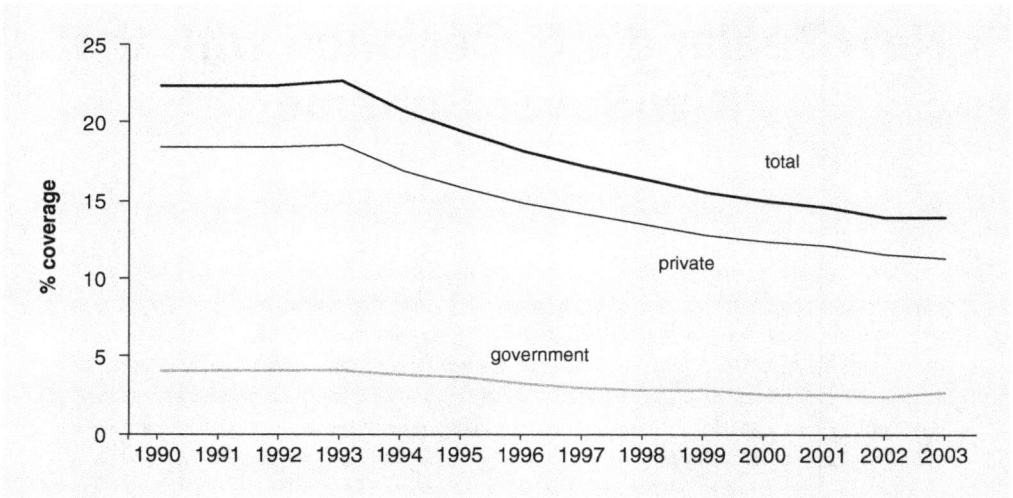

SOURCE: Author, based on data from New Zealand Government Actuary 2006.

NOTE: Figures for 1991 and 1992 are estimates.

it has been of keen interest both in New Zealand and internationally, as a policy falling between compulsion and voluntary saving.

Understanding the design and potential lessons from the KiwiSaver system requires placing this new element of the retirement income system into the appropriate context. In particular, it requires understanding the role played by New Zealand's long-established public pension system, New Zealand Superannuation.

This chapter is organized as follows. The first section describes the history, structure, and outcomes of New Zealand's public pensions system and raises questions about its viability. The second section describes the motivations, development, and structure of the KiwiSaver scheme. The last section summarizes the chapter's conclusions and discusses the policy debate on retirement saving as it has unfolded in New Zealand over the past decade, highlighting concerns raised by the introduction of KiwiSaver.

New Zealand's Public Pension System

HISTORY AND STRUCTURE

New Zealand's public system originated in 1898, when the first old-age pension was introduced.[2] This seminal system provided a means-tested benefit of one-third of the average wage for an individual and two-thirds for a couple. About a third of people over age 65 qualified for benefits. The scheme had other qualifying conditions, including a requirement to provide evidence of good character and provisions designed to exclude criminals, drunkards, and wife deserters.

In 1938, a substantial increase in means-tested payments and a new small universal benefit for people not qualifying for the means-tested benefit was introduced, establishing universal eligibility for some type of old-age income support. In 1977, a system of national retirement was introduced, providing a taxable, universal benefit of 80 percent of the average wage for a couple (48 percent for single person) payable at age 60 after 10 years' residence. Over the ensuing two decades, incremental changes were made to modify benefit levels, link benefit formulas to after-tax earnings measures, and add a surcharge that effectively created an income test, which was later removed. The age of eligibility was increased to 65, a change that was phased in between 1989 and 2001.

The current system reflects this evolution, incorporating the basic design principles and benefit structure of its antecedents. It provides a flat benefit payable at age 65 to all eligible recipients. There is no income or means testing; eligibility is based solely on a residency test. The system is funded through general taxation, with no earmarked social security contributions. Public pension entitlements that have been earned in other countries are, however, deducted from the total benefit.

The level of this flat-rate public pension (sometimes called a demogrant in other settings) is indexed to prices. However, the benefit level is subject to a floor and ceiling that are linked to movement in wages. For a couple, current legislation requires that the net-of-tax value of the benefit as of April 1 is not less than 65 percent and not more than 72.5 percent of a net-of-tax surveyed weekly earnings measure.[3] The net-of-tax rates for single people are set at 65 percent (living alone) and 60 percent (sharing accommodation) of the rate for couples. If movements in prices remain consistently below movements in the net-of-tax surveyed weekly earnings, net-of-tax surveyed weekly earnings effectively become the index. The public pension is subject to personal income tax.

The *OECD Factbook 2011* indicates that public pension spending in New Zealand was 4.3 percent of gross domestic product (GDP) in 2007, the sixth lowest among Organisation for Economic Co-operation and Development (OECD) countries (OECD 2011a). This figure does not include the contributions of about 2 percent of GDP made to a prefunding arrangement, the New Zealand Superannuation Fund (http://www.nzsuperfund.co.nz/), established in 2000 to smooth the emerging increase in the cost of public pensions that will result from the aging of the population. Contributions to this reserve fund come out of government fiscal surpluses. Its size in April 2012 was $NZ 19.46 billion.[4] It is projected to peak at about 40 percent of GDP in 2035, when draw-downs are expected to begin. The time-weighted annualized return on investment since 2000 has been 7.65 percent before tax, some 2.34 percent higher than the return on 90-day treasury bills. The current government ceased making contributions in 2010, however, citing the increase in public debt; it does not plan to resume payments until it is running fiscal surpluses.

Tax claw-backs from New Zealand Superannuation—resulting from taxation of benefits as ordinary personal income and a broad-based consumption tax—are relatively high (about 28 percent of the value of benefits). Hence, the effective fiscal cost of the system is considerably less than the value of the gross benefit payments. The deduction of public pension entitlements accrued in other countries also reduces expenditure, by some 2 percent.

OUTCOMES

New Zealand has the lowest relative poverty rate among people age 65 and over in OECD countries: only 1.5 percent of people this age have incomes that are less than half the median income. New Zealand has more people age 65 and over between 50 and 60 percent median income than in any other OECD country, however. It has the highest minimum pension among OECD countries (39 percent of average earnings). But together with the United Kingdom, the net pension replacement rate for an average worker is the second lowest (after Ireland) in the OECD (OECD 2011b).

As a share of the population, the average income of people in New Zealand over age 65 is 68 percent, the second lowest in the OECD (after Australia). Although inequality among people of working age is the eighth highest in the OECD, among people age 65 and older it is the seventh lowest.

The driver of all these results is the high dependence on New Zealand Superannuation as the primary source of retirement income. Some public servants have government defined benefit pensions, but this scheme was closed to new entrants in 1992. New Zealanders have varying degrees of capital assets, including high (but declining) rates of homeownership, bank deposits, and other financial assets.

Because most assets held by older New Zealanders are not formally classified as retirement savings, they have proved difficult to quantify. Social surveys have suggested hardship levels of about 6–8 percent among older New Zealanders, associated mostly with living in rental housing. Supplementary means-tested disability allowances and accommodation supplements are available through the welfare system, as they are for all New Zealanders.

VIABILITY OF NEW ZEALAND SUPERANNUATION

The main issue faced by New Zealand Superannuation relates to the sustainability of its financing. The increasing ratio of the number of people receiving pensions to the number of people in the labor force will put pressure on the financing of New Zealand Superannuation, whose principal source of support is taxation of labor income. The New Zealand Superannuation Fund will smooth but not fully prefund tax expenditure, and contributions to the fund are currently frozen.

In its *Long-Term Fiscal Report* (New Zealand Treasury 2009), the Treasury consistently draws attention to steadily rising costs, recommending increases in the age of entitlement, changes in indexing, and/or the introduction of means testing. A paper presented at the 2010 New Zealand Retirement Income Conference (Rashbrooke 2010) proposed establishing a fixed-rate pension contribution and maintaining it through progressive increases in the age of entitlement and revenue-targeted means testing. The current government holds that no changes need to be made and that the pension remains sustainable within the time frame over which it is considering policy.

KiwiSaver

DEVELOPMENTS LEADING TO ADOPTION OF THE SCHEME

The KiwiSaver system emerged as a result of a sequence of efforts to expand supplementary private pension coverage to achieve income replacement rates that would enable the broad population to sustain its standard of living in retirement. Private provision for retirement had followed a pattern in New Zealand similar to that in other Anglo-American countries:

a mixture of defined benefit and defined contribution arrangements, with tax concessions for contributions and the investment accrual. In 1974, a Labour Party government introduced a compulsory accumulation scheme, intended to collect 4 percent of earnings from employees and 4 percent from employers. The National Party government elected in 1975 disbanded it, strengthening the tax-funded state pension instead.

Some lack of control over eligibility for the concessional tax treatment for the voluntary regime still in place had become a concern in the 1980s. Rather than plugging the gaps, in the course of introducing a number of market-led reforms, a reforming Labour government instead took the view that retirement saving was no different from any other forms of saving and removed all tax concessions in 1989.

In 1992, the government ordered a review to determine whether compulsory retirement saving, tax concessions, or both should be reconsidered. The review rejected both options but recommended that greater resources be put into educating people about the need to save for retirement. In response, the government established the position of Retirement Commissioner (now Commissioner for Financial Literacy and Retirement Income).

In 1998, as part of a coalition agreement, a referendum was held on whether to introduce a compulsory retirement scheme. The scheme put forward was positioned as a replacement of the existing tax-funded state pension. It received only minimal support.

In the mid-2000s, a Labour government set up a working party to consider whether New Zealanders had a full range of options for retirement saving. The working party assessed the conventional wisdom that deductions from salary were a relatively painless method of forgoing immediate consumption to save for retirement. Its report provided the impetus for KiwiSaver development (Harris 2004).

An early policy decision was to use the pay as you earn (PAYE) tax system as the collection mechanism for employees. Doing so placed Inland Revenue in the lead role as administrator. Policy development was shared by the Treasury, the Ministry of Economic Development (which had regulation of financial services as one of its responsibilities), and the Department of Building and Housing (as there was to be a homeownership component). The government acknowledged the need for adequate funding for evaluation, and Inland Revenue was tasked with conducting it.

In order to identify issues for evaluation, and to confirm the direction of policy development generally, Inland Revenue commissioned a literature review from the Urban Institute (Toder and Khitatrakun 2006). This comprehensive report set out various insights from developments in behavioral economics, as well as other material generally supportive of the KiwiSaver concept. Although the arguments for KiwiSaver were not universally accepted, they were sufficiently persuasive for the government to enact legislation establishing KiwiSaver in 2006, with a commencement date of June 1, 2007.

FEATURES OF THE SCHEME

The KiwiSaver system was intended to provide a supplementary source of retirement income that would extend the basic New Zealand Superannuation benefit in a manner that would achieve a high level of participation without fully mandating coverage. The objective of KiwiSaver, as set out in its governing legislation, is "to encourage a savings habit and asset accumulation among individuals who may not be in a position to enjoy standards of living in retirement similar to those in preretirement." A secondary goal is to support local capital markets by providing an additional source of investment funds. The principal design feature of the system is automatic enrollment; other aspects of the design include specified contribution rates, incentives, and provider provisions. KiwiSaver is explicitly not guaranteed by the government.

Automatic Enrollment

On taking up a new job, all new employees are automatically enrolled in a KiwiSaver scheme; they must opt out if they do not wish to remain a member. The opt-out period is two to eight weeks. If new employees do not opt out within their first eight weeks, they are automatically enrolled. Some safeguards allow later opt-out in specific circumstances, such as not being given an information pack or investment statement in a timely fashion. People aged under 18 or over 65 are excluded from the automatic enrollment procedures. Anyone under age 65, including children under 18, can, however, voluntarily opt in to join a KiwiSaver scheme. The age at which withdrawals of account balances are permitted is age 65 or five years after joining the scheme, whichever comes later.

Members can also withdraw their balances upon permanent emigration, death, serious illness, or significant financial hardship. In addition, all KiwiSaver members who have been making contributions from their pay for 12 months or more are permitted to elect to take a contribution holiday without providing a reason. A contribution holiday can last up to five years. There is no limit on the number of times a contribution holiday can be taken, and it can be renewed at any time. While a member is taking a contribution holiday, the employer is not required to make compulsory employer contributions; individuals can still make voluntary contributions.

Required Contribution Rates

Employee contributions are deducted from pay at the rate of 2 percent, 4 percent, or 8 percent of earnings, as the employee chooses.[5] Originally, the default contribution rate was set at 4 percent; it was reduced in 2009 to 2 percent, although it is scheduled to increase to 3 percent on April 1, 2013. The employer must contribute at least 2 percent of earnings, which will also increase to 3 percent in 2013.

Employee and employer contributions are collected through the income tax system and reconciled monthly. Inland Revenue passes on the contributions to providers. It currently takes about three months for a KiwiSaver contribution to reach a KiwiSaver account, but interest is paid while the contributions are held.

People who are self-employed or not working arrange directly with their KiwiSaver provider how much to contribute; they make payments directly to the financial institution managing the account. Members who are working who want to make voluntary contributions while on a contribution holiday from their wage or salary deductions can likewise, making the minimum contribution required for the member tax credit (described below) if they wish. (This design feature does not appear to have been intentional.)

Financial Incentives

The range of financial incentives has changed somewhat even within the short time KiwiSaver has been in existence (for more information, see http://www.kiwisaver.govt.nz/):

- **$NZ 1,000 "kick start."** The government kick starts accounts with a tax-free contribution of $NZ 1,000. Originally, this amount together with a $NZ 40 a year fee subsidy was intended to be the sole incentive, but others were added just before the 2007 launch.

- **Member tax credit.** From the inception of the system through July 1, 2011, the government matched individual contributions made by people between age 18 and the earliest retirement age (age 65 or five years after joining) by up to $NZ 1,043 a year ($NZ 20 a week). This amount has been reduced to a 50 percent match on the first $NZ 20 of contribution, capping the value of the match at $NZ 521 a year.

- **Compulsory employer contributions.** For contributing member employees, employers are required to contribute an amount equal to at least 2 percent of earnings, although they may contribute more. This minimum employer contribution will increase to 3 percent on April 1, 2013.

- **Partial savings withdrawal for purchase of a first home.** Some own and employer KiwiSaver savings can be withdrawn in order to purchase a first home. The government contribution (the kick-start payment and the member tax credit) cannot be withdrawn.

- **First home deposit subsidy.** After three years of contributing to KiwiSaver, contributors may be entitled to a first home deposit subsidy. The subsidy, administered by Housing New Zealand, is paid on the day the purchase is settled. The subsidy is $NZ 1,000 for each year of contributions, up to a maximum of $NZ 5,000 for five years. A couple buying a house together and both qualifying could receive a combined subsidy of up to $NZ 10,000.

Tax Treatment

Employer contributions to any retirement saving scheme in New Zealand are deductible by the employer for tax purposes but are subject to the Employer Superannuation Contribution Tax. This tax, which has been in place in one form or another since 1990, taxes employer contributions to voluntary retirement schemes on the grounds that these schemes are an additional form of remuneration. Initially, employer contributions to KiwiSaver were given an exemption from the Employer Superannuation Contribution Tax on the compulsory employer contribution of 2 percent of earnings, but this exemption was withdrawn April 1, 2012. No concessional tax treatment of the earnings on investment is provided for any retirement scheme, including KiwiSaver. All retirement schemes are taxed on a proxy basis, as if the payments were the income of the member.

KiwiSaver Providers

Private financial services companies, known as KiwiSaver providers, manage the schemes. Inland Revenue assigns people who do not choose their own scheme and whose employer does not have a scheme to one of the six government-appointed default providers. Allocation to a provider is done one by one on a serial basis.

The companies appointed as default providers were chosen following a competitive tender and a detailed evaluation process. They were selected based on a number of criteria, including security and organizational credibility, organizational capability, scheme structure, administrative capability, fee levels, and investment capacity/capability.

Seven companies applied to be default providers. Although a regulation could have been made under the KiwiSaver Act capping the number of providers, none is apparent, and it is unclear on what basis the limit was set at six.

The default providers' contract with the government requires them to meet additional reporting requirements and limits the fees they can charge. There is also additional monitoring of their default funds (they may also offer other KiwiSaver funds).[6] Default funds are required to be invested conservatively, with the percentage of growth assets to be kept to 15–25 percent of total assets.

The mandate of the existing default providers is to be reviewed in 2014. An initial review, which will commence in late 2012, will set out to answer the following broad questions:

- How have existing default arrangements performed from operational, administrative, regulatory, and policy effectiveness perspectives?

- What should be the objectives for the default provider arrangements, and what are the best institutional arrangements and investment settings for delivering these objectives?

- What is the optimal process for managing any transitions from existing arrangements?

Providers other than the default providers are also required to enter into agreements with the government, setting out their duties and responsibilities, but no limit exists on the number of providers (and although some market observers have suggested amalgamation should be occurring, there is little sign of that). At last count, there were 52 registered providers, including the 6 default providers. These providers may offer more than one investment choice. There is no constraint on the nature of investment choice and assets, but the potential member must receive an investment statement describing the nature of the investment and its risks.

Other

Initially, each member received a fee subsidy of $NZ 40 a year, and employers had their compulsory contribution subsidized through an employer tax credit of up to $NZ 20 a week per member. Both these subsidies were discontinued on April 1, 2009.

Contributors can change their KiwiSaver scheme at any time, but they can belong to only one KiwiSaver scheme at a time. To change their scheme, contributors must apply directly to the provider of the scheme they want to join. The new provider will arrange for savings to be transferred from the old scheme to the new one. With the exception of default funds, the old scheme may charge a transfer fee.

All KiwiSaver schemes are regulated by the Financial Markets Authority, in a similar way as other registered retirement schemes. One difference is that all KiwiSaver schemes are required to pay fees that are "not unreasonable." The process, set out in the KiwiSaver regulations, requires the Financial Markets Authority to compare fees with those of other comparable schemes (which need not be KiwiSaver schemes). The regulations cite a number of criteria for the comparison, including the structure of the scheme, the number of members, and the asset base of the scheme. The fact that the process is based on comparison rather than absolute amounts may not encourage low fees, particularly as information on fees is difficult to standardize. However, providers claim that they cannot afford, under current fees, to remunerate financial advisers to give members individual advice. In the May 2012 budget, the government directed more work on disclosure of fees and investment returns in a standardized fashion.

OUTCOMES

The government set aside funding for a comprehensive evaluation program as an integral part of setting up KiwiSaver. Initial reports were biannual; recently they have been conducted annually.[7] This section summarizes the most recent evaluation report, for the year ending June 30, 2011, and provides some supplementary material on asset allocation.

Enrollment Patterns

People can become KiwiSaver members in three ways:

- Automatic enrollment occurs when employees are automatically enrolled upon employment and they do not opt out. Enrollees can specify a provider or accept the provider sponsored by their employer (if there is one). If they do neither, they will be assigned to a default fund.
- Opt-in through an employer occurs when an employee chooses to join the KiwiSaver scheme sponsored by the employer.
- Opt-in through a provider occurs when people enroll directly through a provider.

Table 5.1 shows the ways in which KiwiSavers have enrolled in the program since its inception.

Opt-in through a provider has been a significant part of enrollment from the outset; after netting opt-outs from automatic enrollments, it has become the predominant means of enrollment. Opt-ins include many people under age 18, as described below, and can reasonably be attributed to the desire to obtain the kick-start subsidy.

Opt-ins through employers were initially high, in large part thanks to the kick-start subsidy and member tax credit. Some employees worked for employers that did not offer a retirement scheme and who would have not required a great deal of motivation to join.

Figure 5.2 shows how opt-in through providers and employers has outstripped automatic enrollment on a cumulative monthly basis. Actual monthly enrollments were broadly stable, at about 25,000 a month from August 2008 through June 2011. Subsequently, enrollments fell to about 10,000 a month, possibly because of a more difficult labor market, tougher economic times, the reduction in member tax credit, or some degree of satiation.

Forty-four percent of the eligible population is enrolled in KiwiSaver. Enrollment is not evenly distributed by age (figures 5.3 and 5.4). People age 25–44 have been the most consistent joiners. Unsurprisingly, people closer to retirement opted in to a greater degree at the beginning, given the five-year minimum membership before being able to withdraw

TABLE 5.1 **Total cumulative enrollment in KiwiSaver, 2008–11**

Enrollment status	2008	2009	2010	2011
Automatic enrollment	273,279	426,629	541,769	646,725
Opt-in through employer	169,410	195,940	211,883	232,131
Opt-in through provider	273,948	477,971	706,290	877,076
% increase over previous year	n.a.	54	33	20
Total net enrollment	716,637	1,100,540	1,459,942	1,755,932
Opt-out	137,762	221,045	245,898	249,549
Closed	1,044	8,240	13,656	25,559
% increase over previous year	n.a.	55	29	18
Total gross enrollment	855,443	1,329,825	1,719,496	2,031,040
Eligible population (age 0–65)	3,746,700	3,787,100	3,814,700	3,823,600

SOURCE: Inland Revenue 2011.

NOTE: Figures are as of June 30. n.a. = not applicable.

FIGURE 5.2 **Total and monthly enrollments in KiwiSaver, 2007–11**

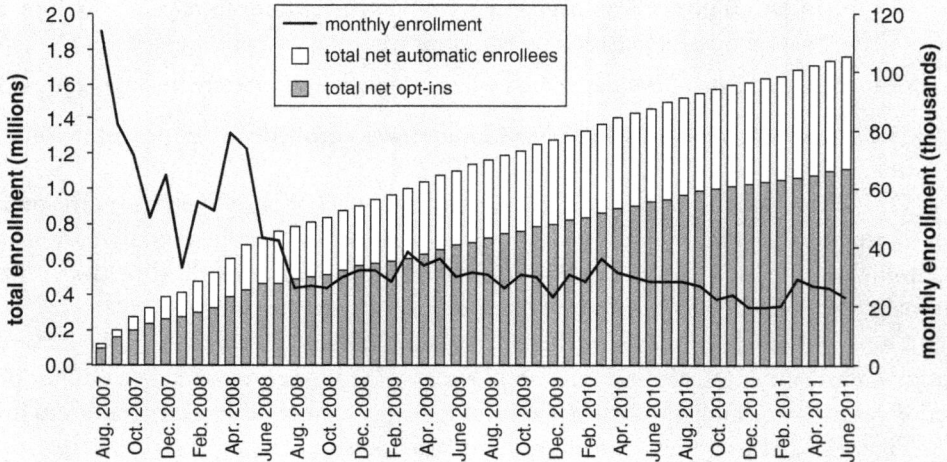

SOURCE: Inland Revenue 2011.

NOTE: Enrollments for July and August 2007 were combined.

savings and perhaps a realization of inadequacy of retirement provision. Enrollment among people under age 18 was slow at the beginning but may have been influenced subsequently by greater awareness of the significant kick-start payment on enrollment. The distribution by sex has been 52 percent women more or less constantly over the period.

FIGURE 5.3 **Age at which member enrolled in KiwiSaver, 2007–11**

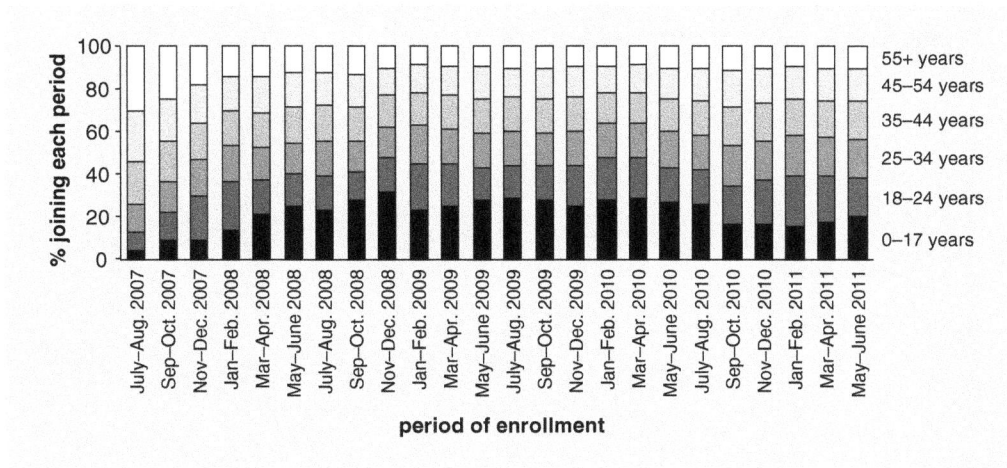

SOURCE: Inland Revenue 2011.

NOTE: All figures are as of June 30.

FIGURE 5.4 **Age distribution of KiwiSaver members and KiwiSaver eligible population, June 30, 2011**

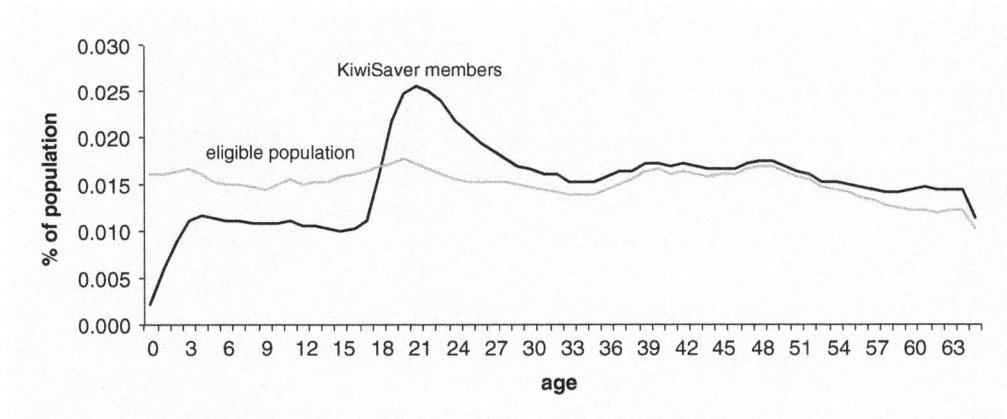

SOURCE: Inland Revenue 2011.

NOTE: The eligible population, taken from the Treasury long-term fiscal model, includes all New Zealand citizens or residents under age 65, regardless of whether they have joined the scheme.

People under age 18 have relatively low rates of enrollment; people entering the workforce (where they are exposed to automatic enrollment) have relatively high rates of enrollment. There is also a slight overrepresentation at older ages, where consciousness of impending retirement is higher (the effect of a shorter time frame in which to obtain the subsidy may have an influence as well).

The age distribution year on year shows a similar pattern, as the number of enrolled members has grown (figure 5.5). Nearly 60 percent of eligible people age 18–24 are members; older people are at or close to the 50 percent mark.

FIGURE 5.5 **Percentage of eligible population enrolled in KiwiSaver, 2008–11**

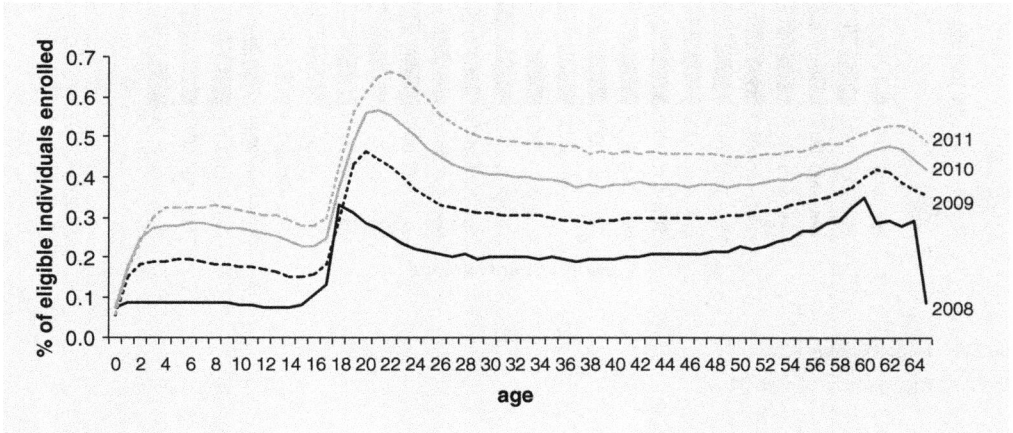

SOURCE: Inland Revenue 2011.

NOTE: The eligible population, taken from the Treasury long-term fiscal model, includes all New Zealand citizens or residents under age 65, regardless of whether they have joined the scheme. Data are as of June 30.

Incomes and Contributions

The incomes of members do not differ greatly from the incomes of the eligible population (figure 5.6). There are slightly lower proportions of KiwiSaver members at low-income levels (up to $NZ 20,000) than in the eligible population, but slightly higher proportions at income levels of $NZ 20,000–$NZ 50,000. These results suggest a minor affordability effect.

Table 5.2 shows the number of KiwiSavers by source of income. More than half (54 percent) had only wage or salary income; 23 percent had no income. Children (people under age 18) made up 73 percent of the no income group. This group also includes full-time students aged 18 and over, who are allowed to make contributions (or have their families make contributions on their behalf) and who are therefore eligible for the member tax credit despite not working or paying income tax.

On April 1, 2009, the default rate for contributions was reduced from 4 percent to 2 percent. Table 5.3 shows the effect of the change.

The data in table 5.3 suggest a marked signaling effect through the change in the default rate. Table 5.4 reinforces this interpretation. The majority of people (62 percent) who joined KiwiSaver before April 1, 2009, still contribute 4 percent of their gross income, indicating a significant degree of inertia in contribution rates, a phenomenon observed in similar saving programs. The majority of members who joined KiwiSaver after April 1, 2009 (80 percent), are contributing 2 percent, reinforcing the importance of the default rate in establishing participation patterns.

FIGURE 5.6 **Income distribution of KiwiSaver members and KiwiSaver eligible population, 2010**

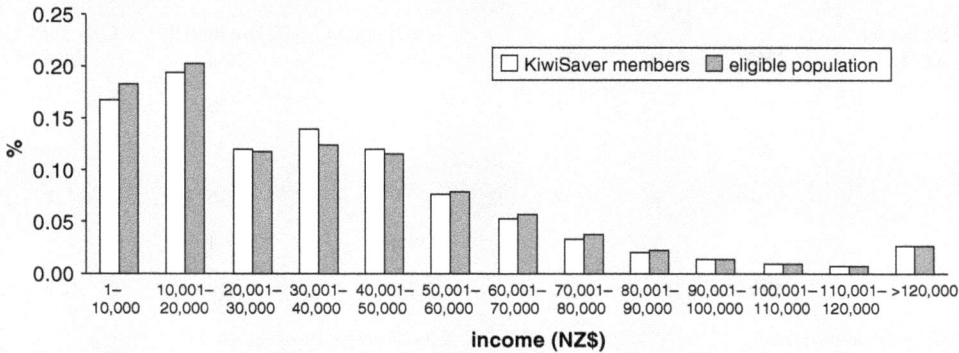

SOURCE: Inland Revenue 2011.

NOTE: Figures are for members as of June 30, 2011. Income relates to the 2010 tax year and includes income from salary and wages (including benefit payments) as well as income from self-employment, royalties, rental income, and other sources. People with no income in 2010 are excluded.

TABLE 5.2 **Income sources of KiwiSaver members, 2010**

Income source	Number of members	Percentage of total
Salary or wage income only	945,917	54
Salary or wage plus other income	324,361	19
Other income only	76,306	4
No income	409,348	23
Total	1,755,932	100

SOURCE: Inland Revenue 2011.

NOTE: Figures are for members as of June 30, 2011. Income relates to the 2010 tax year and includes income from salary and wages (including benefit payments) as well as income from self-employment, royalties, rental income, and other sources.

The median annual contribution in 2009/10 was $NZ 880, with the lowest quartile contributing $NZ 295 and the highest quartile contributing $NZ 1,644 (figure 5.7).

These data relate to members with salary and wage income. People not earning salary or wage income can still contribute and are incentivized to do so (if over age 18) by the member tax credit subsidy. Figure 5.8 shows the annual contributions of people with income from sources other than salary or wages. The two peaks at $NZ 1,040 and $NZ 1,200 suggest that people who do not make contributions through salary or wage deductions are clustered at the maximum thresholds, consistent with contributing to maximize the value of the member tax credit.

People with no income at all also exhibited twin peaks at $1,040 and $1,200, presumably for the same reason (figure 5.9).

TABLE 5.3 **Percentage of KiwiSavers contributing at various rates, 2009–11**

Contribution rate (%)	2009	2010	2011
2	12	41	53
4	83	55	43
8	4	4	4
Other	< 1	< 1	< 1
Total	100	100	100

SOURCE: Inland Revenue 2011.

NOTE: Figures include all members with PAYE deductions as of June 30, excluding members on contribution holidays and members who contribute directly to providers or make ad hoc contributions to Inland Revenue not through the PAYE system. Members' contribution rate at year end is based on at least two contributions over the April–June period. Totals may not sum to 100 percent because of rounding.

TABLE 5.4 **Contribution rates of KiwiSavers by member join date, as of 2011**

Contribution rate (%)	Before April 1, 2009	After April 1, 2009
2	33	80
4	62	18
8	5	2
Other	< 1	< 1
Total	100	100

SOURCE: Inland Revenue 2011.

NOTE: Figures include all members with PAYE deductions as of June 30, 2011, excluding members on contribution holidays and members who contribute directly to providers or make ad hoc contributions to Inland Revenue not through the PAYE system. Members' contribution rate at year end is based on at least two contributions over the April–June period. Totals may not sum to 100 percent because of rounding.

FIGURE 5.7 **Annual KiwiSaver contributions by salary and wage earners, 2009/10**

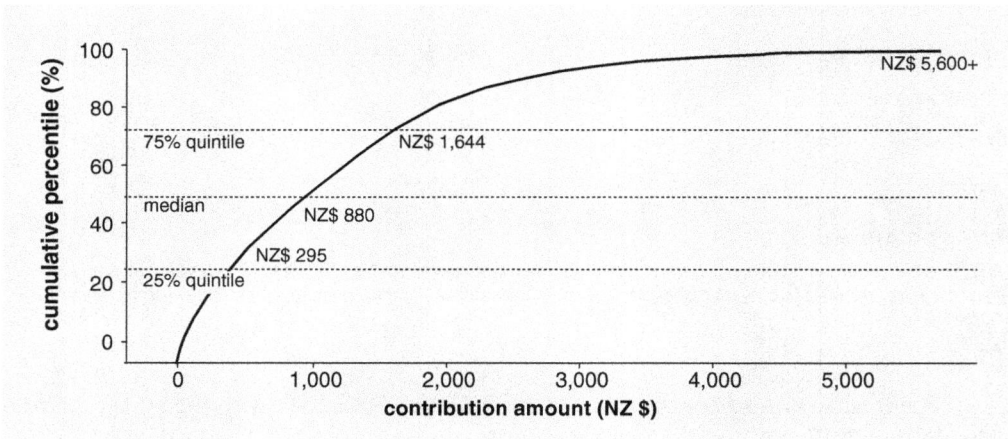

SOURCE: Inland Revenue 2011.

NOTE: Figure includes contributing members with a member tax credit (MTC) claim submitted for 2009/10 with salary and wage income only for the 2010 tax year; beneficiaries are excluded. Only members age 18 and over are eligible to make MTC claims. Contributions include employee deductions through the PAYE system, voluntary contributions directly to providers, and ad hoc contributions to Inland Revenue not through the PAYE process. Figures do not include employer contributions.

FIGURE 5.8 **Annual KiwiSaver contribution for nonsalary and nonwage earners, 2009/10**

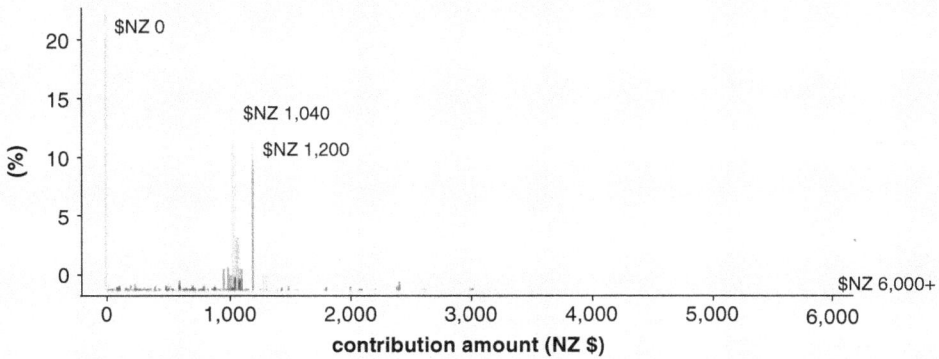

SOURCE: Inland Revenue 2011.

NOTE: Figure includes all KiwiSavers who submitted a member tax credit claim for 2009/10 but for whom no salary or wage income was recorded through the PAYE system for the 2010 tax year.

FIGURE 5.9 **Annual contribution by KiwiSavers with no income, 2009/10**

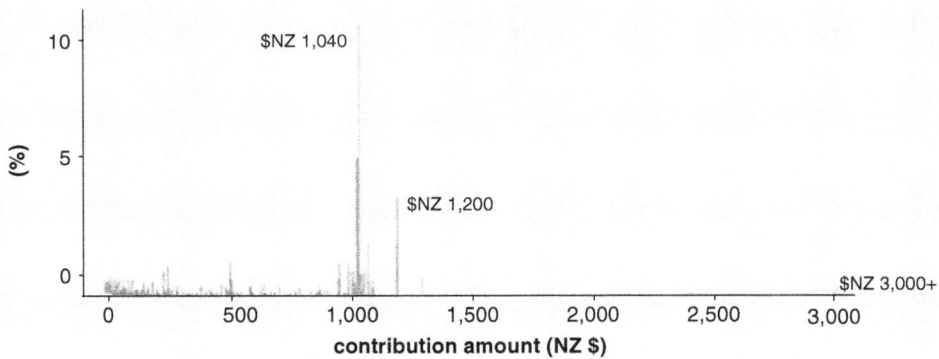

SOURCE: Inland Revenue 2011.

NOTE: Figure includes all KiwiSavers who submitted a member tax credit claim for 2009/10 who earned no income in 2010. Most of the 23 percent of members with no income are under age 18.

Member Tax Credit

Table 5.5 shows the proportion of members who received the maximum tax credit. Claims for the maximum were low in 2008 (14 percent) but rose to 46 percent in 2009 and 45 percent in 2010.

Figure 5.10 shows the distribution of the member tax credit by age. The lower credits paid to younger people are believed to reflect their lower earnings. The higher payments to older people may indicate a focus on maximizing the subsidy as retirement approaches.

TABLE 5.5 **KiwiSavers receiving the maximum tax credit, 2008–10**

	2008		2009		2010	
Member tax credit payment	**Number of members**	**% of total**	**Number of members**	**% of total**	**Number of members**	**% of total**
Maximum payment	83,146	14	359,753	46	420,525	45
Less than maximum payment	505,691	86	414,270	54	511,529	55
Total	588,837	100	774,023	100	932,054	100

SOURCE: Inland Revenue 2011.

NOTE: Figures include all individuals who received member tax credit payments for contributions made in 2009/10, including payments to complying funds (non-KiwiSaver retirement schemes that have all relevant features of KiwiSaver schemes and were in existence before June 1, 2007).

FIGURE 5.10 **Member tax credit granted to KiwiSavers, by age, 2011**

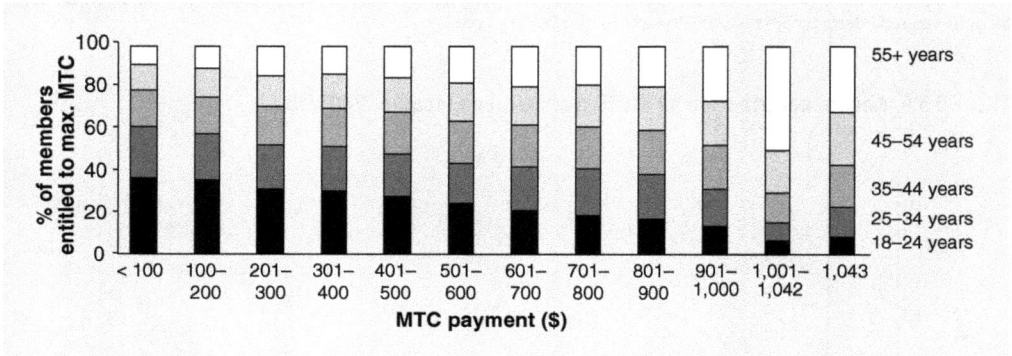

SOURCE: Inland Revenue 2011.

NOTE: Figure includes all members as of June 30, 2011, who had submitted a member tax credit (MTC) claim and were eligible for the maximum MTC of $NZ 1,043 in 2011.

Providers

Since 2008, there has been a steady increase in the share of KiwiSaver members who choose their own scheme. Between 2008 and 2011, the share of members allocated to default schemes declined by 12 percentage points, the share of members in employer-nominated schemes fell by 3 percentage points, and the share of members actively choosing to join the scheme rose by 15 percentage points (table 5.6).

Members are able to transfer between schemes, including transferring from the scheme nominated by their employer to another scheme (table 5.7). Transfer may occur during the eight-week opt-out period following automatic enrollment; members may also transfer from one scheme to another at any time. Transfers across schemes are referred to as "standard" transfers.

Standard transfers number about 110,000 a year, about 6 percent of membership (figure 5.11). Matthews (2011) suggests that people who switch tend to switch to a scheme run by their bank. Providers claim that they are not able to remunerate financial

TABLE 5.6 **Method by which members entered the KiwiSavers scheme, 2008–11**

	2008		2009		2010		2011	
Scheme entry method	Number of members	% of total	Number of members	% of total	Number of members	% of total	Number of members	% of total
Default allocated	268,868	38	369,577	34	419,250	29	458,013	26
Employer nominated	94,895	13	129,963	12	150,157	10	165,500	10
Active choice	352,483	49	600,709	55	890,356	61	1,132,193	64
Unspecified at year end	391	1	291	1	179	< 1	226	< 1
Total	716,637	100	1,100,540	100	1,459,942	100	1,755,932	100

SOURCE: Inland Revenue 2011.

NOTE: Figures show members as of June 30. Totals may not sum to 100 percent because of rounding. Default allocated refers to members who join KiwiSaver through the automatic enrollment process. Employer nominated refers to members who join through active choice into a KiwiSaver scheme sponsored by their employer.

TABLE 5.7 **Number and type of KiwiSaver scheme transfers, 2008–11**

Transfer type	2008	2009	2010	2011
Standard	17,757	50,457	113,555	112,234
Holding period	53,355	12,262	9,753	9,533
Total transfers	71,112	62,719	123,308	121,767

SOURCE: Inland Revenue 2011.

NOTE: Figures are for the period July 1, 2007, to June 30, 2011. Standard transfers are transfers across schemes. Transfers as a result of mergers of scheme providers were excluded.

FIGURE 5.11 **Number of standard KiwiSaver scheme transfers, 2007–11**

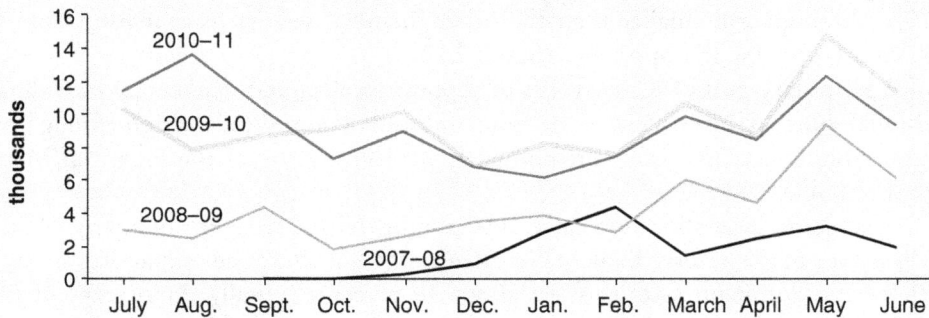

SOURCE: Inland Revenue 2011.

NOTE: Figures are for the period June 1, 2007 to June 30, 2011. Standard transfers are transfers across schemes. Transfers as a result of mergers of scheme providers were excluded.

advisers to persuade people to switch to their scheme; banks seem likely to be able to provide material to their wider customer base more effectively.

Assets

KiwiSaver assets under management reached $NZ 9,187 billion by June 30, 2011.
Table 5.8, compiled by the Financial Markets Authority from provider annual returns,
shows the growth in the number of schemes and assets since 2008.

TABLE 5.8 **KiwiSaver scheme numbers and total assets, 2008–11**

Scheme size (NZ $)	Number of schemes				Total assets (NZ $, millions)			
	2008	2009	2010	2011	2008	2009	2010	2011
< 1 million	17	14	10	10	5	9	2	2
1 million to < 2.5 million	5	6	8	5	9	8	14	8
2.5 million to < 10 million	9	10	5	5	45	51	27	20
10 million to < 25 million	6	6	6	7	89	87	101	122
25 million to < 50 million	3	6	4	4	130	210	132	140
50 million to < 100 million	5	3	5	2	322	221	399	110
100 million to < 200 million	1	4	3	7	101	659	364	1,049
200 million and over	0	5	11	12	0	1,415	4,812	7,736
Total	46	54	52	52	701	2,660	5,851	9,187

SOURCE: Inland Revenue 2011, based on data from the Financial Markets Authority.

NOTE: Figures include all KiwiSaver schemes that provided statistical returns as required under Section 125 of the
KiwiSaver Act 2006 as of March 31 of each year.

Research into the KiwiSaver supply side has identified the increasing role KiwiSaver
is playing in New Zealand's managed funds sector (Ministry of Economic Development
2010). Although still smaller than the other financial sectors (except life insurance),
KiwiSaver is growing in importance (figure 5.12).

A secondary goal of KiwiSaver is to support local capital markets by providing an
additional source of investment funds. Some information on the allocation among investment sectors is available from the annual KiwiSaver reports of the Financial Markets
Authority (table 5.9).

Changes in asset allocation since 2007 can be derived from the quarterly Managed
Funds Survey of the Reserve Bank of New Zealand. Figure 5.13 shows that overseas equity
has been the dominant asset class, at about 30 percent. Initially, 21 percent of funds
were held in local short-term (less than one year maturity) fixed-interest instruments,
and another 18 percent was on deposit with other financial institutions. By 2011, just
15 percent of funds were held in short-term fixed-interest instruments, and 10 percent
were on deposit with other financial institutions. The main gain appears to have been in

FIGURE 5.12 **Managed funds assets in New Zealand, by product category, 2007–11**

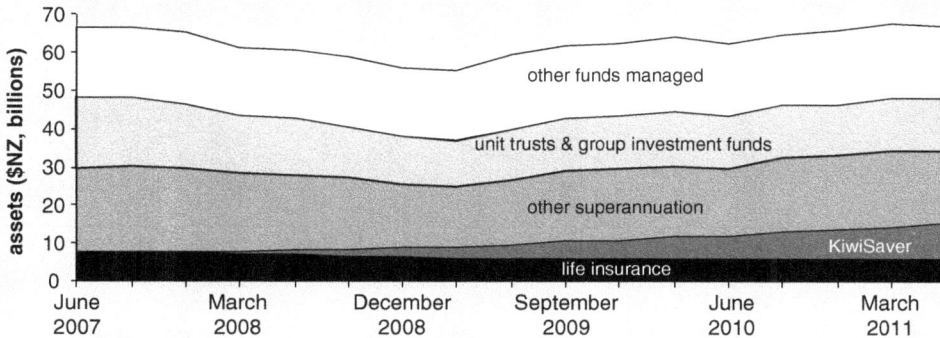

SOURCE: Inland Revenue 2011, based on data from Reserve Bank of New Zealand, Managed Funds Survey.

TABLE 5.9 **Allocation of KiwiSaver assets, 2011**

Fund type	Membership		Assets	
	Number	**% of total**	**Amount ($NZ)**	**% of total**
Default	405,679	17.4	2,250,076,280	24.5
Active default	111,526	4.8	547,147,918	6.0
Conservative	345,816	14.8	1,489,817,370	16.2
Balanced	351,949	15.1	2,056,698,172	22.4
Growth	470,383	20.2	2,053,244,933	22.4
Single-sector funds				
Cash	566,035	24.3	432,834,955	4.7
Shares	23,999	1.0	102,261,060	1.1
Fixed interest	3,060	0.1	7,551,086	0.1
Property	2,108	0.1	9,197,653	0.1
Socially responsible	7,570	0.3	19,538,934	0.2
Other	45,166	1.9	218,268,626	2.4
Total	2,333,291	100.0	9,186,636,988	100.0

SOURCE: Financial Markets Authority 2011, based on returns for year ending March 31, 2011.

foreign and longer-term New Zealand fixed-interest instruments, as investment in domestic equities was about 10 percent of assets under management over the whole period. This distribution is broadly similar to the allocation of other retirement schemes and managed funds.

FIGURE 5.13 **Distribution of KiwiSaver funds by asset class, 2008–12**

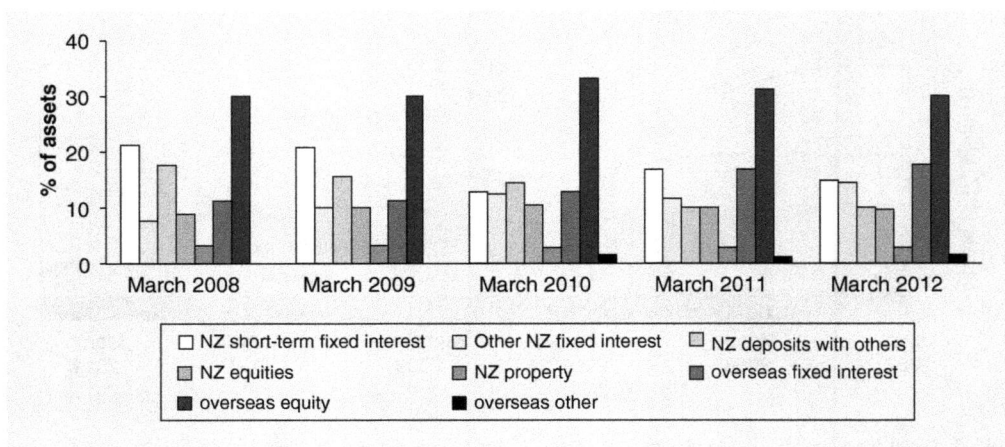

SOURCE: Author, based on Reserve Bank of New Zealand, Managed Funds Survey 2012.

NOTE: Data on overseas assets for March 2008 and 2009 do not distinguish among equities, fixed-interest, and other assets. The assumption of a 30 percent holding in overseas equities for the two years was made based on subsequent data. NZ = New Zealand.

Indeed, the investment patterns for KiwiSaver appear to be similar to the managed funds sector as a whole, with one exception. Figure 5.14 compares the percentages of assets in overseas assets (equities and fixed-interest instruments) for KiwiSaver, other retirement schemes, and all managed funds covered by the survey. It reveals that KiwiSaver holdings in total overseas assets have increased and are comparable with managed funds as a whole. The share remains much smaller than in other retirement funds, however. One might still question whether KiwiSaver's secondary objective of supporting local capital markets is fully being met.

Contribution Holidays

The contribution holiday feature was designed to ensure that potential members were not put off from joining due to a concern that they would have to keep contributing during times of financial or other stress. Two kinds of contribution holiday are possible. The first is a financial hardship holiday, which is subject to consent from the scheme trustees. The second, open to any member who has made at least one year of regular contributions, allows members to cease contributions for a specified time up to five years. As a new holiday can be taken at the end of an existing one, people can drop out for as long as they want (although they do have to keep opting out in this fashion).

The 2011 evaluation report provides the number of members on each type of holiday as of June 30, 2008–11. No figures are provided on the number of members making regular contributions and hence eligible for a contribution holiday. A reasonable proxy is people who enrolled in KiwiSaver either as what was termed in table 5.6 "default allocated" (that is, through the automatic enrollment process) or "employer nominated" (that is, through active choice into a KiwiSaver scheme sponsored by their employer). People

FIGURE 5.14 **Percentage of assets invested in overseas assets by KiwiSaver, other retirement funds, and all managed funds, 2008–12**

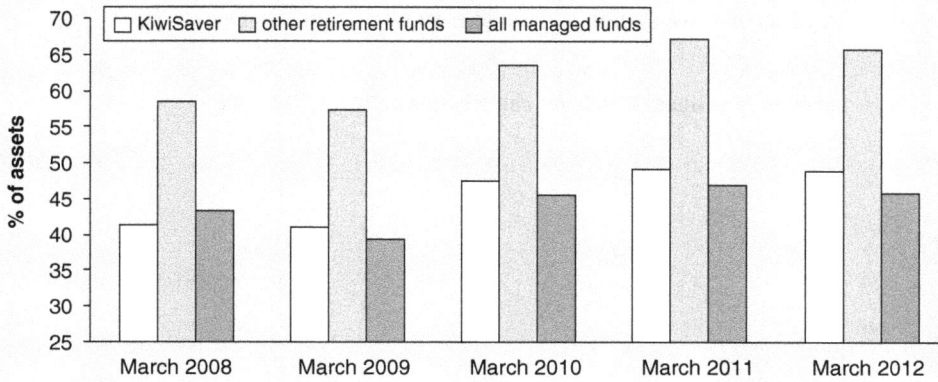

SOURCE: Author, based on Reserve Bank of New Zealand, Managed Funds Survey 2012.

who enter through active choice include all members under age 18, as well as others who joined KiwiSaver through a route other than employer arrangement; this is likely to include some members who are contributing by salary deduction through the PAYE system. The percentages in table 5.10 thus need to be interpreted with some caution.

TABLE 5.10 **KiwiSavers on contribution holiday, 2008–11**

Holiday type	2008		2009		2010		2011	
	Number	% of net enrolled members	Number	% of net enrolled members	Number	% of net enrolled members	Number	% of net enrolled members
Financial hardship	3,280	0.9	813	0.2	494	0.1	383	0.1
Optional	n.a.	n.a.	25,122	5.0	45,069	7.9	63,324	10.1
Total	3,280	0.9	25,935	5.2	45,563	8.0	63,707	10.2

SOURCE: Inland Revenue 2011.

NOTE: Figures include all members who were on contribution holidays as of June 30. Percentages exclude members enrolled through active choice (see table 5.6). n.a. = not applicable.

Only a very small proportion of members (about 0.1 percent) have been granted a contribution holiday on financial hardship grounds. In contrast, 10.1 percent of members took optional contribution holidays in 2011, a figure that has been rising over time. The KiwiSaver Evaluation Group has been carrying out an in-depth investigation into opt-out and contribution holiday behavior. Once released, its report will be posted on its website (http://www.ird.govt.nz/aboutir/reports/research/report-ks/).

Although the proportion of members electing to take a contribution holiday is relatively low (but rising), the duration of the holiday has increased (figure 5.15). This trend may be indicative of the importance of this flexibility to these members. Alternatively, the same pattern of inertia once a choice is made may be at play.

FIGURE 5.15 **Duration of optional KiwiSaver contribution holidays, 2008–11**

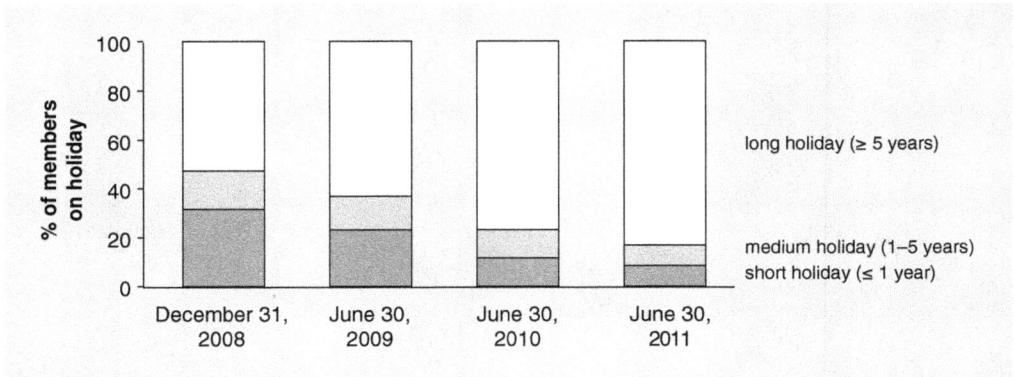

SOURCE: Inland Revenue 2011.

Provision for Housing

Recognizing the potential importance of homeownership for support in retirement, the designers of the KiwiSaver scheme included support for first-time home buyers. These provisions were not triggered until three years after KiwiSaver began. Contributions other than the government subsidy can be withdrawn for a first home purchase, and a grant of $NZ 1,000 per year of contribution, to a maximum of five years, can be obtained for this purpose.

The 2011 evaluation report records that there were 1,274 withdrawals, for a total value of $NZ 12.3 million, between June 1, 2010, and March 31, 2011. The average value of a withdrawal was $NZ 9,640. Over the same period, 619 subsidies of $NZ 3,000 each (the maximum level available after three years of membership) were granted. Unofficially, it has been suggested that in the last quarter of 2010/11 (April 1–June 30), a much higher level of activity occurred, similar in magnitude to the first three quarters combined.

In 2011, Housing New Zealand Corporation conducted an evaluation of some KiwiSaver providers (Laing, Nunns, and Ou 2011).[8] All 5 default KiwiSaver providers whose members applied for housing assistance and 8 of the 25 other providers whose members did so responded to the survey, which revealed that the number of members who withdrew funds to purchase a first home or were approved for a subsidy was higher than forecast. Other evaluation findings included the following:

- Nearly 80 percent of KiwiSaver members who withdrew funds were with default providers.
- Most of the approved subsidy applicants were young.

- Many members experienced problems coordinating subsidy and withdrawal applications.
- Lawyers lacked knowledge about the homeownership package.
- To withdraw funds, a KiwiSaver member has to provide an unconditional sale and purchase agreement. Obtaining the agreement is difficult without knowing the availability of the subsidy or the amount of the withdrawal.

Government Cost

The amount of support from the government is diminishing as a proportion of the total, although it remains substantial, at a little under 40 percent (figure 5.16). This decrease reflects a steady build-up from members' own contributions and increasing investment returns. Members who contribute only the minimum needed to obtain the maximum member tax credit will keep government support higher than it would otherwise be as a proportion of the total.

FIGURE 5.16 **Government KiwiSaver contributions as a percentage of total funds sent to providers, 2007–11**

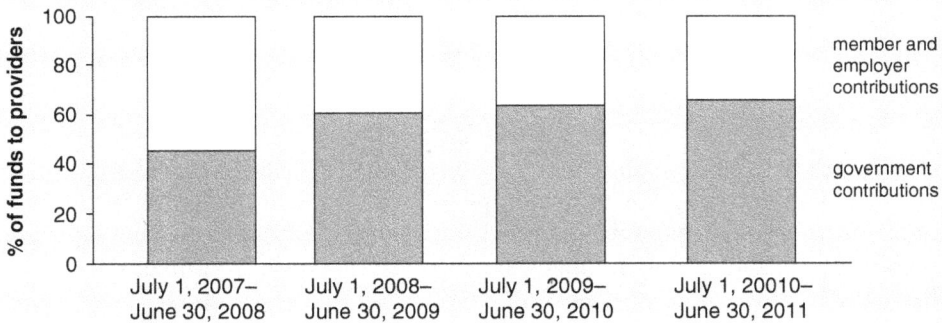

SOURCE: Inland Revenue 2011.

NOTE: Figures show all government contributions to members passed from Inland Revenue to providers between October 2007 and June 2011 (cash basis).

The costs of the KiwiSaver scheme to the government are set out in a little more detail in table 5.11. The impact of discontinuing the employer tax credit is apparent. These figures do not include the cost of the waiver of the employer retirement contribution, which was removed April 1, 2012.

The cost of KiwiSaver subsidies is of particular concern because of the government's commitment to return to fiscal surplus by 2016. A proposal to effect a one-time automatic enrollment of existing non-KiwiSaver member employees that was included in the 2011 budget for implementation in 2012 has been deferred because of the additional cost involved.

TABLE 5.11 **Cost of KiwiSaver to the government, 2008–11**
$NZ, MILLIONS

Cost	2008	2009	2010	2011	2008–11
Payments to members	572	842	970	998	3,382
Employer tax credit	38	206	n.a.	n.a.	244
Total	610	1,048	970	998	3,626

SOURCE: Inland Revenue 2011.

NOTE: Figures show all government contributions to members passed from Inland Revenue to providers between October 2007 and June 2011 (cash basis). n.a. = not applicable.

Conclusions

OBSERVATIONS ON EARLY EXPERIENCE WITH KIWISAVER

After nearly five years of experience and several rounds of evaluations, a number of observations on the impact and dynamics of the KiwiSaver program may now be made. In general, the program has proven very effective in achieving relatively high levels of participation in supplementary retirement saving across a broad spectrum of the population. In a relatively short period, participation has been extended to nearly half the population under age 65 and an even larger proportion of the labor force. As a result, New Zealand now has one of the highest rates of coverage for supplementary retirement saving in the world.

The high level of coverage likely reflects the combination of automatic enrollment and substantial matching incentives. This level of participation is particularly notable as it has occurred in a setting with a long tradition of providing substantial retirement income through a noncontributory public pension system, with effectively no qualifying requirements beyond age and residency. Equally notable is the fact that, in contrast to most other similar settings, New Zealand provides direct subsidies but no tax concessions for retirement savings. The very large share of membership among people age 24–35—who typically have a low probability of contributing to retirement saving schemes—demonstrates the impact of automatic enrollment.

A strong indication of the power of matching incentives is the high proportion (24 percent) of members who indicate no sources of income. These people presumably enrolled to take advantage of the generous kick-start match and the opportunity to contribute the minimum amount to obtain the full member tax credit. The number of members under age 18—a group that typically has a very low propensity to save for retirement—provides similar evidence of the strength of the matching incentives, although it may be that only better-off families are in a position to make the initial contribution.

Lessons from the emerging field of behavioral economics guided the development of KiwiSaver. The evidence confirms the significance of a number of the issues identified in the literature (for a discussion of behavioral economics, see chapter 15). Participants' behavior is consistent with the power of defaults and inertia. A very large proportion of members stick with the default rates for contributions and allow themselves to be enrolled in default provider schemes. The proportion of people who opt out after automatic enroll-ment is relatively low, as is the proportion taking contribution holidays, despite the fact that many (albeit not a majority of) members were automatically enrolled. The fact that many members continued to make contributions at the default rate even after that rate was reduced confirms the stickiness of default parameters in other settings.

Equally instructive is the evidence on the influence of matching thresholds and other parameters on behavior. The remarkable degree to which contributions cluster around the maximum points of matching and tax credits reveals the degree to which members respond to these incentives and their role as a signaling mechanism. It also has implica-tions for the efficiency of the system in increasing saving.

The ramping up of membership of people under age 18 provides evidence of grow-ing awareness of the new system and the potential value of the generous initial kick-start contribution. The increasing exercise of choice, incidence of transfers among providers, and entry of new providers suggests that a few years are needed before a system is accepted and both supply- and demand-side participation become widespread.

BROADER RETIREMENT INCOME POLICY ISSUES

The experience with KiwiSaver has raised some broader retirement policy issues.

Adequacy of New Zealanders' Savings for Retirement

Throughout the 1990s and into the new century, coverage of workers in occupational retirement schemes continued to fall. There was also concern about the general adequacy of private saving levels in New Zealand.

In 2004, as the Savings Product Working Group was delivering its report recom-mending government intervention in the retirement savings market, a Treasury Working Paper (Scobie, Gibson, and Le 2004) was published suggesting that there may not, in fact, be widespread undersaving for retirement. This finding was based on a life-cycle model that derives saving rates as the residual between income and expenditure as reported in the Statistics New Zealand Household Economic Survey. For nearly 40 percent of working-age people, New Zealand Superannuation would provide income equal to or greater than the current level; for this group, saving for retirement would not be a preferred strategy.

Statistics New Zealand strongly recommended against deriving a residual for savings in the manner used in the working paper. A second paper (Bascand, Cope, and Ramsay 2006) found that cross-checking with other data suggested that the Household Economic Survey may have underreported income by 4 percent and expenditure by 17 percent. Attempts to address adequacy using other data sources have not been fruitful, because of data problems.

Complementarity of KiwiSaver and New Zealand Superannuation

The role of the Retirement Commissioner (now the Commissioner for Financial Literacy and Retirement Income) has grown over the years. Since 2007, the commissioner has been tasked with reviewing retirement income policy. The 2007 review expressed some disquiet about the impact of KiwiSaver on the cornerstone (as the commissioner saw it) New Zealand Superannuation. A particular concern was the fact that KiwiSaver is much more complex than the very simple public old-age provision. A response to this concern was provided by a paper in the *New Zealand Journal of Social Policy* (Rashbrooke 2009) that emphasized the complementarity of the two policies, particularly in relation to evidence from *OECD Pensions at a Glance* that made clear that the income adequacy of New Zealand Superannuation fell short of replacement, because preretirement incomes had increased. The paper also suggested that the costs of KiwiSaver were modest compared with subsidies for retirement savings in other countries.

Additionality of KiwiSaver

As part of its ongoing research work, in 2010 the KiwiSaver Evaluation Group commissioned a survey of 825 people (members and nonmembers), asking for their estimates of their expected income in retirement and the amount of income they would need to cover their basic needs or be comfortable. Analysis of these data was published in a Treasury Working Paper (Law, Meehan, and Scobie 2011), and preliminary findings are discussed in the Evaluation Group report. Based on the responses, Law, Meehan, and Scobie estimated that 33 percent of the target population became members based on need and 46 percent became members based on the desire to be comfortable in retirement. For every member in the target population, another 4–14 people from outside the target population are estimated to have joined.

The analysis also explored the impact of the scheme on national saving. It concluded that given the conditions and settings of the scheme in 2011, over the 10 years to 2021 the net contribution of KiwiSaver to national saving would be marginal at best and may actually reduce national saving.

The Treasury paper notes that, as with any survey, there is a risk that some respondents may have answered questions about what they would have done in the absence of the scheme in a way they believed showed them in a favorable light. Certainly the degree of subjectivity raises some questions about the usefulness of the detailed and comprehensive analysis of responses.

The Evaluation Group report also noted the limitations of survey results, which provide a snapshot of respondents' circumstances and expectations about the future at a particular point in time. The results do not provide a comprehensive basis for assessing changes in individual or household saving behavior over time.

Other Research Activities

Work is planned to evaluate the initial impact of KiwiSaver on individuals' saving and net worth. This evaluation is intended to provide a comprehensive basis for assessing changes in individual or household saving behavior over time based on data from the New Zealand longitudinal survey, the Survey of Family Income and Employment.

The Survey of Family Income and Employment was conducted by Statistics New Zealand from 2002 to 2010. The survey collected information on individual and household income, as well as the factors that influence changes in income, such as involvement in the labor force and family composition, and detailed information on assets and liabilities. During the eight years in which the survey was administered, respondents were revisited annually in order to understand how their circumstances changed. Every second year (or wave) of the survey, respondents were asked about their assets and liabilities. In the final year (Wave 8), the survey included specific questions about KiwiSaver.

In 2012, the KiwiSaver evaluation team linked KiwiSaver administrative data from Inland Revenue with survey data in order to gain greater insights into actual saving behavior rather than rely on subjective responses. An evaluation of the types of individuals who opted out and took contribution holidays was released in June 2012.[9] The 2011 evaluation report also noted the intention of the Department of Building and Housing to conduct a follow-up of the initial Housing New Zealand Corporation survey on the homeownership package to assess the impact and effectiveness of the package against its agreed outcomes. The Ministry of Economic Development plans to update its work on the KiwiSaver supply-side evaluation.

An industry survey is also of interest. Matthews (2011) reports on a survey of 1,001 New Zealanders age 18–65 conducted on behalf of the Financial Services Institute of Australasia. This study finds that just over half of New Zealanders age 18–65 were KiwiSavers and that more than half of these people had not been saving for retirement before enrolling. More than half of KiwiSavers joined because they recognized the importance of saving for retirement. Government incentives were also important, with about 90 percent describing the $NZ 1,000 kick-start and just under 90 percent describing the member tax credit as very important or important.

Along with not being able to afford to join, the survey also finds that a key reason why people had not joined KiwiSaver was that they already had sufficient savings and investments for retirement. Uncertainty about the structure of the scheme (as a result of a belief that changes were likely in the future) also discouraged people from joining.

WHAT LIES AHEAD?

New Zealand's public pension system underwent significant changes over the past 35 years. Despite these changes, public pension spending fell by more than in any other OECD country, mainly as a result of the increase in the pension eligibility age.

The universal demogrant approach has considerable and complex challenges. Among other things, it has no inherent buffer mechanisms to absorb shocks, such as declines in employment or wage growth below inflation, let alone increases in longevity. And there is the ever-present pressure on health costs necessary to meet population expectations.

Although the universal benefit appears to be associated with very low poverty rates, significant numbers of pensioners in New Zealand are just above the poverty line. The average incomes of households headed by someone age 65 or over are low, and the vast majority of lower-income retired households (the bottom 50 percent) rely almost exclusively on government benefits. Homeownership has fallen, and income inequality among people of working age has increased significantly.

KiwiSaver provides future governments with some flexibility to deal with these challenges. The evidence suggests that, critics notwithstanding, the scheme is developing in a positive manner. In addition to providing direct benefits, the very introduction of KiwiSaver has led to much greater public awareness of retirement saving and financial services. The Commission for Financial Literacy and Retirement Income has seized the opportunity provided by KiwiSaver to leverage its work on financial education.

Some design issues remain. The availability of the member tax credit when not making regular contributions from pay encourages gaming of the system, and the reduction in the credit from 1:1 to 1:2 reduces the reward to people for whom salary deduction represents some real sacrifice without explicitly addressing the gaming aspect. Standardization of reporting on fees and investment returns is long overdue (the new government initiative in this area will be watched with interest).

The criticism that KiwiSaver perpetuates differences in income and wealth is undeniably true; poorer workers, particularly workers with young children, simply cannot afford to make the payments needed to obtain the member tax credit or employer contributions. This consequence of the program is not in itself an argument against KiwiSaver, but it highlights the need for policy to take a holistic view of outcomes.

No government policy attention has yet been paid to the decumulation aspect of KiwiSaver caused by the fact that benefits will be paid as lump sums. Providers are starting to consider how they might respond, with the likelihood of something like Australian draw-down facilities being made available.[10] The extent to which some New Zealand–relevant regulatory requirements will be needed remains to be seen.

Inevitably, given the politically charged nature of retirement income provision, more changes will be made. But one may cautiously conclude that KiwiSaver is here to stay and that it will make a valued and valuable contribution to retirement income provision in its widest sense.

Notes

1. Retirement accounts are long-term fully funded savings that are accessible only upon reaching some mandated age. In New Zealand and Australia, these arrangements are generally referred to as superannuation schemes.

2. For a good history of New Zealand Superannuation and its forerunners, see Preston (2008).

3. As the result of coalition agreements under New Zealand's system of proportional representation, the net-of-tax value floor is actually 66 percent rather than 65 percent, although no legislative change has been made.

4. Currency values in this chapter are given in New Zealand dollars; $NZ 100 = US$82.

5. These limits were imposed by constraints within the PAYE system adapted to collect contributions.

6. Details of the agreements for the default providers can be obtained from the Financial Markets Authority website, http://www.fma.govt.nz/help-me-comply/kiwisaver/your-obligations/default-providers/.

7. All reports are available at http://www.ird.govt.nz/aboutir/reports/research/report-ks/.

8. The Housing New Zealand Corporation has responsibility for tenancy arrangements and manages the stock of public housing. The Department of Building and Housing has responsibility for policy work.

9. This evaluation, "Opting-Out and Taking Contribution Holidays," is available at http://www.ird.govt.nz/aboutir/reports/research/report-ks/research-ks-opting-out-holiday-contributions.html.

10. In Australia, voluntary take-up of lifetime annuities is very low. The preferred approach is for retirement assets to remain under management and drawn down in regular monthly

payments. If these payments fall between certain minimums and maximums (which depend on life expectancy), some tax advantages remain. Participants can still withdraw lump sums, resetting the monthly payment levels. There is, of course, no further payment if funds are exhausted before death.

References

Bascand, G., J. Cope, and D. Ramsay. 2006. "Selected Issues in the Measurement of New Zealand's Saving(s)." Paper presented at the Reserve Bank of New Zealand Workshop on Saving, Wellington, November 14. www.rbnz.govt.nz/research/workshops/14nov06/2895712.pdf.

Financial Markets Authority. 2011. *Annual Report in Respect of the KiwiSaver Act 2006 for the Year Ending June 30, 2011.* http://www.fma.govt.nz/media/368324/kiwisaver_report_for_the_year_ended_30_june_2011.pdf.

Harris, P. 2004. "A Future for Work-Based Savings in New Zealand." Government of New Zealand, Wellington. http://www.beehive.govt.nz/Documents/Files/WorkplaceSavings.pdf.

Inland Revenue. Various years. "KiwiSaver Evaluation Reports." Wellington. http://www.ird.govt.nz/aboutir/reports/research/report-ks/.

Laing, Patricia, Heather Nunns, and Chris Ou. 2011. "KiwiSaver Home Ownership Package: Process Evaluation. Year One." Housing New Zealand Corporation, Wellington.

Law, David, Lisa Meehan, and Grant Scobie. 2011. "KiwiSaver: An Initial Evaluation of the Impact on Retirement Saving." New Zealand Treasury Working Paper 11/04, Wellington. http://www.treasury.govt.nz/publications/research-policy/wp/2011/11-04/.

Matthews, Claire. 2011. "KiwiSaver and Retirement Savings: A Report Prepared for FINSIA and the IFA." Massey University, Palmerston North. http://www.finsia.com/docs/ecm-files/pol11_13_kiwisaver_web(2)8DFBF9E580A7.pdf?sfvrsn=2.

Ministry of Economic Development. 2010. "Report on KiwiSaver Supply Side Evaluation." Wellington. http://www.med.govt.nz/about-us/publications/publications-by-topic/evaluation-of-government-programmes/kiwisaver-supply-side-evaluation.pdf.

New Zealand Government Actuary. 2006. "Report for the Year Ended June 2006." Wellington. http://www.parliament.nz/NR/rdonlyres/7A582DB3-63D0-4D42-9863-C0700B-199FEC/88258/DBHOH_PAP_14297_36895.pdf.

New Zealand Treasury. 2009. *Challenges and Choices: New Zealand's Long-Term Fiscal Statement.* Wellington: New Zealand Treasury. http://www.treasury.govt.nz/government/longterm/fiscal-position/2009/ltfs-09.pdf.

OECD (Organisation for Economic Co-operation and Development). 2011a. *OECD Factbook 2011.* Paris: OECD.

———. 2011b. *OECD Pensions at a Glance 2011.* Paris: OECD.

Preston, David. 2008. *Retirement Income in New Zealand: The Historical Context.* Wellington: Retirement Commission. http://www.cflri.org.nz/webfm_send/374.

Rashbrooke, Geoff. 2009. "Simple, Effective and (Relatively) Inexpensive: New Zealand Retirement Provision in the International Context." *New Zealand Journal of Social Policy* 36. http://www.msd.govt.nz/about-msd-and-our-work/publications-resources/journals-and-magazines/social-policy-journal/spj36/36-nz-retirement-provision.html.

———. 2010. "Living within Our Means: A Framework for Deciding the Age of Eligibility for NZ Superannuation." In *Retirement Income Policy and Intergenerational Equity*, ed. Judith Davey, Geoff Rashbrooke, and Robert Stephen. Wellington: Institute of Policy Studies.

Reserve Bank of New Zealand. 2012. "Managed Funds Survey." Wellington. http://www.rbnz.govt.nz/statistics/monfin/c15/download.html.

Scobie, Grant, John Gibson, and Trinh Le. 2004. "Saving for Retirement: New Evidence for New Zealand." New Zealand Treasury Working Paper 04/12, Wellington. http://www.treasury.govt.nz/publications/research-policy/wp/2004/04-12/.

Toder, Eric, and Surachai Khitatrakun. 2006. "Final Report to Inland Revenue: KiwiSaver Evaluation Literature Review." Urban Institute, Washington, DC. http://www.treasury.govt.nz/publications/informationreleases/kiwisaver/background/ks-eval-lit-review-dec06.pdf.

CHAPTER 6

The Impact of Matching on Savings in the U.K. Savings Gateway Program

Will Price

The Saving Gateway was a government pilot program that used matching contributions to increase saving by people with low incomes. Two separate pilots experimented with different matching rates, contribution ceilings, eligibility rules, and recruitment mechanisms. The likelihood of joining the pilot doubled as the match rate increased from 20 percent to 50 percent but did not increase further as the match rose to 100 percent. Once in the program, the ceiling on how much a person could contribute each week seemed to have a much larger impact on saving than the match rate. For the low-income target group, the pilots led to new saving rather than a redirection of existing saving from other sources. Important issues of potential selectivity bias need to be considered in evaluating pilot results.

This chapter reviews the experience of the Saving Gateway in the United Kingdom, a government program that used matching contributions to increase saving by people with low incomes (HM Treasury 2001). Two pilots were implemented, the first in 2002–04 and the second in 2005–07. The pilots experimented with different matching rates, contribution ceilings, eligibility rules, and recruitment mechanisms.

In 2008, the Labour government then in power decided to roll out the Saving Gateway nationally (HM Treasury 2008a, 2008b). The launch, scheduled for July 2010, would have covered up to 8 million people, about 20 percent of the population between the ages of 16 and 65. Following the general election in May 2010, the incoming Conservative–Liberal Democrat coalition government canceled the planned scheme as part of its broader program of fiscal retrenchment (HM Treasury 2010).

The Saving Challenge

Successive governments in the United Kingdom have sought to increase both aggregate saving levels and particular forms of saving. There have been a range of policies to encourage both pension and nonpension saving.[1] A common feature of these schemes was the use of tax relief to provide the financial incentive.

Despite these and other interventions, assets, savings, and overall wealth remain unequally distributed in the United Kingdom. Figure 6.1 shows this wide dispersion. It shows that the lowest income deciles have negative financial assets on average.

The Saving Gateway was an experiment in using matching contributions—government cash payments that matched an amount saved by an individual—as a tool that would increase saving levels in a way that was fairer and more effective than tax relief alone (HM Treasury 2004). The approach was to be fairer because the progressive rates of

FIGURE 6.1 **Aggregate wealth in Great Britain, by income decile and type of wealth, 2008–10**

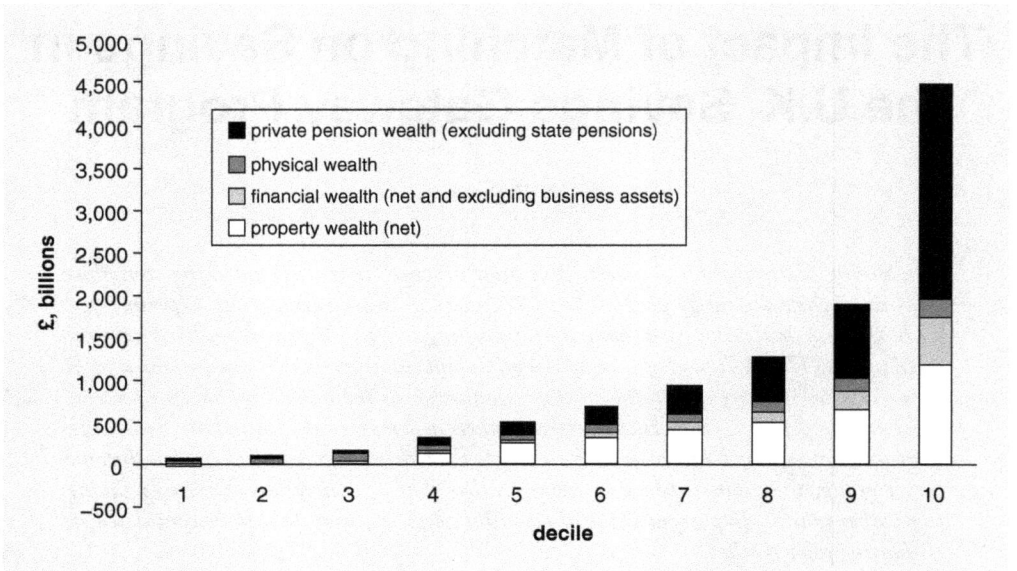

SOURCE: Wealth and Assets Survey, U.K. Office for National Statistics.

income tax in the United Kingdom provide a greater monetary incentive to higher earners through tax relief than lower earners—and gave no incentive at all to nontaxpayers. The experiment with matching contributions aimed to be more effective because the concept of a match was expected to be easier to understand than tax relief. Interest in the concept had been stimulated by examples of matching in Australia and the United States and the general realization that tax-based incentives exclude a significant proportion of the population.

The policy was part of a more all-encompassing strategy on saving that aimed to look across the life cycle and across the different methods through which individuals built up assets. It was also intended to highlight the link between debt and assets. The strategy distinguished between debt held by (usually) wealthy individuals (for example, to finance housing) and often very small amounts of (very high-cost) debt held by low-income individuals. These small but high-cost debts can trap people in a cycle of debt and repayment and prevent the build-up of even low stocks of assets.[2]

The policy was not without critics, even at the outset. The range of arguments against matching design included the need to avoid distorting what might be efficient individual decisions and the fact that a matched saving account may be less effective than other interventions, such as income transfers, increases in spending on programs that target the poor, or financial education programs (Emmerson and Wakefield 2003[3]). Supporters of the matching approach believed that it would provide a fairer and more effective tool with which people, particularly low-income people, could increase saving (see, for example, Sodha and Lister 2006).

The Saving Gateway Pilots

Table 6.1 sets out a timeline of key events in the history of the Saving Gateway. Nine years elapsed between the initial policy proposals and the planned national launch, partly because there were two rounds of pilots (although even with a single pilot, the gap would have been six years), highlighting that the significant benefits of piloting have to be weighed against the inevitable delay it introduces. The progression from the first to the second pilot and then to roll-out was quite swift at each stage. The political window of opportunity can close even for projects whose evaluations indicate that they are successful. In the absence of other policy options that have been as rigorously tested, alternatives may be introduced that are less effective or more expensive, or the negative conditions that motivate the program can remain unaddressed.

PILOT 1

An initial pilot of 1,500 accounts was conducted in 2002–04. A final evaluation report was published in March 2005 (Kempson, McKay, and Collard 2005). The initial pilot had a 100 percent match rate. Participants could save up to £375 over 18 months at up

TABLE 6.1 **Timeline of the Saving Gateway**

Activity	Date
Initial policy proposals	2001
Development of initial pilot	2001–02
First pilot	August 2002–November 2004
Final evaluation of first pilot	March 2005
Second pilot	March 2005—February 2007
Interim evaluation of second pilot	July 2006
Final evaluation of second pilot	May 2007
Announcement of national roll-out in 2010 and consultation on details of the scheme to inform roll-out	March 2008
Summary of responses to consultation announcement of 50 percent match rate	December 2008
Saving Gateway Accounts Act passed	July 2009
Final Labour Budget confirms July 2010 launch	March 2010
U.K. general election	May 2010
First Conservative-Liberal coalition government budget announces that scheme will be canceled	June 2010
Planned launch	July 2010
Saving Gateway Accounts Act repealed	December 2010

SOURCE: Author, based on government documents.

to £25 a month (for example, a maximum of 15 full contributions).[4] The match was then applied at the end of the period. The money could be used for any purpose, in contrast to experiments in other countries that restrict money to certain uses. In four of the five areas, community groups helped find potential low-income participants, who were the target group for the accounts.[5] These groups were part of a separate pilot, called the Community Finance and Learning Initiative. Although financial education services were available for Saving Gateway participants, few people took up the offer, which hence appeared to have little impact on whether people joined the pilot. In the fifth area, letters were sent to people's homes to alert them to the pilot.

The evaluation of the second pilot was largely positive. Its small size limited the design parameters that could be tested and the degree to which the results could be extrapolated to the broader population. The evaluation used a combination of questionnaires, actual data from the matched account provider, and face-to-face interviews. A reference group not offered the account was used as a control.

Relative to the maximum achievable account balance of £375, the mean balance at the end of the pilot (18 months) was £282 and the median was £375.[6] Before the pilot, 56 percent of the people who participated in the pilot had no reported savings, 13 percent had less than £200, and only 17 percent had more than £500.

The pilot increased saving. The question is whether the saving that accrued was additional or money that was transferred from other balances or borrowed.

The evaluation of the program concluded that the pilot "encouraged genuinely new saving among participants. Most were finding the money they saved from their regular income. There was hardly any evidence that people had either borrowed the money or transferred it from other savings accounts" (Kempson, McKay, and Collard 2005, 47).

The government's 2008 consultation on the national roll-out of the scheme concluded that "there was evidence that the scheme led to a change in saving behaviour, with 41 percent of savers still saving three or more months after the pilot had finished and 32 percent of savers saying that they were more likely to plan for retirement." In addition, "a high proportion of account holders (60 percent) agreed that saving into a Saving Gateway account had made them feel more financially secure" (HM Treasury 2008b, 8–9).

Table 6.2 shows the range of responses from qualitative surveys at account opening and account maturity. In general the transitions are positive, meaning that the percentage of people who said they did not save at all fell.[7]

PILOT 2

On the strength of the (interim) evaluation of the first pilot program, the government implemented a new, much larger pilot in 2005.[8] The second pilot included variations in key parameters and contribution levels. It therefore enabled testing of the effects of different match rates and contribution ceilings. It also included people thought to be well outside any potential target group, in order to test whether and at what point diminishing returns from expenditures on incentives set in. The pilot also aimed to test recruitment mechanisms by using telephone and direct mail that could be scalable to a national program. This feature was added because use of community groups and the bundling of financial education in the first pilot were deemed too expensive to include in a national scheme.

TABLE 6.2 **Pilot participants' approach to saving at beginning and end of Saving Gateway Pilot 1**

		Approach to saving at account opening			
		I don't really save at all	I tend to put money away for no particular reason	I save up to buy things I want or need	I tend to put money away for the long term	Total % with each answer at maturity
Approach to saving at account maturity	I don't really save at all	34	20	12	7	18
	I tend to put money away for no particular reason	8	35	10	12	12
	I save up to buy things I want or need	40	33	67	27	50
	I tend to put money away for the long term	18	13	12	53	19
	Total % with each answer at opening	31	8	47	14	100

NOTE: Shaded boxes show the same answer given in each survey (for example, of the people who said at account opening that they don't really save, 34 percent gave the same answer at the end, and 8 percent, 40 percent, and 18 percent reported that they now saved, for a range of reasons). Movement down each column shows an increased attachment to saving after the pilot.

Control and treatment groups were randomly selected from three databases: benefit records; random-digit dialing, using databases of phone numbers; and letters sent to addresses randomly drawn from a directory of household addresses. A control group was selected that had the right mix of the proposed target group. Members of the control group were asked the same questions on saving behavior at the start and end of the pilot but were not offered the account. The treatment group was offered the account. Some refused but agreed to participate in the evaluation, allowing researchers to identify whether being offered an account had any impact even if the offer was refused. Some members of the treatment group accepted and opened the account. The evaluation used surveys of each group at the beginning and end of the pilot, some face-to-face interviews, and administrative account data from the account provider, Halifax Bank, a British bank (now HBOS).

The second pilot was larger, with 22,000 accounts. It tested three different match rates (20 percent, 50 percent, and 100 percent) across six areas of the United Kingdom. It also tested different monthly contribution ceilings (£25, £50, and £125) and included a much wider income range, in order to determine whether and at what point diminishing returns to matching set in.

Table 6.3 shows the mean and median contributions, the match rate, and the contribution ceiling in the six pilot areas. The table shows that there was some evidence that a higher overall match led to higher contributions (but with rapidly diminishing returns).

TABLE 6.3 **Mean and median saving balances in Saving Gateway Pilot 2**

Area	Match rate (%)	Contribution ceiling (£)	Conversion rate (%)	Net monthly contribution (£)		Final balance (before match added) (£)	
				Median	Mean	Median	Mean
1	20	50	6.5	50	33	750	543
2	20	125	10.3	125	89	2,000	1,546
3	50	50	21.8	50	39	800	680
4	50	25	16.2	25	21	400	349
5	50	25	22.8	25	20	400	343
6	100	25	19.7	25	20	400	338

SOURCE: Emmerson and others 2007.

However, the far more dominant impact was the ceiling on monthly contributions. Participants who were offered the lowest 20 percent matching rate for their contributions but were allowed the higher £125 monthly limit made larger contributions than participants offered a 50 percent or 100 percent match but constrained to a lower contribution ceiling. Most people saved up to the contribution ceiling. This result is generally consistent with experience in other settings (see chapter 15), which indicates that the framing of the terms of the match affect behavior.

The higher match rate had a greater impact on the likelihood of opening an account. In the two areas where people were offered a 20 percent match, the average participation rate was less than 9 percent. In the three areas offered a 50 percent match, the average rate was about 20 percent. In the one area with a 100 percent match, the conversion rate was also about 20 percent.[9] These findings suggest that the match rate influences both the participation decision and the amount of saving by people who chose to participate. Higher matches could be offered in the early years of a program to get people into the scheme, with the rate reduced in subsequent years.

Overall, the evaluation of the second pilot showed a 34 percent increase in the probability that people who opened an account would significantly increase their saving. The results showed some decrease in spending by participants on discretionary items, implying that substitution away from other expenditures was a source for the extra saving. There was little or no evidence that participants borrowed to "invest" in the pilot. Set against the positive evidence was the fact that statistical tests could not conclusively demonstrate an increase in the measure of overall net worth, as would be expected if saving had increased. There was evidence that the low-income group appeared to be increasing overall saving by much more than the higher-income group.

Selectivity Bias

Whether these results reflected unobserved differences (selectivity bias) was a key concern. To address this question, the evaluators used two econometric estimation strategies. Their central concern was identifying the impact of the Saving Gateway accounts. The random control group (the group not offered accounts) provided a strong control. It allowed fully randomized experimental comparison of the impact of being offered an account on saving rates, because there was no selection bias.

There were concerns about selection bias in comparing people who opened accounts and people who declined to do so. Indeed, there were observable differences between people who did and did not open accounts when offered the opportunity. Account openers tended to be better educated, earn more, and live closer to a branch of the provider. The econometric results included these observable characteristics in the explanatory variables to try and control for their influence. Of course, they could not account for any unobserved differences in the groups that made account openers more likely to respond to the incentives.

Most of the results presented in the second evaluation report focused on the difference between people offered accounts (regardless of whether they opened one) and the control group. For these two groups, there was no selection bias. But these comparisons do not evaluate the impact of actually opening and participating in the accounts over the period of the pilot. Doing so requires comparing account openers with both control groups—and an assumption or judgment about whether the differences in saving are the result of the policy, of unobservable differences, or a combination of both.

Both sets of results are presented here, each needing a caveat. Most people offered an account chose not to open one. People who did open an account may have unobserved characteristics that introduce selection bias. This bias may affect the results, even though researchers controlled for age, sex, employment, race, housing tenure, education, health, income, household composition, and numeracy.

Impact on Saving, Consumption, and Overall Net Worth

As highlighted above, the impact on saving, consumption, and overall net worth depends on whether the comparison is made between people offered an account or between people who actually opened an account and the control group. Among people offered an account, there is limited evidence of an increased probability of increased saving, some evidence of reduced spending on purchases outside the home, such as dining out, and no evidence of any change in net worth (table 6.4). Among people who actually opened an account, there is strong evidence of an increase in the probability of saving more and reduced spending on food consumed outside the home. But even for this group there is no evidence of a change in net worth.

These results pose something of a conundrum, because in the qualitative evaluations, people generally reported saving more out of current income rather than transferring money from other accounts (though a significant minority of higher-income participants reported recycling existing savings). If people are increasing saving out of current income as a result of the pilot and increasing their balance in the new account, net worth should be rising.

The Planned National Roll-Out

In response to the second evaluation report, the government decided to create a national scheme. A 2010 launch was announced in the 2008 Budget. Alongside the

TABLE 6.4 **Impact of Saving Gateway pilot on saving, consumption, and net worth**

Event	% of all participants offered an account	% of all participants who opened an account
Probability of increasing saving by more than twice the monthly contribution ceiling	5.3*	34.2*
Probability of spending more than £25 ($40) on food outside the home	–4.2*	–21.8*
Probability of increasing net worth	1.0	4.8
Probability of increasing net worth by more than twice the monthly contribution ceiling	–0.2	–1.2

SOURCES: IFS and Ipsos Mori 2006; Emmerson and others 2007.

NOTE: *Significant at 1 percent level.

announcement, a consultation was published on the way in which the national scheme would operate. The government consultation summed up the results of the evaluation that provided the justification for the roll-out as including the following factors (among others):

- Individuals were overwhelmingly positive about the effect of matching as a simple and easily understood incentive to save.
- It was not necessary to offer match rates as generous as pound-for-pound in order to incentivize people to save.
- The pilots led to new saving, particularly among those on lower incomes. However, those on higher incomes were able to recycle existing saving.
- Those living closer to a Halifax branch were more likely to open an account, demonstrating the importance of ease of access.
- Savers learned through learning by doing and welcomed support and guidance at account opening and maturity. However, voluntary opt-in to financial education did not work.
- There were financial inclusion benefits from extending a structured matched savings account to people on lower incomes. Many of these benefits are around formalizing informal savings, promoting regular saving, and getting people to engage with financial institutions for the first time (HM Treasury 2008b).

To ease administration, policy makers decided that eligibility for an existing benefit or tax credit would confer eligibility for a Saving Gateway account. Up to 8 million people—some 20 percent of the working-age population—were to be eligible, making the scheme a potentially very significant intervention. The final match rate announced after the consultation was 50 percent. Accounts would last two years, with a monthly contribution ceiling of £25.

The evaluation results showed that the ceiling had a significant effect on behavior, as many people seemed to treat it as advice or a target level of savings. Consequently, choosing a ceiling that was the lowest tested in the pilots was likely to be an effective way to control costs. Setting a low ceiling would also reduce the problem of savings substitution, in which people with higher incomes and higher existing savings recycled those savings to get the match. In addition, given that some people might try to game the system by recycling savings from noneligible friends or relatives, limiting contributions to the lower level helped constrain costs. However, it would be difficult to prevent such gaming once the system became an established part of the savings infrastructure, given that accounts were short term and complete access was to be allowed at account maturity.

Complete freedom of access to funds in the accounts was in contrast to other countries, which tried to mandate the use of savings for education or home purchase. Although restrictions may have merits, if the aim is to provide people with savings for a "rainy day" and increase flexibility for the unexpected, it is important to allow flexibility on the use of the savings.

The government introduced and passed the legislation to authorize the scheme in 2009 (the Saving Gateway Accounts Act 2009). It then worked with potential suppliers and interested parties, such as groups working with low-income people, to craft the final design and plan the roll-out.[10]

The General Election and the End of the Saving Gateway Scheme

The launch date was set for July 2010. In May 2010, the United Kingdom held a general election, in which a Conservative–Liberal Democrat coalition replaced the Labour government. Against the backdrop of challenging public finances, the new government announced in its first budget in June 2010 that it could not afford to extend the Saving Gateway (HM Treasury 2010).

Although the new government scrapped the scheme, the concept of matched saving for low-income people has appeal across the political spectrum. It has a clear fairness angle in providing incentives for a group typically excluded from tax incentive–based approaches, which typically benefit the better-off. It also has a clear "self-help" rationale. Personal responsibility and control over finances underpin individuals' attempts to improve their own lives; initial assistance from the government creates a virtuous circle that frees the state from the need to provide further assistance when individuals encounter inevitable income shocks. The absence of any controls over the use of the money is consistent with a libertarian view of giving people control over their own decisions. Broad interest in helping people create their own savings on which to fall back on did not translate into proposals to curtail their almost instant access to high-cost credit cards and store cards, which undermines many of the best intentions of would-be savers.

Conclusion and Policy Implications

The Saving Gateway was an attempt to address the long-standing problem of low or negative saving by people with low incomes. It aimed to test matching as a new approach to engage and incentivize saving. The approach offered financial incentives that were easier to calculate and of significantly greater value than tax relief for the target group. Two pilots were conducted, both independently evaluated.

The pilots provided positive qualitative evidence of the impact on people's lives, including increased experiences of emotional well-being and the sense of being in control. Both showed that significant balances could be built up in a savings account by people with relatively low incomes.

The second pilot showed that low-income people who opened accounts significantly increased their savings and reduced their consumption. People with higher incomes were more likely to recycle existing savings, showing the importance of proper targeting of the incentives.

A wide range of observable characteristics were controlled for. However, it is impossible to rule out the chance that some unobserved characteristics could have driven the increased saving. The probability that participants in the second pilot increased overall saving relative to the control group was 34 percent. However, this probability fell to just 5 percent once the impact of being offered but not actually opening an account was tested.

Following the pilots, the previous government decided to roll out the scheme nationally. It was convinced of the benefits—and of the absence of viable alternatives to increase saving for low-income people. The planned roll-out directly incorporated many of the lessons from the pilots. The government elected in May 2010 canceled the national scheme on the grounds that it was unaffordable.

Several key lessons emerge from this experience:

- Matching seems to have a positive impact on saving. It provides a way to reach groups typically excluded from incentives to save based on tax relief. There are issues of deadweight—paying people to do things they would have done anyway—once people outside the low-income target group are included. However, alternative programs (tax relief, direct grants, and financial education) face similar or greater problems and may well cost more. The do-nothing option is very likely to lead to a continuation of low saving and financial exclusion.

- There appear to be strong diminishing returns to more generous match levels—certainly above 50 percent. Contribution ceilings appear to dominate match rates in terms of how much people actually save once they join the scheme, but more generous matches appear to make people more likely to take up the scheme in the first place. Future policy could offer a generous initial match to encourage participation and then reduce it.

- Piloting with independent evaluation is a crucial way to improve policy. There is an inevitable loss of control by policy makers, but there are real benefits to improving scheme design—or not going ahead with a policy that does not seem to deliver the promised benefit.

- Perfect experimental design is difficult if subjects need actively to choose to engage in a program (for example, by transferring their own money into accounts). Selectivity issues inevitably occur even after controlling for a wide range of observable characteristics. There is still value in piloting, however, and using real people in real situations may well be preferable to simulated markets with more control.

- In an ideal world, the behavior of participants would be reviewed 5–10 years later. Testing payoffs such as developing a saving habit or avoiding high-cost debt requires actual experience rather than reported intentions, which are often overly optimistic.

- Pilots increase the lead time between policy formulation and the establishment of a program. During this time, the window of opportunity for action may close, even for good programs. Finding ways to increase the number of pilots financed from research budgets and speed the implementation and evaluation of pilots would be useful.

- Political risk can affect the willingness of the private sector to participate as a delivery channel, because the investment in systems and training may be wasted if the scheme does not go ahead. Gaining some political consensus can help reduce the risk of government failure in delivering and sustaining an intervention.

- "Choice architecture" is important. A generous attention-grabbing match helped enroll people in the scheme—the equivalent of well-established marketing practice in many markets. Once they have an account, individuals seem to view contribution ceilings as contribution targets. Scheme designers may thus have a high degree of control over the balances people accumulate in the accounts.

Notes

1. Schemes included personal equity plans (PEPs), introduced in 1986; tax-exempt special saving accounts (TESSAs), introduced in 1990; and individual saving accounts (ISAs), which effectively replaced tax-exempt special saving accounts and personal equity plans, introduced in 1999.

2. Although the argument was not made in these terms, the aim was to increase people's consumption and saving by helping them avoid wasting money on very high-cost unsecured debt (through credit cards and store credits, for example).

3. Both authors were part of the team selected to produce the independent evaluation report on the second Saving Gateway pilot.

4. Currency values in this chapter are given in U.K. pounds; £1 = $1.6132.

5. People recruited were receiving various forms of employment and unemployment benefits. Maximum individual income was £11,000; maximum household income was £15,000.

6. The median was higher than the mean because most people contributed the maximum but some did not—thus the median was also the maximum.

7. Some people went backward: 7 percent of people who said they tended to put money away for the long term at account opening said they did not save at all when asked at account maturity. This result may reflect the fact that their circumstances changed in the interim, or it may be evidence of significant instability in people's expressed preferences between surveys, which should introduce a note of caution in interpreting survey results.

8. A second pilot was also chosen because by 2005 the public finance environment in the United Kingdom had already started to become tighter. As a result, funds for a national roll-out were not as readily available, despite some political and social pressure to start a national scheme right away.

9. The evaluation included more sophisticated econometric analysis on the conversion rate which did not alter the general message that there was an impact from the generosity of the match.

10. HMRC Saving Gateway news updates were designed "to let you know the what, how and when as we progress towards launch this summer" (HMRC is the U.K. tax authority) (HMRC 2010).

References

Emmerson, C., and M. Wakefield. 2003. "Increasing Support for Those on Lower Incomes: Is the Saving Gateway the Best Policy Response?" *Fiscal Studies* 24 (2): 167–95.

Emmerson, C., G. Tetlow, M. Wakefield, P. Harvey, N. Pettigrew, and R. Madden 2007. "Final Evaluation of the Saving Gateway 2 Pilot: Main Report." Institute for Fiscal Studies and Ipsos Mori, London.

HM Treasury. 2001. "The Modernisation of Britain's Tax and Benefit System." No. 8 and No. 9, London.

———. 2004. "Pre-Budget Report: Opportunity for All: The Strength to Take the Long-Term Decisions for Britain." London.

———. 2008a. "Budget 2008: Stability and Opportunity: Building a Strong, Sustainable Future." London.

———. 2008b. "The Saving Gateway: Operating a National Scheme." March, London.

———. 2010. "Budget 2010: Responsibility, Freedom, Fairness: A Five Year Plan to Rebuild the Economy." June, London.

HMRC. 2010. "Saving Gateway News Updates Designed 'To Let You Know the What, How and When as We Progress Towards Launch This Summer.'" London.

IFS (Institute for Fiscal Studies), and Ipsos Mori. 2006. "Interim Evaluation of Saving Gateway 2: A Report Prepared for Government." London.

Kempson, E., S. McKay, and S. Collard. 2005. "Encouraging Saving among Low-Income Households: Final Report on the Saving Gateway Pilot Project." Personal Finance Research Centre, University of Bristol.

Sodha, S., and Lister, R. 2006. "The Saving Gateway: From Principles to Practice." Institute for Public Policy Research, London.

CHAPTER 7

Matching Defined Contribution Pension Schemes in Japan

Noriyuki Takayama

More than 10 years have passed since Japan began offering defined contribution plans. Contrary to expectations, take-up has been weak, partly because account balances can be cashed out only after age 60. Beginning in January 2012, voluntary defined contribution occupational plans began to implement a new system of matching contributions. The design is very specific to the Japanese context, with workers given the chance to match employer contributions on a tax-preferred basis rather than the opposite design found in other settings. Although it is too early to determine outcomes, experience with the take-up of defined contribution plans in Japan and the lack of incentives for workers to participate suggest that the effects will not be strong.

The use of matching contributions has emerged in a variety of countries as an incentive to extend pension coverage (Palacios and Robalino 2009). In Japan, employer matching contributions in addition to government transfers now play a crucial role in extending social security coverage. This chapter provides a summary of the structure of the Japanese pension system (figure 7.1) and outlines the role of matching contributions within this system.

The Japanese occupational pension system remains significantly oriented toward the provision of retirement benefits in the form of lump-sum payments from an employer at the point of retirement. About 85 percent of employers provide benefit payments in this form, making it a significant part of retirement income, especially for long-term regular employees. According to a 2011 survey conducted by Japan's National Personnel Authority, the average private sector employee with service of 20 years or more received ¥25 million from his or her employer as the present value of all retirement benefits, including annuities.[1] This amount is equivalent to 10–12 times the employee's *annual* benefit from social security.

In January 2012, after many years of development, voluntary defined contribution occupational plans began to implement a new system of matching contributions. The design of these arrangements is very specific to the Japanese context. In contrast to the much longer established employer-based systems in the United States described in chapter 3, where the term *matching contributions* refers to employer contributions, in Japan the term refers to employee contributions to match the employer contributions that provided virtually all payments into occupational pensions until 2011. The new employee

The author is very grateful for the financial support from the academic Project on Intergenerational Equity (PIE), funded by the Grant-in-Aid for Specially Promoted Research from the Japan Society for the Promotion of Science (grant number 22000001).

FIGURE 7.1 **Retirement benefits in Japan as of March 2011**

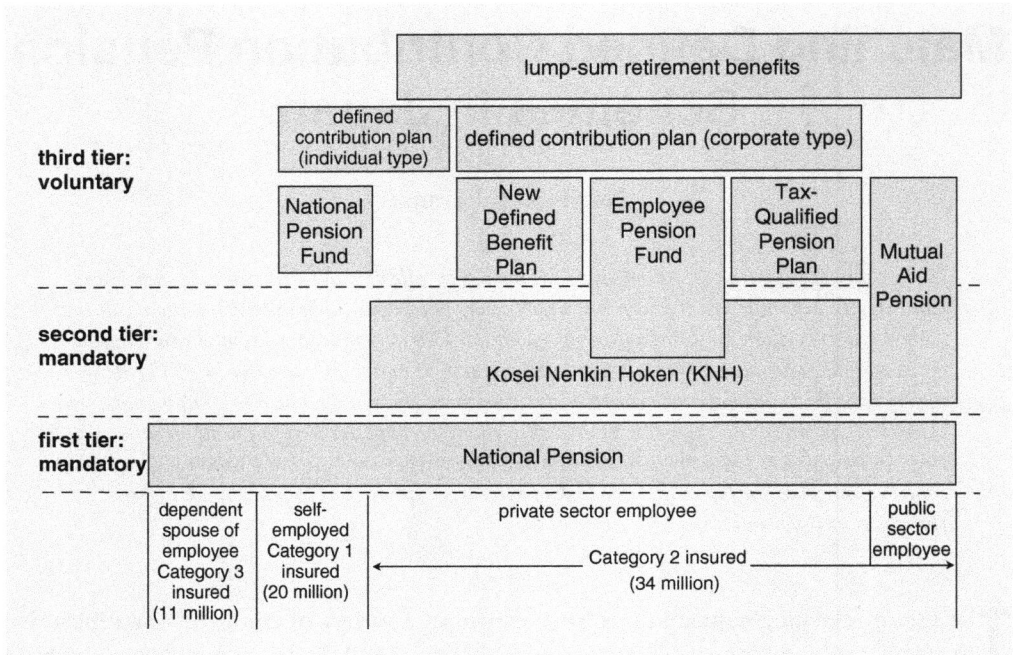

matching contributions have been afforded preferential tax treatment by excluding the contributions from income and deferring taxation in the accumulated fund balances until they are withdrawn. Many Japanese are now waiting to see the effect this new development will have in the field of pensions.

This chapter describes the matching pension schemes in Japan, examines the impact they have had, and considers potential future outcomes. The chapter is organized as follows. The first section provides a brief summary of Japan's social security system. The following section explains how matching contributions from employers and the government have extended the coverage of pensions within this system. The third section provides an overview of occupational and individual pension plans in Japan. The fourth section discusses the new employee matching contributions to defined contribution plans. The last section offers some observations on the future prospects for occupational pensions.

Japan's Social Security Pension Programs

Japan has a two-tier defined benefit system of social security pensions. The first tier provides a flat-rate basic benefit; the second tier provides an earnings-related benefit. The basic figures on social security pensions in Japan are summarized in table 7.1. Eligibility for the first tier is universal for all residents of Japan. It covers not only employees but also the self-employed, the unemployed, and nonemployed adults, including full-time housewives (and househusbands). The only people eligible for earnings-related pensions are regular full-time employees who worked 30 hours or more a week. The system also provides a pension benefit to dependent spouses of regular employees.

TABLE 7.1 **Japanese social security at a glance**

Program type	1965	1985	2008
Kosei Nenkin Hoken (KNH) for private sector employees			
Number of contributors (millions)	19.0	27.0	34.0
Number of old-age benefit recipients (millions)	0.2	3.3	13.0
Contribution rate (%)	5.5	12.4	15.4
Transfer from general revenue as % of aggregate benefits	20.0	20.0	0.0
Annual amount of contributions (¥, trillions)	0.3	7.5	22.7
Annual amount of transfer from general revenue (¥, trillions)	0.01	0.90	0.00
Annual amount of aggregate benefits (¥, trillions)	0.04	6.50	340
Current account surplus/deficit (¥, trillions)	0.34	5.30	−13.50
Funded reserve (¥, trillions)	1.4	50.8	116.6
National Pension			
Number of Category 1 contributors (millions)	17.2	17.6	19.4
Number of old-age benefit recipients (millions)	0.0	6.8	24.0
Amount of contributions per month per person (¥, thousands)	0.10	6.74	14.42
Annual amount of contribution (¥, trillions)	0.02	1.60	1.70
Annual amount of transfer from general revenue (¥, trillions)	0.01	0.80	1.90
Annual amount of benefits (¥, trillions)	0.01	2.80	4.30
Current account surplus/deficit (¥, trillions)	0.04	0.04	−1.30
Funded reserve (¥, trillions)	0.19	2.60	7.20

SOURCE: Ministry of Labor, Health and Welfare 2009.

Only people contributing to the pension scheme for 25 or more years are eligible to receive old-age benefits. The normal pensionable age is 65. The full basic old-age pension is payable after 40 years of contributions. In 2012, the maximum monthly benefit for people with 40 years of coverage was ¥66,000. The annual accrual rate for the earnings-related portion is 0.5481 percent of lifetime average salary. For a typical male retiree (with an average salary earned during 40 years of coverage) and a dependent spouse, the current replacement rate (including basic benefits) represents about 60 percent of lifetime average salary. This average benefit level is set to decrease to 50 percent in the near future.

The contribution rate of the principal program for private sector workers was about 16 percent of salary in 2012, with contributions divided equally between employees and employers (8 percent each).[2] The monthly per person amount of contributions for people covered solely by the flat-rate benefit was about ¥15,000 in 2012. The financing is basically pay-as-you-go, with partial prefunding. The government subsidizes half the total cost of the flat-rate basic benefit and covers all of the administrative expenses.[3]

Matching Contributions for Extending Social Security Coverage

KOSEI NENKIN HOKEN

The principal pension program for private sector employees in Japan is Kosei Nenkin Hoken (KNH). The initial design was based on a funded scheme that would build up reserves by not paying benefits in the early years. One of the main reasons for its establishment in 1942 was to reduce the purchasing power of the Japanese people during World War II through mandatory deduction of contributions from their salary, thereby helping reduce the rate of inflation.

Mandatory occupational retirement benefits with employer contributions were introduced in 1937. They were abolished with the inauguration of the KNH, which mandated both employer and employee contributions.[4] The employers' portion was a partial replacement for their contributions to the previous occupational retirement benefits, effectively establishing the concept of matching contributions. To encourage employees to contribute, the government also implemented a transfer from general revenue, initially set at 10 percent of promised benefits.

The hyperinflation that occurred in Japan just after World War II eliminated any funded reserve of the KNH and had very adverse effects on workers' welfare. Accordingly, in 1948, the (combined) contribution rate was reduced from 11 percent to 3 percent. In response, most employers voluntarily strengthened their occupational retirement benefits. The transfer from general revenue was increased from 10 percent to 15 percent in 1954 and to 20 percent in 1965. These increases were undertaken to extend coverage.[5]

During Japan's long period of rapid economic growth in the late 1950s–1980s, the KNH contribution rate was reinstated to previous levels in a step-by-step process by raising it to 6.4 percent in 1973 and to 12.4 percent in 1986. Coverage of the system was also extended. Before 1988, the KNH was limited to places of business with five or more employees. Since then, the program covers employees at all business establishments.

Contributions from employers and the government, together with industrialization, enabled KNH coverage to expand from 3.5 million contributors in 1942 to 13.5 million in 1970. By 2010, coverage had reached 34.4 million workers.

Some groups, however, still remain outside the system. Employees working less than 30 hours a week or less than two months are not yet covered by the KNH. The current ruling party (the Japan Democratic Party) is considering further extending KNH coverage to include employees working 20 hours or more a week.

NATIONAL PENSION

In 1961, the National Pension was established to cover self-employed workers and the nonemployed, who receive a flat-rate benefit and make flat-rate contributions. To encourage people to participate in the program, the government set contributions at a very low level at the outset, increasing them in stages. It also made a matching contribution from general revenues, initially at a rate of half of each individual's contribution.[6]

The 1961 changes also affected dependent spouses of regular employees, who were allowed to voluntarily participate in the National Pension; since 1986, their participation has been mandatory, albeit with special provisions. Dependent spouses of regular employees (typically full-time housewives) are automatically entitled to the flat-rate basic benefits without being required to make direct individual contributions to the National Pension. The funding for their benefits comes from KNH contributions as well as the transfer from general revenue.[7]

People with low incomes are eligible for contribution exemptions. However, people who do not make contributions are entitled to receive only one-third the flat-rate benefits, equivalent to the value of the transfer from general revenue.[8] Under the various provisions outlined above, the number of people covered by the National Pension increased gradually, from 18.2 million in 1961 to 27.9 million in 1979.

Since 1986, regular employees in the private and public sectors have also participated in the National Pension. Their contributions remain proportional to their earnings; the flat-rate basic benefits of the KNH were harmonized with the flat-rate benefit provided to self-employed and nonemployed people. This arrangement has enabled the financing of the National Pension system to be integrated at the national level.[9] The number of insured people in the National Pension rose from 63.3 million in 1986 to 70.1 million in 2007 (Ministry of Labor, Health and Welfare 2009). Current coverage of social security pensions is near 100 percent.

The development of this national social security system provides only half the story of Japan's retirement income system. Since the bursting of the "bubble economy" at the beginning of the 1990s, Japan has experienced persistent deflation. Many employers have sought to contain their labor costs by reducing the number of regular employees and replacing them with people who work less than 30 hours a week. The movement to more informal (or "atypical") employment was in part motivated by increases in the KNH contribution rate.[10]

Most atypical employees are not covered by the KNH and therefore do not have an earnings-related pension. Their enrollment in the National Pension is mandatory, but many fail to make pension contributions, a practice that will lead to a reduction in social security coverage in the future. In 2010, about 5.5 million people (particularly younger people) were delinquent in making their National Pension flat-rate contributions.[11]

In 2009, the transfer from general revenue was increased from one-third to one-half of the flat-rate basic benefits. This change placed additional burdens on the national budget. Currently, about half the transfer to social security pensions is financed by government borrowing, one factor contributing to the government's increasing deficits.

Occupational and Individual Pensions

Historically, Japanese companies paid lump-sum retirement benefits when workers left their employment. As worker tenure was long and leaving a job before retirement relatively rare, these end of employment arrangements were effectively retirement plans. They were financed through a book-reserve system in which employers estimated the liability but did not set aside dedicated funds to pay the benefit.

In the mid-1960s, two major defined benefit plan types—the Employee Pension Fund (EPF) and the Tax-Qualified Pension Plan (TQPP)—were introduced. Many companies transferred all or part of their lump-sum retirement benefits into the schemes to take advantage of their tax benefits and to smooth cash outflows. In October 2001, a

Defined Contribution Plan was introduced. The following year, the New Defined Benefit Plan was introduced. Each of them differs in terms of applicable laws, regulatory bodies, plan management rules, and taxation.

Some people voluntarily purchase individual annuity products from financial institutions to provide additional sources of retirement income. Since April 1991, self-employed workers have also been able to voluntarily participate in the National Pension Fund to supplement their retirement income. The following section discusses this third tier of the pension system, summarized in table 7.2.[12]

COMPANY-SPONSORED PLANS

Before the 1960s, employer-sponsored retirement benefits in Japan were provided almost exclusively as lump-sum benefits at the time of retirement or separation from employment. In recent decades, defined benefit annuities have also become prevalent. The amount of the benefit is usually lower in the case of voluntary termination (resignation) than in the case of involuntary termination (mandatory retirement, preretirement death, disability, or discharge).

Defined Benefit Plans

The defined benefit plans introduced in the 1960s used to be the predominant employer-sponsored plans in Japan. Their benefit formulas are typically pay related or use a points system. Pay-related plans are based on either final pay or career average pay. Benefits are defined as pensionable pay multiplied by a factor determined by years of service and the reason for termination. In point plans, benefits are equal to the number of accumulated points multiplied by a unit value. Points accrue annually based on the employee's salary grade or job position, age, years of service, or a combination of these factors. Unit value is increased at the employer's discretion or through union negotiation.

In 2002, cash balance plans were introduced in Japan. These plans are technically defined benefit plans, but they resemble defined contribution plans, because they derive benefits from the value of an account balance in relation to a predetermined annuity conversion factor.

Defined benefit plans can be funded through various methods in Japan. The selection of the funding approach can be independent of the plan design. There are five fund types:

- Retirement allowance plans (RAPs)
- EPF plans
- TQPPs
- Fund-type defined benefit plans
- Agreement-type defined benefit plans.

Retirement Allowance Plans

A RAP is an unfunded plan in which the employer's liability is recognized via a book (accounting) reserve. RAP book reserves were tax deductible until March 2002.

The fund reserve is usually not segregated, and security of accrued benefits depends on the financial soundness of the employer. Because benefits are not funded, companies usually administer such plans themselves. For ease of administration, benefit payments are

TABLE 7.2 **Japanese occupational and individual pensions at a glance**

Plan type	2001	2011
Defined benefit plans		
Lump-sum retirement benefits[a]		
TQPP		
Number of plans	73,582	8,051
Number of members (millions)	9.16	1.26
Amount of accumulated assets (¥, trillions)	19	4
EPF		
Number of plans	1,737	595
Number of members (millions)	10.9	4.5
Amount of accumulated assets (¥, trillions)	57	28
New Defined Benefit Plan		
Number of plans	316	10,053
Number of members (millions)	1.35	7.27
Amount of accumulated assets (¥, trillions)	—	42
National Pension Fund		
Number of members (thousands)	787	548
Amount of accumulated assets (¥, trillions)	1.5	2.6
Defined contribution plans		
Corporate type		
Number of plans	361	3,705
Number of members (millions)	0.33	3.71
Amount of accumulated assets (¥, trillions)	—	5.5
Individual type		
Number of plans	7,481	79,639
Number of members (thousands)	14	132

SOURCE: Pension Fund Association 2012.

NOTE: — = not available.

A. Around 94 percent of employees have a lump-sum retirement benefit scheme. In 2011, a private sector employee with 20 years of service or more received ¥25 million from his or her employer as the present value of all retirement benefits, out of which around ¥10 million was paid as lump sum, on average.

usually made in lump-sum form only. RAPs provide employers with more flexibility to change than do other plan types.[13]

Employee Pension Funds

The framework for EPFs was introduced in October 1966. An EPF is a separate independent legal entity established by a single employer or jointly by several employers with approval by the Ministry of Health, Labor and Welfare. It is an externally funded plan whose principal purpose must be the payment of old-age pension benefits to participants.

EPFs are integrated with the social security system. Every EPF contracts out a part of the earnings-related old-age pension under the KNH and provides an additional pension from the fund on top of that portion. In return for paying the earnings-related old-age pension on behalf of the government, an EPF receives a contribution rebate. The entire system under an EPF is called the Daiko system.

For the part of the benefit that is contracted out, the EPF must provide a benefit that is greater than the benefit that would have been received under the social security system (what is known as a "plus alpha benefit") and an additional benefit on top of this contracted-out benefit.[14] The distribution of benefits must be nondiscriminatory. The contracted-out benefits and the plus alpha benefits are called the "basic part"; additional benefits are known as the "additional part."

Eligibility for receiving benefits for the basic part is one month of participation in an EPF. Benefits must be paid in the form of a life annuity. If a participant terminates employment within 15 years of service, the assets equal to the present value of the accrued benefits are transferred to the Pension Fund Association, which takes over the responsibility of paying benefits.[15] For the "additional part" benefits, the maximum allowable eligibility requirements are 20 years of service for an annuity and 3 years of service for a lump-sum withdrawal. Annuity payments must begin no later than age 65. More than half of accrued benefits for the additional portion and the plus alpha portion must be paid as a life annuity, with the maximum guarantee period of 20 years or the maximum guarantee age of 85. Beneficiaries can opt to receive a lump sum instead of a life annuity, but the amount of the lump sum must be less than the present value of the life annuity calculated using the statutory minimum assumed interest rate. An EPF may provide disability benefits and survivor benefits.

Employers usually pay all contributions for plus alpha and additional benefits, although employee contributions are allowed. Employer contributions to an EPF are tax deductible and are not treated as taxable income to employees. Employee contributions can be fully deducted in calculating income tax. This tax treatment distinguishes the EPF taxation from TQPPs and New Defined Benefit Plans (described below).

Investment earnings are tax deferred. Plan assets are generally not subject to an annual special corporation tax. However, plan assets that exceed 2.84 times the contracted-out benefits are subject to a special corporate tax. Lump-sum benefits paid to beneficiaries are taxed as retirement benefits (with a service-year-related deduction), for which the tax rate is lower than for earned income. Annuity benefits are subject to a special income deduction. Survivor benefits are tax free.

Mainly because of an unfavorable investment environment, many EPFs were dissolved during the past 15 years. The Ministry of Health, Labor and Welfare must approve

EPF dissolutions before EPFs settle their assets. Stringent prerequisites must be met before approval of dissolution is granted. If EPF assets are less than the value of the corresponding contracted-out benefits, a one-time contribution to cover the shortfall is required. Once an EPF is dissolved, assets with a value corresponding to contracted-out benefits are transferred to the Pension Fund Association, which takes over responsibility for paying contracted-out benefits. Any residual assets are allocated to participants and beneficiaries according to the rule of distribution stipulated by the EPF plan documents. Participants can choose to receive these benefits as a lump sum or to transfer them to the Pension Fund Association for future annuity payments.

Employers must compensate for the investment loss derived from the contracted-out portion and recognize the projected value of benefits for the contracted-out portion on their books. The contracted-out portion used to bring in extra profits to EPFs. Once the investment environment turned adverse, however, the contracted-out portion began to hurt EPF operation.

Many employers and trade unions lobbied for legislation that allows EPFs to return the contracted-out portion to the original social security regime. Since April 2002, it has been possible for EPFs to do so (Daiko-henjo). Once EPFs return the contracted-out portion, additional benefits and plus alpha benefits are transformed into New Defined Benefit Plans.

The number of EPFs reached a peak of 1,225 in 1997. Thereafter it began to decrease sharply, falling to 568 in 2011, covering 4.4 million employees. The Daiko-henjo amounted to 813 by 2009.

Tax-Qualified Pension Plans

The TQPP, introduced in 1962, used to be one of the two major occupational pension schemes in Japan. It was an externally funded, tax-favored retirement benefit plan. Because there was no minimum participation requirement, TQPPs were popular among small to medium-size companies.

TQPPs had no benefit eligibility requirements (unlike EPFs and New Defined Benefit Plans), and benefits were paid upon termination of employment (in contrast, EPFs and New Defined Benefit Plans pay benefits when participants attain a prescribed age). The form of payment had to be either a fixed annuity of five years or longer or a life annuity (most TQPPs provided only fixed annuities). Beneficiaries could opt to receive a lump sum instead of annuities, but the amount of the lump sum was less than the present value of annuities calculated with the interest rate stipulated in the plan document. TQPPs could provide survivor benefits but not disability benefits.

Policy makers eventually recognized that TQPP regulations were inadequate to protect employees' rights to receive benefits. As a result, employers were required to convert TQPPs to other types of pension plans by March 2012. Some TQPP sponsors switched to other types of pension plans; most simply terminated their TQPPs, leaving employees without any retirement plan.

New Defined Benefit Plans

Two kinds of New Defined Benefit Plans—the *fund type* and the *agreement type*—were introduced in April 2002, in order to unify regulations and enhance protection of vested benefits for participants.

Fund-type plans are similar to EPFs, with separate governing boards but without contracted-out benefits. The legal minimum number of participants for the fund type is 300. Existing EPFs can switch to the plans by surrendering contracted-out benefits to the government.

Agreement-type funds replaced TQPPs, which had problems protecting vested benefits because plan operations were not fully regulated and there were no minimum standards to ensure the annual evaluation and maintenance of full funding status. They are similar to TQPPs. They have a contract with a lead manager, but, unlike TQPPs, they are subject to minimum funding rules, fiduciary duties, and disclosures.

There is no legal minimum number of participants for an agreement-type plan. Benefits must be provided as a fixed annuity of at least five years or as a life annuity. Old-age annuity benefits must begin to be paid between the ages of 60 and 65 for normal retirement but can begin as early as age 50 for early retirees. Beneficiaries can opt for a lump-sum payment instead of annuity payments. The lump-sum value must be equal to or less than the present value of annuities for a guaranteed period. Maximum benefit eligibility requirements are 20 years of service for an annuity and 3 years of service for a lump-sum payout. Survivor and disability benefits are permitted.

To protect vested benefits for participants, strict funding rules apply. Employers make contributions to fund plan assets. Employees are permitted to contribute up to 50 percent of total contributions if plan documents allow them to do so. Actuarial valuation must be performed at least every five years. Each employer determines an assumed interest rate, based on long-term expected investment returns. However, the rate must be equal to or above the minimum assumed interest rate set by the Ministry of Health, Labor and Welfare.

The New Defined Benefit Plan law also permits cash balance–type plans. Pay credit is given to notional accounts, along with an interest credit based on the following rates:

- A fixed rate
- A government bond rate or other objectively measurable stable index (the national wage index or the cost of living index is acceptable; the equity index is not)
- A combination of a fixed rate and a government bond rate
- A fixed or government bond rate with applicable minimums or maximums.

The conversion rate between annuity and lump-sum payments can be indexed regardless of the plan design structure.

In 2011, there were 610 fund-type and 11,593 agreement-type defined benefit plans in Japan, together covering 7.3 million employees.

Defined Contribution Plans

The number of defined contribution plan documents approved by the government has constantly increased since the plans were first introduced in Japan in October 2001. Still, as of the end of October 2011, only 4,013 plans had been approved, covering just 16,000 employers. The numbers of participants were 4.1 million in corporate-type defined contribution plans and 132,000 in individual-type defined contribution plans.

One motivation for this trend is that many companies are replacing seniority pay systems with performance-based compensation. Traditional retirement benefit plans that favor long-term workers are inconsistent with this approach to managing human resources.

More and more companies are trying to reflect individual work performance in the design of retirement benefits. Companies are also trying to improve employees' understanding and appreciation of retirement benefits. More-visible retirement plans, such as defined contribution plans and cash balance plans with individual accounts, are perceived as advancing this objective.

The Japanese labor market is also becoming more fluid and workers more mobile. Traditional retirement plan designs based on a lifetime employment model are not suitable for attracting and retaining talented people.

Mergers and acquisitions have also become prevalent since the deregulation of business reorganization rules. Harmonization of retirement benefits is required in merger and acquisition situations. The need for flexibility to accommodate these organizational changes has provided an important impetus for the emergence of defined contribution plans.

There are two types of defined contribution plans in Japan: corporate-type and individual-type plans. The amount of employer contributions is fixed regardless of its profits: contribution formulas must be a fixed percentage of participants' pay or a fixed amount for every participant. Employee contributions were not originally allowed in corporate-type defined contribution plans, but they have been allowed since January 2012.

In individual-type defined contribution plans, employees or self-employed workers can contribute to the plan at their discretion. Employers, however, cannot make matching contributions to individual-type defined contribution plans. (In Japan, "matching contributions" in defined contribution plans refers to employee contributions that are made to match those of the employer rather than employer matching of employee contributions, as in the United Kingdom and the United States.)

Regular employees who are covered by the KNH are eligible for corporate-type defined contribution plans once their employer establishes such a plan. There are two separate contribution limits for corporate-type plans. If employers maintain an EPF or a New Defined Benefit Plan along with their defined contribution plan, contributions to individual accounts are limited to ¥25,500 a month. If they do not maintain such plans, the limit is ¥51,000 a month.

If employers do not sponsor a defined benefit plan or a corporate-type defined contribution plan, employees are eligible to participate in individual-type defined contribution plans. The contribution limit for these plans is ¥23,000 a month. Self-employed workers can participate in individual-type defined contribution plans, with a limit of ¥68,000 a month on their combined contributions to the plan and to the National Pension Fund. Public sector employees and full-time housewives/househusbands are not eligible for either corporate-type or individual-type defined contribution plans.

Participants select investment options from a list presented for their individual account. At least three options must be provided. Bank deposits, mutual funds (investment trusts), and insurance products are commonly presented as investment options. One of the investment options must be a principal-guaranteed product, such as a time deposit or guaranteed investment contract. Securities of the employer can be one investment option, although they are rarely offered. No real estate investment option is permitted. Participants can change their investment options every three months. Plan administrators must provide information on account balances to participants at least once a year.

Benefits are payable when participants with more than 10 years of participation reach age 60. If participants leave the company before age 60, they must roll over the account balances to a new employer's defined contribution plan or an individual-type defined contribution plan. There are two exceptions to this rule. If an employee leaves with no more than three years of participation and becomes ineligible for any type of defined contribution plan (as would be the case for full-time housewives/househusbands or public sector employees), the vested account balance, if any, can be paid out in cash. If an account balance is ¥500,000 or less, a lump-sum withdrawal payment can be received regardless of the participation period. These exceptions were made to eliminate recordkeeping burdens and the maintenance of small account balances.

Participants can start receiving benefits any time between age 60 and 70, but they must begin receiving benefits by age 70. Benefits are paid in a lump sum or in installments extending over 5–20 years. Life annuities can also be offered. After three years of service, participants are 100 percent vested in corporate-type defined contribution plans.

When a participant in an individual-type defined contribution plan changes jobs to become an employee, his or her account balance must be rolled over to the new employer's corporate-type defined contribution plan. If the new employer does not sponsor a corporate-type defined contribution plan, the account balance remains with the individual-type defined contribution plan.

In corporate-type defined contribution plans, employer contributions are a tax-deductible business expense and are not treated as taxable income for employees. In individual-type defined contribution plans, participants can deduct contributions from their taxable income, and investment earnings are tax deferred. Rollover is tax free. Lump-sum benefits paid to beneficiaries are favorably taxed as retirement benefits (with a service-related deduction). The contribution period is considered as the service period. Annuity benefits are also subject to a special income deduction.

Employee Matching Contributions to Defined Contribution Plans

Pension legislation was enacted in August 2011 that authorized the launch of employee matching contributions under current defined contribution plans beginning in January 2012. This new matching scheme is structured as follows (see Endo 2011 for more details):

1. Employee matching contributions for corporate-type plans are voluntary.
2. Employees' matching contributions cannot exceed their employers' contributions.
3. The combined total of the employee and employer contributions cannot exceed the upper limit for tax privileges.
4. Employers are responsible for ensuring that contributions do not exceed the limit.

5. Employee contributions are deducted by the employer from each employee's salary. They are tax deductible at the contribution stage. Investment earnings are not taxed if they remain in the plan.

6. Benefits are payable only after age 60. They represent taxable income when received, although subject to a special income deduction.

The tax privileges and gains from earlier contributions are two selling points for the new scheme, which is intended to make corporate-type defined contribution plans more attractive. Critics have noted, however, that the second and third requirements make the employee matching contribution redundant. Given that the combined tax limit is ¥51,000 a month, the maximum combined contribution of ¥25,500 from an employer limits the employee maximum contribution to the same amount. If the employer contributes less than ¥25,500, the maximum contribution from the employee must decrease accordingly. Consequently, the employee matching maximum contributions will vary depending on the employer contributions, which can result in a different level of allowable contributions among employees of different firms with the same salary.

The new scheme for matching contributions imposes additional handling costs on employers. If the employer contribution to the defined contribution plan is proportional to the salary of each employee, then every year employers are forced to review and confirm whether their employee matching contributions fall below the approved upper limit.

Tax privileges for employee contributions have become both more complicated and less fair, it can be argued, because individual-type defined contribution plans allow monthly matching contributions of up to either ¥23,000 or ¥68,000, whereas corporate-type plans allow matching contributions up to ¥25,500. The wall between individual- and corporate-type plans has been virtually dismantled, but inequalities among individual employees in making contributions to defined contribution plans remain.

Future Prospects for Defined Contribution Pension Plans and Matching Contributions

More than 10 years have passed since defined contribution plans were introduced in Japan. At the time of their introduction, it was widely expected that they would expand rapidly. This did not happen. In March 2011, the aggregate amount of accumulated assets in occupational plans was only about ¥5.5 trillion for defined contribution plans and about ¥80 trillion for defined benefit plans.

Why has the growth of defined contribution plans been so slow? The major factor is the restriction of cash-out only after age 60. Most small and medium-size companies used to pay lump-sum retirement benefits to early leavers or employees reaching the mandatory retirement age from their occupational pension plans. The fact that defined contribution plans are not able to do so makes them far less attractive to workers and employers than the existing defined benefit plans, which have no such restrictions.

Another factor is the very low maximum imposed on contributions to defined contribution plans (existing defined benefit plans have no maximums). This limit has led potential service providers who might promote the arrangements to believe that defined contribution plans are not a profitable business.

A third factor is that reducing benefits of a defined benefit plan requires the consent of two-thirds of plan participants. When employers want to introduce a defined contribution plan by replacing part of their existing defined benefit plan, this requirement becomes a bottleneck, thereby discouraging them from switching.

A fourth factor is very low (or negative) returns observed in the domestic capital markets for nearly two decades. As of October 2011, about 60 percent of plan participants in Japan had incurred a loss of principal on their accumulated defined contribution assets.

The future of defined contribution plans in Japan will likely depend on whether the design limitations evolve to allow employees to take cash payments at the termination of employment before age 60 and on the potential for a significant increase in the upper limit for contributions. Japan has a long history of not providing tax incentives for personal savings. Saving for retirement is the single exception to this rule. The requirement restricting the ability to cash out before age 60 was imposed in order to provide defined contribution plan contributions with preferential tax treatment similar to that afforded employer-sponsored plans. Individual contributions to defined contribution plans are obliged to follow this rule to receive this tax privilege.

Employer contributions, however, are not necessarily regarded as personal savings but rather as retirement benefits. It is therefore inconsistent with the treatment of other employer-provided benefits to restrict the ability to cash out the benefit upon a change of employment to employer contributions in these plans.

The matching contribution provisions that now apply to defined contribution plans are very recent; the effect these provisions will have on growth within these plans is therefore not yet known. Concerns have already been raised regarding the potential the provisions will have to stimulate meaningful expansion of the nascent defined contribution system. The design of the new arrangement that allows employees to contribute only to the extent that the employer is willing to pay into the plan is the opposite of the approach in other countries, where the sponsor's match provides an inducement for employees to join and contribute. This reversed design does not provide strong incentives for either party, and it imposes additional restrictions and potential burdens on both.

The limited acceptance of these new plans likely will provide a strong example of the importance of context, cultural norms, and perceptions on behavior and the influence that the historical development of a pension system has on the capacity of design innovations such as matching contribution to expand participation and levels of saving. In the presence of a well-established social security system providing meaningful basic benefits to the full population and a relatively high prevalence of supplementary defined benefit arrangements (as indicated in the evidence from other countries in the Organisation for Economic Co-operation and Development presented in chapter 2), there is not likely to be strong demand for supplementary defined contribution savings.

Defined contribution plans could grow in Japan in the long run, but their short-time prospects are weak. Development of these plans crucially depends on the extent to which the schemes evolve to better fit the Japanese environment, meet the needs of participants, and become user friendly.

Notes

1. Currency values in this chapter are given in Japanese yen; ¥ 1 = $0.0128.

2. The contribution rate of Japan's principal pension program for private sector employees, the Kosei Nenkin Hoken (KNH), is to be raised annually until it reaches 18.3 percent in 2017, after which it will essentially become equivalent to a defined contribution plan with pay-as-you-go financing.

3. More detailed explanations of Japan's social security pension system can be found in Takayama (2003, 2004, 2006).

4. Before 1937, old-age security for employees in the private sector and self-employed people in Japan was provided mainly by families. Some companies voluntarily set up their own occupational retirement benefit schemes as a means of strengthening the loyalty of their employees and to pay a lump-sum benefit to employees who were terminated. Public sector workers in Japan have been receiving both pension annuities and a lump-sum retirement benefit since 1875 (see Sakamoto 2011).

5. In the 1960s and 1970s, social insurance coverage worked as a major selling point for employers in recruiting employees.

6. The transfer from general revenue in the National Pension was changed in 1976 because of budget restrictions. It was converted into a matching contribution at the time of benefit payments; one-third of flat-rate pension benefits had begun to be funded by then.

7. This entitlement raises contentious issues (see Takayama 2009 for details).

8. About 5.5 million people were exempted from paying contributions in 2010 (Ministry of Labor, Health and Welfare 2009).

9. The transfer from general revenue to the KNH earnings-related benefits was abolished in 1986, and has been concentrated to match the flat-rate basic benefits of the National Pension.

10. The number of atypical employees in Japan almost doubled between 1990 and 2010, rising from 8.8 million to 17.1 million. The KNH contribution rate rose from 11.3 percent to 15.7 percent over the same period.

11. About 40 percent of nonregular employees and self-employed people are delinquent in paying contributions, equivalent to about 8 percent of the total number of active participants in all social security pension programs in Japan.

12. This section is a revised version of Urata and Takayama (2006). See also Clark and Mitchell (2002).

13. According to a 2008 survey conducted by the Ministry of Labor, Health and Welfare, 64 percent of employers who paid lump-sum retirement benefits utilized RAPs.

14. The plus alpha benefits must be at least 10 percent greater than the contracted-out portion.

15. The Pension Fund Association was founded in 1967 as a federation of EPFs. The main objective of the association is to provide pension benefits to those who seceded from EPFs after a short period and to pay contracted-out benefits to those whose EPFs are dissolved, as well.

References

Clark, R. L., and O. S. Mitchell. 2002. "Strengthening Employment-Based Pensions in Japan." NBER Working Paper 8891, National Bureau of Economic Research, Cambridge, MA.

Endo, T. 2011. "Pension Reform in Japan: The 2011 Law and Future Issues." *Benefits & Compensation International* 41 (5): 15–22.

Ministry of Labor, Health and Welfare. 2009. *The 2009 Actuarial Report on Social Security Pensions*, 2009. (In Japanese.)

Palacios, R., and D. A. Robalino. 2009. "Matching Defined Contributions: A Way to Increase Pension Coverage." In *Closing the Coverage Gap: The Role of Social Pensions and Other Retirement Income Transfers*, ed. R. Holzmann, D. A. Robalino, and N. Takayama, 187–202. Washington, DC: World Bank.

Pension Fund Association. 2012. *Statistical Figures on Occupational Pensions.* (In Japanese.)

Sakamoto, J. 2011. "Civil Service Pension Arrangements in Japan." In *Reforming Pensions for Civil and Military Servants*, ed. N. Takayama, 113–29. Tokyo: Maruzen Publishing Co., Ltd.

Takayama, N., ed. 2003. *Taste of Pie: Searching for Better Pension Provisions in Developed Countries.* Tokyo: Maruzen Publishing Co., Ltd.

———. 2004. "Changes in the Pension System." *Japan Echo* 31 (5): 9–12.

———. 2006. "Reforming Social Security in Japan: Is NDC the Answer?" In *Pension Reform: Issues and Prospects for Non-Financial Defined Contribution (NDC) Schemes*, ed. R. Holzmann and E. Palmer, 639–47. Washington, DC: World Bank.

———. 2009. "Pension Coverage in Japan." In *Closing the Coverage Gap: The Role of Social Pensions and Other Retirement Income Transfers*, ed. R. Holzmann, D. A. Robalino, and N. Takayama, 111–18. Washington, DC: World Bank.

Urata, H., and N. Takayama. 2006. "Pension Regulation in Japan: Issues and Reforms." In *Labour Market Regulation and Deregulation in Asia*, ed. C. Brassard and S. Acharya, 197–218. New Delhi: Academic Foundation.

CHAPTER 8

Matching Contributions and Compliance in Korea's National Pension Program

Hyungpyo Moon

To encourage compliance with its national pension program, the government of the Repub-lic of Korea has been providing matching subsidies to farmers and fishers of up to half of their contribution since 1995. Regression estimates indicate that subsidized groups were more than 10 percentage points more likely to contribute than other self-employed workers, after controlling for other variables, and that differences in contribution rates were larger among low-income workers. The results imply that policy makers can expect contributions to the national pension system to rise if similar subsidies are provided to other groups of workers with low incomes.

Enormous changes are expected in the Republic of Korea as a result of the rapid aging of the population and the extremely low birth rate. The number of people age 65 and older will reach 16.2 million in 2050, 3.7 times the 4.4 million people this age in 2005, according to projections by the National Statistical Office (2006). A rapidly aging popula-tion will increase the importance of old-age income security and significantly affect public pension finance. Korea thus now faces two major policy challenges: enhancing the role of the old-age income security system as early as possible and at the same time improving the financial sustainability of the public pension system.

Although the national pension became applicable to the entire population in 1999, more than a third of all workers are not contributing. A majority of these nonpayers are poor or low-income people with insecure employment, such as atypical workers, the self-employed, and small business owners. Many of them will have difficulty securing pension rights after retirement. Even if they are entitled to pensions, the amount of their benefits may not be enough to support them. Extensive noncompliance increases the risk that many people will fall into poverty in old age.

Recognizing the problems of narrow coverage of the national pension ("pension blind spots"), the government has tried to expand pension coverage and compliance of groups in which contributions are low. In addition to building up the administrative abil-ity to detect the actual income of informal workers and the self-employed, the govern-ment is discussing more radical policy measures. One option is to encourage people who are not currently covered to participate by subsidizing their pension contributions. The main purpose of the contribution subsidy is to prevent old-age poverty rather than provid-ing ex post financial support after people become poor late in life.

Subsidizing contributions to the national pension is not an entirely new idea in Korea. The government has been partially subsidizing the contributions of farmers and fishers to encourage their participation by reducing the contribution burden since compulsory coverage of the national pension was extended to all residents in rural areas in 1995. Has the contribution subsidy increased pension participation of farmers and fishers? This chapter examines the empirical evidence on the effectiveness of the contribution subsidy by comparing the compliance behavior of subsidized farmers and fishers with behavior of nonsubsidized self-employed workers.

The chapter is organized as follows. The first section briefly reviews the narrow coverage of the national pension scheme in Korea. The second section examines the compliance behavior of the insured. The third section empirically investigates the effectiveness of the contribution subsidy on increasing compliance with the scheme. The last section summarizes the chapter's findings.

Coverage of the National Pension

The Korean national pension is a traditional contributory defined benefit pension plan (box 8.1). General coverage of the national pension has grown rapidly since the scheme was first introduced in 1988 (figure 8.1). By 1999, it became a nominally universal pension system, after all working-age Koreans were obliged to contribute to the scheme. The scheme covers all resident citizens of Korea age 18–59, regardless of their income. About

---

BOX 8.1 **The National Pension Scheme in Korea**

The national pension, as a defined benefit scheme which was first introduced in 1988, is designed to function as an income protection system against a wide range of social risks including old age, disability, and death. All residents in Korea from 18 to less than 60 years of age, regardless of their income, are legally covered under the scheme.

The basic pension amount, which is the basis for the calculation of old-age, disability, and survivor pension, is composed of earnings-related and redistributive components. The basic pension amount is in direct proportion to the insured period, but not to the insured person's income. The current income replacement rate of old-age pension of the insured person with median income and a 40-year insured period is approximately 50 percent. The replacement rate is being reduced by 0.5 percentage points annually until reaching 40 percent in 2028. A price indexing system is adopted to maintain the real value of the pension amount. At present, the normal age eligible for an old-age pension is 60, but it shall be gradually increased to 65 by 2033. The expenditure required for payment of benefits is mainly financed from contributions paid by insured persons and their employers. The contribution rate was set low at the initial stage of the scheme (3 percent in 1988) and has been gradually increased to the current 9 percent. It will be adjusted according to the financial recalculation planned to be conducted every five years. The government's financial support is temporarily provided for some portion of contributions paid by farmers and fishers for the purpose of alleviating the financial burden on them.

SOURCE: National Pension Service website (http://english.nps.or.kr).

FIGURE 8.1 **Coverage of Korea's national pension system, 1988–2009**

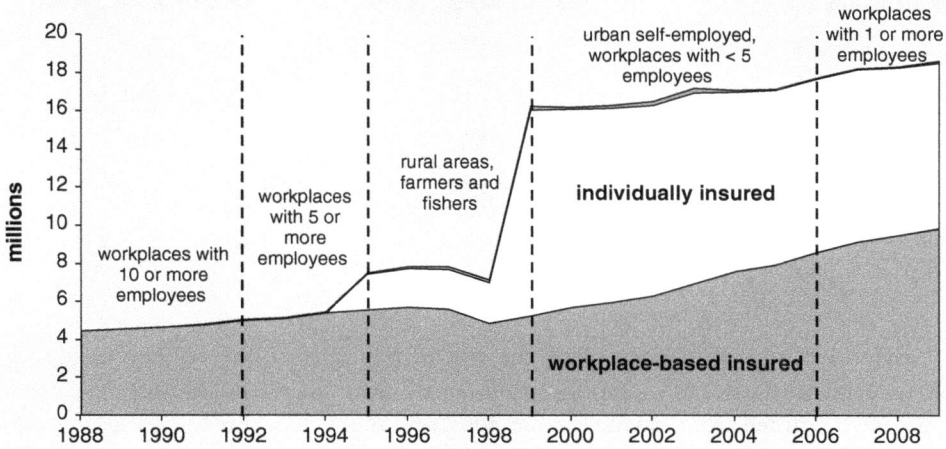

SOURCE: National Pension Service website (http://english.nps.or.kr).

92 percent of the workforce age 18–59 is currently covered by public pension programs. The national pension covers 86 percent of the workforce; the other 6 percent are covered by pension schemes for civil servants, military personnel, and private school teachers.

People insured by the national pension scheme are divided into two main groups: people who are insured through their workplace and people who are insured individually. All employers are required to provide workplace-based coverage if they have even a single employee. The contributions of people covered by workplace-based insurance are shared equally by the employer and the employee. Employers handle the acquisition of pension rights, the loss of insured status, and the payment of contributions. All self-employed workers are individually insured. They are supposed to pay both halves of their contribution and report their income status themselves.

The category of individually insured people includes those who are exempted from making contributions. Where a mandatorily insured person has temporary difficulty making a contribution because of termination of business, loss of employment, or a calamity or accident, he or she can be exempted from doing so during the relevant period without losing coverage. Once the person earns income again, he or she should then report to the National Pension Service and resume making contributions. According to official statistics, 5 million people were exempted from making contributions in 2009, 27.1 percent of all insured people and 58.2 percent of all individually insured people (table 8.1).

Among income reporters, a large number of insured people remain delinquent. As of 2009, the system collected 92 percent of the amount it should have collected (from both workplace-based and individually insured workers), but only 62 percent of all individually insured people made their contributions (National Pension Service 2009). About half of the people who failed to pay contributions are long-term delinquents with more than two years of deferral.

TABLE 8.1 **Number of people insured by Korea's national pension, 2009**

Type of insured	Number covered (millions)	Proportion covered (%)
Workplace based	9.87	53.0
Individually insured	8.68	47.0
Income reporter	3.63	19.9
Contribution exemption	5.05	27.1

SOURCE: National Pension Service 2009.

Extensive noncompliance raises the risk of falling into poverty late in life. Such risks are evident in cases of exemption from contribution payment. Almost 90 percent of the people exempted from payment were poor, and more than three-fourths were jobless (table 8.2). The number of unemployed among the exempted from contribution payments is much higher than the national unemployment rate (3.6 percent in 2009). A direct comparison may not be fair, however, given that the number of insured but exempted from payment includes the economically inactive population (who paid contributions while employed) as well as the unemployed. Nevertheless, the large gap between the two numbers implies the limited capability of the government to gather accurate information on the personal income of income earners. The majority of informal sector workers and self-employed small business owners evade income reporting or underreport their incomes in order to avoid contributing to the pension plan. Their actual incomes are very difficult to measure because of the poor administrative capability of the pension system. As a result, although they are engaged in economic activities, many informal workers and small business owners are exempt from paying contributions to the system.

TABLE 8.2 **Reasons for exemption from contributing to Korea's national pension plan, 2009**

Reason for exemption	Number of exemptions (thousands)	Percentage of total
Jobless	3,817	75.6
Business closure	433	8.6
Student	278	5.5
Temporary leave	92	1.8
Livelihood difficulties	7	0.1
Other[a]	422	8.4
Total	5,052	100.0

SOURCE: National Pension Service 2009.

A. Includes military personnel, inmates, missing people, hospital patients, and others.

Who Contributes to the National Pension System and Who Does Not?

This section examines the characteristics of people who contribute to the national pension and the reasons why people do not contribute. It is based on data from the 2008 Korea Welfare Panel Study, the largest source of panel data in Korea. The survey, which has followed more than 7,000 households since 2006, includes farming and fishing households, which makes it suitable for this study.[1] This analysis extracts 4,115 individuals age 18–59, the target age of the national pension, from the 2008 data.

About a third (31 percent) of the population in the sample did not contribute to the national pension (table 8.3). Among people insured through their workplace, 99.8 percent contributed. In contrast, just 34.4 percent of individually insured people did so, mainly because 57 percent of all individually insured people were exempt. However, even among people who reported their income, the delinquency rate was almost 20 percent, much higher than the rate for people insured at their workplace.

More than half of respondents classified as exempt engage in economic activities, indicating the seriousness of "blind-spot" problems arising from poor administrative capability in gathering accurate information on income status. Among the individually insured, 33.4 percent are actually wage workers, the majority of whom are legally entitled to workplace-based insurance. These workers remained individually insured because their status reports were not submitted properly.

The compliance rate of the individually insured shows considerable differences by occupational status. The noncompliance rate of wage workers averaged 72.2 percent—1.7 times the 41.5 percent noncompliance rate among the self-employed. The noncompliance

TABLE 8.3 **Number of people covered by Korea's national pension plan, by occupational and participation status, 2007**

| | | Non–wage worker | | | Wage worker | | | |
Category	Total	Sub-total	Employer	Self-employed	Sub-total	Regular worker	Temporary worker	Daily laborer	Other[a]
Workplace based	2,156								
Contribution	2,152	62	57	5	2,081	1,888	171	22	9
Noncontribution	5	1	1	0	4	4	0	0	0
Individually insured	1,959								
Contribution	674	406	129	277	182	92	29	62	85
Noncontribution	1,285	288	64	225	474	161	136	176	523
Exemption	1,111	195	46	149	412	146	115	151	504
Delinquent	169	92	18	75	60	15	20	25	17

SOURCE: Author, based on data from the Korea Welfare Panel Study 2008.

A. Includes unpaid family workers, unemployed, and economically nonactive population.

rate of wage workers was 63.6 percent for regular workers, 74.1 percent for daily labor-ers, and 82.7 percent for temporary workers. These data suggest that nonregular workers should be considered the primary target in developing policy measures to reduce pension blind spots.

Table 8.4 shows the characteristics of individually insured and uninsured people (exempt payers and delinquents). The characteristic that stands out most is that the aver-age disposable income of individually uninsured people is more than 20 percent lower than that of individually insured people. Also, as household incomes decrease, the non-compliance rate increases rapidly, meaning that economic status is a significant determi-nant of participation in the pension system. Individually uninsured people tend to have a higher education level than insured people, and younger people have lower compliance rates than older people (the noncompliance rate of people in their 30s or younger is as high as 95 percent). The compliance rate of women is about 20 percent lower than that of men, meaning there are bigger blind spots among women.

A regression analysis using the probit model was conducted in order to examine the effects of individual characteristics on compliance behavior. The results show the estima-tion of the compliance probability of 1,993 individually insured people (table 8.5). As expected, the compliance probability of individually insured people is highly sensitive to variables such as sex, age, and income. The probability of compliance appears to rise significantly with income and age; it is also higher for men than women. The estimated coefficients on educational background are negative and statistically insignificant, indicat-ing that education has little impact on compliance.

The compliance probability of individually insured people varies significantly with occupational status. The compliance probability of daily laborers is not statistically sig-nificantly different from that of temporary workers (whose probability of compliance is 17.4 percent). In contrast, the probability of compliance increases by 18.4 percentage points for regular workers and by 31.3 percentage points for the self-employed. Even after controlling for individual characteristics, among individually insured people the compli-ance probability of wage workers and the self-employed shows considerable differences. The compliance probability of temporary and daily laborers is particularly low.

How Effective Has the Government's Contribution Subsidy to Farmers and Fishers Been?

Recognizing that expanding coverage of the national pension is essential to preparing for a rapidly aging society, the government has made efforts to reduce the blind spots in the national pension. As part of such efforts, the Ministry of Health and Welfare recently undertook a review of a matching contribution subsidy that would provide low-income individually insured people with a subsidy that covers up to half of their contributions.[2] This program may serve as an incentive for low-income workers.

The government has been subsidizing monthly contributions by farmers and fishers to reduce the burden of pension contribution and encourage their participation ever since the national pension extended its compulsory coverage to all rural residents in 1995.[3] The subsidy plan is financed by revenues from an earmarked tax in the Special Accounts

TABLE 8.4 **Demographic characteristics of individually insured and noninsured people in Korea's national pension plan**

Category		Total No. of samples	%	Individually insured No. of samples	%	Noninsured No. of samples	%
Total		1,959	100.0	674	100.0	1,285	100.0
Age	18–30	205	10.5	11	1.6	194	15.1
	31–40	684	34.9	166	24.6	519	40.4
	41–50	650	33.2	264	39.2	385	30.0
	51–59	420	21.5	233	34.6	187	14.6
	Average	42.4		46.5		40.3	
Education	Uneducated, elementary, middle school	329	16.8	156	23.1	173	13.5
	High school	957	48.8	319	47.4	637	49.6
	College diploma or higher	673	34.4	199	29.5	475	36.9
	Average years of school	12.35		11.98		12.54	
Sex	Male	1,235	63.0	511	75.8	724	56.4
	Female	724	37.0	163	24.2	561	43.6
Spouse	Yes	1,509	77.1	575	85.3	935	72.7
	No	450	22.9	99	14.7	351	27.3
No. of family members	Average (people)	3.51		3.61		3.46	
Householder	Yes	1,205	61.5	518	76.8	687	53.5
	No	754	38.5	156	23.2	598	46.5
Economic activity participation status	Regular worker	253	12.9	92	13.7	161	12.5
	Temporary worker	165	8.4	29	4.2	136	10.6
	Daily laborer	238	12.2	62	9.2	176	13.7
	Self-employed	695	35.5	406	60.3	288	22.4
	Others	608	31.1	85	12.7	523	40.7
Disposable income[a] (W 10,000)	≤ 1,000	291	14.8	73	10.8	218	16.9
	1,000~2,000	823	42.0	248	36.8	575	44.7
	2,000~3,000	526	26.8	185	27.5	340	26.5
	3,000~4,000	173	8.8	77	11.5	95	7.4
	≥ 4,000	148	7.5	90	13.3	58	4.5
	Average	2,178.7		2,547.9		1,985.2	

SOURCE: Author, based on data from the Korea Welfare Panel Study 2008.

A. Adjusted for family size using $\sqrt{n}$. W 1,125 ≈ $1.

TABLE 8.5 Probit regression estimations of determinants of compliance with Korea's national pension plan among individually insured people

Dependent variable		Individually insured or noninsured			
		Model 1		Model 2	
		dy/dx	Standard error	dy/dx	Standard error
Male		0.0758***	(0.028)	0.0736***	(0.028)
Age		0.0375**	(0.016)	0.0355**	(0.016)
Age 2		−0.0002	(0.000)	−0.0002	(0.000)
Economic activity participation status (Basis: temporary workers)	Regular workers	0.1835***	(0.063)	0.1822***	(0.063)
	Daily laborers	0.0023	(0.058)	0.0048	(0.058)
	Self-employed	0.3129***	(0.052)	0.3150***	(0.052)
	Other[a]	−0.0513	(0.052)	−0.0492	(0.052)
Education (Basis: middle school or below)	High school	−0.0475	(0.037)		
	College or higher	−0.0399	(0.042)		
Years of schooling				−0.0146	(0.021)
ln (disposable income)[b]		0.1144***	(0.023)	0.1140***	(0.023)
Number of observations		1,933		1,933	
Log pseudo-likelihood		−979.729		−980.054	
Pseudo R^2		0.2127		0.2124	

NOTE: ***$p < 0.01$, **$p < 0.05$, *$p < 0.1$.

A. Includes unpaid family workers, unemployed, and economically nonactive population.

B. Adjusted for family size using $\sqrt{n}$.

for Agriculture and Fishery Structure Adjustment. People who are entitled to the subsidy work in the agriculture, forestry, livestock, and fishery businesses and are individually insured (or voluntarily and continuously insured). The subsidy is scheduled to be terminated by the end of 2014.

Initially, farmers and fishers were assisted with a third of the lowest contribution amount; later the amount gradually increased. Currently, they are given half of the total contribution, up to an income ceiling; when income exceeds the ceiling, a fixed amount is applied (table 8.6).

If the matching subsidy has positive effects on increasing the compliance rate of farmers and fishers, the expansion of such a subsidy program to other noncompliant groups may be an effective policy instrument that could reduce blind spots in national

TABLE 8.6 **Size of matching subsidy to farmers and fishers in Korea**

Standard monthly income	Size of subsidy
Less than W 790,000	4.5% of income (half of total contribution)
More than W 790,000	W 35,550 (about $32)

SOURCE: http://english.nps.or.kr.

NOTE: W 790,000 (about $700) corresponds to the 18th of the 45 grades in the standard monthly income table.

pension coverage. Differences in compliance between the group of farmers and fishers who are individually insured and receive the subsidy and other self-employed groups that are individually insured but do not receive a subsidy are therefore studied.

CONCEPTUAL FRAMEWORK

Intuitively, a contribution subsidy should provide incentives for pension compliance, especially to workers who are not currently making contributions. The effect of the subsidy can be divided into two parts. First, it can help reduce delinquency among people who are already individually insured but are not able to make their contributions because of economic difficulties. The current contribution rate of 9 percent of income can be burdensome to low-income households. Reducing this contribution to 4.5 percent through a matching subsidy would reduce liquidity constraints (the "contribution effect").

Second, a substantial portion of individually insured people who earn income decide to remain exempt by concealing their income from the national pension system. Providing a contribution subsidy to these groups would make it more advantageous to them to register with the scheme by reporting their income to the authorities. The contribution subsidy would provide incentives for voluntary income reporting, reducing the blind spots in pension coverage. The magnitude of this "extensive margin" will depend partly on the generosity of the benefits provided.

The contribution subsidy could also encourage people in the targeted groups to report their income levels more honestly. Underreporting of income levels, with short-sighted intentions to reduce current contribution burdens, is believed to be prevalent among individually insured people. It is possible because of the government's limited ability to gather accurate information on personal income. A contribution subsidy might induce people to report their income more truthfully by reducing the economic burden of doing so. This "intensive margin" will be greater if the contribution subsidy increases with the level of reported income.

A natural experiment can be exploited by comparing the behavior of individually insured people who received the matching subsidy with that of individually insured people who did not. A few strong assumptions are necessary—namely, that all individually insured people are ex ante homogeneous in compliance, regardless of the type of work they do, and that non-observables (for example, differences between the groups in "choice architecture," such as ease of contribution payment) are not relevant.

DATA

Empirical analysis of the effects of the contribution subsidy requires detailed information on individual characteristics and compliance behaviors of various types of individually insured people, including farmers and fishers. The Korea Welfare Panel Study is the only source of data that contains detailed information on compliance with the national pension and on farmers and fishers. This study conducted a quantitative analysis using these data. The sample included 704 self-employed workers age 18–59 who were individually insured by the national pension. Among these workers were 142 farmers and fishers who received the contribution subsidy in 2007.

The narrow coverage of the national pension is indeed a serious problem among the self-employed, with 40 percent not contributing (table 8.7). The average delinquency rate of farmers and fishers was 9.2 percent—far lower than the 13.9 percent of other self-employed workers. The proportion of exempt payers was also significantly lower (18.3 percent for farmers and fishers versus 29.9 percent for other self-employed workers). The rate of contributors among farmers and fishers was 16.3 percentage points higher than that of other self-employed workers.

TABLE 8.7 Compliance with Korea's national pension by subsidy recipients and nonrecipients, 2007

Category	Total	Farmers and fishers	Other self-employed
Contributors	419 (59.5)	103 (72.5)	316 (56.2)
Noncontributors	285 (40.5)	39 (27.5)	246 (43.8)
Delinquents	91 (12.9)	13 (9.2)	78 (13.9)
Exempt payers	194 (27.6)	26 (18.3)	168 (29.9)
Total	704(100.0)	142(100.0)	562(100.0)

SOURCE: Author, based on data from the 2008 Korea Welfare Panel Study.

NOTE: Figures in parentheses are percentages of the total.

Table 8.8 compares the major characteristics of farmers and fishers with those of other self-employed workers. The average age of farmers and fishers surveyed was 50.9, considerably higher than the average age of other self-employed people (44.5). More than half of farmers and fishers were 50 or older.[4] The average disposable household income of farmers and fishers was about three-quarters that of other self-employed workers. These data imply that, on average, rural households were more likely than other households to face binding liquidity constraints in paying pension contributions and in saving for post-retirement consumption. The average education level of farmers and fishers was significantly lower than the average level of other self-employed people, and the percentage of men was higher.

TABLE 8.8 **Demographic characteristics of recipients and nonrecipients of subsidized contribution to Korea's national pension plan, 2007**

Category		Total		Farmers and fishers		Other self-employed	
		No. of samples	%	No. of samples	%	No. of samples	%
Total		704	100.0	142	100.0	562	100.0
Age	18–30	19	2.7	0	0.0	19	3.4
	31–40	170	24.2	9	6.3	161	28.7
	41–50	296	42.1	52	36.6	244	43.4
	51–59	219	31.1	81	57.0	138	24.6
	Average (years)	45.8		50.9		44.5	
Educational Background	Middle school or lower	177	25.1	76	53.5	101	18.0
	High school	332	47.2	59	41.6	273	48.6
	College diploma or higher	195	27.7	7	4.9	188	33.5
	Average years of schooling	11.8		9.6		12.4	
Sex	Male	582	82.7	128	90.1	454	80.8
	Female	122	17.3	14	9.9	108	19.2
Spouse	Yes	603	85.6	128	90.1	475	84.5
	No	101	14.4	14	9.9	87	15.5
Family size	Average (people)	3.7		3.9		3.6	
Householder	Yes	588	83.5	129	90.9	459	81.7
	No	116	16.5	13	9.2	103	18.3
Disposable income[a] (W 10,000)	≤ 1,000	113	16.1	39	27.5	74	13.2
	1,000~2,000	284	40.3	62	43.7	222	39.5
	2,000~3,000	181	25.7	26	18.3	155	27.6
	3,000~4,000	57	8.1	6	4.2	51	9.1
	≥ 4,000	69	9.8	9	6.3	60	10.7
	Average	2,311.0		1,842.6		2,429.4	

SOURCE: Author, based on data from the 2008 Korea Welfare Panel Study.

A. Adjusted for family size using $\sqrt{n}$. W 1,125 ≈ $1.

EMPIRICAL RESULTS

This study uses a probit regression model that includes dummies for farmers and fishers. The model estimates differences between the group of individually insured farmers and fishers and other self-employed groups. The effect of the contribution subsidy can be decomposed into the contribution effect and the registration effect, each of which is estimated separately.

Table 8.9 summarizes the estimation results for the entire sample of self-employed people. The first column reports the result when the probability of contribution payment is estimated for income reporters. The result reveals that among income reporters, disposable income is the most important variable affecting the decision to make a pension contribution. Other variables, such as age and education, have some explanatory power, but their statistical significance is relatively weak. The coefficient of the dummy variable for farmers and fishers is positive and statistically significant within the confidence interval of 90 percent. After controlling for individual characteristics, the probability of making a pension contribution was 7.4 percentage points higher among the subsidized farmers and fishers than it was among other nonsubsidized. The contribution subsidy thus had a nonnegligible effect on reducing delinquency among the subsidized group by lightening the financial burden of participating.[5]

TABLE 8.9 **Contribution, registration, and total effects of subsidy on pension behavior of farmers and fishers in Korea**
PROBIT REGRESSION RESULTS

Dependent variable	Contribution effect		Registration effect		Aggregate effect	
	dy/dx	Standard error	dy/dx	Standard error	dy/dx	Standard error
Male dummy	−0.0309	0.041	0.0565	0.047	0.0278	0.051
Schooling years	0.0110*	0.007	−0.0082	0.007	0.0004	0.007
Age	−0.0442*	0.025	0.0259	0.023	−0.0097	0.027
Age2	0.0006**	0.000	−0.0002	0.000	0.0003	0.000
ln(Disposable income)a	0.0677**	0.027	0.0696***	0.027	0.1088***	0.031
agri_dummy	0.0742*	0.038	0.0669	0.045	0.1108**	0.051
Number of observations	501		691		691	
Log pseudo-likelihood	−218.104		−387.327		−435.833	
Pseudo R^2	0.0694		0.0469		0.0649	

SOURCE: Author, based on data from the 2008 Korea Welfare Panel Study.

NOTE: ***p < 0.01, **p < 0.05, *p < 0.1. The contribution effect (the probability of contribution payment) is estimated for income reporters. The registration effect (the probability of income reporting) is estimated for the entire sample. The aggregate effect is estimated for the entire sample, including people who are exempt. Adjusted for family size using √n.

The estimates of the registration effect are reported in the second column of the table. When the probability of income reporting is estimated for the entire sample, the coefficient of the dummy variable for the subsidized group is positive, as expected, implying that the subsidized group is 6–7 percentage points more likely to report income to the national pension system than the nonsubsidized group. The estimate is not statistically significant, however.

The third column in the table reports the estimation results of the overall effect of the contribution subsidy when the probability of contribution payment is estimated for the entire sample, including exempt payers. The estimated coefficient of the subsidy dummy is greater in absolute value and is statistically significant: the estimated probability of paying a contribution was 11 percentage points higher for farmers and fishers and statistically significant at the 95 percent level. The empirical evidence on the positive effect of the contribution subsidy seems to be stronger in this case.

Differences in compliance are illustrated in figure 8.2. Compliance rates of the subsidized farmers and fishers are higher than those of the nonsubsidized group across all income levels. The average compliance gap between the two groups is more than 16 percentage points.

The estimation results imply that the contribution subsidy plays a significant role in encouraging participation of farmers and fishers. One would expect the subsidy to

FIGURE 8.2 **Payment of pension contributions by subsidy recipients and nonrecipients in Korea, by level of income, 2007**

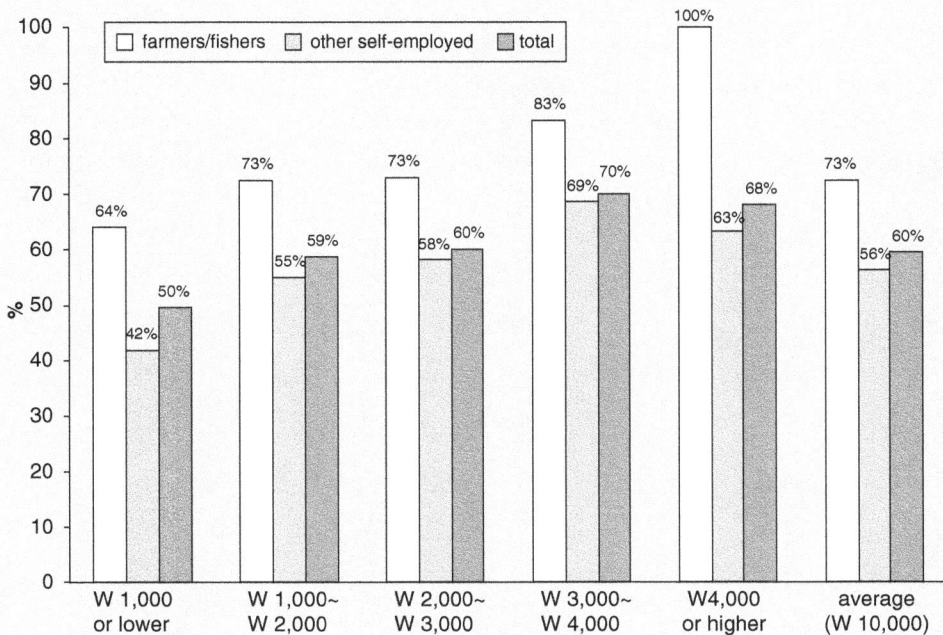

SOURCE: Author, based on data from the 2008 Korea Welfare Panel Study. W 1,125 ≈ $1.

have a greater effect on lower-income households. The estimation results are reported in table 8.10.

As expected, among income reporters, the difference in contribution probability between subsidized farmers and fishers and the nonsubsidized group is substantially larger when the regression samples are restricted to low-income households: the estimated coefficient for the contribution effect case is 12.2 percent (4.8 percentage points higher than the results shown in table 8.9) and statistically significant. No statistically meaningful change was found in the estimate of the dummy variable for differences in the probability of income reporting, however (column 2). The registration effect of the contribution subsidy does not seem larger among low-income classes. Among low-income self-employed workers, the probability of paying contributions is 13.5 percentage points higher for farmers and fishers. This value is 2.4 percentage points, or 22 percent, greater than the estimate in table 8.9.

The results in table 8.10 show that the difference in compliance behaviors between subsidized and nonsubsidized groups is more apparent among low-income classes. This evidence is consistent with the expectation that the marginal impact of the contribution subsidy should be larger for poorer households, which have more difficulty paying pension contributions.

TABLE 8.10 **Effects of income on pension behavior of self–employed workers in Korea**
PROBIT REGRESSION RESULTS

Dependent variable	Contribution effect		Registration effect		Aggregate effect	
	dy/dx	Standard error	dy/dx	Standard error	dy/dx	Standard error
Male dummy	0.0047	0.068	0.0289	0.066	0.0293	0.072
Schooling years	0.0061	0.010	−0.0023	0.009	0.0024	0.010
Age	−0.0754**	0.038	0.0241	0.032	−0.0368	0.037
Age2	0.0010**	0.000	−0.0002	0.000	0.0006	0.000
ln(Disposable income)a	−0.0188	0.056	0.1133**	0.050	0.0673	0.058
agri_dummy	0.1220**	0.056	0.0630	0.058	0.1347**	0.066
Number of observations	261		365		365	
Log pseudo–likelihood	−130.096		−209.744		−236.605	
Pseudo R^2	0.0755		0.0383		0.0578	

SOURCE: Author, based on data from the 2008 Korea Welfare Panel Study.
NOTE: ***$p < 0.01$, **$p < 0.05$, *$p < 0.1$. Adjusted for family size using $\sqrt{n}$.

Conclusion

Vast blind spots remain within Korea's national pension. About a third of the country's self-employed and nonregular workers fail to make contributions. The fact that most of them have low incomes suggests that many may fall into poverty in old age.

Compliance with the national pension may gradually increase, as public awareness and the government's ability to gather accurate information on personal incomes grow. However, to prevent the spread of old-age poverty, more active measures are needed for improving the compliance of groups among which compliance is low (nonregular low-income workers and self-employed small business owners). In addition, the administrative capacity for gathering more accurate information on their income status needs to be reinforced (Moon 2011).

One measure for increasing compliance, which is under active discussion in Korea, is to provide economic incentives to participate in the national pension by subsidizing the contribution of low-income individually insured people. The subsidy could encourage compliance by people who are currently financially unable to make contributions.

Since 1995, the Korean government has been providing matching subsidies to farmers and fishers worth up to half of their pension contributions. Simple empirical tests suggest that the subsidy may have significantly contributed to increasing the compliance rate of farmers and fishers. In particular, the rate of delinquency among income reporters was significantly lower for farmers and fishers, after controlling for other variables. The effect of the subsidy on the probability of reporting income was positive but statistically insignificant. Overall, the probability of contributing to the national pension system was more than 10 percentage points higher among (subsidized) farmers and fishers than among nonsubsidized self-employed workers. The difference in compliance rates was more pronounced among low-income workers.

The results suggest that providing subsidies to other self-employed groups with low incomes could increase compliance with the national pension scheme. These preliminary results need to be supplemented by more rigorous empirical investigations before the contribution subsidy program is expanded, however.

Notes

1. This section relies heavily on chapter 2 of Moon (2011).

2. Although a matching contribution subsidy is commonly applied to defined contribution schemes with individual accounts, it would not necessarily be confined to them. It can also be used for defined benefit schemes, as long as they are contributory schemes, as a measure to encourage pension participation of poor or vulnerable workers by alleviating their financial burden. This section examines the effectiveness of a contribution subsidy in promoting the participation of the concerned group when it is applied to the publicly provided defined benefit scheme in Korea.

3. The government spent W 87 billion (about $79 million) in 2011 on contribution subsidies to 219,000 farmers and fishers.

4. The difference in age between farmers and the other self-employed in the sample is natural as it reflects the fact that farmers in Korea are much older than workers in other sectors. This

difference would not affect the regression results because age and sex variables are controlled in the analysis.

5. Dummies for farmers and fishers might capture individual characteristics that are explained by other variables as well as the effects of the contribution subsidy. For instance, there could be differences in income instability between the households of farmers/fishers and other workers. If the incomes of farming and fishing households are more stable than the incomes of other self-employed workers, the compliance rate of farmers and fishers should be higher, everything else being equal. In this case, the coefficients of the dummies for farmers and fishers will over-estimate the effect of the contribution subsidy.

References

Korea Institute for Health and Social Affairs. 2008. *Korea Welfare Panel Study.* (In Korean.)

Moon, Hyungpyo. 2011. "Managing Pension and Healthcare Costs in Rapidly Aging Depopulating Countries: The Case of Korea." Paper presented at the ERIA-SP Project Workshop, Economic Research Institute for ASEAN and East Asia, Singapore, March 5–6.

National Pension Service. 2009. *National Pension Statistics.* (In Korean.)

National Statistical Office. 2006. *Population Projections for Korea: 2005–2050.* Seoul.

PART III

Middle-Income
Country Experience

Complementing Chile's Pensions with Subsidized Youth Employment and Contributions

Hermann von Gersdorff and Paula Benavides

Replacement rates of Chile's pension system have been lower than expected, forcing the government to top off the pensions of a significant share of retirees. Chile's recent experience with youth employment subsidies provides some useful evidence on the effects of employment subsidies on social security coverage and replacement rates. That experience indicates that most of the impact was short term, raising questions about the suitability of subsidies in promoting social security among the target population. Except for some impact on employment and labor force participation, it is unlikely that the subsidies will provide a relevant alternative to the solidarity pillar as an instrument for addressing the issue of low pensions. Youth employment subsidies seem more suitable as a countercyclical policy in times of high unemployment.

This chapter describes and analyzes two youth employment subsidy schemes in Chile. The first, Subsidio Previsional a los Trabajadores Jóvenes (Social Security Subsidy for Young Workers—SPTJ), was established in 2008, through Law No. 20.255, which deepened Chile's pension reform. The second, Subsidio al Empleo Joven (Youth Employment Subsidy—SEJ), was established in 2009, through Law No. 20.338. Both subsidies have the objective of promoting formal youth employment through incentives for both the supply of and demand for labor. The SPTJ provides an explicit and direct subsidy for social security contributions.

The chapter is organized as follows. The first section describes Chile's pension system and provides some indicators on the youth labor market in Chile. The second section describes the objectives and design of both subsidy schemes and examines the effects of the subsidies on social security coverage, employment, and fiscal costs. It presents the results of an impact evaluation of the SEJ that could provide valuable lessons for reform of the schemes. The last section summarizes the experience with the programs.

The Chilean Pension System and the Labor Market for Young Workers

THE CHILEAN PENSION SYSTEM

Since the latest pension reform in 2008, the Chilean pension system has had three pillars: a mandatory, a voluntary, and a solidarity pillar. The mandatory pillar—established through Law No. 3.500 of 1980 and reformed in 2008 through Law No. 20.255—is a defined contribution system with individual capitalization and private management of pension funds under strong public regulations of both asset and accounts management. Membership in and contributions to the system are mandatory for all dependent workers and gradually for independent workers. As of 2012, independent workers are required to make contributions for pensions and workers' compensation on the first 40 percent of their taxable income unless they formally opt out. The percentage of their income subject to contributions will increase to 70 percent in 2013 and 100 percent in 2014. Beginning in 2015, contributions will be mandatory, without the possibility of opting out. Beginning in 2018, contributions for health insurance will also become mandatory. People without labor income may also join the pension system, on a voluntary basis.

The pension contribution rate is 10 percent, paid entirely by the employee; employers contribute 1.49 percent for disability and survivorship insurance of the employee. The management fee of the asset manager is paid by the worker as a share of his or her wage (not a share of assets under management); it ranges from 0.77 percent to 2.36 percent of wages.[1] Including health insurance contributions (7 percent) and workers' compensation (0.95 percent), total social security contributions represent about 21 percent of wages. Mandatory contributions are capped at a wage of about $3,000 a month in 2012.

As of August 2011, assets under management were $150 billion, which represents 60 percent of gross domestic product (GDP). About 8.9 million people participated in the pension system. Of the 4.4 million people making contributions in July 2011, 98 percent were dependent workers and 61 percent were men (Superintendencia de Pensiones 2011) (table 9.1).

The number of funded pensions paid in March 2011 was 887,255, two-thirds of which were old-age pensions; about half of old-age pensions received a complement from the government (figure 9.1). The average pension was $353 a month. The average value of pensions is low because of the significant number of women who benefited from a public transfer for each child but made few contributions into their pension accounts.

The voluntary pillar includes several saving mechanisms, including Voluntary Savings Accounts (1987), Voluntary Pension Savings (2002), and Collective Voluntary Pension Savings (2008). As of June 2011, the number of voluntary accounts was of 927,558, with total assets of $7 billion.

The Collective Voluntary Pension Savings is a new pension saving mechanism that allows enterprises to match pension savings of their employees. Offering the plan is

TABLE 9.1 **Number and average income of contributors to Chile's pension program, July 2011**

Sex	Number of contributors (millions)	Average income ($)
Men	2.70	1,060
Women	1.74	936
Total	4.44	1,010

SOURCE: Superintendencia de Pensiones.

FIGURE 9.1 **Number and percentage of pensioners in Chile, by type of pension**

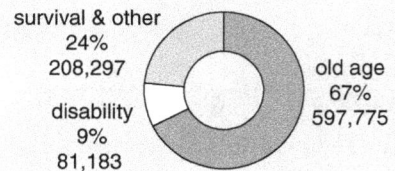

survival & other
24%
208,297

old age
67%
597,775

disability
9%
81,183

SOURCE: Authors, based on data from Superintendencia de Pensiones 2011.

voluntary for the enterprise, which can define the terms of the plan.[2] However, once the plan is part of the labor contract, the employer has to make the committed payments. Employees have the right, not the obligation, to individually join the plan offered by the employer. This mechanism has been slow in taking off, with only 1,904 accounts in place as of June 2011.

The 2008 pension reform included tax benefits and subsidies to promote voluntary pension saving. Workers who do not take advantage of the tax benefits but who do make voluntary pension savings can obtain a matching contribution into their pension savings account of 15 percent of the saved amount, with a maximum of $470 a year.

The solidarity pillar covers people who did not save enough for their pension to protect them from poverty in old age or in case of disability. These benefits are integrated with those of the individual capitalization system. Once a person in the poorest 60 percent of the population complies with age and residency requirements, he or she can receive a basic pension (Pensión Básica Solidaria [PBS]), for people who have no pension at all; or a social pension complement (Aporte Previsional Solidario [APS]), for people who have a pension funded by their own savings that provides less than the maximum pension with social complement (Pensión Máxima con Aporte Solidario [PMAS]). Four types of pensions are provided: an old-age basic pension, a disability basic pension, an old-age social pension complement, and a disability social pension complement.

As of December 2011, 1.08 million Chileans were beneficiaries of the solidarity pillar (figure 9.2). Public spending on these pensions was 0.7 percent of GDP. Beneficiaries of the old-age social pension complement were the largest group (436,791). The basic pension was $157 a month; the average monthly complement for the old-age social pension complement was $92.

FIGURE 9.2 **Number of beneficiaries of Chile's solidarity pension pillar, by type of benefit, December 2011**

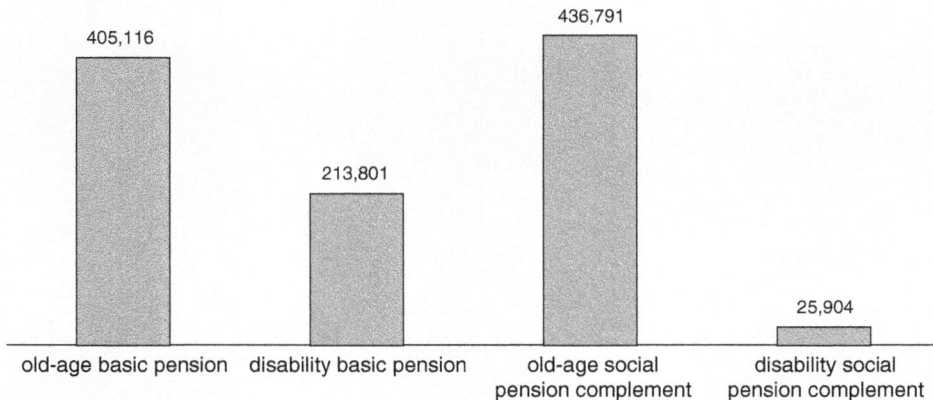

SOURCE: Authors, based on data from Superintendencia de Pensiones 2011.

THE YOUTH LABOR MARKET IN CHILE

Chile's population was 17.1 million in 2010. The population is projected to grow by about 19 percent, to 20.4 million, by 2050, with the share of the population older than 65 growing faster than the population as a whole. The number of economically active people will continue to grow, however, because the largest cohorts of the population are currently age 15–24.

The average labor force participation rate for people age 15–64 was 66.2 percent in 2011. The rate for men was 78.6 percent, very close to the average for Organisation for Economic Co-operation and Development (OECD) countries (79.7 percent in 2010). The rate for women was 53.9 percent, a low rate relative to the OECD average (61.8 percent in 2010). The average unemployment rate was 8.4 percent in 2010 and 7.4 percent in 2011. The participation rate among people age 15–24 was 38.4 percent, well below the average participation rate in Chile of 66.2 percent (see annex) in 2011. This rate was lower than the participation rate for the same age group in the OECD, which was 47.4 percent in 2010.

The unemployment rate among people age 15–24 was 17.5 percent in 2011, more than twice the 7.4 percent rate for people age 15–64. The rate was higher than the 16.7 percent unemployment rate for the same age group in the OECD in 2010 (figure 9.3).

FIGURE 9.3 **Unemployment rate among people 15–24 in selected countries, 2010**

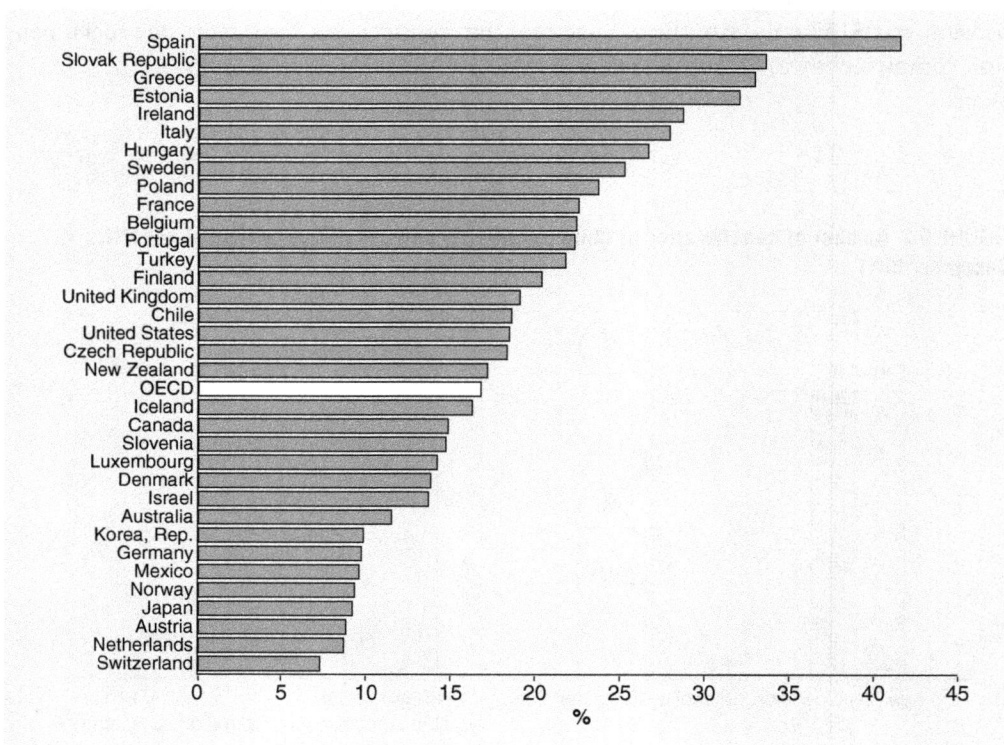

SOURCE: OECD 2011.

Data from the 2009 National Socioeconomic Survey reveal significant differences among participation rates at different income levels (figure 9.4). In particular, the differences between labor participation rates by the first four deciles and the other six deciles are large for people age 18–29. The differences are smaller in the age 18–24 group, because people in the upper deciles are more likely to be enrolled in higher education, which keeps them out of the labor market.

FIGURE 9.4 **Labor participation rate for young workers in Chile, by income decile, 2009**

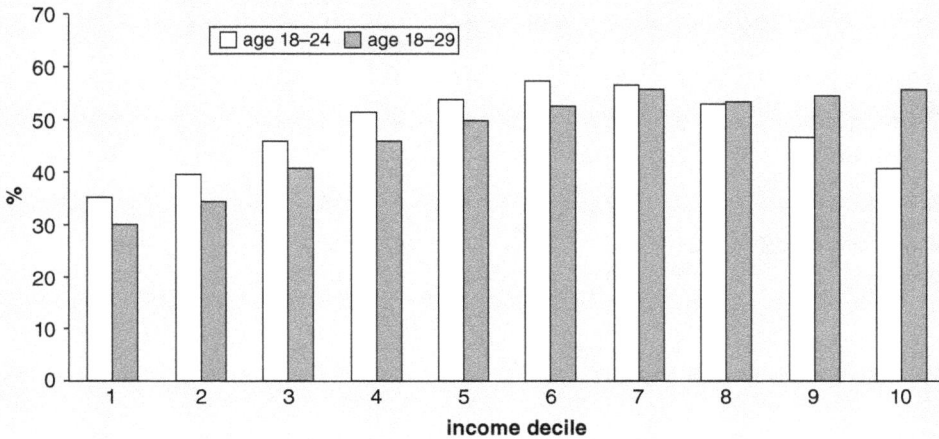

SOURCE: National Socioeconomic Survey 2009.

Low-income youth have the most difficulty entering the labor market (figure 9.5). The 18–24 age group has the highest inactivity and unemployment rates. In the lowest decile, 56 percent of the population is either inactive (37 percent) or looking for work and not attending school (19 percent). This low-income age group is at high risk of remaining unemployed. The share of unemployed declines with each decile, reaching 9 percent in the 10th decile. The unemployment rate of people age 18–24 in the first income quintile was more than 50 percent in 2009 (figure 9.6).

These labor market conditions for youth are not unique to Chile; many OECD countries face similar challenges. However, in Chile, the situation of young workers in the lower quintiles is particularly grave, prompting recent efforts to bring these workers into the labor market and under the coverage of the social security system.

Youth Employment Subsidy Schemes

The introduction of employment subsidies was triggered by the discussion of Chile's low pension levels and the need to promote contributions into pension funds to improve future pensions.[3] Policy makers debated whether this labor subsidy should be provided ex ante or ex post. The solidarity pillar introduced an ex post subsidy that rewards pension

FIGURE 9.5 **Activity of population age 18–24 in Chile, by income decile, 2009**

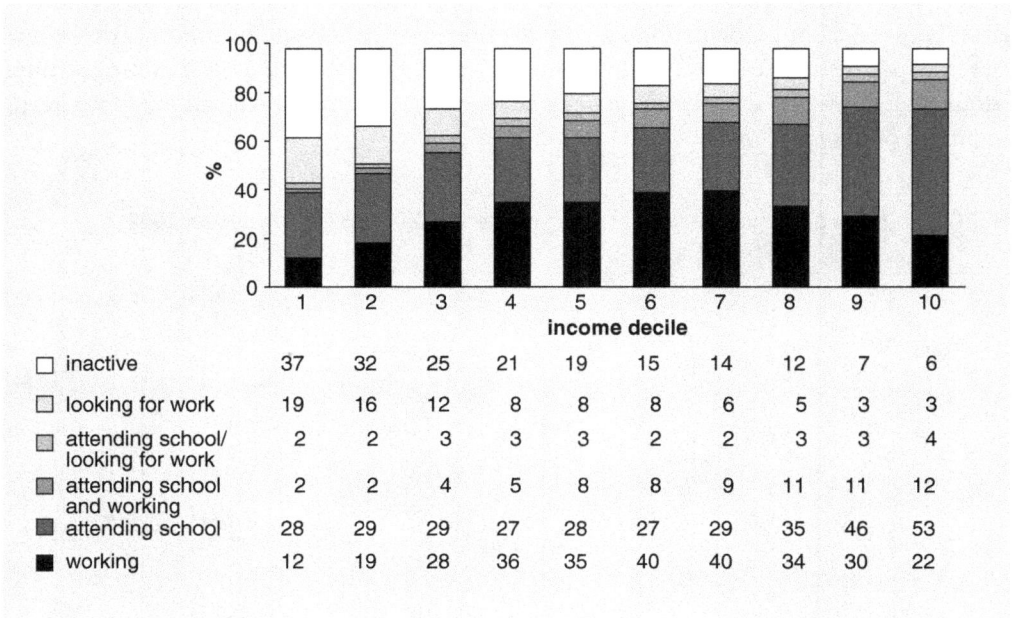

	1	2	3	4	5	6	7	8	9	10
☐ inactive	37	32	25	21	19	15	14	12	7	6
☐ looking for work	19	16	12	8	8	8	6	5	3	3
▨ attending school/ looking for work	2	2	3	3	3	2	2	3	3	4
▨ attending school and working	2	2	4	5	8	8	9	11	11	12
▨ attending school	28	29	29	27	28	27	29	35	46	53
■ working	12	19	28	36	35	40	40	34	30	22

SOURCE: National Socioeconomic Survey 2009.

FIGURE 9.6 **Unemployment rate among people 18–24 in Chile, by income quintile, 2009**

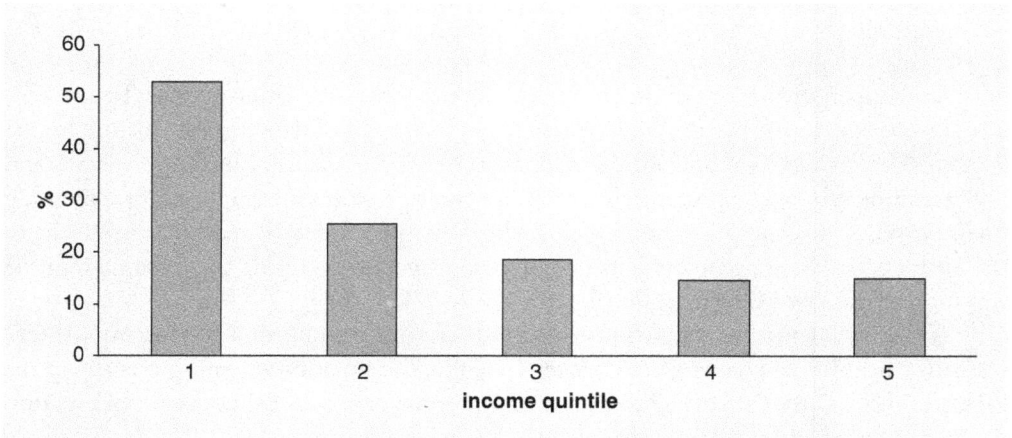

SOURCE: National Socioeconomic Survey 2009.

saving and provides low-income workers with incentives to contribute by topping up the pension so as not to fully tax away the additional savings until the pension reached a maximum level. Similarly, the child benefit for women is paid only at retirement. The main arguments for ex post subsidies are that they delay the fiscal cost of the measure and reduce the cost of providing a subsidy for a target group that has a high probability of having to rely on social assistance for old-age income anyway; it does not make much administrative sense to set up a system to pay the subsidy ex ante each time a contribution is made and to pay management fees to pension fund managers if most beneficiaries will not collect a pension based only on their own savings.

The debate was settled in favor of an ex ante subsidy for young workers, for two main reasons. First, one of the objectives was to establish a culture of contribution among young workers. Seeing a growing pension savings account without lower net wages was expected to provide this incentive; the learning effect of contributing regularly into the pension account was expected even with a subsidy that could be paid for as quickly as 24 months. Second, Chile created a pension reserve fund to cover future public pension liabilities. Making the subsidy ex post for young workers would generate future pension liabilities that would at least offset some of the payments made into the pension reserve fund. The economic crisis of 2008, together with the findings of an equity commission, increased the priority of countercyclical labor market measures, settling the decision for a more generous ex ante labor employment subsidy that was expected to have a more immediate impact on the unemployment rate.

THE SOCIAL SECURITY SUBSIDY FOR YOUNG WORKERS

A key element of the pension reform of 2008 was a stronger solidarity pillar. The demand for this improvement arose because of the large number of low pensions the pension system was producing. A key explanation for the low pensions was the low density of contributions by workers due to few contributions during youth and the frequent movement of workers between the formal and informal labor markets.

The SPTJ was established during the pension reform of 2008 to promote formal employment and increase social security coverage and pension savings of the target population. It has two independent components, which were implemented at different points in time.

The first component was launched October 1, 2008. It provides a subsidy to employers who hire workers age 18–35 earning less than $540 a month (1.5 times the minimum wage of $360). The subsidy is equivalent to 50 percent of pension contributions at the minimum wage and is paid on the first 24 contributions of the worker into the pension system. Payment of the subsidy to the employer is made only for months in which the employer pays the worker's contribution on time. The subsidy was started with a payment to the employer to get workers hired by lowering the effective wage before the second component was implemented.

The second component, a subsidy to the contribution, was launched July 1, 2011. It is received by workers who comply with the same requirements as the first component. Workers can apply for the subsidy independently of employers. This component, which is equal in value to the subsidy to employers, goes directly into the worker's pension account. Every time the young worker returns to formal employment, the subsidy kicks in for a total of 24 contributions.

Figure 9.7 shows the average number of monthly beneficiaries of the subsidy and the amount paid for the period between March 2009 (when payments started) and December 2011. The average subsidy was $12.50 a month. Most subsidies were paid between

FIGURE 9.7 **Number and average amount of subsidies paid in Chile under the Social Security Subsidy for Young Workers, March 2009–December 2011**

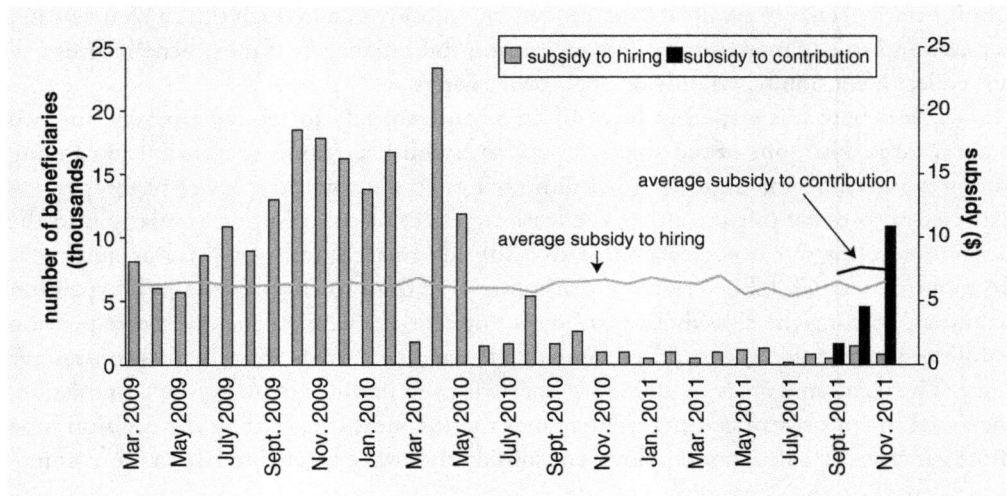

SOURCE: Authors, based on data from Superintendencia de Pensiones.

October 2009 and February 2010, although there was a peak, at 23,317, in April 2010. The number of subsidies for hiring dropped sharply starting in mid-2010, when the SEJ was introduced. The SEJ pays a higher subsidy, and employers may use only one of the two subsidies. Activation of the subsidy to contributions is noticeable by the end of 2011 because employees can have access to both the SPTJ and SEJ subsidy schemes. During the period, 55 percent of the beneficiaries were women. Public expenditure on the subsidy peaked in 2009, with annual expenditure of $1.8 million (table 9.2).

THE YOUTH EMPLOYMENT SUBSIDY

To address the consequences of the economic crisis, and following recommendations by the Equity Commission, in March 2009 the government implemented a new employment subsidy, the SEJ, for dependent young workers and their employers and for self-employed

TABLE 9.2 **Public expenditure on Chile's youth employment subsidies, 2008–11**
$, MILLIONS

Year	SPTJ	SEJ
2008	0.0	0.0
2009	1.8	10.6
2010	1.3	71.6
2011	0.8	88.1

SOURCE: Chilean Budget Office.

young workers. The SEJ subsidy is similar to the SPTJ and has similar objectives, but its introduction was motivated more by high unemployment among the target group than by concerns about the pension system. The SEJ, launched in July 2009, was aimed at promoting formal employment of young low-income workers.

To qualify for the subsidy, a dependent worker must fulfill three requirements: be age 18–25, belong to a household that is among the 40 percent poorest in Chile, and earn gross monthly wages of less than $740 and total yearly gross wages of less than $8,880. To qualify for the subsidy, the employer has to pay social security contributions on time for all its workers, not just the ones for which it is receiving the subsidy. Self-employed workers have access to the subsidy under the same conditions. They must provide evidence that they have paid their social security and health insurance contributions on time.

Two-thirds of the subsidy goes to the worker and one-third to the employer. The amounts start at 30 percent of the wage on which social security and health contributions have been paid for wages below $328 (figure 9.8). The subsidy is flat, at $98.40 for wages up to $410. For higher wages, the subsidy falls to zero for monthly wages of $740.

FIGURE 9.8 **Monthly SEJ subsidy in Chile, by level of income**

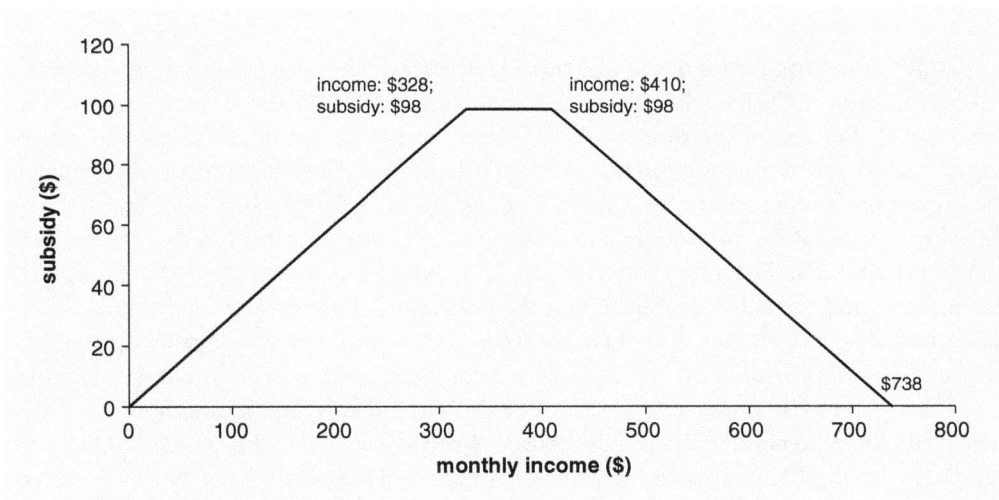

SOURCE: Authors, based on legislation.

Workers with more than one employer receive only one subsidy, the amount of which is calculated based on total monthly gross wages. For workers, the monthly payment of the subsidy is an advance of 75 percent of the subsidy. Once a year, the subsidy is recalculated based on gross annual wages. Workers can receive the subsidy after age 25 for each year they were enrolled in higher education and for time on maternity leave after age 18. In 2010, on average 67,048 young workers received the subsidy each month, and the average subsidy was $33 (figure 9.9).

Public spending on this subsidy has been growing. In 2011, it reached about $88 million (table 9.2).

FIGURE 9.9 **Number and average amount of SEJ subsidy paid in Chile**

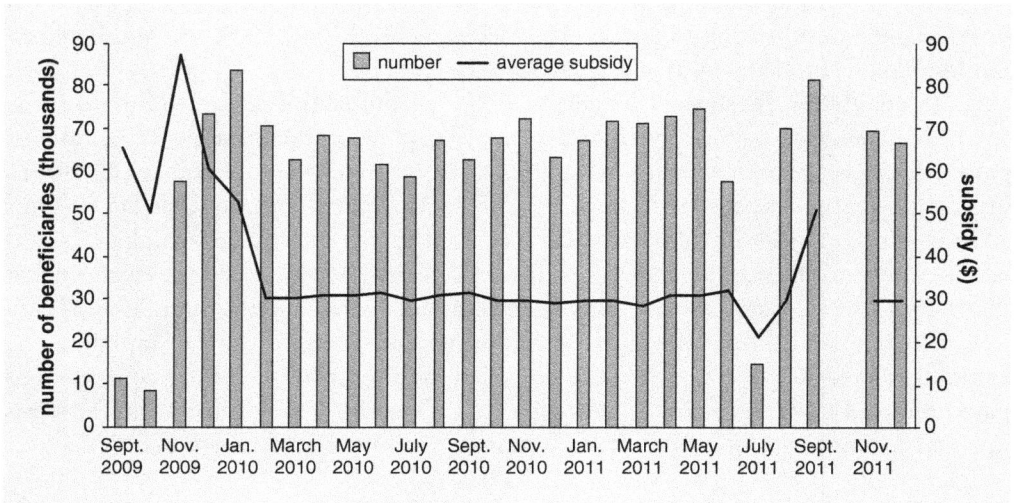

SOURCE: National Employment and Training Service.

Given the importance of the SEJ subsidy in terms of both fiscal spending and public policy, the Budget Office asked for an impact evaluation in 2011 (see Centro de Micro-datos 2011). Because of the short period of time that has passed since the subsidy scheme was launched, the terms of reference for the evaluation did not include an assessment of the impact on future pensions or potential savings from social pensions. The focus was on the labor impact of the subsidy. The evaluation used administrative data from unemploy-ment insurance, the Ficha de Protección Social (Social Protection Index—FPS) targeting mechanism, and the subsidy itself. Using the regression discontinuity method, beneficia-ries at the margin of the age limit were compared with people over the age limit; people at the margin of the cut-off score of the FPS were compared with people who did not qualify.

The evaluation shows that coverage of the SEJ subsidy was low, at about 4.6 per-cent of the eligible population in 2009 and 4.8 percent in 2010. The share of employed people in the eligible population that received the subsidy was 21.2 percent in 2009 and 21.3 percent in 2010. The subsidy benefited mostly young workers with more stable jobs, raising questions about how many of these workers would have had formal employment in any case and about the deadweight loss of the subsidy.

Use of the subsidy by enterprises was very low (3.75 percent): subsidy of the demand for labor had less coverage than subsidy of the supply of labor. Enterprises asked for the subsidy for only 10 percent of the total number of workers who received it in 2009 and for just 11 percent in 2010. Among companies that used the subsidy, 44 percent were microenterprises with fewer than 10 workers.

The results of the evaluation using the age factor show no significant impact of the SEJ, possibly because the SPTJ covers workers up to age 35. The FPS, which relies heavily on self-reporting, is a weak targeting mechanism, because the bottom two quintiles end up including almost 60 percent of Chile's population. This weakness also puts into ques-tion the results of the impact evaluation.

Bearing this caveat in mind, the impact evaluation of the SEJ shows a positive impact on the supply of labor: employment and labor force participation rates among the eligible population rose, particularly in 2009. The evaluation estimated an average increase in the probability of employment of 4.5 percentage points in 2009 and 2.1 percentage points in 2010. The peak in terms of increased probability of employment was in August and September 2009, suggesting that the initial advertising of the subsidy and identification of beneficiaries had an immediate impact that quickly waned.

There seems to have been a significant impact on the rate of formal employment, which was one of the objectives of the subsidy, measured as the proportion of time the worker was contributing while working. The number of months contributed increased by 6.6 percentage points among people receiving the subsidy. In contrast, the increase among those not receiving the subsidy was only 4.8 percent. The labor force participation rate rose by an estimated 3.0 percentage points in 2009 and 2.7 percentage points in 2010.

The evaluation concluded that, in times of high unemployment, the SEJ could be a useful tool for promoting employment of low-income workers but that the reduction in the impact in 2010 leads to questions about the need to retain the subsidy in times of high employment creation and falling unemployment. An unanswered question is whether the larger impact of the SEJ in 2009 was caused by the instrument itself or a strong public effort to place young workers using the subsidy during a year marked by economic crisis and presidential and congressional elections. The evaluation concludes that the SEJ is not a suitable instrument for addressing social security and pension issues, which are longer term in nature.

COMPARATIVE ANALYSIS AND INTERACTION BETWEEN SUBSIDY SCHEMES

Table 9.3 summarizes the main characteristics of both youth employment subsidy schemes. The subsidies share the objective of promoting formal youth employment and in particular on-time payment of social security contributions; the expectation is that they could lead to a culture of contribution that will eventually result in better pensions. However, because of the long lag in results, the subsidies will not replace the minimum pension guarantees put in place in 2008.

As employers can pick only one of the subsidies, if they use a subsidy at all they will probably choose the SEJ, which provides larger subsidies and results in a larger reduction of the effective wage paid by the employer. Workers can access both subsidy schemes at the same time. There are no data on the incidence of either subsidy. The net impact on future pensions is thus not clear. Young low-income workers who are not in the bottom two income quintiles, workers age 25–35 who have not made 24 contributions, and workers who are not employed under the labor code (for example, public sector workers) can access only the SPTJ.

Conclusion

Chile's experience with youth employment subsidies is interesting because Chile is an emerging economy and its programs target the poorest 40 percent of the population. The results of the impact evaluation are in line with international experience. The impact on formal employment and labor market participation was positive, but the design of

TABLE 9.3 **Comparison of Chile's youth employment subsidy programs**

Feature	SPTJ	SEJ
Start date	Subsidy to employer: October 2008; subsidy to worker: July 2011	Subsidy to employer and worker: July 2009
Age requirement	18–35	18–25; extension for maternity and education (expires at age 21 if secondary education incomplete)
Targeting	None	Bottom two quintiles according to FPS vulnerability measure
Wage requirement	< $540 (1.5 × monthly minimum wages)	< $740 a month, measured as average for the year
Length of benefit	First 24 contribution payments, continuous or discontinuous	No limit as long as above requirements are fulfilled
Benefit	5% of the minimum wage (50% of pension contribution), about $19 paid monthly to employer and 5% of minimum wage into worker's pension fund account	30% of current wage for wages up to $328, $99 for wages of $328–$410, $99 less 30% of the difference between actual wage and $410 for wages $410–$740; 20 percentage points of the subsidy go to the worker and 10 percentage points to the employer
Type of worker	Dependent	Dependent workers under labor code; independent workers who pay income tax and are current with their contributions for pension and health insurance

the subsidy and its targeting (using the FPS, which relies on self-reporting) could have been better. The initial design of the employment subsidies considered using a targeting mechanism specific to the employment subsidies. In the rush to launch the employment subsidies before the elections of November 2009, however, the decision was made to start with the FPS. A new targeting mechanism has not yet been developed; in light of the results, it may not be developed until a complete revision of both employment subsidies is undertaken.

Another issue to be considered is the overlap in the objectives of the two subsidies. The SPTJ subsidy is much more explicit about promoting pension fund contributions, but the higher benefits of the SEJ and the similarity of the benefits requires an evaluation of the continuity of the SPTJ and the possibility of double-dipping by a significant share of beneficiaries. Another issue that needs to be addressed is the low utilization of the subsidy by enterprises.

There are indications that the subsidies may have been used as an electoral campaign mechanism. The number of allocated subsidies peaked just before the elections, after which the effort to promote the mechanism declined. The design of an improved scheme should take this factor into account.

The evaluation of the SEJ and international experience show that most of the impact of employment subsidies is short term. This evidence raises questions about the suitability of employment subsidies to promote social security among youth. Although the subsidies may have some impact on employment and labor force participation, they are unlikely to provide a meaningful alternative to the solidarity pillar in addressing the problem of low pensions. The subsidies seem more suitable as countercyclical policy in times of high unemployment.

Notes

1. The 0.77 percent management fee is the result of the last auction among asset managers for new workers entering formal employment. The 2008 reform introduced an auction system that registers all new workers with the asset manager that bid the lowest management fee for a period of two years. The latest bidding process resulted in a management fee of 0.77 percent for all new workers during 2012 and 2013. Other workers can join the asset management firm at the same management fee.

2. The plan may establish a minimum period before employees vest the amounts contributed by the enterprise.

3. Globally, the experience with employment subsidies has not been positive. A review by Bucheli (2005) of labor market programs in a variety of countries concludes that recipients of employment subsidies do not have better outcomes than people in control groups, except people with disadvantages (the long-term unemployed, women). Puerto (2007) provides evidence that the international experience with youth employment subsidies has been more positive in emerging economies than in industrial countries, where results have been mixed. Along the same line, Marx (2001) concludes from a review of the literature of empirical evidence that the net impact of employment subsidies is considerably smaller than most theoretical models would predict. The main problem is that most subsidized workers would have obtained jobs without the subsidy (deadweight loss). Adequate targeting of the subsidies is essential for positive results.

References

Bucheli, Marisa. 2005. "Las políticas activas de mercado del trabajo: un panorama internacional de experiencias y evaluaciones." Serie de estudios y perspectivas de CEPAL, Comisión Económica para América Latina y el Caribe, Montevideo.

Centro de Microdatos, Departamento de Economía, Universidad de Chile. 2011. "Informe final de evaluación de impacto del programa de subsidio al empleo joven."

Marx, Ive. 2001. "Jobs Subsidies and Cuts in Employers' Social Security Contributions: The Verdict of Empirical Evaluation Studies." *International Labour Review* 140 (1): 69–83.

OECD (Organisation for Economic Co-operation and Development). 2010. *Off to a Good Start? Jobs for Youth*. Paris: OECD.

Puerto, Olga. 2007. "International Experience on Youth Employment Interventions: The Youth Employment Inventory." Background paper for the World Bank's 2007 Economic and Sector Work on Sierra Leone Youth and Employment, World Bank, Washington, DC.

Superintendencia de Pensiones. 2011. "Panorama Previsional de Septiembre de 2011." http://www.spensiones.cl/portal/informes/581/w3-article-7793.html.

Annex: Composition of Chile's Labor Force, 2010 and 2011

Sex/age	Participation rate (labor force/population)		Occupation employment/ population		Unemployment rate (unemployed/labor force)	
	2010	2011	2010	2011	2010	2011
Total						
15–19	19.4	20.2	14.9	15.8	23.1	21.7
20–24	57.5	57.4	47.8	48.2	16.9	16.0
25–29	77.0	78.0	68.2	70.0	11.5	10.3
30–34	80.1	81.7	73.9	75.7	7.7	7.3
35–39	79.9	80.5	74.4	76.0	6.9	5.6
40–44	78.9	80.1	74.3	76.0	5.9	5.1
45–49	76.1	78.6	72.1	75.4	5.3	4.1
50–54	73.7	75.4	69.5	72.3	5.7	4.2
55–59	67.7	68.6	64.7	65.9	4.4	3.9
60–64	52.2	54.4	50.1	52.3	4.1	3.8
65–69	34.5	37.1	33.4	35.9	3.2	3.2
70+	13.1	15.2	12.9	14.9	2.1	1.8
15-24	37.5	38.4	30.5	31.7	18.6	17.5
15-64	64.8	66.2	59.3	61.3	8.4	7.4
Men						
15–19	23.4	23.8	18.8	19.3	19.6	19.0
20–24	67.1	66.2	56.7	57.1	15.5	13.7
25–29	87.2	87.9	77.9	79.6	10.7	9.5
30–34	93.5	94.8	87.3	89.3	6.6	5.7
35–39	94.4	94.5	89.0	90.4	5.7	4.4
40–44	94.5	93.7	90.1	90.0	4.6	3.9
45–49	93.6	94.2	89.6	91.1	4.2	3.3
50–54	91.8	92.3	87.3	88.9	4.9	3.7
55–59	87.5	87.7	83.5	84.5	4.6	3.6
60–64	75.6	77.2	72.4	74.1	4.2	4.0
65–69	51.3	54.4	49.5	52.5	3.5	3.5
70+	22.6	24.7	22.1	24.2	2.5	2.0
15-24	43.8	44.3	36.6	37.6	16.6	15.2
15-64	77.8	78.6	72.1	73.6	7.4	6.3
Women						
15–19	14.9	16.0	10.5	11.8	29.5	26.3
20–24	47.1	48.1	38.2	38.8	19.0	19.4
25–29	66.8	68.0	58.5	60.3	12.5	11.3
30–34	66.0	68.8	59.9	62.3	9.3	9.3
35–39	66.1	67.4	60.5	62.6	8.4	7.2
40–44	64.0	66.6	59.1	62.1	7.6	6.8
45–49	59.8	63.7	55.8	60.3	6.8	5.3
50–54	57.2	59.3	53.2	56.4	6.9	4.9
55–59	48.9	51.2	46.9	48.9	4.2	4.3
60–64	31.4	33.7	30.2	32.5	3.7	3.6
65–69	18.9	21.1	18.5	20.6	2.4	2.5
70+	6.1	7.8	6.0	7.7	0.9	1.4
15-24	30.4	32.0	23.8	25.3	21.7	21.1
15-64	51.8	53.9	46.7	49.1	9.9	8.9

SOURCE: National Institute of Statistics.

CHAPTER 10

Matching Contributions in Colombia, Mexico, and Peru: Experiences and Prospects

Luis Carranza, Ángel Melguizo, and David Tuesta

Although Colombia, Mexico, and Peru introduced major structural reforms in the mid-1990s, they still exhibit very limited levels of social protection coverage (28 percent of the labor force in Colombia, 27 percent in Mexico, and 22 percent in Peru). These figures reflect the limited effectiveness of basing a pension scheme on employer withholding of contributions in environments in which most employment relations are informal. Better design of matching defined contribution schemes could increase the level of pension savings by the nearly 20 million middle-income workers in the informal sector in the three countries. Such an approach is preferable to ex post solutions to the growing problem of old age as the region ages rapidly, which are not sustainable and strengthen incentives for informality.

Colombia, Mexico, and Peru implemented structural reforms of their pension systems at almost the same time. Between 1994 and 1997, all three countries introduced mandatory funded systems for retirement based on individual defined contribution accounts. In Colombia and Peru, the reform allowed participants to choose between the existing defined benefit pay-as-you-go system (with some parametric adjustments) and the new defined contribution scheme. In contrast, in Mexico the introduction of privately run savings involved closing the pay-as-you-go system.[1]

These reforms had three explicit objectives: to ease the pressure generated by the pension system on public expenditures, to provide pensions that are more directly linked to the history of contributions, and to create incentives for greater participation in the formal labor market and therefore the pension system. Although the first two objectives were to a large extent achieved, the reform fell short in addressing the problem of low coverage.[2] Coverage rates (measured as the number of contributors as a share of the economically active population) remain low (28 percent in Colombia, 27 percent in Mexico, and 22 percent in Peru in 2010). These levels of participation in the pension system are not only low but slightly below those observed before the implementation of the reforms in Mexico and Peru.

The authors would like to thank Consuelo del Carmen Hoyo (BBVA Research) and Christian Daude and Juan de Laiglesia (Organisation for Economic Co-operation and Development Development Centre) for their helpful comments and suggestions, as well as Maria Claudia Llanes and Rosario Sanchez (BBVA Research) for their assistance in the empirical analysis for Colombia and Peru. The views expressed herein are the sole responsibility of the authors and do not necessarily reflect the opinions of their institutions.

The lack of coverage by large segments of the population represents an enormous public policy issue in these countries. It reflects the often very difficult challenges associated with achieving high coverage rates among low- and middle-income groups and in environments characterized by high levels of informal employment, which are common at this level of development (figure 10.1).[3]

FIGURE 10.1 **Pension coverage in Colombia, Mexico, and Peru**

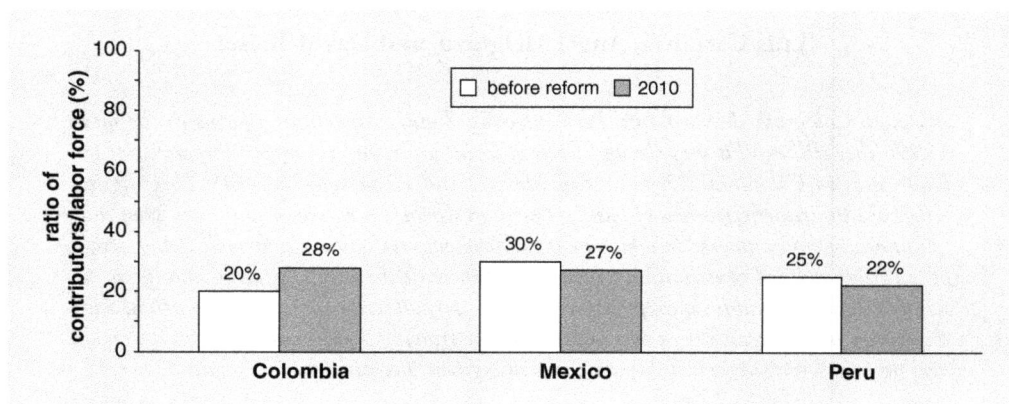

SOURCE: National supervisors.

NOTE: Year of reform is 1993 for Colombia, 1996 for Mexico, and 1992 for Peru.

The willingness of individuals to contribute voluntarily to a pension system is a significant, albeit less readily quantifiable, factor in determining the observed coverage levels in these countries. Assuming that people at all levels of income have some capacity to consume less and allocate resources for old-age savings, participation in any retirement savings system will to a large extent depend on the features of the product offered and individuals' perceptions of the need to create a formal (as opposed to a family-based) source of support when they are elderly. The willingness to participate in a pension system is also known to increase with age.

An important factor in determining the demand for pension products may also be the type or level of immediate monetary incentives, the most prevalent of which are matching defined contributions (MDCs). These incentives can come from either public or private sources. They represent an important policy instrument, in combination with other interventions, to encourage people in groups that are currently not participating in pension systems to begin saving for retirement.

This chapter reviews the attempts by Colombia, Mexico, and Peru to develop MDC-type pension schemes. It also looks at the extent to which such schemes could be extended to groups that are currently not contributing to the system. The chapter begins by analyzing the reasons why MDC schemes may be relevant in Latin America, focusing on the three countries. It then reviews the experience of MDC schemes in the three countries, including projects that have been implemented, regulatory development in progress, and other initiatives that have been abandoned for the time being. The following section uses household survey data from Colombia, Mexico, and Peru to consider the potential for developing MDC-type schemes and identify groups in the labor force that could be the focus of such an initiative. The last section draws some conclusions.

Matching Schemes and Structural Problems behind Low Pension Coverage in Latin America

Latin America has low coverage in social insurance and social protection, particularly in the case of pensions (Rofman, Lucchetti, and Ourens 2008; Rofman and Oliveri 2012). Even though there is a strong correlation (about 80 percent) between the level of coverage and gross domestic product (GDP) per capita (Forteza, Luchetti, and Pallares-Miralles 2009), with the exception of Chile, Latin American countries exhibit pension coverage rates that are below those of other countries with similar per capita GDP levels (figure 10.2).

FIGURE 10.2 **Pension coverage as a percentage of the labor force and GDP per capita in selected countries, early 2000s**

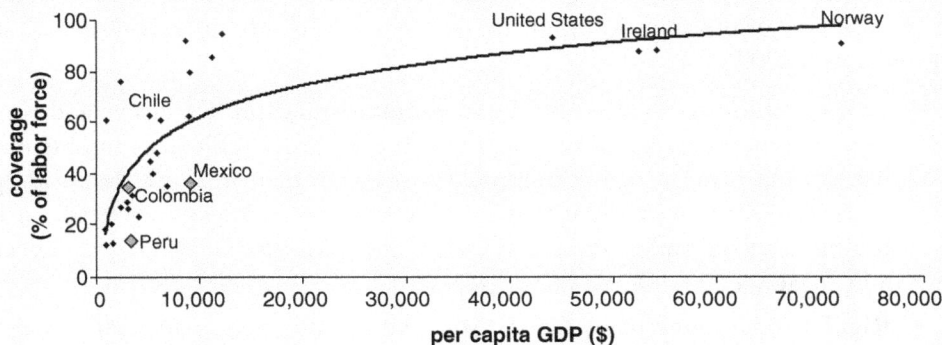

SOURCES: Holzmann, Robalino, and Takayama 2009; World Bank Development Indicators database.

THE CHALLENGE OF INFORMALITY

A number of factors lie behind the problem of low pension coverage in the region. One is the capacity to save, which is closely related to per capita income, among other factors (Costa and others 2011; Ribe, Robalino, and Walker 2010; Robalino and Holzmann 2009; Tuesta 2011a). A second is government inefficiency in various areas (Carranza, Chávez, and Valderrama 2006). Behind the problem of low income generation are poor economic management and ill-conceived growth strategies, a deficient institutional structure, and inadequate policies for dealing with poverty, health, education, and sex (Acosta and Ramírez 2004). A third, particularly serious, problem within the institutional arena is the extent of the informal economy, which makes it infeasible to impose a mandate for pension contributions because the state cannot enforce compliance (Costa and others 2011; Levy 2008; Tuesta 2011b). As shown in figure 10.3, there is a negative correlation between the level of labor informality and pension coverage rates. Peru is ranked among the economies with the highest levels of labor informality in the world.

FIGURE 10.3 **Labor informality and pension coverage in selected countries, early 2000s**

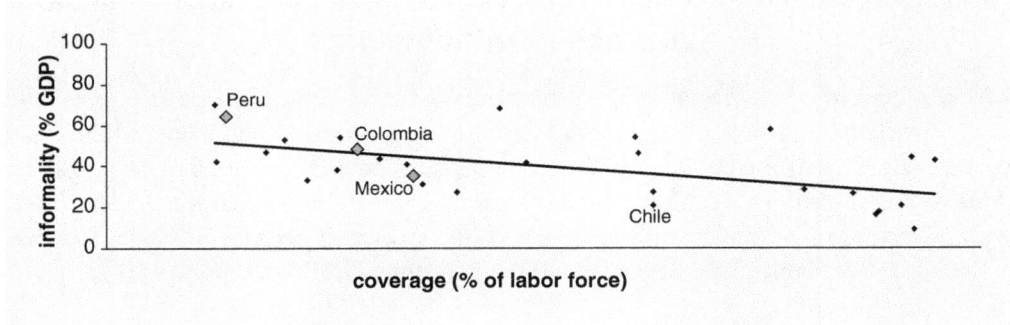

SOURCES: Holzmann, Robalino, and Takayama 2009; Schneider, Buehn, and Montenegro 2010.

Several factors explain the high levels of labor informality in Colombia, Mexico, and Peru (for a survey of the empirical evidence on labor informality in Latin America, see Perry and others 2007):

- **Low institutional quality and burdensome regulation.** Expensive and complicated procedures for creating and winding up firms, difficulties in obtaining licenses and permits, registration problems, and inadequate protection of property rights create an environment that is not favorable for doing business or establishing new companies (Breceda, Rigolini, and Saavedra 2008; Loayza, Serven, and Sugawara 2009; World Bank 2012).

- **Rigid and complex labor legislation.** The combination of minimum wages, relatively high employment benefits, low labor productivity, and restrictions on hiring and firing is conducive to labor informality (Breceda, Rigolini, and Saavedra 2008; Carranza 2012; Chong, Galdo, and Saavedra 2007; Loayza, Serven, and Sugawara 2009).

- **Imperfect land and water markets.** In areas where the land market does not operate properly, it is impossible to accumulate land. In areas where water rights are not transparently assigned, landownership is concentrated among farmers with small holdings or in farming communities. The result is inefficient farming operations with very low productivity and without the capacity to generate levels of income that enable workers to participate in a social security system (De Soto 1989; Loayza 2007; Oviedo 2009).

- **Recent history of high macroeconomic volatility.** Macroeconomic problems include volatile prices, unexpected changes in the tax system, erratic demand, and restrictions on capital flows and foreign exchange regimes that limit the development of financial markets. All these factors have meant that companies cannot easily or predictably comply with their social security or tax obligations. The greater macroeconomic stability achieved over the last decade has improved average incomes, developed capital markets, and led to a steady reduction in labor informality, but formalizing the economy remains a very slow process (Loayza 2007).

- **Explicit or implicit incentives to informality.** The significant number of people who remain in the informal economy generates the political temptation to offer financial assistance and subsidies, either explicit (such as public purchase programs, special tax schemes, subsidies, or programs to write off agricultural debt for small producers) or implicit (exemptions from labor and tax inspection, special application of regulations to physical establishments where informal activities are being carried out) (Carranza 2012; Loayza 2007; Oviedo 2009).

This high rate of labor informality, particularly in rural areas, has generated the following structural characteristics:

- A two-tier business structure, in which many very small companies with low labor productivity account for a high percentage of jobs and a few very large companies with high labor productivity account for a high percentage of output

- Small companies that have informal relations with their workers, because low labor productivity does not allow them to pay minimum wages or provide other types of required benefits

- Large companies that have formal relations with their workers but encounter problems when they attempt to expand to take advantage of economies of scale in sectors in which they compete with small informal enterprises (services, retail trade)

- Employment legislation that allows temporary formal employment without benefits; this form of employment tends to be popular among both employers (because of the potentially lower labor costs and more flexible ability to terminate workers) and workers (who usually choose to receive higher cash income in the short term by not participating in social security systems, even when there is typically greater overall value over the longer term in establishing eligibility for the benefits), and affects the level of social security coverage and the employer's incentives to invest in training.

Although macroeconomic growth and stability in Latin America are generating conditions conducive to formalizing the economy—and Colombia, Mexico, and Peru have been examples of stability and growth for more than two decades—formalization is a very gradual process. Moreover, growth alone is not enough to achieve it. Structural reforms are required to introduce greater flexibility to factor markets, establish uniform and simple tax systems, and make it easier to do business. These reforms may be delayed or simply not implemented for political economy reasons.

Formalization is important because, like many industrial economies, Colombia, Mexico, and Peru have established systems that use employers as contractual agents to ensure social security coverage, mandating participation as a condition of employment and collecting contributions through deductions from wages. Informal firms—or firms that maintain informal relations with their employees—do not act as agents of the state in enforcing compliance with the law. As Latin America ages, the high level of informality is leaving a growing number of people without social protection (in terms of pensions, health, and unemployment).

CAN A MATCHING SCHEME INCREASE COVERAGE?

Given these structural difficulties, some countries have given up on looking for schemes that oblige or create incentives for workers to contribute to a social protection scheme during their active lives. Instead, they have opted for ex post solutions aimed at providing means-tested noncontributory pensions for the elderly or people who do not otherwise qualify to receive a pension.[4]

Such solutions are problematic for several reasons. First, if the rate of informality remains high and life expectancy continues to rise, public expenditure will face significant political pressures in the future. Second, ex post solutions reinforce the economic incentives for not moving into the formal economy and impose rigid thresholds that could create disincentives for saving by people who might otherwise be capable of and inclined to do so. Third, to the extent that there is a social program with broad groups that are actual or potential beneficiaries, there will be considerable political pressure for new initiatives and additions to these programs, which will extend coverage and increase benefits. Development of these social pensions is thus not a long-term solution for the problem of coverage related to the capacity and desire to save during one's active working life (Levy 2008).

The most adequate way to extend coverage in the long term is to find new mechanisms that can increase participation in saving for old age during the period of active employment. Mandatory contribution schemes could play a role, although they have clear limitations in a context of high levels of informality that are likely to be meaningfully reduced only over the long term. A smarter proposal could therefore be to promote voluntary saving by a broad range of groups that are not currently saving by trying to identify the factors that could encourage them to participate.

In a context of limited fiscal resources, particularly in medium- and low-income countries such as Colombia, Mexico, and Peru, the aim should be to identify groups that require government assistance for saving for old age and that are more likely to respond to incentives. Among people who currently do not participate in mandated pension schemes, some independent workers with high income have sufficient resources to make contributions. For such workers, it is probably a good idea to develop strategies or implement changes to the law to make participation mandatory.

The situation differs for low- and middle-income independent workers who have low productivity and unstable relationships with informal enterprises, which makes it difficult for them to generate income, thus limiting their possibility to save. This large group will probably represent the biggest challenge for the government in terms of designing incentives, considering that the incentives to remain in the informal sector and to not contribute are great and difficult to counteract.

Some workers in this group are probably in a better position than others and may be able to save for old age if the incentives are appropriate and well designed. MDC-type systems that have significant government support and provide meaningful economic incentives that complement the savings of workers who decide to contribute voluntarily are an option. It is important that incentives be sufficiently attractive to encourage pension saving among low-income groups, where the opportunity cost with respect to other alternatives is usually high (Mitchell and Utkus 2004). Not only the willingness to save but also the adequacy and design of a financial product (that will be used only when people are old enough to retire) are needed. Saving for pensions tends not to be very popular, because it absorbs limited current resources in return for benefits at a distant point in time, which some people will never reach (Selnow 2004).

An MDC scheme may be relevant if it interacts with other incentives that help informal workers overcome other needs that may be more urgent in the short term. Some pension systems that have considered using MDC schemes have complemented them with the possibility of using pension funds to help purchase a first home or access health care. Other schemes have also allowed access to these savings when people suffer negative shocks to their short-term income or experience liquidity needs because of illness or other factors.

MDC schemes should be considered a mechanism for encouraging saving as part of a set of broader instruments. Particularly in the cases of Chile and Colombia, the probability of household saving increases when saving offers access to the future acquisition of a home, health care services, or improved educational opportunities (Cardoso 2007; Fuentes 2010).

REVIEW OF MATCHING CONTRIBUTION SCHEMES IN COLOMBIA, MEXICO, AND PERU

Pension legislation in Colombia, Mexico, and Peru has addressed the problem of low coverage through a variety of different initiatives. Each approach has to take into account the specific characteristics of the country and respond to the situations of workers both during their working life (ex ante) and at the time of retirement (ex post). In general terms, reforms must provide a comprehensive response to social, employment, and macroeconomic aspects. At the same time, although reducing labor informality should continue to be a goal and incentives may be introduced for this purpose, transformations must focus on guaranteeing adequate and sustainable pensions for the population (OECD 2010; Ribe, Robalino, and Walker 2010).

Given that employment informality is widespread and old-age poverty is persistent in Latin America, reinforcing the solidarity pillar in the short term is an inevitable first step in strengthening the retirement income system. The Inter-American Development Bank has proposed establishing a general social protection system financed through consumption taxes (Levy 2008; Pagés 2010); the Economic Commission for Latin America and the Caribbean proposes extending existing minimum pensions (ECLAC 2006). One way of strengthening this pillar could be to reduce the number of years of contributions required to obtain a minimum contributory pension. Another would be to introduce social noncontributory pensions, although this option would require the commitment of significantly more public resources (1–2 percent in the case of very small cash transfers to the elderly population in poverty according to estimates). As broad fiscal commitment to a basic noncontributory pension could become a strong disincentive to formality, it may be advisable for minimum pensions to be directly linked to contributions up to a certain level, as they are in Chile.

One of the few ways of providing a solution to the lack of coverage that is sustainable socially and economically in the long term is to increase the savings of people working now. Ex ante policies thus appear to offer more room for maneuvering toward a reform of pension systems.

The most direct political option is to make it mandatory for self-employed workers to be members of the system. Such workers represent about half of informal urban middle-income workers in Colombia, Mexico, and Peru (8.8 million, of which fewer than 0.7 million have completed tertiary education).[5] However, the case of Brazil, which has introduced mandatory payment, shows that coverage continues to be unequally distributed, as high-income independent workers contribute significantly more than low- and middle-income ones. Clearly, it is not easy to introduce this policy effectively (Costa and others 2011). Ensuring that workers make contributions is difficult, and requiring them to do so may not be the best or a sufficient way to provide for their old age, given their limited capacity for saving. Some countries have considered a semi-mandatory hybrid option, in which workers are automatically registered but may decide to quit the system. This option may be accompanied by modifications to adapt to special cases, such as greater flexibility in the amount and frequency of contributions or permission to withdraw payments in some circumstances, such as long-term unemployment or health problems (Hu and Stewart 2009).

In recent years, the debate has begun to focus on the use of matching contributions to enhance participation in defined contribution pensions by introducing transfers from the government that are contingent on the level of voluntary contributions made to individual pension accounts. Unlike minimum pensions and social pensions, MDCs can have a significant impact on informal sector middle-income workers (Ribe, Robalino, and Walker 2010). However, the likely effect will depend on the size of the coverage problem and the factors behind it.

The sources of finance of these incentives may be diverse, and they may differ in scope and form. The experiences in Colombia, Mexico, and Peru have been specific to each country's circumstances. The fiscal prudence shown by their finance ministers has influenced the design and limited the progress of these programs. The often contrasting vision of experts and policy makers has also played a role in each country. In many cases, matching contribution projects, and even laws already approved, have not been implemented because of a lack of consensus. As a result, MDC schemes in the three countries have so far been fairly limited; in no case have they ended up being generally applicable.

It is important to underscore that matching schemes—or any other incentive that seeks to increase participation without solving the underpinnings of labor informality—will not be enough. Structural reforms (for example, in the labor market or on the regulatory side) beyond pension policy will be necessary to effect real change and spur workers to save for old age.

Colombia

Since the Act of 1993, when structural pension reforms were implemented, the Colombian pension system has implemented two core mandatory schemes. One was the new private mandatory defined contribution scheme known as the Individual Savings System with Solidarity (Régimen de Ahorro Individual con Solidaridad—RAIS). The other was the pay-as-you-go public scheme known as the Average Premium System (Régimen de Prima Media—RPM). Workers must choose and contribute exclusively to one of these schemes. They contribute 16 percent of their base income, although the percentage allocated to savings for old-age pensions is different in each scheme: 11.5 percent of income is allocated to the individual account in the RAIS; 13 percent goes into the RPM. The remaining amount is allocated to the payment of administrative costs in both schemes and to disability and survivors' insurance, to the Minimum Pension Guarantee Fund (Fondo de Garantía de Pensión Mínima—FGPM) in the RAIS and to disability and survivors' pensions in the RPM. In both systems, the employer is responsible for 75 percent and the employee for 25 percent of the contribution. Independent workers are responsible for all their own contributions to the system (Llanes and Alonso 2010).

Based on this structure, three MDC pension schemes can be identified in Colombia. Two already work as part of the RAIS and the RPM; the third, which is in the process of implementation, is intended to be part of a more general scheme aimed at boosting saving for old age outside of the formal pension system.

The two MDC pension schemes currently in operation are associated with contributions to (1) the private individual accounts system through the FGPM of the RAIS and (2) the Pension Solidarity Fund (Fondo de Solidaridad Pensional—FSP), which is supported by contributions of workers from the RAIS and the RPM. The aim of the first is to benefit pensioners in the RAIS who contributed to their individual accounts but whose accumulated account value is insufficient to obtain a minimum pension under the requirements of the law (frequency of contributions and age).[6] The matching mechanism for RAIS members operates ex post, by activating the use of the FGPM once the pensioner has used up his or her individual account fund. The FGPM is funded from 1.5 percent of the worker's monthly income (part of the 16 percent contribution). Because the RAIS is fairly new, few pensioners have accessed the minimum pension guarantee.[7]

The second type of matching scheme operates through the FSP, which is divided into two subaccounts. The first, the solidarity subaccount (a matching scheme), temporarily subsidizes contributions to the pension system for some groups deemed to have financial limitations. The second, the subsistence subaccount, which has been in place since 1993, is intended to provide protection against poverty in old age. For this account, a previous contributory history is not required (this subaccount is not a matching contribution scheme). These subaccounts are financed by contributions of workers to the public (RPM) or private system (RAIS) who earn more than four times the minimum wage. The subsistence subaccount is also financed by the resources of contributors who earn more than 16 times the minimum wage.

The solidarity subaccount is designed exclusively to subsidize the monthly contribution of workers who meet certain conditions (earning a monthly payment less than a minimum salary, among others) who have difficulty making required contributions and thus may find themselves ineligible for a pension. The matching benefit is provided ex ante; it makes up for the contributions that are lacking to qualify for pension benefits. In order to qualify for this benefit, the member is also required to have previously contributed for a certain number of weeks (table 10.1).

The target population of the matching contribution from this subaccount includes people with very low contribution densities, including rural workers, people with disabilities, and women providing care for children (*madres comunitarias*—community mothers).[8] To access the matching contribution, pensioners must first be over the age of 55

TABLE 10.1 **Requirements for accessing the solidarity subaccount of Colombia's Pension Solidarity Fund**

Population group	Requirements		Benefits	
	Age	Previous weeks	Length of subsidy (weeks)	% of subsidy
Self-employed in rural and urban sectors	RPM: 35–55 RAIS: 35–58	250	650	75
Municipal councilors, administrative categories 4.5 and 6	RPM: > 55 RAIS: > 58	500	500	75
Disabled workers	n.a.	500	750	95
Community mothers	n.a.	0	750	80
Unemployed	RPM: > 55 RAIS: > 58	500	650	70

SOURCE: Departamento Nacional de Planeación 2009.

NOTE: To access the FSP, a worker must be affiliated with the General System of Social Security for Health. n.a. = not applicable.

(RPM) or 58 (RAIS) and have contributed to the system for a minimum of 500 weeks (based on the 16 percent of income contribution). In 2009, these conditions were relaxed, and the minimum age was reduced to 35 years. Other groups were added, such as councillors in certain local councils. The percentage of the value subsidized depends on the specific population group eligible for the subsidy.

To qualify for the subsistence subaccount, beneficiaries must be Colombian, have lived in Colombia for the past 10 years, be at least three years younger than the retirement age,[9] and be classified as having a standard of living at the lower two levels.[10] The local authority selects beneficiaries (after verifying their social conditions) and determines the level of the subsidy. In order to increase coverage, the Ministry of Social Welfare selects beneficiaries residing in welfare centers for the elderly, after completing notice and verification requirements. The grants covered by this subsidy include money and basic social services, such as food and medicine. The value of the subsidy cannot exceed 50 percent of the monthly legal minimum wage.

Another potentially interesting scheme, for which the implementing regulations have not yet been passed, is the Periodic Economic Benefits (Beneficios Económicos Periódicos—BEP) scheme.[11] Once enacted, this program will provide monthly payments equal to less than the minimum wage to elderly people who do not meet the conditions required to receive a pension. Since by constitutional mandate, a pension has to be at least equal to the legal minimum wage, the BEP scheme is thus not a pension. The BEP scheme seeks to meet the needs of people working in informal low- and middle-paying jobs, who typically have inadequate income and few incentives to save for old age. It would provide incentives of around 20 percent of accumulated savings at the time of retirement (up to 0.85 times the minimum wage) to stimulate people to make voluntary contributions to the scheme.[12] The goal is to reach some of the low and middle-income groups that are not reached through the participation mandate of the pension systems. The financing of the match will come from government resources rather than a special fund.

Mexico

At least two matching-type schemes in Mexico function within the general mandatory defined contribution pension system established in the reforms of the late 1990s. The first, which targets low-wage workers, is the Social Contribution (Cuota Social), which is part of the defined contribution scheme administered by the Mexican Social Security Institute (Instituto Mexicano de Seguridad Social—IMSS). The second, "solidarity savings," is included in the defined contribution scheme of the Institute for Civil Servant Social Insurance and Services (Instituto de Seguridad Social y Servicios Sociales de los Trabajadores del Estado—ISSSTE). It targets workers who opt to increase their contributions voluntarily (table 10.2).

TABLE 10.2 **Matching schemes in Mexico**

Financial scheme	IMSS	ISSSTE
General contribution rate	6.5% SBC	11.3% SBC
Matching scheme		
Social Contribution	Progressive scheme for workers up to 15 MW	5.5% MW 97[a] indexed to inflation, for all workers
Solidarity Savings (confirmed by the state)	No matching contribution	3.25 times the worker's contribution[b]
Guaranteed pension	Mex$2,096 monthly	Mex$3,626 monthly

SOURCE: OECD 2011.

NOTE: SBC = basic contribution salary (*salario base de cotización*); MW = minimum wage.

A. 5.5% of minimum salary in 1997, indexed to inflation (Mex$3.50 daily).

B. The allowed worker's contribution is up to 2% of SBC.

The Social Contribution is a matching payment by the federal government to the individual accounts of lower-income workers. It consists of a government subsidy of 5.5 percent of the minimum wage in the Federal District for each day of work, adjusted quarterly by the rate of inflation. The Social Contribution significantly increases the retirement savings of lower-income workers. When the new IMSS defined contribution system began operating in July 1997, the Social Contribution was introduced as a welfare instrument for all workers holding pension rights. However, in May 2009, the federal government limited payment of the Social Contribution to workers who earned less than 15 times the minimum wage in the Federal District. The value of the contribution is progressive, decreasing by steps with multiples of the minimum wage.[13]

The Social Contribution scheme can be considered a matching scheme in which the government complements the worker's contribution to the defined contribution system. As this is a public contribution to workers who are already paying into the system, this assistance may be interpreted as more of an incentive to prevent workers already in the system from stopping their contributions rather than a scheme for attracting new contributors. The scheme's matching does not reduce the cost of formality; it increases future benefits for people who enter the system and contribute.

The Social Contribution provides increased pension benefits for many lower-income workers affiliated with the pension system. The 2009 reform establishing an income cap as an eligibility requirement tightened the scheme's focus on lower-income groups. The policy could be better targeted by, for example, having the state contribute 11 percent of the 1997 minimum wage instead of the current 5.5 percent for people earning up to three times the minimum wage (Herrera 2010). Under such a reform, the fiscal cost of increasing the Social Contribution for people with salaries up to three times the minimum wage would be fully compensated by eliminating benefits by workers earning more than this amount.

In the scheme run by the ISSSTE, the match originates with the reforms implemented in 2007. The new system is based on funded defined contribution individual accounts for public sector workers. It includes the establishment of the National Pension Fund for Civil Servants (PENSIONISSTE), a public body that is an offshoot of the ISSSTE. The National Commission for the Retirement Saving System (Consar) regulates and supervises the fund's operation, administration, and execution. PENSIONISSTE is thus a state body. It operates in a manner similar to the Afores, the private pension fund administrators that manage the funds for private sector workers.

PENSIONISSTE is financed through the collection of fees from member accounts. The law stipulates that for each Mex\$1 workers contributes voluntarily to their individual pension accounts, the state will contribute Mex\$3.25. This voluntary contribution has a ceiling of 2 percent on the employee contribution base and a maximum match from the employer that cannot exceed 6.5 percent. This matching scheme, which is attractive for the worker, can increase a pensioner's replacement rate by up to 20 percentage points if it is maintained over a full working life. This ex ante–type matching scheme aims to increase the mandatory pension contributions of public sector workers.

In addition to these schemes, firms in Mexico can develop employer pension plans. Various types of matching contribution schemes encourage worker participation. These plans are registered at Consar. In 2010, more than 1,830 of these plans were operating, accounting for about 3 percent of GDP (Turner 2011). The plans may be defined benefit, defined contribution, or mixed, depending on the firm. More than half of all plans operate under schemes in which contributions are shared by employer and employee.

In 2006, Mexico proposed the Mechanism for Saving for Retirement Opportunities (Mecanismo de Ahorro para el Retiro Oportunidades—MAROP), as part of the Oportunidades human development program (Secretaria de Desarrollo Social 2006). Under the scheme, Mexicans between the ages of 30 and 69 who were participating in the Oportunidades program who saved Mex\$20–Mex\$50 a month would receive equal matching contributions from the state. Seven million people would have been eligible for the scheme. With savings of Mex\$50 a month and an equal match from the state, savers would have received pensions of Mex\$1,000 a month at age 70. In the end, the project was not approved, because of doubts regarding the consistency of including a saving objective for groups in the Oportunidades program, who lived in poverty.

Peru

In June 2008, Legislative Decree No. 1086 established the objective of promoting the competitiveness, formality, and development of micro- and small enterprises (known as the Spanish acronym MYPES, from *micro and pequeñas empresas* which are firms with up to 10 workers for microenterprises and between 11 and 100 workers for small enterprises).

One main component of the decree was to create a permanent regime for the support of MYPES. Registration requirements were made more flexible for firms with up to 100 workers and annual sales of no more than 1,700 tax units (Unidad Impositiva Tributaria), which in 2012 represents sales of S/. 6.2 million (around $2.3 million). Some 95 percent of all Peruvian companies fall within these limits, but most of them do not contribute to any pension scheme although it is mandatory. This behavior, common in high-level informal economies, has been explained by the lack of enforcement by the Peruvian state and the obvious income constraints of employees working in very low-productivity firms. Thus, the decree's objective was to introduce incentives for workers and firms to follow the law by directly reducing the cost of labor by giving wage complements of 50 percent (nonsalary payments) and a third of severance payments for each worker hired. A key aspect for implementing this component had been to define a different minimum wage for these enterprises by the National Employee Council. However, this never occurred, and the Ministry of Finance, which promoted this law, lost interest in implementing it (Carranza 2012).

A second interesting component of the decree was the introduction of the Welfare Pension System (Sistema de Pensiones Sociales) for workers and owners of microenterprises, which was never implemented. This component of the 1998 decree was taken up in the recent Private Pension Reform Law No. 29903 of July 2012.[14] The Welfare Pension System is now obligatory for workers in microenterprises who are less than 40 years old and voluntary for those who are older. The workers in these firms will contribute according to a graduated contribution rate (to be defined by regulation) of up to 4 percent of the legal minimum wage. The government will then match that contribution by giving a percentage of it (also to be defined by regulation) through a recognition bond to be redeemed when the worker reaches retirement. This matching is only provided to workers who receive less than 1.5 times the legal minimum wage. Workers can make additional contributions exceeding the matching limit, but those contributions will not be matched. For microenterprises, the formalization process has not gained momentum, for two reasons. First, the National Employment Council has not created a different minimum wage for microenterprises, a move that would allow for a more market-based approach. Second, no pension contributions have been collected by the Welfare Pension System, because the National Pension Office (Oficina de Normalización Previsional) has not been able to implement the operational system to manage individual contributions of independent workers.

Assessment of Matching Schemes in Colombia, Mexico, and Peru

Of the three countries analyzed in this chapter, only Colombia and Mexico have implemented matching schemes for pensions. The schemes in Colombia—the FGPM and the solidarity subaccount—have been aimed largely at increasing the savings of groups of contributors to the system who could end up ineligible for a minimum pension or receive a very limited benefit in old age. The financing source for the matching payments has been higher-income savers, without any support from employers or the state in the case of Colombia. In Mexico, the target population is the same (low-density, low-income affiliates), but the funding of the more general schemes, such as the Social Contribution of the Retirement Savings System and the solidarity saving of PENSIONISSTE comes from the state.

Participation in these programs was limited by two factors. First, fiscal resources for implementing more ambitious programs were scarce, because of the transition from the old public pay-as-you-go systems to the new funded private systems. Second, the matching programs implemented in Colombia and Mexico were designed for people who participated in mandatory schemes; they failed to take account of the high barriers to participating in the formal economy (Levy 2008). Where these costs are high, matching schemes are not enough to bring "outsiders" (informal workers) into the system.

More ambitious matching schemes have not succeeded in advancing beyond the planning stage, and some laws—including the MAROP in Mexico, the BEP scheme in Colombia, and the Welfare Pension System in Peru—have not been implemented. It is difficult to speculate as to whether these matching programs would have provided enough incentives to increase pension participation.

It is important to put in context the importance of MDC schemes in incentivizing pension participation. Given the very large size of the informal sector in these economies (almost 70 percent in Peru), it is difficult to imagine that a monetary incentive to contribute could solve a core structural socioeconomic problem. Bringing workers who are currently not covered by pension systems into the system requires creating incentives that really matter to them. Money (a matching program) could be an incentive, but other factors could provide "nudges" (Thaler and Sunstein 2009) to contribute. Countries such as China, Germany, and New Zealand achieved success by including other incentives, such as allowing partial withdrawals from pension savings in case of liquidity constraints or the financing of a first mortgage.

In developing a policy, perhaps the first step is to determine which workers in the informal sector are in the best position to save and to tailor a program for them. The next section examines this point.

FOCUSING ON THE MIDDLE CLASSES

Among the groups of workers with the greatest potential to respond to voluntary MDC-style savings schemes are middle-income workers, defined as people with per capita income of 50–150 percent of the average.[15] These workers have some capacity to save, and many lack adequate pension coverage. According to household survey data, just 43 percent of workers age 14–64 in Colombia make pension contributions. This percentage is even lower in Mexico (37 percent) and Peru (17 percent).[16] These three countries have among the lowest coverage levels in Latin America (Rofman, Lucchetti, and Ourens 2008; Rofman and Oliveri 2012). The proportion of middle-income households that make regular pension contributions is 39 percent in Colombia, 33 percent in Mexico, and 9 percent in Peru (figure 10.4).

The low affiliation and contribution rates partly reflect informality, which is common among even among the urban middle class. Only a third of middle-income workers in Colombia and Mexico, and slightly more than 20 percent in Peru, are formally

FIGURE 10.4 **Pension coverage in Colombia, Mexico, and Peru, by household income level**

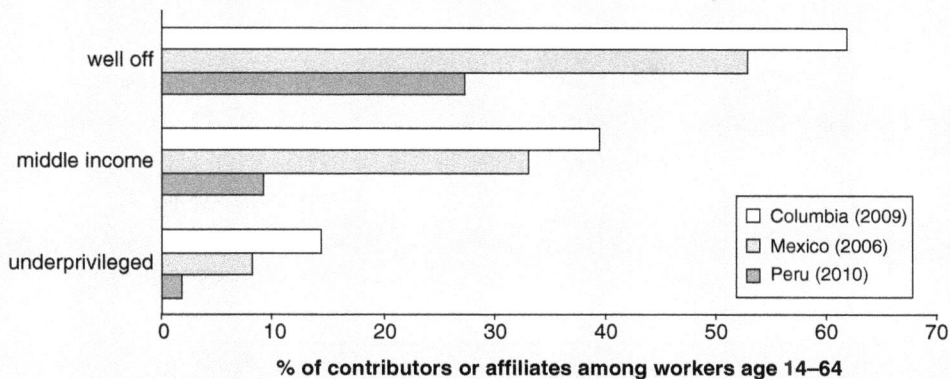

% of contributors or affiliates among workers age 14–64

SOURCES: Costa and others 2011 for Mexico; authors' calculations for Colombia and Peru, based on data from national household surveys.

NOTE: Figures includes affiliates who are paid a wage (*sueldo*) in Mexico and contributors in Colombia and Peru.

employed (defined as having a written employment contract) (figure 10.5).[17] The vast majority of middle-income workers in the three countries are dependent workers without a contract or independent workers, with about equal numbers employed in each group.

Informality not only implies significantly lower rates of affiliation and contribution, it can also have a regressive impact on the pension system. Inequality in Latin America has fallen somewhat since 2000, as a result of the increase in social expenditures, particularly conditional cash transfers programs, and a decline in the returns from education (López-Calva and Lustig 2010). But inequality still remains very high. In the absence of further pension reforms, the contributory social insurance systems will continue to be regressive, as (formal sector) workers with higher incomes are more likely to participate in the system (and by definition contribute at higher levels) than low- and middle-income workers in the informal sector.

Among the 33.3 million middle-class workers in Colombia, Mexico, and Peru, 19.8 million are informal (4.4 million in Colombia, 11.9 million in Mexico, and 3.5 million in Peru). Many workers alternate frequently between periods of employment and unemployment as well as between formal and informal employment. In Mexico, for example, the probability of remaining in the same employment situation between 2002 and 2005 was 63 percent for independently employed men (it was much lower among all types of workers analyzed) (Jütting and de Laiglesia 2009).

Among informal middle-income workers, independent workers who completed tertiary education have higher coverage rates than other informal workers (figure 10.6). These rates are still low, however: 20 percent in Colombia, 1 percent in Mexico, and 5 percent in Peru. They are far below those of formal workers in the same countries: 78 percent in Colombia, 81 percent in Mexico, and 56 percent in Peru. Except in Mexico, where the coverage rate of informal nonagricultural workers is 18 percent, informal workers rarely contribute to a pension system.

FIGURE 10.5 **Nonagricultural middle-income workers in Colombia, Mexico, and Peru by employment category**

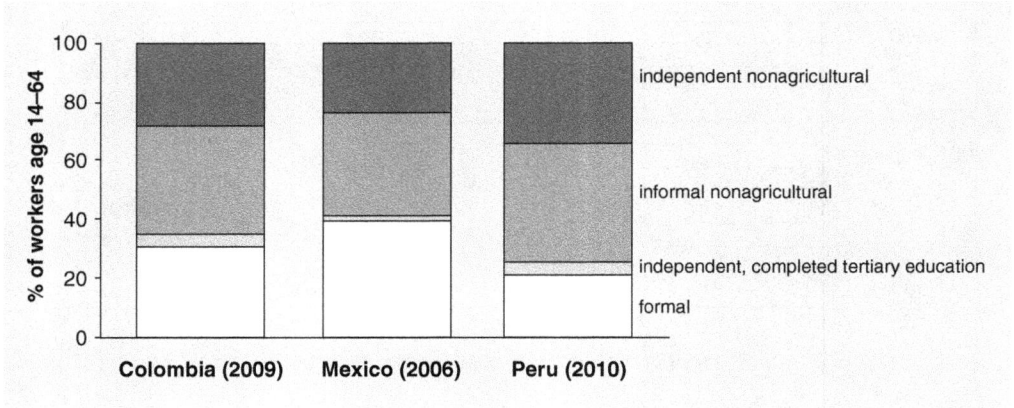

SOURCES: Costa and others 2011 for Mexico; authors' calculations based on national household surveys for Colombia and Peru.

FIGURE 10.6 **Pension coverage of middle-class nonagricultural workers in Colombia, Mexico, and Peru, by type of employment**

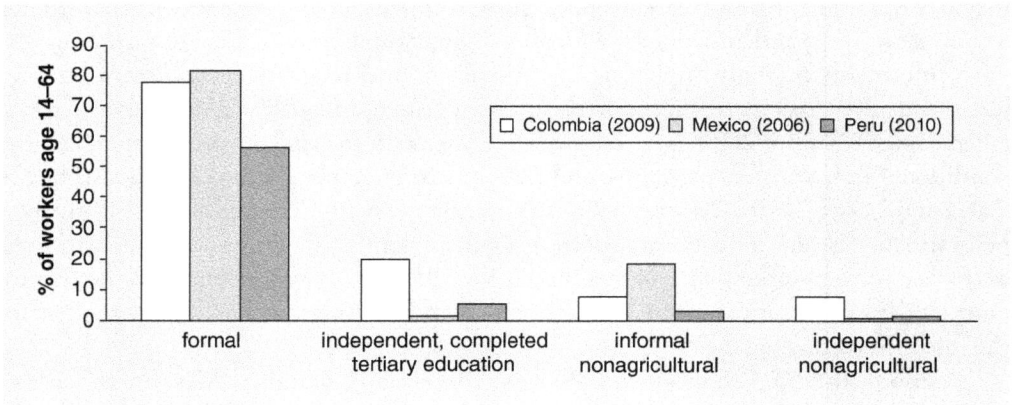

SOURCES: Costa and others (2011) for Mexico; authors' calculations based on national household surveys for Colombia and Peru.

NOTE: Figures are for affiliates who are paid a wage (*sueldo*) in Mexico and contributors in Colombia and Peru. Figures for Mexico include only workers who also earned wages and should therefore be interpreted with caution.

Informal middle-income workers are therefore the group on which matching defined contributions could have the greatest impact. This group numbers about 19.8 million workers in these three countries. On average, the remuneration of these workers is similar to the minimum wage in Colombia and Peru and up to twice the minimum wage in Mexico. Their labor income alone places them significantly above the national poverty threshold, suggesting that they could respond positively to incentives for pension savings.

Conclusions

Although Colombia, Mexico, and Peru introduced major structural reforms in the mid-1990s, they still exhibit very limited levels of social protection coverage (28 percent of the labor force in Colombia, 27 percent in Mexico, and 22 percent in Peru). These figures reflect the limited effectiveness of basing a pension scheme on withholding of contributions by employers in environments in which most employment relations are informal.

A high level of labor informality in the region is the result of various factors, including weak institutions; excessive regulation; rigid and complex employment legislation; the combination of minimum wages, relatively high employment benefits, and low labor productivity; imperfect land and water markets; the still recent history of high macroeconomic volatility; and incentives to informality, whether explicit (such as public purchase programs, special tax regimes, subsidies, or programs to write off the debt of small farmers) or implicit (exemption from employment, tax, and building inspections). This combination of factors has had several worrisome consequences. It has led to a two-tier firm structure, made up of a large number of very small companies, which employ workers with low productivity, and a small number of very large companies, which employ workers with high productivity. It has also incentivized small companies to maintain informal relations with their workers, because low labor productivity does not allow them to pay the minimum wage and provide benefits. It has made it more difficult for large companies to compete with informal enterprises (services, retail trade). As some employment legislation allows formal hiring temporarily without benefits (for example, the law promoting nontraditional exports in Peru), employers tend to choose this method of employment relation, reinforcing the low level of coverage of social security and the lack of employer investment in training employees.

Addressing the lack of social protection cannot rely solely on the formalization process, which will be gradual. Several programs in the three countries aim to support savings for old-age income through ex post or ex ante incentives and subsidies. Ex post policies provide direct subsidies when benefits are calculated on the basis of the value of savings accounts at retirement or establish a noncontributory pension for people who reach the retirement age without having participated in a pension system. Rather than attempt to provide universal coverage, these kinds of programs could target specific groups. Implementation of ex post schemes should take account of their fiscal effects, the distortions they could generate in assigning resources, and the disincentives to saving that could result for groups that are currently saving or who have the potential to do so.

Ex ante schemes provide a preferable alternative, not only because they reduce distortions and are more manageable from the fiscal point of view but also because they address the basic problem of limited participation and long-term savings within the pension system. In order to design an adequate reform, it is important to identify the limitations of the existing mandatory schemes, study the level and types of informality, and take into account the inherent economic conditions potential savers face. These conditions include low productivity, high exposure to economic shocks, difficulty in accumulating a continuous employment history, the need to cover basic shorter-term demands (for housing, education, and health services), and others.

MDC schemes could be appropriate for some workers who are not currently making contributions to the pension system, provided that the monetary transfer by the state is sufficiently attractive to encourage saving. An MDC scheme could be of significant value if it includes certain features, such as allowing funds to be withdrawn to purchase a first home, access health services, or weather negative shocks to short-term income.

Colombia, Mexico, and Peru have very limited experience with matching-type schemes, which have focused mainly on increasing the savings of groups of workers who are already participating in some part of the pension system. These schemes do not seem attractive enough to people who are not contributing or are not even affiliated.

Future reform efforts should target groups that have the capacity to save and might respond to government incentives. The emerging middle class, among whom pension coverage remains very low, is beginning to show some capacity for saving. The nearly 20 million informal middle-income workers in Colombia, Mexico, and Peru could well benefit from MDC schemes.

Notes

1. In Mexico, workers belonging to the old pay-as-you-go system until 1997 who were transferred to the new funded system could choose the form in which their pension was calculated, based on either the rules of the pay-as-you-go system or the savings they had accumulated in their individual accounts.

2. For a complete review of the origin of the reforms in Latin America, see Gill, Packard, and Yermo (2004); Holzmann and Hinz (2005); Tuesta (2011a); and World Bank (1994).

3. The term informality covers a range of employment, from illegal activity to exchanges that are outside formal or contractual environments, such as mutual aid between neighbors.

4. One example of this type of scheme is the recently approved Pensión 65 plan in Peru, aimed at very poor people age 65 and older. Bjeletic and Tuesta (2010) review other schemes.

5. Independent workers in Colombia are required to contribute to both pension and health insurance schemes.

6. The minimum pension in Colombia is the legal minimum wage, which is annually discussed in a tripartite commission made up of representatives from the government, unions, and employers. If they do not reach agreement, the wage is set by a government decree.

7. The public defined benefit pay-as-you-go scheme (RPM) does not have a similar fund. The reserves of the social security were depleted in 2004. When a worker completes the number of weeks of contribution required and reaches the age of retirement, the government pays the minimum pension through a transfer from the budget.

8. Community mothers are women hired by the Welfare Family Institute to provide child care in a community.

9. The age for retirement is 62 for men and 57 for women.

10. According to the Identification System of Potential Beneficiaries of Social Programmes (Sistema de Identificación de Potenciales Beneficiarios de Programas Sociales), a tool that classifies individuals according to their living standard. It is used to objectively select potential beneficiaries of social programs managed by the state.

11. Legislative Act 01 of 2005 and Decreto 4944 of December 18, 2009.

12. Among the incentives policy makers are considering is the possibility of allowing the funds to be used as a guarantee for obtaining credit, including for housing.

13. The progressive incremental scheme starts with a daily amount equivalent to Mex$57 ($4.35) for workers earning up to 1 minimum wage (MW); Mex$54 ($4.16) for workers earning 1–4 MWs; Mex$52 ($3.98) for workers earning 4–7 MWs; Mex$50 ($3.80) for workers earning 7–10 MWs; and Mex$47 ($3.62) for workers earning 10–15 MWs.

14. Law No. 29903 takes into account various modifications of the private pension system, such as industrial organization, investment regime, corporate governance, and law enforcement, among others. The Welfare Pension System is one of the issues considered by this law.

15. Empirical studies on poverty and income distribution often use half the average income as the poverty line. Middle-classes workers represent 41 percent of workers in Peru, 50 percent in Colombia, and 55 percent in Mexico.

16. The figure for Colombia (the number of contributors) comes from the 2009 Great Integrated Household Survey, which covered 13 cities. The figure for Mexico (number of affiliates receiving a wage) comes from the 2006 National Household Income and Expenditure Survey. The number for Peru (number of contributors who declared having made contributions during the year) comes from the 2010 National Household Survey. See Costa and others (2011) for a detailed description of the methodology and an analysis of pensions and informality in Bolivia, Brazil, Chile, and Mexico.

17. Using this criterion to define formality facilitates international comparisons, as it reflects a form of regulation that is common to Latin American countries: the obligation to formalize and register an employment relationship.

References

Acosta, O., and J. Ramírez. 2004. "Las redes de protección social: modelo incompleto." Development Finance Series, Economic Commission for Latin America and the Caribbean.

Bjeletic, J., and D. Tuesta. 2010. "Pension Reform in Peru." In *Pension Reforms in Latin America: Balance and Challenges Ahead*, ed. Eduardo Fuentes, Alicia García Herrero, and José Luis Escrivá. Madrid: BBVA. http://www.bbvaresearch.com/KETD/fbin/mult/Pensionreformsin-latinamerica_tcm348-238550.pdf?ts=2292012.

Breceda, K., Rigolini, J., and Saavedra, Jaime. 2008. "Latin America and the Social Contract: Patterns of Social Spending and Taxation." Policy Research Working Paper Series 4604, World Bank, Washington, DC.

Cardoso, Miguel. 2007. "Pension Systems and Incentives for Independent Workers: An Analysis for the Chilean Economy." Presentation prepared for the Latin American and Caribbean Economic Association and Latin American Meeting of the Econometric Society, parallel meeting, Bogota, October 5.

Carranza, L. 2012. "La Ley Mypes 2008 en el Perú." Draft note. Universidad San Martin de Porres-USMP.

Carranza, L., J. Chávez, and J. Valderrama. 2006. "The Political Economy of the Budget Process: the Peruvian Case." IADB Publications 15178, Washington, DC, Inter-American Development Bank.

Chong, A., J. Galdo, and J. Saavedra. 2007. "Informality and Productivity in the Labor Market: Peru 1986–2001." RES Working Papers 4526, Inter-American Development Bank, Research Department.

Costa, R. Da, J. R. de Laiglesia, E. Martinez, and A. Melguizo. 2011. "The Economy of the Possible: Pensions and Informality in Latin America." Working Paper 295, Organisation for Economic Co-operation and Development Development Center, Paris.

Departamento Nacional de Planeación. 2009. "Requisitos de Acceso al Programa Subsidiado de Aporte a la Pensión Financiado con los Recursos de la Subcuenta de Solidaridad del Fondo de Solidaridad Pensional." Documento Conpes 3605, Consejo Nacional de Política Económica y Social República de Colombia, Bogotá.

De Soto, H. 1989. *The Other Path: The Invisible Revolution in the Third World.* Harpercollins.

ECLAC (Economic Commission for Latin America and the Caribbean). 2006. "La protección social de cara al futuro: acceso, financiamiento y solidaridad." ECLAC, Santiago.

Forteza, A., L. Luchetti, and M. Pallares-Miralles. 2009. "Measuring the Coverage Gap." In *Closing the Coverage Gap: The Role of Social Pensions and Other Retirement Income Transfers*, ed. R. Holzmann, D. A. Robalino, and N. Takayama. Washington, DC: World Bank.

Fuentes, E. 2010. "Creating Incentives for Voluntary Contributions to Pension Funds by Independent Workers: An Informal Evaluation Based on the Case of Chile." 10/12, BBVA Research Working Papers. Madrid: BBVA.

Gill, I., T. Packard, and J. Yermo. 2004. "Keeping the Promise of Social Security in Latin America." World Bank, Washington, DC.

Herrera, C. 2010. "Towards Stronger Pension Systems in Mexico: Vision and Proposals for Reform." In *Pension Reforms in Latin America: Balance and Challenges Ahead*, ed. Eduardo Fuentes and others. Madrid: BBVA.

Holzmann, R., and R. Hinz. 2005. "Old Age Income Support in the 21st Century." World Bank, Washington, DC.

Holzmann, R., D. A. Robalino, and N. Takayama. 2009. *Closing the Coverage Gap: The Role of Social Pensions and Other Retirement Income Transfers.* Washington, DC: World Bank.

Hu, Y., and F. Stewart. 2009. "Pension Coverage and Informal Sector Workers: International Experiences." Working Papers on Insurance and Private Pensions 31, Organisation for Economic Co-operation and Development, Paris.

Jütting, J. P., and J. R. de Laiglesia, eds. 2009. "Is Informal Normal? Towards More and Better Jobs in Developing Countries." Organisation for Economic Co-operation and Development, Paris.

Levy, S. 2008. *Good Intentions, Bad Outcomes. Social Policy, Informality and Economic Growth in Mexico.* Washington, DC: Brookings Institution Press.

Llanes, M., and J. Alonso. 2010. "Confidence in the Future: Proposals for an Improved Pension System in Colombia." In *Pension Reforms in Latin America: Balance and Challenges Ahead*, ed. Eduardo Fuentes and others. Madrid: BBVA.

Loayza, N. 2007. "The Causes and Consequences of Informality in Peru." Working Papers 2007-018, Banco Central de Reserva del Perú.

Loayza, N., L. Serven, and N. Sugawara. 2009. "Informality in Latin America and the Caribbean." Policy Research Working Paper Series 4888, World Bank, Washington, DC.

Lopez-Calva, L. P., and N. Lustig, eds. 2010. *Declining Inequality in Latin America: A Decade of Progress?* Baltimore: Brookings Institution Press and United Nations Development Programme.

Mitchell, O., and S. Utkus. 2004. "Lessons from Behavioral Finance and Retirement Plan Design." In *Pension Design and Structure: New Lessons from Behavioral Finance*, ed. Olivia Mitchell and Stephen Utkus. Oxford: Oxford University Press.

OECD (Organisation for Economic Co-operation and Development). 2010. *Latin American Economic Outlook 2011: How Middle-Class Is Latin America?* Paris: OECD Development Center.

———. 2011. "Pensions at a Glance 2011: Retirement-Income Systems in OECD and G20 Countries." www.oecd.org/els/social/pensions/PAG.

Oviedo, A. M. 2009. "Economic Informality: Causes, Costs, and Policies: A Literature Survey of International Experience" Draft background paper prepared for Turkey Country Economic Memorandum—Informality: Causes, Consequences, Policies. World Bank, Washington, DC.

Pagés, C. 2010. *The Age of Productivity: Transforming Economies from the Bottom Up.* New York: Inter-American Development Bank and Palgrave Macmillan.

Perry, G., W. Maloney, O. Arias, P., Fajnzylber, A. Mason, and J. Saavedra-Chanduvi. 2007. *Informality: Exit and Exclusion.* Washington, DC: World Bank.

Ribe, H., D. A. Robalino, and I. Walker. 2010. *From Right to Reality: Achieving Effective Social Protection for All in Latin America and the Caribbean.* Washington, DC: World Bank.

Robalino, D. A., and R. Holzmann. 2009. "Overview and Preliminary Policy Guidance." In *Closing the Coverage Gap: The Role of Social Pensions and Other Retirement Income Transfers*, ed. R. Holzmann, D. A. Robalino, and N. Takayama. Washington, DC: World Bank.

Rofman, R., L. Lucchetti, and G. Ourens. 2008. "Pension Systems in Latin America: Concepts and Measurements of Coverage." Social Protection and Labor Discussion Paper 0616, World Bank, Washington, DC.

Rofman, R., and M. L. Oliveri. 2012. "La cobertura de los sistemas previsionales en América Latina: Conceptos e indicadores." Serie de Documentos de Trabajo sobre Políticas Sociales No. 7, World Bank, Washington, DC.

Schneider, F., A. Buehn, and C. Montenegro. 2010. "Shadow Economies All over the World: New Estimates for 162 Countries from 1999 to 2007." Working Paper No. 322, University of Chile, Department of Economics.

Secretaria de Desarrollo Social. 2006. "Decreto por el que se establece el Mecanismo de Ahorro para el Retiro Oportunidades." March 27, 2006, Diario Oficial.

Selnow, G. 2004. "Motivating Retirement Planning: Problems and Solutions." In *Pension Design and Structure: New Lessons from Behavioral Finance*, ed. Olivia Mitchell and Stephen Utkus. Oxford: Oxford University Press.

Thaler, Richard, and Cass Sunstein. 2009. *Nudge: Improving Decisions about Health, Wealth, and Happiness.* New York: Penguin Books.

Tuesta, D. 2011a. "A Review of the Pensions Systems in Latin America." 11/15 BBVA Research Working Papers.

———. 2011b. "Matching Arrangements in Mexico, Colombia, and Peru." Presentation, MDC Conference, World Bank, June 6.

Turner, A. 2011. "Planes privados de pensiones en México: situación actual y perspectivas." Presentation by Instituto Tecnológico Autónomo de México, Ninth Conference of the International Center for Pension Research, April.

World Bank. 1994. *Averting the Old Age Crisis.* Washington, DC: Oxford University Press.

———. 2012. *Doing Business in a More Transparent World.* Washington, DC: World Bank.

PART IV

Developing Country Experience

CHAPTER 11

China's Pension Schemes for Rural and Urban Residents

Mark C. Dorfman, Dewen Wang, Philip O'Keefe, and Jie Cheng

China's recent establishment of national pension schemes for its rural and urban residents represents a major step toward its ambitious objective of universal pension coverage. The design includes a locally financed matching subsidy linked to a flat defined benefit pension after a vesting period or through "family binding" provisions requiring retirees' adult children to contribute. The policy design supports broad coverage, in part by providing modest basic benefits and a channel for an integrated scheme that can accommodate the wide variation in economic needs and circumstances across China. The benefit level and financing plan balance benefit adequacy against a very modest fiscal commitment while enabling local authorities to supplement benefits. The design may be able to broaden coverage, but its benefits may not be sufficient to provide adequate financial protection in old age for substantial numbers of beneficiaries. Looking forward, universal pension coverage at the individual level will depend in large part on the incentives for sustained participation and the authorities' ability to enhance portability and eventually integrate pension programs across schemes and across space, and pool risk.

Since economic liberalization in the early 1980s, China has faced substantial disparities in pension coverage between urban and rural areas and across regions, and it has implemented multiple reforms of its pension system. As in many former command economies, labor force coverage of China's contributory pension scheme declined sharply in the 1980s. After experimenting with a number of pilot programs in the early 1990s, the government established a national framework for urban contributory pensions, albeit one allowing for regional variation. In the last few years, the authorities have articulated principles for reform, including broad coverage, basic protection, multilayering (urban systems), flexibility (rural systems), and sustainability. These principles underpin the commitments made at the 17th Party Congress toward a comprehensive and integrated social security system by 2020.

As part of its ongoing social protection reforms, in September 2009 the authorities established a national framework for rural pensions, the Rural Pension Pilot Scheme (RPPS), now the National Rural Pension Scheme (NRPS); in July 2011, it introduced an Urban Resident Pension Scheme (URPS). Both schemes fall under the broader umbrella of the 2010 Social Insurance Law. These voluntary schemes include a matching defined contribution element and a heavily subsidized flat basic pension. Both schemes are being rapidly rolled out, with a target of full national geographic coverage by 2013. Early numbers on participation are impressive: by early 2012, the NRPS had more than 250 million contributors, and more than 100 million people were receiving basic pensions.

China's introduction of the NRPS and URPS has arguably been one of the world's most ambitious voluntary pension saving and minimum elderly assistance schemes in a low- or middle-income country. The sheer scale and speed of coverage expansion has already exceeded the initial targets of the Chinese authorities.

The design supports broad coverage as a core objective. Consistent with this objective, minimum contributions are low, benefits are very modest, and fiscal costs are low for all but the poorest local communities. The design links a basic defined benefit to a minimum contribution history. In a unique variation, it also includes a "family binding" provision, whereby the pension eligibility of a contributor already over pensionable age is determined by whether the contributor's adult children contribute to the new system. The financing structure provides the flexibility for communities with additional resources to provide more generous benefits while guaranteeing a minimum level of basic benefits through central government financing. Although initial participation levels suggest considerable momentum for registration, only time will tell if such participation levels are sustained.

This chapter is organized as follows. The first section provides a historical context for the national guidelines established in 2009 for urban and 2011 for rural areas. The second section outlines the design features of the reforms. The third section assesses the design elements and initial experience of the reforms, including benefit adequacy, worker and fiscal affordability, and institutional issues. The last section evaluates the lessons from the Chinese experience and considers their applicability to other countries.

Evolution of Pension Provision for Rural and Urban Residents

PENSION PROVISION IN RURAL AREAS

The pension system in rural areas has experienced two milestones. The first was the old rural pension scheme, introduced by the Ministry of Civil Affairs (MOCA) in 1992. The second is the new rural pension scheme, introduced by the Ministry of Human Resources and Social Security (MHRSS) in 2009.[1] Both schemes built on a typical Chinese policy process of bottom-up local experimentation, which informed the development of national guidelines. The national guidelines in turn attempted to impose greater standardization of scheme design and management, with only partial success in the case of the old system. Perhaps the major distinction between the old and new schemes is the significant financing commitment of the central authorities in the new scheme, which for the first time provides a strong incentive to local authorities to follow a nationally harmonized scheme design.

The old pension scheme experienced steady, if unspectacular, expansion in the 1990s, before coverage growth stagnated and the scheme design fragmented beginning in the late 1990s before the establishment of the new rural pension scheme. This evolution unfolded in various stages.

Initiation and Expansion of Rural Pensions: 1986–98

The initial policy directions on rural pensions were set out in the Seventh Five-Year Plan (1985–90), in which the Chinese government committed to exploring ways to provide basic pensions for rural residents.[2] The plan was built upon through county-level pilots led by MOCA in the Beijing and Shanxi provinces, which emphasized mixed financing responsibility by government, collectives, and individuals, with most of the responsibility falling on individuals.

There was a clear policy push in the early 1990s to expand rural pension schemes, with the large majority following a simple defined contribution design with a small subsidy from the collective in some areas. The initial pilots were followed in 1991 by measures assigning MOCA the lead role on rural pensions and the establishment of pilots in five counties of Shandong Province. The various pilots contributed to a major MOCA policy document in 1992—"The Basic Approach of Rural Pension Schemes at County Level (Trial)"—that outlined a set of principles for rural pension schemes while allowing for regional variations. As a result of this policy initiative, coverage of rural pensions expanded significantly during the 1990s, with programs established by the end of 1998 in 31 provinces and 2,123 counties (just under three-quarters of all rural counties). This period was also the high point of coverage before the NRPS, with more than 80 million rural workers contributing and more than 600,000 people receiving pensions (figure 11.1).

FIGURE 11.1 **Rural pension participation and coverage, 1994–2010**

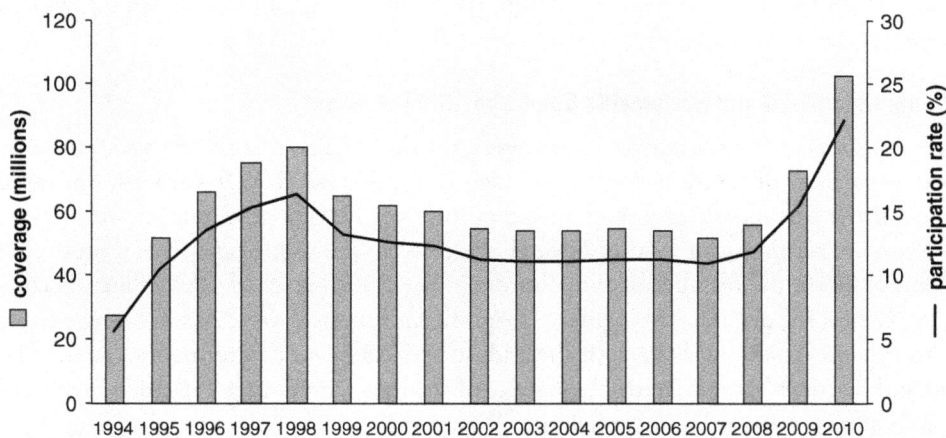

SOURCE: NBS 1995–2011.

Concerns soon began to emerge about the operation of local schemes and the lack of a sound governance framework; the Asian financial crisis in 1997 underscored the need to rethink the program (see Chen 2002; Liang 1999; Ma 1999; and Shi 2006 for a discussion of the shortcomings of previous rural pension schemes). Responsibility for rural pensions was subsequently switched from MOCA to the Ministry of Labor and Social Security (now the MHRSS) in the 1998 administrative restructuring.

Contraction and Stagnation: 1999–2002

As a result of concerns about the effectiveness and sustainability of rural pension schemes, a sharp policy shift took place in the late 1990s to limit their expansion. By 2001, the shift in policy contributed to a steep decline in coverage to just under 60 million participants, with the number stabilizing in the low to mid-50 millions through 2007 in roughly 1,900 counties (see figure 11.1). Despite this contraction, new participants continued to enter the system, and accumulated funds from existing schemes continued to increase, more than doubling between 2000 and 2007. The number of pension beneficiaries approached 4 million by 2007 as existing schemes matured.

Renewal: 2003–09

Renewed impetus toward a new rural pension system emerged with new guidelines from the Ministry of Labor and Social Security in 2003 ("Notice on Seriously Improving Work on Current Rural Pensions"). The new rural pension schemes established during this period fall broadly into three types: social pooling plus individual accounts, flat universal pensions in combination with individual accounts, and individual accounts only. The schemes differed in terms of the financing role of the government at the accumulation and payout stages. The Chinese government reviewed the local pilots before introducing the new national pilot.[3] Although no rigorous evaluation was undertaken, a number of deficiencies in the rural pension system during this phase undermined the achievement of policy objectives and influenced the design of the local and national pilot programs that followed.

National Guidelines and Nationwide Coverage: 2009–Present

The introduction of a nationwide framework for the NRPS in 2009 marked a milestone in the expansion of pension system coverage in rural areas. The framework has rapidly expanded the participation of rural residents and, for the first time, put all localities on a more sustainable financial footing through the injection of significant central funding. By the end of 2010, the number of contributors in the NRPS reached 103 million, accounting for 22 percent of rural employment, a significant increase over 2008. Coverage continued to expand rapidly in 2011 with the addition of 2,343 rural counties and county-level cities and districts (more than three-quarters of the total), including 258 million contributors and almost 100 million beneficiaries (Wen 2012).[4]

PENSION PROVISION IN URBAN AREAS

Earlier pension reforms targeted urban enterprise workers and employees. Based on pilot experiments, in 1998 the government set national guidelines for China's urban social insurance programs. These guidelines provided for five types of social insurance for urban formal sector workers: pensions, health care, maternity, unemployment, and workplace injury. The contributory urban pension insurance program had two components, a basic redistributive defined benefit pension ("social pooling") and a state-managed defined contribution funded individual account scheme.

The urban pension program witnessed steady coverage expansion among wage earners, including within private and foreign enterprises. However, the program excluded the vast majority of people working for themselves in the informal sector, or for small private businesses, as well as the unemployed (collectively known as "urban residents" in the social insurance system). Civil servants and public service unit workers continued to have distinct schemes.

Around 1997, local governments—in Beijing, Chengdu, Guangzhou, Shanghai, and elsewhere—began to establish pilot programs for voluntary contributory and basic benefits for nonwage urban residents.[5] Shanghai's program provided old-age poverty protection for all urban elderly with no other source of income, financed solely by the local government. Guangzhou also set up an urban pension program for the elderly with no other fixed sources of income.[6] The design adopted in Beijing in 2009 was similar to that of the urban old-age insurance scheme for wage-based workers, with a monthly basic pension of Y 280 financed by the local government.[7] These pilot experiences generated useful inputs for the design of the 2011 national framework for the pilot URPS.

In June 2011, the government established nationwide guidelines for the URPS ("Guiding Opinions on Piloting Social Pension Insurance for Urban Residents, State Council"), with the objective of extending minimum basic income protection to all urban elderly, including the unemployed and people without support from social insurance. The broad design of the scheme mimics the NRPS (table 11.1), which provides a harmonized policy framework to facilitate subsequent integration of the pension schemes for rural and urban residents. The program is expected to cover at least 50 million urban residents not otherwise covered or insufficiently covered by the scheme for urban workers. After only six months of operation, there were more than 13 million participants, including 6.4 million pension recipients (Wen 2012). The authorities have set an ambitious goal of expanding the program to all urban areas by the end of 2012.

Several pilot programs established during the 2000s transcended the urban and rural distinction by providing an integrated pension scheme for rural and urban citizens within individual prefectures.[8] In rapidly expanding areas, such schemes have merged urban and rural schemes to achieve an integrated pension scheme for all residents, in a number of cases with benefit levels that are equivalent for people with urban and rural *hukou*. Like the NRPS and URPS, such initiatives are useful vehicles for expanding pension coverage to the nonwage sector and promoting the vision laid out by national policy makers of rural-urban integration. Almost all of these local programs adopted the national NRPS/URPS guidelines or some close variant, though there were some exceptions. In Chengdu, for example, the city adjusted its local program broadly in line with the NRPS framework but retained differences in the details of the scheme design in both the NRPS and the URPS (Wang, Chen, and Gao 2011).

Design Features of Pension Schemes

The old rural pension scheme was voluntary and financed mainly from individual contributions of Y 2–Y 20 a month, with a matching contribution of Y 2 by the collective. Retirement ages were to be 60 for both men and women, and elderly farmers were entitled to receive a monthly pension benefit paid from the bank until death. Administration was by the local bureau of civil affairs (typically at the county level, resulting in highly fragmented scheme management); administrative costs were paid for by contributions (with

TABLE 11.1 **Comparison of old and new pension schemes for rural and urban residents of China**

Feature	Old rural pension scheme	NRPS	URPS
Principles	Basic protection	Basic protection, broad coverage, flexibility, and sustainability	Same as NRPS
Coverage	Rural residents age 20 and older	Rural residents age 16 and older, except students	Urban residents age 16 and older, except students
Financing	Individual contribution plus collective subsidy	Individual contribution plus government subsidies and/or subsidy from rural collectives	Individual contribution plus government subsidy
Individual contribution	10 levels, Y 2–Y 20 a month	5 levels, Y 100–Y 500 a month; family binding (parents collect benefits only if all adult children are contributing to pension scheme)	10 levels, Y 100–Y 1,000 a month
Government subsidy	Y 2 a month from collectives; tax reduction for township and village enterprises and collective economy	Y 30 matching to individual account annually; Y 55 a month basic pension benefits	Same as NRPS
Qualifying conditions	Pensionable at age 60; immediate vesting	Pensionable at age 60; vesting period: 15 years	Same as NRPS
Benefits	Accumulation divided by 120, but benefits maintained until death	Accumulation divided by 139 plus Y 55 a month basic pension	Same as NRPS
Fund management	Specific account at county level	Specific account at county level	Specific account at city level
Portability	Very limited	In theory, portable within NRPS and between NRPS and URPS; little portability to and from urban workers pension scheme	Same as NRPS

SOURCE: Authors' compilation, based on policy documents.

a cap of 3 percent, set subsequently). Oversight and regulation of the scheme sat largely with the implementing agency itself, subject to the internal controls of the Ministry of Finance and internal auditing.

Several design problems undermined achievement of the government's policy objectives:

- Coverage was highly imbalanced geographically, with four coastal provinces accounting for about 45 percent of total participation and 64 percent of total accumulations. Matching contributions from collectives were often not made, and their incidence was highly skewed toward a small number of richer provinces.

- Pension benefits were very low, and even those benefits could not be paid in full in at least 200 counties (Wang 2000). Returns to investment were also low.

- The administrative cost was as high as 3 percent of contributions, and supervision was weak. By the end of 2000, about 20 percent of accumulations had been invested in unauthorized assets, including real estate, stocks, enterprise bonds, and nonbank financial agencies. With county-level management, risk pools were highly fragmented.

In 2009, the State Council issued policy guidelines for the RPPS (now the NRPS); in July 2011, it issued guidelines for the URPS. The guidelines scaled up multiple local and provincial pilot programs into a national framework. The diverse experience with rural pension schemes at the subnational level offered important lessons for policy makers at the national level that have been reflected in significant measure in the design of the national guidelines.

The underlying design principles of the guidelines were basic insurance and wide coverage with flexibility and sustainability. Key features of the URPS design include the following (table 11.1):

- Participation is voluntary, with incentives. All rural residents over the age of 16 are eligible to participate if they are not already covered by a contributory urban scheme. Participation incentives include matching subsidies; 15-year vesting requirements to receive the basic benefit; and family binding provisions, whereby the pension eligibility of contributors already over retirement age is determined by whether the contributor's spouse and all adult children contribute to the new system (family binding).

- The scheme design has two components: individual pension accounts with matching contributions and a basic flat pension for workers who have contributed for 15 years or meet other qualifying conditions. The initial value of the basic pension under the scheme is Y 55 a month, which can be topped up by local governments from their own revenues. Individual accounts have a rate of return equal to the one-year deposit interest rate; benefits will be computed by dividing the accumulation at age 60 by 139 (as in the urban scheme). Indexation is somewhat vague, to be set in accordance with "economic development and changing prices."[9]

- Participants become eligible for benefits at age 60. People over 60 at the time the scheme is introduced can receive the basic pension benefit if their children are contributing to the scheme (family binding). People with less than 15 years left before reaching age 60 should contribute during their working lives and then make lump-sum contributions to make up any shortfall on the vesting period of 15 years of contributions.

- Financing of the scheme comes from a combination of central subsidies to support the basic pension (in full for central and western regions and 50 percent for eastern regions); individual contributions (of Y 100–Y 500 a year determined by the worker); a partial match on the individual contribution by local governments of at least Y 30 a year (independent of the contribution level chosen by the worker) or at a higher rate as locally determined; and collective subsidies, which are encouraged but not mandated, with no level specified.

- Fund management for individual account accumulations will begin at the county level, with the aim of shifting responsibility to the provincial level as quickly as feasible. Supervision of funds would be by the local offices of the MHRSS. The guidelines suggest the importance of gradually raising the level of management with the scaling up of the programs and indicate the importance of establishing systems for accumulating individual account entitlements and facilitating benefit portability.

The URPS shares almost the same design as the NRPS, with exactly the same basic pension level (determined by the central government), the same financing design, and the same matching contribution provided by local authorities. The scheme aims to provide minimum voluntary pension savings arrangements to cover the unemployed, other urban workers without employment contracts, and urban retirees without alternative sources of retirement income. Significantly, the URPS is open only to people with local urban *hukou*; migrant workers from rural or other urban areas are eligible to participate, but only in their area of *hukou* registration.[10] One characteristic that is distinct for the urban scheme is that contribution tiers can range up to Y 1,000 a year.

Assessment of Schemes and Initial Experience

COVERAGE

The authorities have set a goal of achieving full geographic coverage for both the rural and urban resident schemes by the end of 2012.[11] Given the voluntary nature of the scheme, full geographic coverage does not automatically imply full coverage of all individuals, but the authorities are committed to maximizing individual participation in the scheme, especially for workers uncovered by other forms of old-age income protection. Geographic coverage is ensured largely by offering the schemes throughout China and supporting registration and contributions with an administrative apparatus.

The authorities appear on track for meeting this geographic coverage target. By the end of the first quarter of 2012, 376 million people were participating in the rural and urban resident pension schemes, with 107 million receiving pension benefits. Sixteen provinces had achieved full geographic coverage, and 10 provinces had integrated their rural and urban resident schemes (*China Labor and Social Security News* 2012). Early starters—such as Beijing, Hainan, Jiangsu, Ningxia, Qinghai, Shanghai, Tianjin, Tibet, and Zhejiang—generally have high participation rates. In Jiangsu, for example, which started to implement the RPPS very early, coverage is reported to have reached 97 percent (Huang 2010) (table 11.2).

Notable differences are evident in the participation rates in pilot counties between rates reported in administrative data and rates estimated on the basis of survey data, with estimated rates usually lower. Reported local coverage or participation rates therefore need to be interpreted with some caution. Fieldwork by the authors reveals that local officials are prone to calculate coverage in nonstandard ways—including only people over 45 in the

TABLE 11.2 **Participation rates in selected local rural and urban schemes**

Location	Participation rate (from surveys or administrative data) (%)	Source
Rural schemes		
Jiangsu Province	97.0	Huang (2010)
Jiangxi (11 pilot counties/districts)	73.6 among enrollees in local RPPS	Mu and Lu (2010)
Shenmu and Yao Counties, Shaanxi Province, Jimo District of Qingdao City	75.0	Wu (2011)
Guqiao Town, Henan Province	96.5	Li (2011)
Urban schemes		
Chengdu	27.8	Wang, Chen, and Gao (2011)
Pilot counties, Anhui Province	Average just above 50; lowest 20.1	Luo (2011)
1,942 rural households in 68 villages in 68 pilot counties in 20 provinces	Average 57.6	Rural Research Center of the Central China Normal University (2010)
Pilot counties, Xian City, Shaanxi Province	54.9 among rural migrants	Liu (2011)

SOURCE: Cheng 2012.

denominator (due to the 15-year vesting rule), for example, or including people receiving pensions in the total program coverage figure, potentially blurring the line between current contributors and pension recipients. In figure 11.1, the coverage rate calculation uses total rural employment as the denominator.

PARTICIPATION INCENTIVES

Incentives for participation of the elderly reflected the existence of earlier pilot programs, the policy design, financing structure, and pressure on local social security authorities to offer the schemes. The age profile of participants and the choices of the contribution level have also been affected by the scheme design.

Both the 15-year contribution requirement for vesting into the basic benefit pension and the low rate of return on individual contributions would suggest that workers would begin contributing to the scheme at about age 45 (somewhat earlier if they expected periods of unemployment). Limited empirical studies from several provinces of the new rural scheme provide initial evidence of this effect. For example, a 2010 survey of Chengdu in the early stages of the rural pension pilot suggested that people age 50–59 had the highest participation rate and that participation across the life cycle rose (figure 11.2). A survey of rural Guangdong in 2011 finds a similar pattern, though neither survey reveals a spike in

FIGURE 11.2 **Rural pension system coverage in Chengdu and Guangdong**

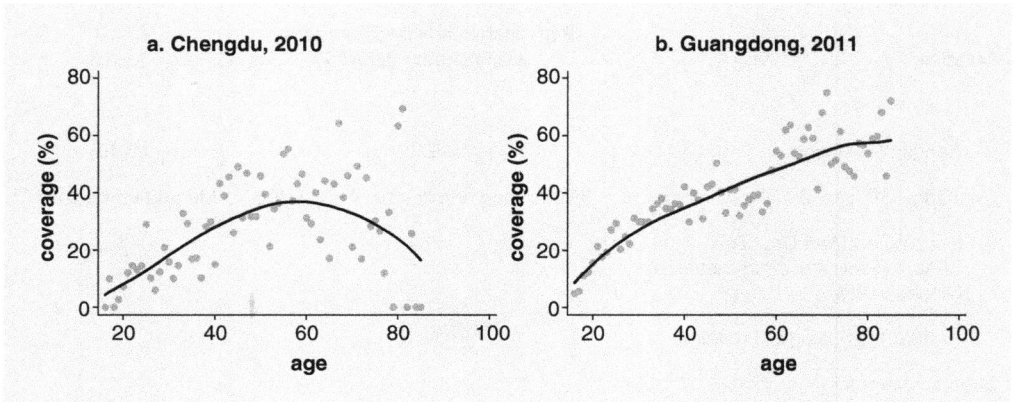

SOURCES: Wang, Chen, and Gao 2011, based on the 2010 Chengdu Rural Pension Survey 2010; Wang, O'Keefe, and Thompson 2012, based on the Guangdong Social Insurance Survey 2011.

NOTE: "Coverage" includes both people currently contributing to a rural pension scheme and people receiving benefits.

participation at exactly age 45 (perhaps because of family binding considerations) (Wang, Chen, and Gao 2011; Wang, O'Keefe, and Thompson 2011). A survey of pilot counties in Anhui Province suggests that 49 percent of participants are age 45–49, with only 6.7 percent under age 29 (Luo 2011). The survey of pilot counties in Zhejiang suggests that in some counties, 85 percent of participants were over age 45 and only about 1 percent were under age 35 (Feng 2010).

Contributors need to contribute only at the lowest level of Y 100 a year in order to satisfy the vesting requirements for the basic benefit pension, and matching subsidies are generally limited to the lowest contribution level. In this way, the rates of return on contributions above the lowest contribution level are limited to the rate of return on pension assets, which is specified as the one-year bank deposit rate (Li 2011). There is thus a strong incentive to choose the lowest contribution level (Y 100). Overall returns on contributions made at the mandated minimum for the 15-year vesting period (including matching subsidies) make for a very high 16 percent internal rate of return on contributions (Wang, O'Keefe, and Thompson 2012). If family binding is also in play, the internal rate of return for the pensioner is even higher. Almost 75 percent of benefits (93 percent of the subsidy) is provided through the basic benefit of Y 55 a month after 15 years of contributions, suggesting that unless the parameters of the scheme are adjusted, the incentives for workers to contribute more than 15 years or more than Y 100 a year will be very low.

The matching subsidy of Y 30 for annual contributions of Y 100 may be too low to incentivize workers to contribute beyond the 15-year vesting period for the basic benefit. It is lower than in other developing countries, such as India, where a 1:1 match is more common. The flat match and absence of a match above the threshold also act as a weak incentive for making contributions above the Y 100 minimum, although it has merit from an equity perspective. It will be important to monitor participation to see whether the

Y 30 match is sufficient to incentivize higher individual contributions and contributions beyond 15 years.

The empirical findings support the assertion that contributors have very weak incentives to contribute at levels above the minimum of Y 100 per year. According to a 2010 survey in Chengdu, 46 percent of participants from pilot counties chose the lowest contribution rate, and only 8 percent chose the highest rate (Y 500 a year). A survey of pilot counties in Anhui Province shows that more than two-thirds of participants chose the lowest contribution rate (Luo 2011).

The current design concentrates incentives on the ex post subsidy (that is, the financing of a basic pension benefit) and has the advantage of simplicity. For mobile rural populations, however, ex ante subsidies (that is, the matching of individual account contributions) can be more useful. Once the system matures, rural workers who enroll in an urban scheme upon migration—or intent to move—would not benefit as much from the incentive effect of the ex post subsidy under the current design, where portability of entitlements to other schemes is still unclear. Portability may be an important consideration with an increasingly mobile and urbanizing population. Increasing the ex ante subsidy by increasing matching would reduce this possible disincentive effect.

An obvious question raised by a shift in the balance of public subsidies from ex post to ex ante is the impact on the poverty alleviation objective of the basic rural pension. If greater public subsidies were shifted ex ante, maintaining a neutral fiscal impact would require a lower basic pension. The Y 55 benefit is already well below the rural poverty line; reducing it leaves the basic benefit below the average per capita *dibao* threshold, which could have additional negative incentive effects.[12]

This problem could be dealt with in at least two ways. First, it may be possible to effect a partial benefit reduction for individuals above a certain income threshold to ensure a higher benefit level for poorer elderly people. Second, local authorities may be able to top up the basic benefit to ensure that it exceeds the local *dibao* threshold.

Four stylistic mathematical projections of individual accumulations and benefits are summarized in table 11.3. Scenario 1 evaluates the current monthly contributions and matching subsidies, projected basic and total benefits, and the net present value of central government subsidies and total central and local government subsidies. Scenario 2 increases the matching (ex ante) subsidy from 30 percent to 100 percent for the first Y 100 in contributions while leaving the subsidized ex post basic benefit at Y 55 per month. Under this scenario, the net present value of total central government subsidies increases somewhat, with a stronger incentive created for contributors and a small increase in projected monthly benefits. Scenario 3 would remove the ex post basic benefit entirely and replace it with a substantial increase in the ex ante matching subsidy aimed at achieving the same monthly benefit as the current scheme for a worker who contributes for 15 years. This arrangement could have the effect of reducing the government's cost in present value terms by about 10 percent (depending on the real discount rate), as a result of the return on the matching subsidy which would be invested during the accumulation period (assuming a 3 percent real rate of return, which has not been consistently the case in China). Alternatively, if the central government authorities retained the same level of subsidy in present value terms but shifted the subsidy from the basic pension benefit to a

TABLE 11.3 **Stylized Examples of Matching Subsidy Options**
Y PER INDIVIDUAL

	Scenario			
	1	**2**	**3**	**4**
Individual annual contribution	100	100	100	100
Local annual matching subsidy (accumulation phase)	30	30	30	30
Central government annual matching subsidy (accumulation phase)		70	548	825
Monthly individual account benefit in retirement	13.8	21.2	68.8	98.2
Monthly basic benefit in retirement	55.0	55.0		
Total monthly benefit in retirement	68.8	76.2	68.8	98.2
NPV local matching subsidy	358	358	358	358
NPV lifetime central government ex ante matching subsidy		836	6,184	9,491
NPV lifetime central government subsidy for basic benefit	9,490	9,490		
NPV total government subsidies	9,848	10,684	6,542	9,849

NOTE: Scenario 1: Current NRPS/URPS parameters and subsidies; Scenario 2: matching ex ante subsidies provided by the central government at 70% of contributions increasing the total central/local subsidy to 100% of contributions; Scenario 3: matching ex ante subsidies provided by the central government at 548% of contributions with central government–financed basic benefit eliminated; Scenario 4: matching ex ante subsidies provided by the central government at 825% of contributions with central government–financed basic benefit eliminated. In all scenarios, the authors projected individual contributions of Y 100 a year and local government matching subsidies of Y 30 a year. A 3 percent real interest rate and real discount rate was assumed in all scenarios. Other assumptions included 15 years of contributions at eligibility age, an eligibility age of 60, and life expectancy at age 60 of 19.1 years for both men and women. NPV = net present value.

matching subsidy during the accumulation phase (Scenario 4), the monthly benefit would increase by about 43 percent, depending on the interest rate assumed.

Public awareness of the schemes has a substantial impact on enrollment. Farmers still have very limited knowledge about the NRPS, as suggested by a survey of pilot counties in Jilin, which showed that 45 percent of local farmers did not have a clear knowledge about the policy and 6 percent had never heard about it (Liu, Wu, and He 2011). A survey of pilot counties in Hebei revealed that only 27 percent of farmers knew that the government provides subsidies for the RPPS (Geng 2011). Farmers were not familiar with the NRPS in pilot or nonpilot counties at the beginning. In order to increase their awareness, the central government asked local governments to disseminate this new policy through various channels, including broadcasting, television, posters, brochures, and village campaign activities. Thanks to the media and administrative campaigns, farmers are largely informed of the NRPS program.

ADEQUACY OF BENEFITS

Benefit adequacy—how effective the benefit is in ensuring that the elderly are shielded from absolute or relative poverty—is difficult to measure. Two metrics often considered are the locally determined poverty line and an international metric such as income.[13] At the individual level, there is a natural tension between benefit adequacy and affordability. A benefit that is completely effective at ensuring the elderly against poverty will likely come at a high cost if shouldered entirely by the individual and his or her family. Moreover, a benefit that is barely adequate for some people will prove inadequate for others. Benefit adequacy also depends not only on the benefit level but on the adjustment of such levels over time, in line with prices, wages, or per capita income. Bearing in mind these trade-offs, setting a target benefit level is challenging in China, where local economic conditions vary substantially.

Benefit levels vary greatly by locality, as different counties and cities offer different contribution levels above the national maximum, different matching subsidies, and different levels of basic benefits. Moreover, the benefit accruing to individuals will depend on the level and duration of contributions, the rate of return, the matching subsidies and supplementary financing provided by localities, and the annuity factor used to calculate the benefit. Based on several basic assumptions and bearing these caveats in mind, the authors calculated that a minimum benefit of about Y 73 a month would be obtained by a worker making a Y 100 contribution a year for 15 years.[14] This projected benefit would only partially achieve the unstated objective of protecting against poverty in old age. In 2011, this amount represented 13 percent of net rural per capita income, 30 percent of the absolute poverty criterion of about Y 20/day, 51 percent of the national average *dibao* threshold, and 38 percent of the national rural poverty line.

Before the introduction of the national scheme, pilot local programs often adopted a rule of thumb that pension benefits should be at or slightly above the average *dibao* threshold in the locality. Together the anticipated basic benefit and funded individual account accumulations should yield a benefit that is expected to raise total pensions notably above the *dibao* level. The level of benefits will vary based on local fiscal capacity (for example, Beijing sets its flat pension portion at 35 percent of rural average income).

With respect to indexation, guidelines established for the rural and urban schemes note the importance of adjustments to the basic pension, but they do not specify criteria or parameters. The basic benefit of Y 55 a month, put in place in September 2009, has not been adjusted, despite annual inflation in 2010 and 2011 of 5–6 percent.

Survey data provide limited insights into actual benefit levels. A study of 18 counties in Hebei Province indicates that as many as 55 percent of rural pensioners claim only the Y 55 basic pension; less than 15 percent of pensioners had a monthly pension of more than Y 100 (Geng 2011). A 2010 survey of Chengdu suggests that despite the steady increase in the benefit levels of local programs, which are higher than the national average, about three-quarters of pensioners still receive a monthly benefit of less than Y 150, a replacement of rural per capita net income of 31 percent. A survey of pilot counties in Anhui Province reveals that the average monthly benefit is Y 60.4 and that 71 percent of the elderly believe that the current benefit level is inadequate to meet their essential needs (Luo 2011). Farmers cannot depend solely on their income from the NRPS; they have to rely on other income sources, such as family members, farming income, property rental income, and support from communities.

The RPPS was scaled up only in 2010; too little time has passed to evaluate the scheme's impact on the incomes and well-being of elderly people in rural areas.[15] Moreover, benefit levels of Y 55 a month would likely have a very modest impact on all but the poorest rural elderly.

Despite the low level of benefits, survey data suggest that rural recipients of pension benefits in earlier schemes indicated that they felt a stronger sense of security and self-regard (Zhang and Tang 2008). Scheme benefits help them with living expenditures, increase economic stability, and reduce some of their reliance on other sources of income. A 2010 study of Chengdu suggests that more than half the elderly claim their pension on a monthly basis, some rely largely on pension income support, and 71 percent indicate that the most important uses of their pension benefits were food, followed by health care, production materials, and savings.

FISCAL COSTS AND WORKER AFFORDABILITY

Five sets of fiscal costs are associated with the NRPS and URPS:

- Central government financing of the basic benefit, initially set at Y 55 a month per person
- Local government financing of matching subsidies, which are at least Y 30 per year per contributor
- Local government financing of individual contributions for *dibao* recipients and possibly others deemed locally to be entitled to a contribution subsidy
- The subsidy required to finance the difference between the annuitized benefit using the current annuity factor of 139 and a more appropriate and actuarially fair annuity factor
- The payment to survivors of any remaining balance in a deceased worker's individual account.

Presumably, the local authorities will bear the costs of the fourth and fifth items, which will come payable only over time.

An unresolved issue is the future fiscal affordability of the new schemes. Initial calculations suggest that the central government's commitments are affordable, although as suggested above, such affordability may come at the price of insufficient adequacy for many beneficiaries. The cost to the central government of the portion of the basic benefit for which it is responsible is low and likely to remain so despite a growing elderly population. Simulations using different system parameters find that spending on pensions consumes 1.0–2.5 percent of central general revenues (Cheng 2011).[16] Providing Y 55 a month to everyone in China over age 60 would cost the central government about 0.26 percent of gross domestic product (GDP).[17] These costs are projected to grow over time, as the elderly population increases in China. However, if the benefit level were to grow at the same rate as GDP growth and the central authorities were to finance 100 percent of the basic benefit, an estimate of the cost would still be less than 0.75 percent of GDP in 2050. Keeping such costs low and affordable over the coming decades will inevitably depend on the expansion of the importance of the NRPS/URPS saving provisions as well as other saving options for nonwage citizens.

Fiscal affordability at the county and municipal levels is more uncertain, as the level of matching contributions for individual accounts and the fiscal situation varies greatly across localities. The current matching is evenly shared by provincial, city, and county-level governments. The cost to local governments of minimum matching subsidies is very low relative to GDP, although it depends on local revenue-generating capacity.[18] The minimum fiscal commitment therefore should be affordable in the aggregate, although it remains to be seen whether the required commitment will be met in every locality. The obvious challenge is to avoid a situation in which poor counties fail to match individual account contributions (resulting in lower accumulations for the poor) while still maintaining enough local interest in the scheme to encourage accountability at the county level.

A third subsidy is implicit in the annuity factor used to calculate benefits for the individual account pension. The guidelines specify that the coefficient used to determine the benefit is 139 months (the same coefficient used to calculate benefits from workers' individual accounts in the urban workers scheme), based on a life expectancy calculation at age 60 and a 4 percent expected rate of return on funds during retirement. Unisex life expectancy tables published by the World Health Organization for China indicate that life expectancy at age 60 in 2009 was 19.1 years (229 months), suggesting that the 139 figure is much too low.[19] There is thus a substantial subsidy embedded in the annuity factor for the individual account pension of about 65 percent of the benefit amount (Wang, O'Keefe, and Thompson 2012). This subsidy would be the responsibility of the authorities administering the scheme, which in the short term would be local authorities.

No simple metric measures worker affordability. For workers themselves, minimum contributions of Y 100 a year represented only 1.4 percent of rural per capita income in 2011. They should therefore be affordable for all but the lowest deciles of rural workers. Of course, many rural workers will be liquidity constrained or concerned about the risk that the benefits received after 15 years of contributions may turn out to be far different from intended at the outset. Such a contribution would be more affordable for urban workers, who generally have much higher income levels.

FUND MANAGEMENT AND GOVERNANCE

The initial approach under the new schemes of allowing fund management at the county level has a range of drawbacks, including investment risk and the risk that funds are used for other pressing purposes, leaving accounts that are in practice empty. Localized management also complicates the portability of account balances for rural workers who move beyond their home counties. In addition, demographic trends in rural areas suggest that a sizable reserve fund will likely be necessary, which is best managed at higher levels.

Raising the level of risk pooling—which can occur only gradually—would have substantial benefits in terms of both the soundness of the system design and implementation capacity.[20] Gradual steps should probably be considered to upgrade the pooling level from county to prefecture (as has already happened in the urban workers scheme and in some prefectures for all schemes); from prefecture to province; and from province to the national level. Some cities or provinces, such as Beijing, Hunan, and Shanghai, have already been managing the funds at the provincial level.

The experience of local pilot programs with respect to scheme administration and fund management demonstrates a modest degree of capacity and continuity, but regulation demands greater attention. Administration of new schemes has remained with the Social Security Bureau, with roles for villages (for collection of contributions and in some cases payment of benefits), townships (for consolidation of collections, approval of benefits and registration), counties (for general oversight and scheme design), and banks (for payment of contributions and delivery of benefits in many cases). There also appears to have been a general improvement in scheme information systems, in particular with the issuance of standard software by the MHRSS for the scheme.

Within this general administrative structure, there are a variety of local innovations in administration. For example, farmers in Guangdong and Suzhou have been able to make contributions directly through banks rather than village officials, and post offices (including mobile facilities) are being used in areas with lower banking penetration. Some schemes also allow for the seasonality of farmer incomes, so that schemes such as the one in Baoji collect payment only once a year.

In addition to the drawbacks of subprovincial fund management, the use of the one-year deposit rate of interest as the rate of return for individual accounts is likely to prove problematic over time (as it has for urban schemes), because it has typically provided a negative real rate of return, which affects both the return on contributions and the adequacy of benefits. Although very secure, the low rate virtually guarantees a low individual account balance at retirement, thereby weakening participation incentives for rural workers. Other approaches, such as nonfinancial or notional defined contribution plans, can in principle provide benefit promises based on higher rates of return, but such returns would require additional fiscal subsidies. Another option would be to invest reserves in a much riskier pool of assets, which would subject members to additional risk and require substantial additional institutional infrastructure and oversight.

PORTABILITY OF PENSION RIGHTS

Portable pension rights reduce pension losses for individuals who move across space and in and out of formal sector employment. Portability is therefore important to the overall participation incentives in the rural and urban resident pension schemes as well as to addressing gaps in the overall set of pension instruments, including the urban old-age insurance system. Portability of vested rights and individual account balances—both across rural areas and between rural and urban schemes—is important given China's increasingly mobile labor force. Conceptually, it is much easier to achieve portability of pension rights within rural and urban resident pension schemes, as they would have the same essential design and compatible institutional infrastructure; it is more difficult achieving portability between separate pension schemes, such as between the NRPS/URPS on the one hand and the urban workers pension scheme on the other.

The NRPS/URPS guidelines anticipate but do not address the portability of pension rights under the schemes. In 2009, the Chinese government established an initiative for pension portability within the urban worker's pension scheme.

The next policy priority will focus on making pension rights portable within and across programs; MHRSS is developing regulations along these lines, which the government plans to introduce in 2013. Ensuring portability will require the rapid development of systems to reliably transfer information and funds across localities, integrating rural and urban schemes and integrating both schemes with urban social insurance. Provinces such as Guangdong are already working on development of the provincial management information systems needed to do so.

The lack of a national policy has contributed to pension system fragmentation and weak incentives for participation. Fragmentation between the urban and rural pension schemes has become an important barrier for coordinated urban-rural development and urbanization (Deng and Liu 2011; Wang 2006). A number of provinces and cities have integrated pension schemes for rural and urban residents. What is needed is a national policy to guide the transfer and portability of pension rights within and between pension schemes.

Distinct local policies have been adopted to address this issue. Suzhou, for example, initiated a simple 2:1 rule for farmers wishing to transfer their social pooling rights from the rural to urban scheme; transferring their rights is simple, because the rural contribution base has been exactly half that of the urban system. The 2:1 rule means farmers will receive half of their social pooling benefits when transferring into the urban scheme because their contributions are exactly half that of their urban counterparts. Beijing has made provisions for portability, albeit only at the point of retirement. Former farmers who have accumulated enough years in the urban system at retirement will receive an urban pension (with an allowance for lower rural contributions); their urban contributions will be credited with a rural pension scheme if the accumulation period in the urban system is less than 15 years. In principle, the funded portion of all schemes could easily be made portable.

The clear direction of policy is toward eventual integration of the schemes for rural and urban residents; some prefectures have already done so.[21] The Social Insurance Law promulgated in July 2011 spells out unequivocally: "The government needs to set up a robust pension program for urban residents. Provincial government[s] or the governments of municipalities directly under the central government may, in line with their local conditions, establish an integrated pension program for urban and rural residents." Such integration is an important objective for China's pension reform.

INSTITUTIONAL CHALLENGES

Little information is available about institutional capacity, although several key challenges are clear:

- Local capacity needs to be increased, particularly at the county level and below. The massive and very rapid expansion of the system places demands on local implementation and delivery capacity. The government intends to introduce rural social security service centers at least down to (and ideally below) the county level. However, existing staffing ratios imply service loads in an expanding system well above levels observed in similar schemes in other countries. Experiences from provincial partnerships with the banking sector may assist in helping spread the administrative burden of managing client contributions and basic recordkeeping. For example, Guangdong has a generalized service agreement with the Postal Savings Bank, which accepts contributions, is the vehicle for payment directly into pensioners' accounts, and has an information system linked to the Department of Human Resources and Social Security.

- Collection and payment systems need improvement. Incomplete penetration of financial and banking services in some rural areas likely affect implementation, by constraining contribution collections and payments. The MHRSS is working actively on this issue, in cooperation with national banks such as the partnership with the Postal Savings Bank, but even banks with wide coverage do not have branches in all townships.

- Information systems and links to related programs—such as to the New Cooperative Medical Scheme—and other localities need strengthening. The government's stated intention is to extend the systems to the grassroots level; doing so will require increasing system capacities and training personnel. If the system is not closely managed, information systems could be fragmented (the standardized software from the MHRSS should help promote greater coherence than has been observed in urban schemes).

Lessons for Other Countries

China's adoption of national pension programs for rural and urban residents in 2009–11 may provide insights for other countries considering similar reforms. Lessons include the need for high-level political commitment, iterative and gradual policy development, an incentive structure for voluntary participation, policy design to achieve rural-urban integration, and assignment of financing responsibilities of central and local governments in a decentralized environment. At the same time, it is important not to be overly mechanical in interpreting these lessons, as they reflect idiosyncratic characteristics of China's labor market, political, and fiscal systems.

As China moves from a middle-income to a high-income country, the acceleration of pension programs aims to narrow coverage gaps between rural and urban areas and across regions and promote more integrated development. This effort has been driven by China's ambitious policy goal to provide basic social protection for all by 2020. Such high-level political commitment is key for developing countries seeking to approach universal coverage and allow all people to share the fruits of economic development. The innovative design of China's matching defined contribution plus basic benefit scheme has already dramatically increased the registration of rural and urban residents. Only time will tell if such high voluntary participation is sustained.

The process and mechanism of policy reform in China has followed an iterative and gradual paradigm. China has conducted subnational piloting, accumulating experience and lessons for policy design at the national level and subsequent roll-out. For a large country, local experiments are useful to accommodate diverse conditions and decentralized environments. Few countries are as fiscally and administratively decentralized as China (DRC and World Bank 2011; Lou and Wang 2008). Many countries may be sufficiently centralized that they can prescribe more uniform designs and financing for such programs. Even in these cases, however, countries could benefit from piloting designs and "learning by doing," as China as done.

China is now trying to coordinate and integrate its systems for urban and rural workers. In other countries, it may be possible to avoid the initial split between rural and urban schemes for informal workers, which in China is a legacy of a broader social policy framework of separate programs for rural and urban people linked in part to the *hukou* system.

The main difference between China's old and new rural pension schemes is that the ex ante and ex post financing from central and local governments has helped assure participants of the credibility of the scheme. The ex ante subsidy to individual accounts is financed by local governments (province, city, and county); the ex post subsidy to the basic pension is financed totally by central governments for inland provinces and shared by central and provincial governments for coastal provinces. The financing responsibilities of central and local governments are clearly defined. Both central and local financing have been important because many Chinese lost confidence in earlier rural pension programs that depended entirely on individual responsibilities and local collectives. The lesson for other countries is that a significant and credible public subsidy may be necessary to incentivize the voluntary participation of nonformal workers. The commitment of the central authorities to a significant subsidy has also added credibility to the pension commitment. In other countries, government support may not be sufficient to give individuals the confidence to contribute.

A related question is the appropriate balance between ex ante and ex post public subsidies and the extent to which the ex post subsidy is best "bundled" with a matching defined contribution ex ante subsidy (as in the NRPS and the URPS) or potentially delinked through a noncontributory social pension approach. The initial success in achieving substantial registration in rural China can be attributed to the structure of incentives of government subsidies, vesting requirements, and family binding provisions. Family binding provisions may prove of particular importance in China, where the proportion of rural migrants of working age is substantial and many of the rural elderly have remained in rural areas.

Linkages between voluntary matching defined contribution schemes and a basic defined benefit pension represent an innovative design that deserves consideration by countries with comparable needs, conditions, and the administrative apparatus to carry such a design forward. At the same time, preliminary empirical findings show that rural young people are less likely to participate in the NRPS, suggesting that the incentives may not be strong enough. Given the relatively low participation of younger rural workers to date, it may be worth considering rebalancing the public subsidy from an ex post toward an ex ante subsidy.

A bigger question for China and other developing countries is whether it may be worth going even farther and converting the basic pension benefit into a full-blown noncontributory social pension largely delinked from the matching defined contribution portion of the schemes. To reduce elderly poverty, China could consider a social pension (World Bank forthcoming).

China's pension schemes for rural and urban residents appear to be financially stable, because they focus on fiscal and worker affordability while providing only a very modest benefit. This situation will be changing with the rapidly aging population. Fiscal affordability will also depend on the future levels at which the authorities provide ex ante subsidies, the returns on individual account accumulations they commit to, and future adjustments to the level of basic pension benefits. Whether the fiscal costs of ex ante and ex post subsidies are affordable and appropriate for other countries will depend on their characteristics, including the working age and elderly income distribution and household composition.

The limited adequacy of benefits may leave a substantial portion of the elderly insufficiently protected against poverty. Potential remedies include increasing the ex ante matching subsidy, which induces individuals to save for their own retirement, and strengthening the linkages between the pension and *dibao* programs.

Other challenges China faces include pooling and managing funds, strengthening institutions and capacity for service delivery, and managing funds while rapidly increasing the geographic coverage of the program. These challenges are common in developing countries. A key lesson of earlier schemes in China is that overly decentralized fund management, pooling, and regulation pose real risks that need to be managed, preferably through higher-level pooling and scheme management. Institutional penetration in remote areas of China—including the presence of finance bureaus, labor and social security bureaus, banks and other funds transfer agents, and a strong system of identification and registry—was another important asset. Not all developing countries have this administrative and financial sector infrastructure, raising questions about the possibility for achieving such wide coverage expansion so quickly and the relative roles of government and nongovernmental partners in the process. Even in China, partnering between government and financial sector players has proven important in achieving accelerated scheme expansion. Although China's experience demonstrates the potential of a voluntary and incentive-driven approach to expanding coverage, its specific political economy has probably been a significant factor in the impressive initial performance. Although the NRPS and the URPS are voluntary, China retains a degree of moral suasion to encourage participation that may not be present in many developing countries. These enabling conditions—and not just the design characteristics—may have supported these pension programs. At the same time, such suasion was present in earlier rural schemes, which failed to achieve significant penetration, suggesting that the NRPS and URPS design features of are likely to be important factors in the early success of the schemes.

Conclusions

China's recent establishment of national pension schemes for its rural and uncovered urban populations represents a major step toward its ambitious objective of universal pension coverage by the end of 2012 and provision of basic social security for all by 2020. The policy designs support the principle of broad coverage, in part by providing modest basic benefits. The urban and rural designs have already achieved substantial momentum in increasing the registration and participation of previously uncovered populations. The common policy framework has provided a channel for an integrated pension scheme for rural and urban residents. Such a framework also appears able to accommodate the wide variation in economic needs and circumstances across China.

Although the NRPS and the URPS have several innovative features and represent milestones in social policy in China, there remains scope for improvement and refinement of some policy parameters if China is to fully achieve its objectives. Looking forward, whether China will be able to achieve universal pension coverage at the individual level will depend in large part on the incentives for sustained participation, the authorities' ability to enhance portability and eventually integrate the programs, and their ability to strengthen institutions and capacity for service delivery and management.

The authorities have established a benefit level and financing plan that can achieve broad coverage, but the benefit may not be sufficient to protect substantial numbers of elderly beneficiaries from poverty. In setting the benefit level and guaranteeing the financing of the basic benefit for most provinces, the authorities have balanced benefit adequacy against a very modest fiscal commitment while at the same time enabling local authorities to supplement benefits where local fiscal situations and priorities permit. One means of promoting a higher replacement rate could be to increase the matching subsidy in the pension savings scheme, including perhaps providing financing by the central government to enhance the match. Doing so would both increase incentives to contribute more than 15 years and improve benefit adequacy. But such a move would need to be accompanied by gradual relaxation of portfolio rules to allow investment of accumulations in vehicles that ensure a positive real rate of return, which is not currently the case.

The linkages between the vesting requirements and family binding provisions for the savings scheme on the one hand and the basic benefit on the other likely provide strong incentives for participation while at the same time creating a significant administrative challenge for a very modest benefit. Further evaluation is needed of the costs and challenges of linking the two components of the scheme. Increasing the matching subsidy (and target replacement rate) could enhance the benefits of linking the two elements.

Decentralized and fragmented fund management in China cannot achieve risk pooling, which is essential for ensuring benefits over the long term. Measures are needed to raise the level of fund and risk management to at least the provincial level in order to achieve risk pooling and portability, two important objectives for China's increasingly mobile labor force and diverse local fiscal circumstances. A higher level of participation in fund management and regulation can increase professionalism and system robustness within given capacity constraints.

Notes

1. This section draws extensively on Cai and others (2012) and World Bank (forthcoming).

2. The term "resident" has a specific meaning in the context of social insurance, because residency in China is defined based on a person's *hukou* (household registration) status and type of employment. In this chapter, the term refers to all rural workers (except local officials) and self-employed, informally employed, and nonworking people with local *hukou* in urban areas. Residents are contrasted with workers, who are covered under the urban workers pension scheme.

3. There were five major variants in local schemes during this renewal phase: (1) flat pensions plus individual accounts with government financing at the payout stage only; (2) flat pensions plus individual accounts with government financing by matching contributions to individual accounts or at the payout stage through the financing of flat pensions from general

revenues; (3) individual accounts with social pooling, with government financing in the accumulation phase; (4) individual accounts combined with social pooling, with government financing by matching contributions to individual accounts or at the payout stage; and (5) individual accounts only, with government matching for contributions to such accounts. This simple design lacks risk pooling of any form. For descriptions of the systems in Beijing, Baoji, Suzhou, and Yantai, see Wu (2009). For a detailed discussion of the Baoji pilot rural pension experience, see Zhang and Tang (2008).

4. China's definitions of scheme coverage and participation are not consistent with international norms, as total figures for scheme participation tend to include both working-age people still contributing and people already receiving pensions and no longer contributing, as discussed later in this chapter.

5. Other cities launched their own pilots before the establishment of national RPPS guidelines in 2009. They include Lianshan, in Shandong Province; Zhengzhou, in Henan Province; Yulin, in Shaanxi Province; and Wuhu, in Anhui Province. These urban programs generally adopted a design of matching defined contribution savings arrangements and basic benefits (social pooling), but they varied greatly in terms of the financing and contribution rate; the central government did not provide any financial support. There was significant variation in benefit levels resulting from differences in local economic circumstances and the fiscal position of local governments.

6. This system combines a basic pension and individual account, with a flat individual contribution rate of Y 2,400 a year and immediate vesting. Participants could claim a monthly pension of Y 400 the same year they began to make contributions. Contributions during working life were waived for *dibao* household members (people participating in the minimum living guarantee social assistance program).

7. Currency values in this chapter are given in Chinese yuan; Y 1 = $0.1591.

8. Pilots were run in Zhejiang Province, Chongqing and Chengdu in Sichuan Province, Qingdao City in Shandong Province, and Taizhou City in Jiangsu Province.

9. This is the same method used in urban schemes. It reflects the assumptions of a notional life expectancy at age 60 and an assumed draw-down interest rate of 4 percent.

10. Survey evidence from selected major cities in China for 2010 confirms that a proportion of migrant workers reporting participation in pension schemes were in fact contributing to schemes in locations other than that of their surveyed residence (Giles, Wang, and Park forthcoming).

11. Geographic coverage refers to offering the scheme to all workers and the elderly people in certain geographic areas. Full geographic coverage refers to offering the scheme to workers and the elderly throughout China.

12. *Dibao* refers to the minimum living guarantee social assistance program for China. The *dibao* threshold is the subsistence level below which household incomes are topped up.

13. Ideally, an elder assistance benefit should be sufficient to cover the poverty gap for such individuals.

14. Assumptions include a contribution of Y 100 a year, a matching subsidy of Y 30 a year, and retirement at 60 based on life expectancy in 2012. The benefit in 2012 for 15 years' accumulations would be about Y 18 a month, and the basic benefit would be Y 55 a month. The adequacy of benefits provided by individual account pensions will depend on the contribution level, the rate of return on individual accounts, and the annuity factor used to determine the pension benefit.

15. Studies show that households with social security tend to have a low savings rate, suggesting that pension provision could reduce saving and boost household consumption (Cai and others 2012).

16. The assumptions underlying these simulations merit note. Chen uses a projection model based on data from Jiangsu Province that assumes that one-quarter of the increase in general revenues would be needed for rural pension subsidies to support a universal pension for men at age 60 and women at age 55. Assuming that this figure represents 2.5 percent of general revenues, a universal farmers' pension of Y 825 a year could have been provided in 2010 compared with a minimum basic benefit of Y 660 under the national scheme.

17. The 0.26 percent of GDP figure is likely to be overstated, for several reasons. First, the central government is responsible for only 50 percent of the basic benefit for beneficiaries in coastal provinces. Second, recipients of the urban contributory old-age pension are not eligible for the URPS. Third, the NRPS or the URPS is not likely to cover all elderly people.

18. In this case, the estimated cost of providing a minimum annual pension of Y 30 per person for all working people age 18–59 would be 0.4 percent of GDP in 2012. This figure would gradually decline, as the projected working-age population is projected to decline over the coming years.

19. See http://www.worldlifeexpectancy.com/your-life-expectancy-by-age.

20. The authorities indicated that "in the pilot phase, the new rural pension funds can be managed by counties…and with the rolling out of the pilot, management can be transferred to higher levels; provincial management can be practiced in places with the required conditions." Funds were "to be deposited into the fiscal account of social security funds, and managed in a way of separating revenue from expenditures with separate book-keeping and auditing and inflation-proofing and appreciation according to relevant regulations" (State Council 2009).

21. The 2009 State Council decision states:

    The way the new rural pension scheme can be dovetailed with the urban workers basic pension scheme and other pension schemes should be decided by the Ministry of Human Resources and Social Security together with the Ministry of Finance. There is also a need to dovetail the new rural pension scheme with other policies and systems, such as social security of farmers whose land has been requisitioned; policies for reservoir resettlement; preferential policies toward households practicing family planning in rural areas; Wubao [the five guarantees program for the elderly, people with disabilities, and youth who lack the ability to work, sources of income, and sources of support, such as assistance from family members; about 5.5 million people have been covered by such benefits in recent years] in rural areas; social special care; and *dibao*. The specific methods will be studied and decided by the Ministry of Human Resources and Social Security and the Ministry of Finance, together with other relevant departments.

References

Cai, Fang, John Giles, Philip O'Keefe, and Dewen Wang. 2012. *The Elderly and Old Age Support in Rural China*. Directions in Development. Washington, DC: World Bank.

Chen, Ping. 2002. "Establishing a Unified Social Security System Is a Shortsighted Policy." *China Reform* 4: 16–17. (In Chinese.)

Cheng, Jie. 2011. "RPPP Fiscal Burden Estimates: Possibility of Universal Coverage during the 12th Five-Year Plan Period." *Social Security Studies* 1: 57–66. (In Chinese.)

———. 2012. "Overview of China's New Rural Pension and Urban Residents' Pension Scheme." World Bank, Washington, DC. (In Chinese.)

China Labor and Social Security News. 2012. Issue 4883, April 27.

Deng, Dasong, and Yuanfeng Liu. 2011. "Risk Analysis on the Social Security System: Close-up Analysis of the RPPP." *Journal of Chinese Economic and Business Studies* 4: 84–89. (In Chinese.)

DRC (Development Research Center), and World Bank. 2011. *China 2030: Building a Modern, Harmonious and Creative High-Income Society.* Beijing and Washington, DC: World Bank.

Feng, Jing. 2010. "The RPPP: Policy Design and Implementation Effect." *World Economy, World Economic Situation* 8: 14–19. (In Chinese.)

Geng, Yongzhi. 2011. "Follow-up Survey on RPPP Pilots: Rural Households in 18 Counties." *Research on Financial and Economic Issues* 5: 125–28. (In Chinese.)

Giles, John, Dewen Wang, and Albert Park. Forthcoming. "Expanding Social Insurance Coverage in Urban China." World Bank Policy Note, Washington, DC.

Huang, Hongfang. 2010. "Jiangsu Province Has Realized the Full Coverage of the New Rural Pension Scheme." *Xinhua News Daily,* October 29. (In Chinese.)

Li, Wei. 2011. "Survey on the Implementation of RPPP." *Economic Review* 6: 80–83. (In Chinese.)

Liang, Hong. 1999. "Economic Analysis of Current Rural Community Security of China," Ph.D. diss., University of Fudan. (In Chinese.)

Liu, Junwei. 2011. "Analysis with Rational Choice Theory on the Determinants for the Enrollment Behaviors of Farmers into the RPPP." *Zhejiang Social Sciences Journal* 4: 77–83. (In Chinese.)

Liu, Shangkui, Zhiqihui Wu, and Shengcai He. 2011. "Issues Arising from the Implementation of the RPPP and Countermeasures—A Survey on 5,000 Rural Households in Jilin." *Survey World* 2: 30–33. (In Chinese.)

Lou, Jiwei, and Shuilin Wang, eds. 2008. *Public Finance in China: Reform and Growth for a Harmonious Society.* Washington, DC: World Bank.

Luo, Xia. 2011. "Empirical Study on the RPPP: Case Study on Sixian City of Anhui Province." *Social Security Studies* 1: 67–73. (In Chinese.)

Ma, Limin. 1999. "Slowing Down Rural Pension." *Exploration and Debate* 7: 11–12. (In Chinese.)

Mu, Liangze, and Ren Lu. 2010. "Policies Beneficial for Farmers and Restructuring for the Rural Management Resources—Analysis on the RPPP." *Theory and Reform* 6: 71–74. (In Chinese.)

NBS (National Bureau of Statistics). 1995–2011. *China Labor Statistical Yearbook.* Beijing: China Statistics Press. (In Chinese.)

Rural Research Center of the Central China Normal University. 2010. Survey. http://www. juejingushi.com/znews/vvfnews-106026. (In Chinese.)

Shi, Shih-Jiunn. 2006. "Left to Market and Family—Again? Ideas and the Development of the Rural Pension Policy in China." *Social Policy & Administration* 40 (7): 791–806.

State Council. 2009. "Guidelines of Developing the New Rural Pension Scheme Pilot." (In Chinese.)

Wen, Jiabao. 2012. "Report on the Work of the Government." Delivered at the 5th Session of the 11th National People's Congress, March 5. http://news.xinhuanet.com/english/china/2012-03/15/c_131469703.htm.

Wang, Dewen. 2006. "China's Urban and Rural Old Age Security System: Challenges and Options." *China & World Economy* 14 (1): 102–16.

Wang, Dewen, Jiaze Chen, and Wenshu Gao. 2011. "Social Security Integration: The Case of Rural and Urban Resident Pension Pilot in Chengdu." World Bank, Washington, DC.

Wang, Dewen, Philip O'Keefe, and Lawrence Thompson. 2012. "China's Pension System Integration: The Case of Guangdong." World Bank, Washington, DC.

Wang, Guojun. 2000. "Defects of Current Rural Pension System and Reform Thinking." *Quarterly of Shanghai Academy of Social Science* 1: 120–27. (In Chinese.)

World Bank. Forthcoming. "China 2011. A Vision for Pension Policy Reform." World Bank, Washington, DC.

Wu, Yufeng. 2011. "Empirical Studies on Social Interactions and Enrollment Behaviors of the RPPP." *Huazhong University Journal of Science and Technology* 4: 105–111. (In Chinese.)

Wu, Yyuning. 2009. "Rural Pensions." Background paper for the World Bank report on the rural elderly, Washington, DC.

Zhang, Wenjun, and Dan Tang 2008. "The New Rural Social Pension Insurance Program of Baoji City Shaanxi Province." HelpAge International–Asia/Pacific, Chiang Mai, Thailand. www.helpage.org/download/4c48ab08674c1/. (In Chinese.)

CHAPTER 12

Learning from the Early Experience of India's Matching Defined Contribution Scheme

Robert Palacios and Renuka Sane

In an attempt to expand pension coverage, in 2010 the government of India introduced a matching defined contribution scheme. Preliminary analysis of the New Pension Scheme strongly suggests that women are more likely than men to participate; that higher income and more education are positively associated with take-up; and that having other potential sources of income for old age, including land, housing, and sons, reduces take-up, with other factors held constant. The data do not allow exploration of many others factors that may contribute to take-up, including the importance of the credibility of the intermediary (aggregator) and the role of information.

The challenge of expanding pension coverage is immense in India, where less than 10 percent of the labor force participates in formal pension schemes, according to most estimates. Private, formal sector workers are covered by both defined contribution and defined benefit schemes run by the Employee Provident Fund Organization (EPFO). Until recently, government employees were covered by the civil service pension system inherited from the British—a defined benefit system financed directly from the budget. Although a new defined contribution scheme was introduced in 2004, it applied only to new entrants, leaving the defined benefit scheme in place for many workers for the next few decades.

Like many countries, India has tried to expand coverage of formal sector pension schemes. These attempts have largely failed. In the 50 years since the Employees' Provident Fund Act (1952) was introduced, coverage increased from roughly 1 percent to 5 percent of the labor force. This level of coverage is typical of countries at India's income level (figure 12.1).

Moreover, EPFO coverage is highly concentrated among upper-income workers. Only a very small proportion of lower-middle-income or poor people, who make up the majority of India's population, have ever contributed to a formal pension scheme (figure 12.2).

One response to the failure to expand pension coverage was the introduction of the National Old Age Pension Scheme in 1995. This cash transfer scheme targets people age 65 and older living in households deemed to be below the poverty line. Currently, roughly

The authors would like to thank Kshetriya Grameen Financial Services (KGFS) for its cooperation and support and Parthasarathi Edupalli for research assistance.

FIGURE 12.1 **Coverage of contributory pension schemes, by income level**

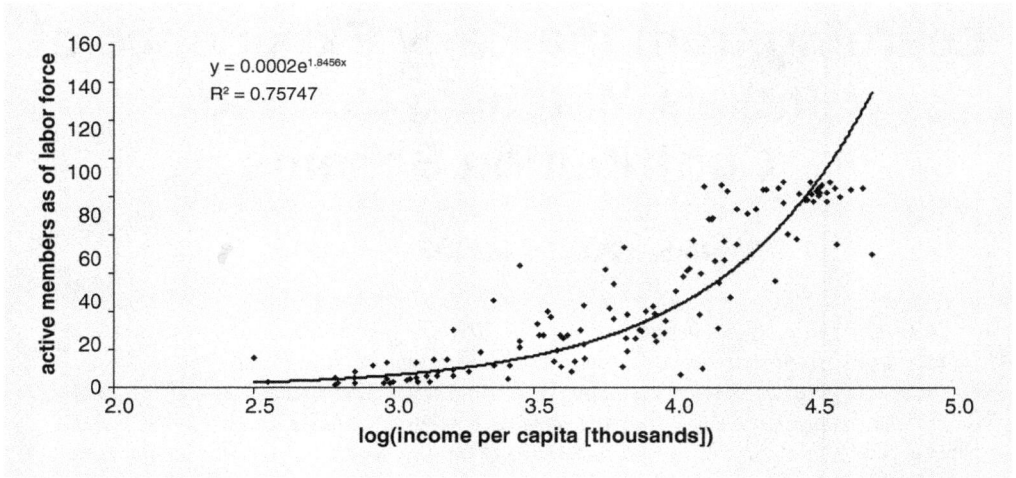

$$y = 0.0002e^{1.8456x}$$
$$R^2 = 0.75747$$

SOURCE: Pallares-Miralles, Romero, and Whitehouse 2011.

FIGURE 12.2 **Pension system coverage in India, by income level, 2010**

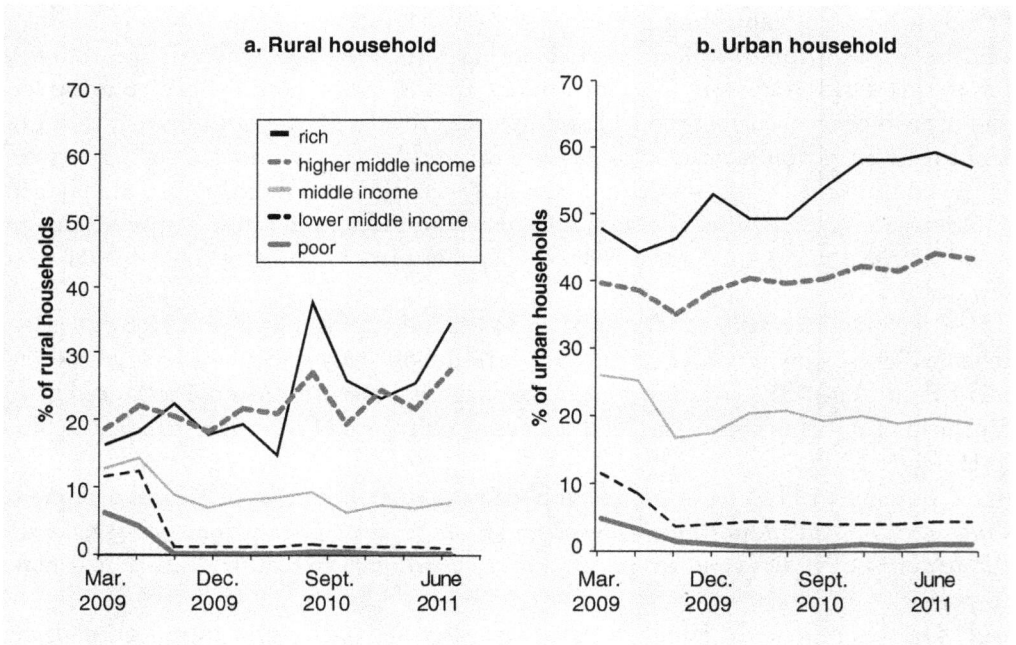

a. Rural household

b. Urban household

- rich
- higher middle income
- middle income
- lower middle income
- poor

SOURCE: Center for Monitoring Indian Economy.

one in every five elderly people in India is receiving a cash transfer of about Rs 200–300 a month. The National Old Age Pension Scheme benefit can at best supplement other sources of support required to survive.[1]

For most older people in India, income support in old age comes from family. Co-residence rates are high, with elderly women especially dependent on their families for support. Poor families find it difficult to support the elderly, and there is some evidence that they do not always provide support even when they are able to do so.

The gaps in family support may increase with the decline in fertility rates, increases in life expectancy, and urbanization. Although there is wide regional variation across the country, India's population is aging. Over the last two decades, policy makers have begun to introduce new features and to reform the system to prepare for the future.

In 2001, the government set up a special committee to provide recommendations to address the increasingly obvious gap in pension coverage. The Dave Committee proposed a new approach that would allow workers in the informal sector (known in India as the "unorganized sector") to contribute to a defined contribution plan managed by the state (Shah 2006). This New Pension Scheme (NPS) was first adopted for civil servants in a major reform implemented in 2004. Under the reformed civil service retirement system, all new central government employees are required to contribute 10 percent of their wages to a defined contribution account. This mandatory contribution is then matched with an equivalent contribution from the government.

In addition to controlling the liability of the government for benefits through a transition to a defined contribution structure, an important feature of the new scheme was the unbundling of recordkeeping and asset management. Over the next few years, most state governments adopted this model.[2] An interim regulator, the Pension Fund Regulatory and Development Authority, was set up along with a new recordkeeping infrastructure, known as the Central Recordkeeping Authority. A competitive bidding process resulted in contracts with three public sector asset managers; private firms were brought in later.

The second phase of NPS implementation was intended to use its infrastructure to extend coverage to informal sector workers throughout the country. In 2009, the NPS was officially opened to any worker not covered by a formal pension scheme.[3] Post offices, public sector banks, and other entities were enlisted to allow workers to open NPS accounts. In addition to its regulatory and oversight role, the Pension Fund Regulatory and Development Authority undertook efforts to inform workers about the system and encourage their participation.

Despite these efforts, take-up was extremely low the first year, largely as a result of the lack of incentives for providers and individuals. Other saving products received more favorable tax treatment, and the cost of opening and maintaining accounts made the NPS unattractive to most informal sector workers. Although investment returns were good and the systems were gradually coalescing for account administration for civil servants, by 2010 the Indian press was widely reporting the failure of the NPS to achieve meaningful coverage expansion among informal sector workers.

To address this challenge, in the spring of 2010, the government of India announced that it would deposit matching contributions of Rs 1,000 a year into the NPS accounts of individuals who made contributions of Rs 1,000–Rs 12,000 per fiscal year (April 1–March 31).[4] These accounts were called NPS-lite, as they differed from those of civil servants in several ways. Civil servants were able to view their accounts online and had other services that were not available to NPS-lite members. Most important, fees for basic retirement savings accounts were significantly lower than the fees on civil servants' accounts. The fee for opening an account was Rs 70, and the first 12 transactions were free. In contrast, the account opening fee for civil servants was Rs 350. (Annex A displays the range of charges, which include asset management fees.) Other changes made to the tax treatment of NPS accounts put them on an equal footing with similar saving products, although restrictions on withdrawals (intended to ensure that the savings were preserved for retirement income) were more restrictive.[5] These changes did not address the lack of outreach or incentives for providers to market the NPS to the informal sector, and the increase in take-up remained relatively modest.

In August 2010, the government set up a committee to review the performance of informal sector pensions. The committee made various recommendations in areas ranging from marketing to reduction of costs. It paid special attention to incentives for providers, including pension fund managers, and to "points of presence" (places where subscribers can open accounts).

In late 2010, the government launched a new initiative. To extend coverage of the system, it established incentives to encourage the introduction of entities that would serve as account "aggregators." These aggregators were mostly nongovernmental organizations that had met predefined criteria that qualified them to undertake outreach, marketing, and enrollment functions (see annex B). These aggregators are paid at least Rs 50 per enrollee and a volume bonus of Rs 10 up to 120,000, Rs 17 up 200,000, and Rs 22 up to 500,000. It remains to be seen whether these incentives are adequate to motivate aggregators to actively pursue enrollment and whether the reduced costs of NPS-lite combined with the matching contribution will be sufficient to encourage low-income informal workers to enroll in the system on a large scale.

Early Experience with Matching Defined Contributions in India

The NPS concept that emerged in 2001 began as an attempt to reach the massive informal labor force in India with a suitable vehicle for saving for old age. Arguably, however, the two key ingredients for successful implementation of such an approach—particularly in regard to the inherent limitations faced in reaching a predominantly low-income and largely rural target population—were missing. The first was a financial incentive to encourage workers with limited liquidity to tie up their limited savings over the extended period required to produce meaningful retirement income. The second was a supply-side incentive to motivate entry into the market and effective marketing of the product to inform people and make it easy to enroll in the program. These pieces of the puzzle were put into place only in late 2010.

What does the limited evidence since late 2010 show? No systematic evaluation process is yet in place to study what determines take-up of NPS-lite. Collectively, aggregators enrolled about 300,000 workers in 2011. It is not possible to estimate the take-up rate from these figures without information on the potential number of participants, but clearly it represents a tiny fraction of the potential pool. At the same time, the number of enrollees has expanded sixfold since the new incentive mechanisms were introduced.

A study of the determinants of enrollment patterns as the NPS unfolds and an analysis of how different segments of India's very heterogeneous unorganized sector are likely to respond to the design of the program would help policy makers understand the dynamics and scope for expanding coverage. Combining evaluation with national-level survey data would help policy makers obtain a more accurate idea of the potential size of the program and craft a better strategy. The next section presents a preliminary quantitative analysis of the differences between people who have enrolled in the NPS and people who have not.

DATA

The data presented here are from Kshetriya Grameen Financial Services (KGFS), a financial services provider that operates in five districts in three states in India.[6] In addition to selling insurance and loan products, KGFS functions as an aggregator for the NPS.

KGFS institutions are promoted by the Institute for Financial Management and Research Trust, a foundation whose mission is to ensure that every individual and enterprise has access to financial services. All KGFS institutions have a common parent company, which provides equity capital to each. Each institution is an autonomous, self-contained regional operation with its own management team hired locally.

When a customer enrolls in the KGFS system, information on his or her demographics, income, and financial goals is recorded. With the help of an in-house algorithm, a financial well-being report is generated that provides recommendations on which products the individual should buy. These products include loans (joint-liability loans, emergency loans, and gold loans), savings products (money market mutual funds), and insurance (personal accident insurance, term life insurance, and livestock insurance). Individuals often buy products that are different from the ones KGFS recommends.

The data used in this chapter are on all customers in the various locations in which KGFS operates. (For detailed descriptive statistics, see annex C.) All customers were told about the NPS and shown how to sign up for the scheme.

Figure 12.3 displays the number of people that enrolled in the NPS each month between November 2010 and April 2012. In the early months of January–March 2011, there was a surge in participation, perhaps because individuals had to enroll before the end of March to receive the Rs 1,000 co-contribution (although the peak was in February, not March).

Annex C compares people who enrolled in the NPS with people who did not. Enrollment is much higher among women (30 percent) than among men (9 percent); among women, it is higher among "housewives" (women who do not work outside the home) (32 percent) than among wage laborers (25 percent). In the states in which KGFS operates, Tamil Nadu has the highest participation rate (25 percent), followed by Orissa (21 percent); Uttarakhand (8 percent) lags far behind. The regions in Tamil Nadu are better off than the regions in Orissa and Uttarakhand, perhaps explaining their residents' greater willingness to set aside money for old age. Enrollees in the NPS have slightly higher median income (Rs 94,625) than non-enrollees (RS 90,000).

The proportion of households subscribing to the NPS increases marginally with household income, falling slightly at the highest part of the distribution (figure 12.4). Although the sample is not representative of the population even in these three states, it is striking that a substantial portion of the poorest people were willing to participate.

The NPS may be the only long-term saving product held by KGFS customers, or it may be held along with several other loan and insurance products (table 12.1). Background

FIGURE 12.3 **Monthly enrollment in India's New Pension Scheme, 2010–12**

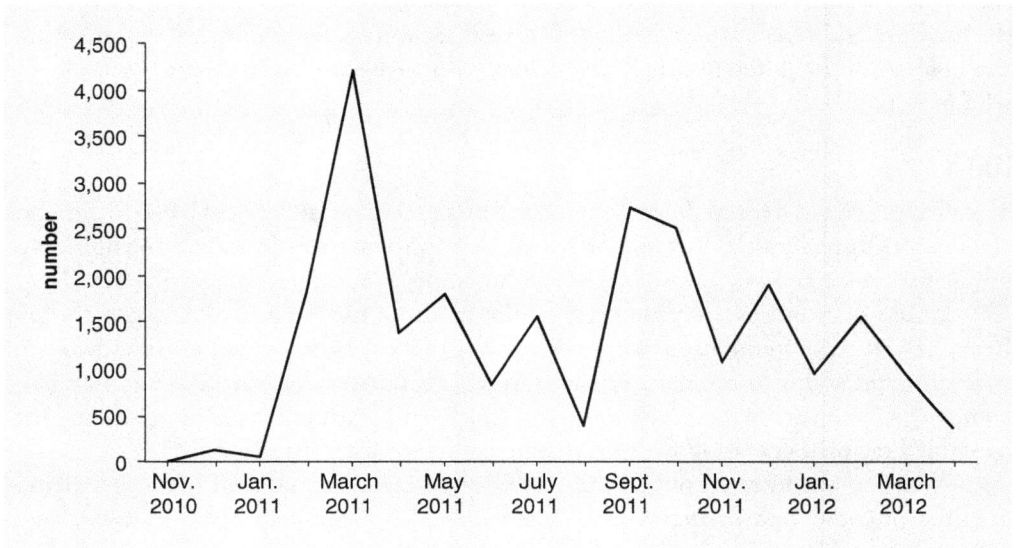

SOURCE: Authors' calculations, based on KGFS data.

FIGURE 12.4 **Participation in India's New Pension Scheme, by per capita income, 2011**

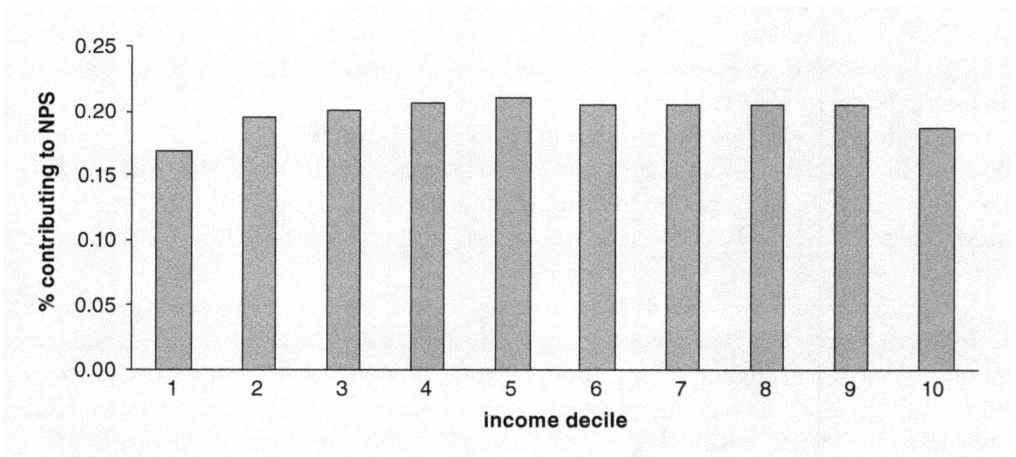

SOURCE: Authors' calculations, based on KGFS data.

risk and liquidity constraints are important determinants of household portfolio choice (Angerer and Lam 2009; Heaton and Lucas 2000; Zeldes 1997).

Purchasers of accident insurance and joint liability group loans—a common type of microfinance group loan in India—are more likely to participate in the NPS than people who do not buy the two products. The numbers are particularly stark for joint liability group clients, 33 percent of whom enrolled in the NPS. In contrast, among people

TABLE 12.1 **Participation in India's New Pension Scheme by people with and without other financial assets**

Financial asset	Did not buy NPS	Bought NPS	Number of observations
Personal accident insurance			
Bought	77	23	79,073
Did not buy	79	21	18,240
Life insurance			
Bought	63	37	39,943
Did not buy	87	13	57,370
Joint liability group loan (microfinance)			
Bought	67	33	58,448
Did not buy	92	8	38,865

SOURCE: Authors' calculations, based on KGFS data.

NOTE: Figures show only KGFS assets. However, given that KGFS opens branches only in areas that are not typically served by the formal financial sector, it is unlikely that households had access to insurance products other than those sold by KGFS.

without a joint liability group loan, just 8 percent were enrolled. Two factors may account for this pattern. On the one hand, people who are very well off do not need to take such a loan and may also feel no need to contribute to the NPS. On the other hand, people with a joint liability group loan are better able to cope with liquidity demands and are therefore better able to set aside money for old age.

Full analysis of NPS enrollment requires data on persistence (the percentage of people who continued to contribute the year after enrolling). Such data are not yet available.

STATISTICAL ANALYSIS OF PEOPLE WHO DO AND DO NOT ENROLL IN THE NEW PENSION SCHEME

Many factors affect the decision to join the NPS. The following logit model is estimated to identify them:

$$c^* = \beta 0 + \beta 1 X + \varepsilon c = 1 \text{ if } c^* > 0$$

The dependent variable, c, indicates whether the respondent contributed to the NPS. The variable X includes demographic indicators (age, sex, marital status, education, occupation, and family size and composition).

Of interest is the impact of income and wealth on participation. Household income is measured as the sum of the income of all household members. Three sets of variables capture household wealth: socioeconomic status (captured by whether the household has an electricity connection, whether it uses gas or wood for cooking, and whether it has a private toilet), land- and homeownership, and ownership and value of consumer durables (ownership of a CD player, a mixer and grinder, a mobile phone, a sewing machine, a television, a refrigerator, a washing machine, and a computer and the value of jewelry and livestock owned).

Log values are used for land and housing assets and income, because variation in percentage terms is more useful than variation in absolute levels. All values are scaled so that observations with a value of zero are not lost. The regression also controls for the region in which the household resides (table 12.2).

The results in table 12.2 are generally consistent with international evidence on the relationship between pension contributions and age, marital status, education level, and income. Age, for example, is positively associated with participation, as is education and marital status (Munnell, Sundén, and Taylor 2002). The age effect is nonlinear, increasing until the early 40s and falling thereafter (figure 12.5), a pattern witnessed in the Organisation for Economic Co-operation and Development (see chapter 2).

Although income is positively correlated with participation, the correlation between participation and regular income is negative (people with regular income are more than 50 percent less likely to contribute to the NPS). This result reflects the eligibility conditions of the program, which in principle at least, apply only to people not covered by the EPFO or other pension schemes. People with regular wage income are more likely to be covered by the formal pension scheme. The fact that they already contribute to a pension likely reduces their interest in the NPS, regardless of whether such a rule is enforced.

The value of land and housing is also negatively correlated with participation. A straightforward interpretation would be that these assets are viewed as a potential source of income in old age or as a resource to be used as part of a bequest strategy by which the owner extracts support during old age from his or her children (Bernheim, Schleifer, and Summers 1985; for empirical evidence in rural Kenya, see Hoddinott 1982).[7] This interpretation does not apply to wealth held in the form of jewelry or livestock.

The negative correlation between NPS participation and the number of children is strong, but only with regard to sons. This result is consistent with Indian cultural norms, which assume that sons will be the main source of parental support.[8] As the number of sons increases, there is less of an incentive to set aside money for old age.

The estimations confirm the dramatic difference between the take-up rates of men and women shown in annex C. There are several possible interpretations of this result, including the higher risk aversion and longer life expectancies of women. It may also reflect a desire among women to control at least part of the household's savings by opening these accounts in their names (Bannerjee and Duflo 2011).

Prospects for Matching Defined Contributions in India

Experience with NPS-lite has been mixed, possibly because of inadequate incentives or lack of confidence in aggregators. A rigorous evaluation is needed to assess the determinants of success or failure.

A first step in formulating a frame of reference for such an evaluation is recognizing that the unorganized sector is very heterogeneous. It includes tens of millions of subsistence farmers and a similar number of small-scale urban vendors. It includes people at the highest and lowest ends of the income distribution as well as people of all ages and education levels.

TABLE 12.2 **Logit regressions for determinants of participation in India's New Pension Scheme**

Variable	Estimate	Standard error	z–value	Marginal effect[a]	Error	t–value
(Intercept)	−7.90	0.22	−36.20	−1.21	0.13	−9.61
Age	0.14	0.01	19.61	0.02	0.00	8.89
Age2	−0.002	0.0001	−19.63	0.00	0.00	−8.89
Female	1.39	0.02	58.48	0.19	0.02	9.57
Married	0.42	0.06	6.51	0.06	0.01	5.46
Up to 12th standard	0.25	0.02	10.80	0.04	0.01	7.34
Graduate and above	0.08	0.06	1.31	0.01	0.01	1.30
Wage labor	0.20	0.02	8.27	0.03	0.01	6.36
Regular income	−0.48	0.05	−8.70	−0.06	0.01	−6.79
Housewife	0.19	0.03	6.29	0.03	0.01	5.21
Others	0.12	0.03	3.74	0.02	0.01	3.50
Hindu	0.25	0.04	6.61	0.04	0.01	5.51
Number of children	0.08	0.01	8.41	0.01	0.00	6.43
Number of sons	−0.04	0.01	−3.14	−0.01	0.00	−2.99
Electricity connection	−0.05	0.03	−1.63	−0.01	0.01	−1.61
Gas as cooking medium	−0.15	0.02	−6.04	−0.02	0.00	−5.16
Private toilet	−0.15	0.02	−6.18	−0.02	0.00	−5.25
Owns shop	0.24	0.04	6.23	0.04	0.01	5.13
Log(per capita household income)	0.13	0.01	10.46	0.02	0.00	7.21
Owns land	0.51	0.07	7.17	0.08	0.01	5.77
Log(value of land)	−0.05	0.01	−7.65	−0.01	0.00	−6.07
Owns house	0.99	0.18	5.62	0.15	0.03	4.89
Log(value of home)	−0.06	0.01	−4.64	−0.01	0.00	−4.21
Number of consumer durables	0.10	0.01	16.45	0.02	0.00	8.52
Factor(region_id)3	0.31	0.03	9.98	0.05	0.01	7.02
Factor(region_id)4	−0.45	0.04	−10.09	−0.06	0.01	−7.21
Factor(region_id)5	−13.26	58.69	−0.23	−0.19	0.02	−11.84
Factor(region_id)6	−13.32	69.19	−0.19	−0.19	0.02	−10.01

SOURCE: Authors' calculations, based on KGFS data.

NOTE: Marginal effects represent the change in the probability of participation from a one-unit change in a continuous variable evaluated at the mean or the shift in a dichotomous variable from zero to one.

FIGURE 12.5 **Probability of participating in India's New Pension Scheme, by age and sex at mean income**

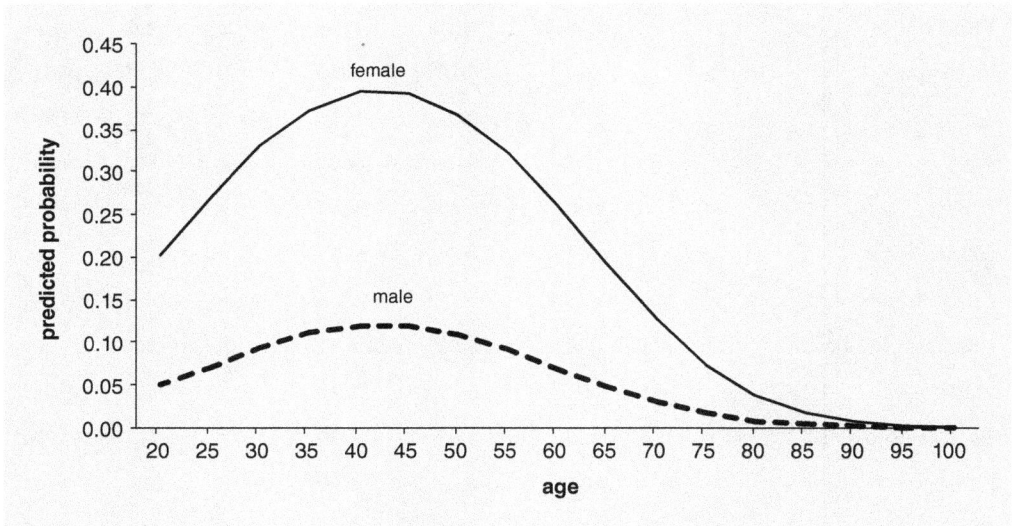

SOURCE: Authors' calculations, based on KGFS data.

To assess potential demand for pensions by the various segments of the informal sector, in 2004 the Asian Development Bank financed a national survey of 40,000 households. It also commissioned an analysis aimed at identifying the parts of the informal workforce most likely to participate in the NPS as it existed at the time. Figure 12.6 divides India's workforce into workers who are, or should be, covered by the EPFO and workers who fall into three categories: unpaid family workers, workers in small firms that are not covered by the EPFO, and the rest. According to the author of the study (Butel 2010), the potential market for the NPS is about 372 million workers.

The study asked workers to state whether they would be interested in participating in the NPS. Roughly 40 percent of respondents expressed a "keen interest" in doing so.

The same survey reveals important variations across this population in terms of ability to contribute and saving capacity. For the purposes of the analysis, the informal sector is defined as salaried employees of the state or central governments and salaried employees in private firms with 10 or more workers.[9] Based on this definition, 84 percent of all workers in India are in the unorganized sector.

In considering potential participation in the NPS, it makes sense to focus on informal sector workers between the ages of 20 and 50. These workers, whose median age in the sample was 35, are able to accumulate significant balances in their individual accounts before reaching old age and are more easily insured for mortality and health shocks than older workers. They make up about 85 percent of the unorganized labor force.

Table 12.3 shows the distribution of unorganized sector workers across income deciles. The deciles were computed using incomes of all workers in the organized and unorganized sectors. This method produces a distribution of unorganized sector workers

FIGURE 12.6 **Disaggregation of India's workforce, 2004**

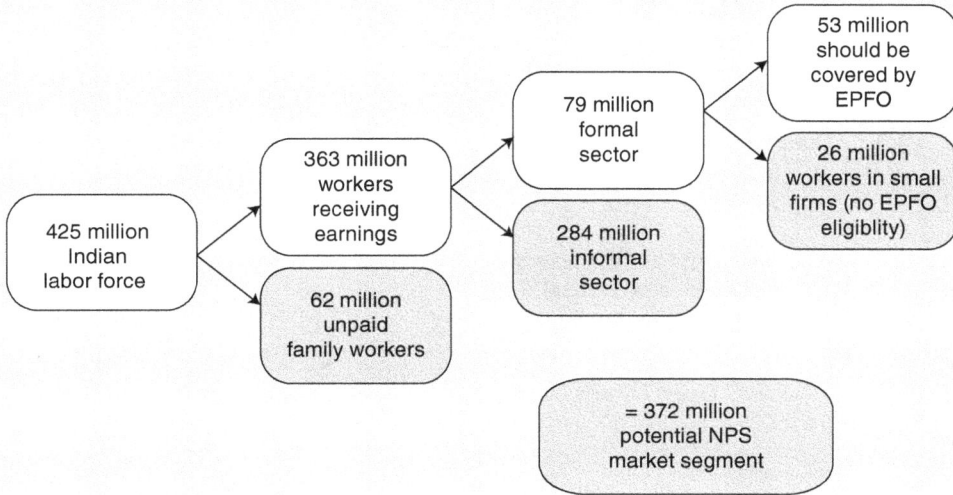

SOURCE: Butel and Bhardwaj 2010.

TABLE 12.3 **Distribution of workers in India's unorganized sector by income decile, 2004**

Income decile	Income (Rs)	Share (%)	Cumulative share (%)
1 (lowest)	≤ 11,000	11.8	11.8
2	> 11,001–16,800	11.0	22.8
3	> 16,801–21,600	11.6	34.4
4	> 21,601–27,000	11.6	46.1
5	> 27,001–35,000	11.6	57.7
6	> 35,001–42,000	10.6	68.2
7	> 42,001–54,000	8.6	76.8
8	> 54,001–72,000	8.9	85.8
9	> 72,001–105,000	6.8	92.6
10 (highest)	> 105,001	7.4	100.0

SOURCE: Authors' calculations, based on 2004 Asian Development Bank survey.

concentrated in the lower part of the income distribution. Nevertheless, the table clearly shows that the unorganized sector is heterogeneous with respect to income distribution.

At the higher end of the distribution, the top two deciles earn, on average, more than Rs 72,000 a year. The median saving rates are 15.3 percent for the top decile and 21.6 percent for the second decile, with median savings of at least Rs 10,000 a year. The saving rate of the top decile is twice the average saving rate, and the saving rate of the second decile is 1.5 times the average. Median savings are nearly 10 times higher than savings for the bottom two deciles.

Deciles 3–8 include workers with incomes of Rs 16,800–Rs 72,000 a year. These workers display saving and insurance behaviors that are relevant for assessing the feasibility of voluntary participation. The median saving rates for these deciles is 11.7–15.8 percent, and the share of workers with life insurance policies is 8–36 percent. Clearly, there is some capacity for insurance and saving in this part of the income distribution.

TABLE 12.4 **Median saving rate and life insurance coverage of workers age 20–50 in India's unorganized sector (middle-income deciles), 2004**

Income decile	Median saving rate (%)	Life insurance coverage (%)
3	11.7	7.9
4	12.0	13.6
5	13.2	18.3
6	14.3	24.0
7	15.0	27.8
8	15.8	35.7

SOURCE: Authors' calculations, based on 2004 Asian Development Bank survey data.

Figure 12.7 shows a simple example of an Rs 5 per day (Rs 1,825 a year) pension contribution for deciles 3–8, expressed as a percentage of earnings that workers would have to contribute.[10] In all cases, the rate is lower than the median saving rate of individuals in each decile. However, in the lower deciles, making the contribution would require

FIGURE 12.7 **Minimum pension contribution as share of income in India**

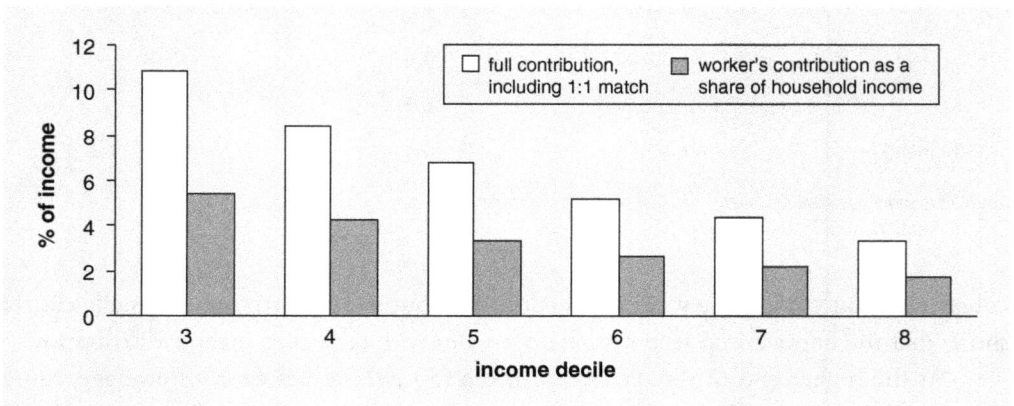

SOURCE: Authors' calculations, based on 2004 Asian Development Bank survey data.

individuals to shift most of their savings into the designated pension savings accounts, and some individuals would have to increase their overall saving rate. Doing so would tie up a significant part of the small savings of these liquidity-constrained lower-income workers—suggesting the need for a matching contribution to increase take-up, especially at lower income levels. Given a 1:1 government match of the Rs 1,000 currently offered through the NPS-lite program,[11] a large share of informal workers in the middle of the income distribution would be able to make the minimum contribution given a 1:1 match (see figure 12.7).

If a significant segment of the informal sector participated in India's version of a matching defined contribution, the cost could become significant. In NPS-lite, the annual match from the government would be Rs 1,000 per participating worker. If all informal sector workers took up the program—extending coverage to several hundred million workers and their families—the annual cost would reach 0.3–0.4 percent of gross domestic product (GDP). If 23 percent of workers took up the program (the take-up observed in the KGFS population, which would triple pension coverage in India), the cost of the match would be 0.07–0.10 percent of GDP. To put these figures in perspective, the central government provides an annual subsidy to the EPFO of about 0.04 percent of GDP.

Conclusions

The idea of the NPS is more than a decade old, but implementation started only in 2009, and the key incentives were introduced only at the end of 2010. There has been little time to test the matching defined contribution concept, which continues to evolve.

Slightly less than a quarter of the sample population analyzed contributed to a retirement account in 2011. This figure may be as low as it is because the program has no track record, requiring participants to sacrifice liquidity and trust that the funds will be well invested. If the program produces the desired results, take-up rates may increase, as confidence in the program grows. Conversely, poor performance should lead to lower take-up.

The limited analysis presented reveals certain patterns, albeit in a sample that is not representative of India's population or of the informal sector. There is strong evidence that women are more likely to participate in the NPS than men; that higher income and more education are positively associated with take-up; and that having other potential sources of income for old age, including land, housing, and sons, reduces take-up rates, other factors held constant.

The data do not allow exploration of other salient issues that should contribute to take-up, including the importance of the credibility of the intermediary (aggregator) and the role of information. Qualitative analysis that disentangles the reasons behind high take-up among women, apparent reliance on sons, and other suggested determinants would be very useful.

Of course, enrolling in the NPS is only a small part of the story. Persistence of contributions over time will ultimately determine whether the scheme succeeds in providing its members with a significant source of income during old age.

Among the lessons learned from the experience to date is the need for incentives—not only for potential participants but also for providers. Provider incentives have to be aligned with customer interest; too often, the distribution of financial services has been plagued by the selling of inappropriate financial products to fool individuals. Studying the determinants of enrollment patterns as the program unfolds and analyzing how different segments of India's very heterogeneous informal sector respond to the program's design should help policy makers better understand the potential dynamics and scope for expanding coverage. Combining evaluation with national-level survey data can help them obtain a more accurate idea of the potential size and cost of the program and craft a better strategy.

A number of parallel developments in India may affect the ultimate outcome of this initiative. India is experiencing strong economic growth, which is raising incomes and putting a larger share of the population in a position to save and insure against risks. The government appears to be strongly committed to expanding social insurance and pension programs, as shown by passage of the Social Security for Unorganized Sector bill in December 2008 and the massive expansion of health insurance coverage during the following three years.[12]

Another important development is the emergence of technologies that may allow India to leapfrog richer countries in certain areas, such as identification and payment systems. The Unique Identification Authority of India has issued about 120 million unique numbers tied to sophisticated biometrics; applications being piloted would allow for reliable transfers of funds to and from citizens who are difficult to reach through formal financial channels. This technology may be useful for programs such as the NPS as they mature.

Notes

1. At the time of writing, an active lobby was seeking to increase the scope of the National Old Age Pension Scheme and to make it universal (*Hindu Business Line* 2012).

2. Kerala and West Bengal are the two major exceptions.

3. Although the eligibility criteria are not clearly specified, they seem to apply to special government schemes such as the Coal Miners' Provident Fund in addition to the civil service pension schemes at the state and federal levels and the EPFO.

4. Currency values in this chapter are given in Indian rupees; Rs 1 = $0.0191.

5. Restrictions include a rule that at least 40 percent of the balance must be annuitized (Ananth Ananth, Chen, and Rasmussen 2012).

6. The institutions operating in 2012 are in the Thanjavur and Thiruvarur districts of Tamil Nadu (South India), which are fertile agrarian economies; the Ganjam and Khurda districts in Orissa (East India), which are characterized by subsistence agriculture supplemented by domestic migration; and five sparsely populated hilly districts in Uttarakhand (North India), which are dominated by trade and services.

7. A large body of literature examines the role of children as a source of income support in old age. For a recent review, see Galasso, Gatti, and Profetta (2008).

8. Börsch-Supan, Coppola, and Reil-Held (2012) find that there is a strong demand for Riester pensions (another matching defined contribution) in Germany among parents with more than two children. This result, however, reflects the fact that the Riester subsidies increase linearly with the number of children.

9. EPFO extends coverage only to workers in firms with at least 20 employees.

10. Crudely adjusting for the change in nominal incomes during the time period considered would result in the Rs 1,000 a year required by the NPS-lite program.

11. The subsidy is actually part of a program known as Svalambadam.

12. Three years after it was established, the National Health Insurance Scheme (RSBY) uses biometric identification and a voucher-like smart card to provide cashless hospitalization insurance to more than 100 million people. Policy makers have expressed a desire to bundle this program with the NPS as well as life insurance to harness the scheme's technology and outreach to informal sector workers.

References

Ananth, Bindu, Gregory Chen, and Stephen Rasmussen. 2012. *The Pursuit of Complete Financial Inclusion: The KGFS Model in India.* Access to Finance Forum, Report by Consultative Group Assist the Poorest and Its Partners 4, CGAP and IFMR Trust, Chennai.

Angerer, Xiaohong, and Pok-Sang Lam. 2009. "Income Risk and Portfolio Choice: An Empirical Study." *Journal of Finance* 64 (2): 1037–55.

Bannerjee, A., and E. Duflo. 2011. *Poor Economics.* Cambridge, MA: MIT Press.

Bernheim, D., A. Schleifer, and L. Summers. 1985. "The Strategic Bequest Motive." *Journal of Political Economy* 93 (December): 1045–76.

Börsch-Supan, Axel H., Michela Coppola, and Anette Reil-Held. 2012. "Riester Pensions in Germany: Design, Dynamics, Targeting Success and Crowding-In." NBER Working Paper 18014, National Bureau of Economic Research, Cambridge, MA.

Butel, Chris. 2010. *India: Pension Reforms for the Unorganised Sector.* Asian Development Bank Project Report, Final Report TA 4226-IND, 99–164. Manila: Asian Development Bank.

Butel, Chris, and Gautam Bhardwaj. 2010. *Overview Report. India: Pension Reforms for the Unorganised Sector.* Asian Development Bank Project Report, Final Report TA 4226-IND, 1–35. Manila: Asian Development Bank.

Galasso, V., R. Gatti, and P. Profetta. 2008. "Investing in Old Age: Pensions, Children and Savings." Econpubblica Working Paper 138. http://papers.ssrn.com/sol3/papers.cfm?abstract_id=1338058.

Heaton, John, and Deborah Lucas. 2000. "Portfolio Choice in the Presence of Background Risk." *Economic Journal* 110 (460): 1–26.

Hindu Business Line. 2012. "Sonia for Universal Pension for Aged Poor." May 22. http://www.thehindubusinessline.com/industry-and-economy/economy/article3445791.ece.

Hoddinott, J. 1992. "Rotten Kids or Manipulative Parents: Are Children Old Age Security in Western Kenya?" *Economic Development and Cultural Change* 40 (3): 545–66.

Munnell, Alicia H., Annika Sundén, and Catherine Taylor. 2002. "What Determines 401(k) Participation and Contributions?" *Social Security Bulletin* 64 (3): 64–75.

Pallares-Miralles, M., C. Romero, and E. Whitehouse. 2011. "International Patterns of Pension Provision II: Worldwide Overview of Facts and Figures." Draft, World Bank, Washington, DC.

Shah, Ajay. 2006. "Indian Pension Reform: A Sustainable and Scalable Approach." In *Managing Globalisation: Lessons from China and India*, ed. D. A. Kelly, R. S. Rajan, and G. H. L. Goh. New Delhi: World Scientific.

Zeldes, Stephen P. 1997. "Consumption and Liquidity Constraints: An Empirical Investigation." *Journal of Political Economy* 97 (2): 305–46.

Annex A Fee Structure of India's New Pension Scheme

Intermediary	Activity	Charges	Method of deduction
Central Recordkeeping Agency (CRA)	Account opening charges	Rs 35 (digitization performed by CRA)	Cancellation of units from each subscriber pension account
	Annual maintenance charges[a]	Rs 70 per year with 12 free subscriber contributions each fiscal year	
	Transaction charges[b]	None for first 12 transactions; Rs 5 per transaction beyond 12 free subscriber contributions per year	
Trustee bank	Per transaction originating from a non–Reserve Bank of India location[c]	Rs 15 per transaction for collection of funds at non–Reserve Bank of India centers	Net asset value deduction
Custodian[d] (on asset value in custody)	Asset servicing charges	0.0075% per year for electronic segment; 0.05% per year for physical segment	Net asset value deduction
Pension fund manager (PFM)	Investment management fee[e]	0.0009% per year (PFMs receive a fee of Rs 90,000 for every Rs 1,000 crores of fund they manage)	Net asset value deduction

NOTE: Service tax and other levies, as applicable, will be levied as per existing tax laws.

A. When the number of accounts in the CRA reaches 15 lakh, the service charges—exclusive of service tax and other taxes as applicable—will be reduced to Rs 50 per account for annual maintenance. The CRA account maintenance charge covers maintenance of electronic information on balances, incorporation of account details received electronically, annual hard copy transmission of account information, and so on.

B. The cost will be reduced to Rs 4 and Rs 3 per transaction when the thresholds of 15 lakh and 30 lakh subscribers, respectively, are attained.

C. Trustee bank charges are not charged to the subscriber directly. The transaction refers to the entire chain of activities starting from receipt of electronic instructions/receipt of the physical instrument to the transfer of funds to the designated PFMs. On the outflow side, it includes all activities leading to crediting of the beneficiary account.

D. Charges for demat/remat; receipt of shares and Securities and Exchange Board of India charges are extra.

E. This fee includes all transaction-related charges such as brokerage, transaction costs, and so on, except custodian charges and applicable taxes. The fee is calculated on the basis of the average monthly assets managed by the pension fund.

Annex B Aggregators in India's NPS-Lite System as of March 21, 2011

Aggregator name	Government/nongovernment
Adhikar Microfinance Pvt Ltd	Nongovernment
Alankit Assignments Ltd	Nongovernment
APB & Other Construction Workers Welfare Board, Hyderabad	Government
Banaskantha District Co-op Milk Producers Union Limited	Nongovernment
Bandhan Financial Services Pvt Ltd	Nongovernment
Bandhan Konnagar	Nongovernment
Computer Age Management Services (CAMS)	Nongovernment
Department of Women & Child Development	Government
Department of Post	Government
ESAF Microfinance	Nongovernment
Financial Inclusion Network and Operations Ltd (FINO)	Nongovernment
IFMR Holding Private Ltd	Nongovernment
Karnataka State Unorganized Workers Social Security Board (KSUWSSB)	Government
LIC Housing Finance Ltd	Government
MP State Electronics Development Corporation Ltd (MPSEDC)	Government
Samhita Community Development Services	Nongovernment
Society for Elimination of Rural Poverty (SERP)	Government
SEWA Bank	Nongovernment
South Indian Bank	Nongovernment
SREI Sahaj e-Village Ltd	Nongovernment

Annex C Demographic and Other Characteristics of Enrollees and Non-enrollees in India's New Pension Scheme

Characteristic	NPS noncustomers	NPS customers	Number of observations
Number of KGFS customers	75,097	22,216	97,313
% of sample with account at KGFS	77.3	22.7	97,313
Age (median)	41	52	97,313
Sex (%)			
Male	91	9	33,754
Female	70	30	63,559
Marital status (%)			
Married	76	24	92,321
Single	94	6	4,992
Education (%)			
Illiterate	78	22	17,113
School	76	24	76,900
Graduate and above	88	12	3,300
Occupation (%)			
Wage labor	75	25	44,974
Agriculture based	81	19	17,622
Housewife	68	32	13,008
Regular income	90	10	4,868
Other	82	18	16,841
State (%)			
Orissa	79	21	11,204
Tamil Nadu	75	25	75,878
Uttarakhand	92	8	10,231
Sanitation (%)			
Private toilet	82	18	24,800
Public/open toilet	75	25	72,513
Median household income (Rs)	90,000	94,625	97,313
Household size (median)	4	4	97,313
Number of children (median)	2	2	97,313
Number of sons (median)	1	1	97,313
Landownership (%)			
Owns land	78	22	39,800
Does not own land	77	23	57,513
Median land value (Rs)	0	0	97,313
Homeownership (%)			
Homeowner	77	23	95,873
Nonhomeowner	83	17	1,440
Median home value (Rs)	99,000	99,000	97,313
Median number of consumer durables	2	3	97,313

SOURCE: Authors' calculations, based on KGFS data.

CHAPTER 13

Using Prepaid Contributions to Cover Mobile Workers in Cape Verde and Tunisia

Antoine Delarue

The informal sector is often characterized as one of marginal jobs and precarious workers, typically populated by workers who do not want, and usually cannot afford, to pay taxes. Analysis of this sector in Cape Verde and Tunisia finds that it is more accurately described as one in which highly mobile workers use their mobility to survive and prosper in a quickly changing economic environment. In these settings, the employer's main role is that of a temporary "equipment provider." In this relationship, workers claim no long-term security, and the equipment provider avoids any long-term commitment or other aspects of the traditional role and attendant responsibilities of an employer. As no one is willing to take on the administrative burden of declaration and contribution collection, the traditional approach to providing and financing pension (or health) schemes has to be completely reconsidered. A new type of pension scheme decouples financing from the accrual of pension rights, through prepaid contribution vouchers that minimize the administrative cost of the scheme while drastically reducing the declaration obligations of the equipment provider. The design has won praise from social security institutions but has yet to be implemented.

Informal sector activities are thriving in developing countries. Unlike the formal or modern sector, which accepts social security obligations, the informal sector appears to resist not only the traditional social security approach but many customized approaches that intend to accommodate their presumed economic specificities. This chapter provides insight into why efforts to enforce compliance or reduce the cost of participating in pension schemes have failed.

Informal economies, which can be globally competitive, are individually very fragile. They have developed novel forms of labor relations to address the high level of uncertainty they face. They rely on temporary clusters of "mobile workers" who are employed short term by "equipment providers." As risk sharing is essential, mobile workers do not claim long-term security, and equipment providers are not willing to assume the traditional role played by employers. Mobile workers, who often operate in teams, moving from one "user" to the next, do not consider their employers clients or view themselves as independent workers. The relationships between these workers and the firms that hire them preclude the use of traditional recording and contribution collection techniques, which social security institutions have successfully developed with salaried or independent workers, irrespective of the economic burden involved.

This chapter proposes an alternative approach, based on contribution prepayment techniques that overcome the administrative challenge of registering mobile workers and contributions at an acceptable cost. The techniques are shown to be politically feasible, as

261

they can be turned into organized schemes between mobile workers and the firms that use them. Although they are unwilling to play the role of traditional employers, equipment providers are often aware of their collective responsibility and the economic interest in securing mobile workers for their sector. Some sectors indeed offered to pay a tax on their gross income as a proxy for the employer's contribution.

Evidence from Case Studies

This chapter draws on two reports based on missions to Cape Verde in 2005–06 and Tunisia in 2002–03 (SERVAC 2006, 2003). In both countries, SERVAC, a French consulting firm, was mandated to study the extension of social security schemes to informal workers after classical extension strategies had been taken to their limits and failed. It found that the main cause of these shortcomings was the innate inability of traditional pension schemes to account for the new type of labor relation that characterizes informal economies.

CAPE VERDE

Cape Verde has a private pension and health insurance scheme, the National Institute of Social Protection (Instituto Nacional de Previdência Social—INPS), which proved remarkably successful with the modern sector of the economy. Monthly contributions trigger very complete health coverage, including third-party payment for medication purchased at private pharmacies.

Cape Verde's main problem was that the INPS was the only scheme that reimbursed medication (public workers had free access to hospitals and in theory could obtain medication there; in practice, medication was never available). As a result, many people, both within the civil service and from the informal sector, found ways to charge their medication to a family member or a friend covered by the INPS.

In 2002, the INPS and its members—who represented just 20 percent of active workers—were responsible for 80 percent of spending on medication outside of public hospitals. There was therefore a great incentive for the INPS to register as many informal workers as possible, as it was in effect already paying for their health expenses; any contribution, no matter how small, would have been a plus. The informal sector included 30,000 noncovered independent workers who could have afforded coverage had it been offered.

INPS first relied on a strategy of enforcing compliance, backed by improved information technology and data collection processing but using the same model of monthly declarations and contributions. This model—which is easy enough for a modern enterprise with stable employment to comply with (each monthly declaration is largely identical to the previous month's)—is not well adapted to Cape Verde's informal sector.

Cape Verde's informal sector stems from its wealth of very small employers, each employing fewer than five people, who move frequently between jobs. This high turnover challenges the timely recording of contributions and its possible use as a condition for accessing health benefits. (If access is immediate upon registering, people will register only when they need services; if it is not, informal workers end up being excluded from coverage if their records are incomplete or face administrative hurdles if the scheme has difficulties tracking them between employers.) It also challenges the administrative capabilities of small employers, who often lack experience with the strict bookkeeping required. Controls and inspections of employers have decreasing returns in terms of population coverage: large employers are easy to find, but small employers are not, particularly if they never turn in contributions. Moreover, each inspection solves only a few cases and is therefore not cost-effective. Another problem with the INPS is that it did not introduce a minimal declared salary, leaving itself wide open to underdeclaration of income.

The INPS found itself overwhelmed with a haphazard flow of employers' declarations with which it could not hope to cope, both because of their sheer volume and because records were incomplete and of poor quality. The INPS did not provide the medical coverage to which transient workers might have been entitled had their declarations been complete, destroying the scheme's credibility. The sheer volume of declarations made controlling them, if only to clarify them, impossible. Strictly speaking, insurees were a loss for the scheme, at least for health insurance, but the INPS assumed that insurees were already finding ways of charging their medical expenses to it. As both a health insurance and pension scheme, the INPS included new members in pension coverage, which suffered from the same declaration problem.

The INPS's second answer to its problem was the creation of a scheme tailored for self-employed professionals. Contributions were based on an average estimated income for each profession (all lawyers pay the same contribution, for instance). The scheme also mandated a minimum of 15 years of contributions to receive a pension, ignoring the fact that many self-employed workers do not remain self-employed their entire working life. This scheme met with no success, as self-employed professionals remained very reluctant to register, probably because no effort was made to tailor the scheme to their actual economic conditions.

In 2005, the INPS mandated SERVAC to study its extension to both self-employed workers and informal salaried workers. In both cases, SERVAC found that the underlying problem was applying a traditional (and excellent) scheme tailored for large companies with a regular income to populations that were completely different.

The problem was probably not the income of these workers but their situation. Self-employed workers often regard their employment as precarious (even if their income is high); they need a flexible scheme, with contributions that can be adjusted to their current income. Above all, they need a scheme that requires no minimum contribution period, as many self-employed workers have held, or expect to hold, salaried jobs at some point in their career and may remain self-employed only for a few years.

For their part, informal workers often have multiple employers, who see a high turnover of employees. These workers are mobile workers; attempting to treat them as stable employees of modern enterprises is counterproductive, as it generated an unacceptable administrative burden for both the informal sector and the INPS.

TUNISIA

Tunisia has a highly segmented system of mandatory pension schemes (one per activity), which in theory covers everyone. Three segments of the population had very low affiliation rates, however: fishers, agricultural workers, and domestic workers. Affiliation in these schemes, while at first sight mandatory, was in fact conditioned by a minimum activity of 45 days of work per quarter for agricultural workers, a given number of fishing trips for small ships, and other rules. In practice, these rules were impossible to verify, leading to underreporting by workers. Moreover, highly mobile workers might never meet the requirements. SERVAC was mandated to study the problem and offer solutions.

Fishers

Tunisia's fishing sector makes perhaps the best case for a new and adapted scheme. Tunisia employs three separate schemes, depending on the ship's size. The system is ill suited to a population of mobile workers who change ships (and therefore schemes) often, and it imposes heavy administrative burdens on shipowners, who must register frequently changing crews. The union of owners, the Tunisian Union of Agriculture and Fishing (Union Tunisienne de l'Agriculture et de la Pêche—UTAP), declared itself willing to see employers' contributions, and the detailed declarations that must accompany them, replaced with a tax on caught fish. Tunisian shipowners were sensitive to their collective need to maintain a ready workforce by keeping the profession attractive.

The Tunisian fishing sector is healthy economically, employing an estimated 50,000 fishers for an estimated 7.5 million work days annually.[1] It is, however, a very weather-dependent activity. Because idle periods, during which no crews are hired, may last for weeks, a very mobile workforce is needed. The fishing sector globally represented TD 311 million in 2001, about half of which came from coastal fishing, the category most dependent on mobile workers.[2]

Agricultural Workers

Tunisia's agricultural sector produced an estimated TD 2.54 billion of goods in 1998. It employed about 280,000 salaried workers, 50,000 of them full time, and another 1 million family workers, 312,000 of them permanent workers.

A mandatory pension scheme exists, but farmers (like shipowners) are obligated to report workers only if they employ them for more than 45 days per trimester. As employment is impossible to verify, affiliation can be considered voluntary in practice.

SERVAC (2003) estimated informal (and undeclared) labor in the agricultural sector at about 55 million work days a year, including both occasional salaried workers and occasional family workers.[3] Introducing a branch tax might be difficult because of the diversity of the sector, but it would be a viable means of financing a pension scheme.

Domestic Workers

Domestic workers were not covered by any scheme in 2002. The number of domestic workers in 2001 was estimated at about 52,000 (the number would be higher if part-time workers whose main occupation is not domestic work were included).[4] The number is difficult to pin down, as there is a gray area between occasional help and regular employment on the one hand and between help from family or friends with payment in kind and actual salaried work on the other. SERVAC estimated that there were about 10 million work days a year in the sector. No hard data were available on the sector's economic value.

Summary

Workers in these three categories are characterized less by the precariousness of their employment than by their mobility. They have multiple employers, sequentially or concurrently, without durable ties to any of them. Having multiple employers allows them to manage the risk they face and cushion themselves from the precariousness of each of their jobs. These workers have regular incomes, albeit from multiple sources. They are therefore good candidates for a social insurance scheme (as opposed to assistance).

At the time SERVAC conducted its study, Tunisia tried to induce precarious workers to register in customized low-cost pension schemes. These schemes had minimum and flexible contribution requirements and very attractive benefits. To the authorities' surprise, the schemes attracted very few new participants. SERVAC discovered that enrollment was limited because the administrative burden on employers was heavy. Turnover of fishers and small-scale agricultural laborers is very high, with workers hired for a few days at a time; in agriculture, work is highly seasonal. Domestic workers often have several employers concurrently, none of whom would be willing to take responsibility for handling their registration.

SERVAC's discussions with UTAP set it on a search for alternative solutions. UTAP suggested replacing traditional contributions (taken from wages) by a tax on gross fishing income (directly on the catch). A 2 percent tax would generate TD 6.2 million a year, or TD 116 per year per worker (about TD 0.6 a day). By way of comparison, the guaranteed agricultural minimum wage was TD 6 a day. Assuming a fisher would draw about the same pay, the contribution was equivalent to about 10 percent of wages, a typical figure for traditional employer contributions. Unlike those contributions, however, the earmarked tax would be levied regardless of the amount of mobile work used on a boat.

SERVAC suggested adding an employee's contribution of TD 0.12 a day, based on prepaid contribution vouchers (see below). The incentive for employees to participate in the pension scheme would have been great, as their employer would have contributed five times as much, albeit indirectly.

LESSONS LEARNED

Cape Verde and Tunisia adopted different approaches to the informal sector and the problem of getting employees to declare. Cape Verde showed that enforced compliance, which relies solely on employers' declarations, does not work. The reason for its failure stems not so much from the fact that it adds only "bad risk" insurees to the scheme—people with low declared (and unverifiable) income, who will cost the scheme more than they can hope to bring in in contributions; many of these people were already finding ways of charging their expenses to the scheme. The problem was the difficulty (and high cost) of keeping track of such a volatile segment of the population, which enters and leaves the scheme frequently, making it difficult to start and end its health coverage. Forcing an ill-fitting mold of monthly individual declarations on employers of flexible workers only clogs the system with a large number of declarations, often of poor quality and dubious accuracy.

Tunisia tried to prompt declaration with a low-cost approach, creating what it saw as a very enticing scheme. It failed to see that the main problem, particularly in the fishing sector, stemmed from the heavy administrative burden of declaring highly mobile workers, not the unwillingness of employers to make contributions. The real barrier was administrative, not economic.

In neither country was the income of informal workers the problem. In Cape Verde, most health expenses were already being borne by the scheme, so any contributions at all were welcome. In Tunisia, the economic branches involved were willing and able to pay for the scheme.

Maintaining Competitiveness through Mobile Work

The problems noted above, which are encountered in a variety of settings, stem from a gap between the administrative requirement of the traditional approach for a social security scheme that relies heavily on employers' goodwill and the flexible labor relation through which informal economies deal with systemic risks. A key operational challenge for social security schemes is finding a way to collect contributions and handle the corresponding data flows needed to compute individual benefits at an acceptable administrative cost. The traditional answer is to rely on employers to register insured workers, assess and collect their contributions, and consolidate their contributions into regular payments. Such a system works well in a modern sector of stable enterprises; it is inefficient in sectors in which high economic uncertainty excludes long-term labor relations.

MEETING THE ORGANIZATIONAL CONSTRAINTS OF LARGE-SCALE OLD-AGE INSURANCE

A large-scale old-age insurance scheme entails regular and stable contributions on the one hand and regular declarations of insured members (so that their individual pension contributions can be computed and recorded) on the other. To keep costs as low as possible, these data flows need to be processed together. Doing so represents a considerable organizational challenge that involves collecting and checking contributions for accuracy and compliance, recording and checking data pertaining to rights, and making the appropriate computations.

Such mass treatment is possible only if the data are aggregated and homogeneous. In typical social security schemes, employers aggregate the data. They are responsible for collecting and paying contributions (both their own and those of their employees).

This method of handling pension contributions is effective in a modern sector, where the number of employees per company is large and turnover is low. It is ineffective for other sectors. For self-employed workers, there is in effect one employee per company, so the costs of aggregation fall heavily on the social security scheme (although employees report their own declarations). Informal workers, among whom turnover is very high, are far less able to cope with the declaration process, and no employer is willing to do so for them. Another form of organization is needed, one that is flexible enough to handle informal activities yet standardized enough to minimize operating cost.

UNDERSTANDING THE ECONOMY OF INFORMAL LABOR

A good metaphor for mobile workers is that of herders and farmers. Farmers stay put and wait for the rain; herders follow it wherever it falls. In arid regions, herders are more successful, because no matter how rare and irregular, it always rains somewhere, and they can move their herds there to take advantage of it.

Similarly, informal workers are not so much precarious as mobile. Fishers, small farmers and farm laborers, domestic workers, and others—as well as the firms that employ them—may individually have precarious income. But collectively the demand for their services is strong: entire branches of the economy rely on them, and these branches are growing. Informal workers are therefore a working economic answer to a very volatile work environment beset by economic, climatic, and other hard-to-insure risks.

A perfect example is found in Tunisia's fishing sector, where weather keeps ships in port for weeks at a time and some fishing activities are seasonal. By not being tied to any one ship, but going from one to another to follow the work as well as going back to other land-based work if fishing work becomes entirely unavailable, workers manage to earn a regular income in a very volatile sector. These workers exemplify a new type of labor relation characterized by the following features:

- Work effort is specialized but segmented, located by the user (who does not view him- or herself as an employer in the traditional sense).
- Demand for labor fluctuates (because of weather, for example).
- Employers and employees share risk.
- Workers have multiple employers/users, with no durable ties to any of them.
- Incomes fluctuate but are globally strong, as a result of the economic competitiveness of the sector and workers' willingness to change employers and even activities.

These features mean that informal workers are neither true employees nor self-employed. The multiplicity of missions and employers makes them similar to self-employed workers, but unlike artisans or shop owners, they often work as part of a team, and their place of work is determined by an employer, albeit one who does not take on the responsibilities traditional employers assume.

Mobile workers are, by definition, mobile: their work relations are short and change often; they have no fixed or even primary employer. But they do not view themselves as self-employed, and they are not able to take on the burden of making their social security contributions.

The people who hire them do not view themselves as employers, because of the short duration of the link between them. They refuse any individual responsibility toward them but are aware that the availability of mobile workers is key to the economic survival of their activity.

Traditional contribution schemes rely heavily on employers to collect contributions and fill out declarations. Without them, the whole system collapses. An overhaul of the traditional approach is therefore needed to handle mobile workers.

Contribution Prepayment Techniques

There are two main difficulties in creating a scheme for a mobile population. The first is keeping administrative costs under control. The second is convincing people to join. Enforcing compliance is very difficult and failed in Cape Verde, despite an excellent data system; relying only on generous matching terms from employers (and, indirectly, the government, which guaranteed it) failed in Tunisia.

The most delicate issue is the second one. In Tunisia, the scheme the government introduced was deliberately generous, but from both the employers' and the employees' point of view, it was more of the same: a red-tape burden. As Thaler and Sunstein (2009) explain in their book *Nudge*, people in this situation tend to focus on the elements they recognize and have already rejected (in this case, the traditional structure of the scheme), the importance of which they inflate.

Perhaps the most important lesson from their book, and from the case studies, is that people should be nudged toward entering the scheme (and, in the case of mobile workers, to remain in it when they change employers) by making it as easy as possible to do so. Regardless of the economic value of a scheme, people will often ignore a new program if they find the registration process too cumbersome.

THE MOBILE PHONE PARADIGM

When mobile phones were introduced, companies required subscribers to have a bank account, and they marketed them to people with regular incomes. The invention of prepaid cards changed that paradigm: it eliminated any solvency concern on the part of the mobile phone company, allowing it to market to people without bank accounts or fixed incomes. Mobile phones have been spectacularly successful in the informal economy. The use of prepaid cards removes the need to ensure that subscribers will (or even can) pay, thereby obviating the need to collect information on them. In a way, it is now the phone that pays.

A similar technique could play the same role for pension contributions, taking the place of traditional contribution collection while keeping the information data flow minimal, and thus manageable for a very mobile population. Under this system, it would no longer matter who the employer is. Contributions would be based on how much work was performed. This type of mechanism allows the administration of a pension scheme to be divided into two separate fields: financing and keeping track of rights.

EARMARKED BRANCH TAXES AS PROXY FOR EMPLOYER CONTRIBUTION

Employer contributions could be replaced by a collective contribution in the form of a branch tax, freeing employers from having to declare employees and wages. An example of an activity tax would be a tax on fish captured, which would be assessed when a ship returned to port. For domestic workers, the tax could be part of the land or housing tax. For small agricultural workers, taxes could be imposed on the products they produce. In the transportation sector, the tax could be imposed on each bus (or taxi) leaving the central station of the city.

Another possibility is to tax projects rather than sectors. Construction companies employ a large number of (often clandestine) workers for a given project or part of a project. A tax on the project rather than the sector would cover workers who worked on the project. This mechanism would be particularly easy to implement if the project were publicly financed, as the procurement process provides an estimate of the number of workers and days needed.

Unlike a regular employer contribution, these taxes have no direct link with the actual workers involved. Information on the workers, which is of course needed to calculate rights, would be provided by contribution vouchers, described in the next section.

Branch taxes require government intervention. Where a sound taxable base cannot be found, the government might have to step in with subsidies.

TRIPARTITE CONTRIBUTION VOUCHERS AS EMPLOYEE CONTRIBUTION

The proposed scheme replaces the employee contribution with contribution vouchers, which collect the minimal information needed to calculate pension rights. They also collect the employee contribution (kept low to ensure the scheme's attractiveness) and serve as a legal work contract. Figure 13.1 shows a draft design of a voucher.

FIGURE 13.1 **Sample tripartite contribution voucher**

Employer Slip	Employee Slip	Pension Scheme Slip	
Employer Reg #	Employer Reg #	Employer Reg #	Prefilled portion
# Voucher	# Voucher	# Voucher	
Contribution Value (employee contribution)	Contribution Value (employee contribution)	Contribution Value (employee contribution)	
Number of points	Number of points	Number of points	
Worker Name:	Worker Name:	Worker Name:	Portion to be filled out
Worker Reg #:	Worker Reg #:	Worker Reg #:	
Quarter worked:	Quarter worked:	Quarter worked:	

The vouchers are tripartite, with one part each for the employer, the employee, and the pension scheme. Employers "buy" the voucher from the pension scheme, paying the employee contribution (which they later withdraw from employee salaries). But the voucher is not tied to any particular employee. The employer fills in the name and registration number of the worker and gives the worker the employee slip and the pension scheme slip. Workers retain their part and at their convenience present the third slip to the social scheme, together with any other pension scheme slips collected during the period. The scheme already knows that the employee's contribution has been paid and does not need to check if and by whom it is matched on the employer's side; it needs only to record the employee's pension contribution.

The tripartite voucher makes prepayment administratively feasible. It has legal status as a short-term work contract. It is purchased in advance by employers and given to employees with their wages. Workers bring their vouchers to the social security scheme when convenient and their contributions are recorded, all at a low operating cost.

The voucher also takes care of the need to control employee registration and employers' payment of employee contributions. Being prepaid and of fixed value, it makes certain that the correct contributions are paid. Employees are registered once, obviating the need to monitor their employers (monitoring could be done by checking the employer's registration number on the voucher, but it need not be done systematically).

A point scheme is a pay-as-you-go pension scheme that awards points to participants in proportion to their contributions. In effect, the participant buys points with his or her contributions, using a purchase value set by the scheme, which can be adjusted each year for inflation or other factors but is the same for all adherents regardless of age.

Keeping track of an individual's contributions through a point scheme is necessary because the use of a branch tax neither requires nor provides information on the people who work in the sector. The service value of the point (the value paid to retirees) can be adjusted each year to keep the scheme balanced.

To accommodate different lengths of work, vouchers of different colors and values could be issued. For instance, vouchers could be for 1, 6, and 12 points, each a different color for one day, one week, and two weeks, where 1 point equals 1 day of work. The voucher could be read by an optical reader or simply counted by hand, reducing the administrative cost.

The point mechanism makes the prepayment of vouchers acceptable. It records small and potentially irregular contributions. The link between contributions and rights is transparent, and there is no threshold; even a small contribution increases the value of the pension. Awarded points accrue in an individual account at the scheme. When the pension is liquidated, the annual pension is equal to the number of accrued points multiplied by the service value of the point, which is based on what a regular employee with similar contributions would receive.

Each participant's points are summed, year after year. There is no funding of points or interest compounded on them, but points have an implicit return that is linked with the growth of the contribution base. When pension benefits are first paid out, they are calculated by multiplying the number of points by the service value of the point. In the following years, the pension remains based on the number of points acquired; it is the service value that is adjusted each year to account for inflation (or average salary evolution, whichever index is preferred).

The point scheme has three main advantages. First, the system is transparent for users, who know at any time how many points they have acquired and can estimate their pension value by multiplying the number of points by the current service value. Second, the system can adjust to changing economic conditions by changing the purchase value, the service value, or both. Third, because all rights are recorded in points, the scheme knows at all times what its engagements are, both in number of points and, by using simple actuarial techniques, points served by year (and therefore in monetary value).

PENSION AND HEALTH SCHEMES FOR MOBILE WORKERS

The combination of an earmarked branch tax and prepaid contribution voucher solves the two problems pension schemes face: securing stable financing and gathering the information needed to calculate pension rights while keeping administrative costs low. Building a scheme based on these tools will require the cooperation of social partners, to ensure that the tax is correctly applied throughout the branch and vouchers are wisely used. The price of the vouchers should be high enough to prevent opportunistic buying, yet low enough to make their prepayment affordable by users of mobile work.

The scheme should also be attractive enough that mobile workers will want to request vouchers from their employers. Making it attractive should be made easier if the branch tax represents the greater part of financing—something that will need to be put forward when introducing the scheme to mobile workers. The scheme is strictly contributive by design, which will make explaining it to its users easier.

Unlike traditional schemes, the mobile workers scheme centers on the employee, not the employer. The employee is responsible for reporting his or her pension contributions. Each declaration increases his or her future benefits.

The incentives to participate resolve the compliance problem, as the employer is no longer part of the information loop. Unlike traditional schemes, the mobile workers scheme collects all information from the employee. This makes it easier to keep track of each person's contributions and to calculate pension benefits upon retirement. Focusing on the employee is particularly crucial for mobile workers, who have dozens of employers during their active lives, some of whom may submit incomplete declarations or fail to keep full records, making reconstruction of the employee's contributions very difficult.

Because each branch has its own specific tax, a separate scheme, or at least section within a scheme, will be needed for each sector. Sectors can be grouped under a common umbrella and linked by a common service value of the point, but the overall approach needs to be customized, adjusting the voucher price to the yield of the branch tax.

As for health schemes, the thorniest issue, beyond the problem of financing, is that of initiating and terminating rights to health coverage. Coverage should be continuous for the scheme to remain credible.

Under a system of prepaid contribution vouchers, workers are responsible for turning in their vouchers each quarter. Once a worker reaches a minimum number of vouchers, he or she is entitled to coverage during the next quarter. There is no need to track workers across numerous employers. Workers have an incentive to collect and submit their vouchers.

Simultaneously, third-party payment cards could be issued, with a credit limit directly linked to the contribution vouchers turned in. As long as the credit stands, the expenses are directly charged to the scheme. Once the credit is used up, the worker needs to advance the money for additional treatments and submit a form for reimbursement; preliminary clearance would be required for large expenses.

Third-party payment cards are perfect for routine treatments and low-cost medications. They work particularly well with a voucher system: users' cards are credited when they submit vouchers, incentivizing them to submit as many vouchers as possible and to refrain from charging other people's expenses on their cards.

The challenge is to set the right limit and voucher value to ensure that the scheme stays solvent. This is a governance issue. In many cases, simply getting informal workers to register would be a huge improvement over the current situation.

TRANSITION TO THE NEW SCHEME

This new approach marks the replacement of enforced employer compliance with a more client-based relation with employees. All the information gathering and collating for the scheme is based on the employee, not the employer, which will make liquidating pensions much easier. Pension rights shift from being based on the duration of contribution to being linked directly to the value of these contributions through a point system. This transition is not an easy one for a traditional pension scheme.

Implementation Issues

Despite intellectual recognition by national social security authorities of the relevance of the diagnosis and feasibility of the proposed solution, mobile workers schemes have failed so far to materialize, for several reasons. The first difficulty is logistic. For an existing social security scheme, creating a mobile workers scheme requires an information technology and procedural overhaul, which is costly, both financially and in terms of retraining existing employees. Prepaid contribution vouchers need to be designed, printed, and distributed; optical reading systems (or a similar, less expensive system to read and collate vouchers) need to be found and made compatible with the existing information technology infrastructure; and new data collection software needs to be implemented to collate rights. (These costs are offset by the expected lower administrative cost of the scheme.)

The second difficulty is reluctance to adopt the scheme—not from the scheme's directors, who tend to be enthusiastic about it, but from the rank-and-file staff, who fear losing control over employers and losing tracks of employees. Such reluctance will need to be addressed unless the scheme is a completely new one, possibly through extensive communications with the scheme's staff.

Controlling employers and having them turn in contributions and registration is part of social security culture. The new scheme makes no provision for enforcing compliance and is in practice almost voluntary, requiring a more client-oriented approach on the part of the staff.

In Tunisia, there is one scheme for each branch (or, in the case of fishing, several schemes for one branch). The new scheme would overlap several existing schemes, as it would track employees across them, and the specific occupation of workers would no longer be relevant past the employer's purchase of the contribution voucher. Adoption of the new scheme would mean that a firm may have traditional employees who remain part of a traditional scheme and mobile workers who are affiliated with the new mobile workers scheme. Having workers at the same firm enroll in different schemes goes against long-accepted practice.

A third issue involves the monitoring and governance of the schemes: ensuring that the branch tax is collected and represents adequate financing, and keeping track of the vouchers to ensure that the number turned in is equal (or at least close) to the number of vouchers bought and that the number of vouchers bought represents the actual amount of work done in the branch. The price of vouchers will need to be carefully weighed. They should be cheap enough to be affordable for employers yet expensive enough to deter opportunistic purchases that would lead to inflated attribution of rights. Avoiding such an outcome is particularly important because the whole approach is new, meaning the signal flags indicating problems are not yet part of social security institutions' cultures.

SERVAC's work in Tunisia suggested that the best way to monitor the schemes would be to monitor the number of days worked rather than the number of affiliated members—who come and go, possibly to other, more permanent work and the schemes associated with such work. Each day worked carries the same pension right, so tracking their volume (cross-referenced by the age of the worker) is the easiest way to monitor the overall health of the scheme.

Prepayment appears feasible, but it requires full-scale experimentation. Developing countries with extensive informal sectors of mobile workers provide large natural opportunities. The hesitancy of national social security institutions with regard to such a paradigm shift will disappear once successful pilot plans are initiated, through transnational settings or in developed economies in the many areas where mobile workers strive.

Notes

1. UTAP and Social Security estimate that Tunisia had 50,000 fishers in 2001. The average fisher worked 150 days a year.

2. Currency values in this chapter are given in Tunisian dinars; TD 1 = $0.6383.

3. These data come from the 1994 and 2001 Institut National de la Statistique Employment Census (the 1994 one is more detailed) and the Ministry of Agriculture's 1997/98 Survey. As part-time work is massive, the volume of work days is the meaningful measure in economic terms. It requires crosschecking sources, as census data usually provide the numbers of people who declare their main activity as agriculture with their occupational rates, but groups whose main activity is not agriculture are also involved. The Ministry of Agriculture survey estimates thus indicate large employment figures (1 million family workers and 280,000 other workers) with only a small core of permanent workers (312,000 family workers and 50,000 other workers). Occasional work remains significant even in large farms, which supposedly belong to the modern sector. The Ministry of Agriculture survey estimates the average number of annual days worked at 220 for permanent agricultural workers and 60 for other agricultural workers.

4. These data, which include 16 percent known part-time workers (who still declare domestic work as their main occupation), are from the 1994 census.

References

SERVAC. 2003. "Extension de la couverture sociale aux marins pêcheurs, ouvriers agricoles et employés de maison" ("Extension of Social Security to Fishers, Small Agricultural Laborers, and Domestic Workers"). Restricted mission report prepared for the World Bank, Washington, DC.

———. 2006. "Stratégie d'extension de la couverture sociale au Cap Vert" ("Strategy to Expand the Coverage of Social Security in Cape Verde"). Restricted mission report prepared for the World Bank, Washington, DC.

Thaler, Richard, and Cass Sunstein. 2009. *Nudge: Improving Decisions about Health, Wealth, and Happiness.* New York: Penguin Books.

CHAPTER 14

Thailand's Matching Defined Contribution Programs for the Informal Sector

Mitchell Wiener

Thailand's current pension system predominantly covers civil servants, the military, and formal sector workers. Informal sector workers, who represent two-thirds of the workforce, are covered only by a social pension. For many workers, the benefit from the social pension will not be sufficient to allow them to retire, avoid poverty, or maintain the same standard of living following retirement. To address the problem, the government of Thailand created two new pension programs for informal sector workers. It hopes that high participation rates in the new programs will eventually allow it to phase out the social pension. Unfortunately, the programs are unlikely to meet the government's stated objectives, because the pension programs for the informal sector are voluntary, the two programs compete with each other, and the programs are not designed with the savings needs of the informal sector in mind. Participation rates are likely to be low, the primary participants will probably be self-employed professionals and other wealthier informal sector workers, and the programs will likely have little impact on coverage rates or old-age poverty. The government match will mostly go to people who are not poor. The programs are unlikely to replace the social pension as the primary source of retirement income, particularly for the elderly poor.

Over the past 10 years, governments in Asia and elsewhere have begun to focus more attention on the need to increase pension coverage. In many countries in Asia, the informal economy makes up 60–90 percent of the total workforce, and informal workers are typically not covered by formal pension programs. In the past, the government's strategy for increasing coverage centered on increasing the size of the formal economy. Confounding expectations, however, the size of the informal economy has been increasing in many countries, including Thailand.

Over the next 20–30 years, the population of Asia will also age dramatically, thanks to vastly lower birth rates and longer life expectancy throughout the region. As a result, the number of elderly people will increase substantially, and most of them will have worked in the informal sector.

Other economic forces are also increasing the vulnerability of the elderly. Smaller family sizes and economic development have resulted in increased urbanization and a breakdown in the family support system. Consequently, there is more pressure than in the past to develop retirement income strategies for people in the informal sector.

In 2011 and early 2012, Thailand introduced two new voluntary pension programs for informal sector workers. The National Savings Fund is sponsored by the Ministry of Finance and has a well-established legal structure, but has not yet begun. The other is sponsored by the Social Security Office under the Ministry of Labor and is a restructuring of an existing program under Article 40 of the Social Security Act. The legal structure of the Article 40 program is based on a single article of the law and royal decrees. Consequently, many of the key features of the program can be easily changed, including the benefits, cost, and employer matching provision. Both are defined contribution programs and encourage voluntary participation by providing government matching contributions. However, the match under the Article 40 program can easily be stopped at any time, while the match under the National Savings Fund is based on law. These programs are often referred to as matching defined contribution programs.

The stated purpose of these programs is to allow for the eventual phaseout or targeting of the existing universal pension scheme, to improve the level of pension coverage and benefits, and to reduce old-age poverty. Early evidence indicates that these programs are not likely to meet any of these objectives. It appears that participation rates will be very low and that most of the participants will be self-employed professionals and other wealthier members of the informal sector. As of February 2012, only 600,000 of an estimated 24 million informal sector workers had joined. Consequently, the programs are unlikely to significantly increase coverage rates, the universal social pension will remain the main source of retirement income for Thailand's elderly poor, and the government match will largely benefit wealthier informal sector workers. Therefore, the most-vulnerable will remain outside the supplemental pension systems.

Several actions should be considered to improve the overall effectiveness of the matching defined contribution programs. The government should be clearer about their purpose and their interaction with the universal social pension. The design features should vary depending on whether these programs are intended to replace or supplement the universal social pension and whether the social pension will remain universal or be targeted.

The existence of two competing programs is a source of confusion for informal sector workers. The administrators of the two programs are separately and aggressively marketing their programs to the same group of eligible participants. Workers do not understand why there are two programs, how they differ, and how they are to choose between them. It would be helpful if the government gave guidance to potential participants about the features of the two programs and how to select between them rather than allowing the sponsors to separately and competitively market the two programs.

The government should also reconsider some of the features of the two programs, which appear to be designed with the needs of the formal sector in mind. They do not take into account the savings methods, needs, or priorities of the informal sector, particularly workers in the bottom four income deciles. Greater withdrawal flexibility is needed if the programs are to achieve higher coverage rates.

Pension Programs for Formal Sector Workers

Before the introduction of the new voluntary pension programs for the informal sector, the government of Thailand already sponsored numerous retirement programs. For the formal sector, these include the Old Age Pension under the Social Security Office, the Government Pension Fund, voluntary provident funds, and retirement mutual funds. The informal sector is eligible for retirement mutual funds and for the universal social pension under the Old Age Act.

The Old Age Pension program is a mandatory defined benefit program covering formal sector workers. The retirement age is 55, and a minimum of 15 years of contributions is required to be eligible for a pension benefit. The program began in 1999, so the first pensions will be paid in 2014. The program provides a benefit of 20 percent of final average pay for workers retiring with 15 years of contributions and an additional 1.5 percent of final average pay for each year of contributions in excess of 15.

Civil servants are eligible for both a defined benefit pension payable from the state budget and a defined contribution program administered by the Government Pension Fund. From the defined benefit program, civil servants receive a benefit equal to 2 percent of their final five-year average pay for each year of service, up to a maximum of 70 percent. Payouts at retirement can be received as an annuity or as a lump sum. In addition, a contribution of 8 percent is made to the Government Pension Fund each year. The government contributes 5 percent and civil servants contribute 3 percent. The government contribution to the Government Pension Fund is reduced by 2 percent if workers choose to take the defined benefit plan payout as a lump sum.

Voluntary provident funds are established by employers for the benefit of their employees. Most of these funds were established by state-owned entities and large corporations that are listed on the Thai stock exchange. These programs require both employer and employee contributions, and the employer contribution must be equal to or greater than the employee's contribution. Employees can receive the accumulated funds at retirement (age 55) or earlier employment termination.

Retirement mutual funds are voluntary defined contribution programs that are available to both formal and informal sector workers. However, the structure of the programs is inappropriate for workers with low or irregular income or in vulnerable employment. Retirement mutual funds are offered and managed by mutual fund companies; they must offer participants a choice of funds with varying risk profiles. They offer tax privileges but only under stringent conditions. Units must be purchased continuously until age 55, except under certain limited conditions, and there is a minimum annual contribution requirement. Consequently, these programs have attracted limited interest and are designed for wealthy individuals.

The government also sponsors a universal social pension under the Old Age Act. Before 2008, the program was targeted, and benefits were limited to B 200 a month. In 2008, the program became universal, and the benefit was increased to B 500 a month. The benefit is payable to everyone age 60 and older who is not eligible for any of the mandatory social insurance programs (primarily the Old Age Pension and Government Pension Fund programs).

Benefits were increased at the beginning of 2012. Monthly payments now vary by age, with people age 60–69 receiving B 600, people age 70–79 receiving B 700, people age 80–89 receiving B 800, and people age 90 and older receiving B 1,000.

Pension Programs for Informal Sector Workers

The government recently introduced two new voluntary pension programs, the National Savings Fund (NSF) and a modified program under Article 40 of the Social Security Act. There are two options under the Article 40 program. Option 1 provides insurance benefits and no pension savings. Option 2 provides the same insurance benefits as Option 1, plus a pension savings program. Only informal sector workers are eligible for these programs, and workers cannot participate in both NSF and Article 40, Option 2, but must choose their desired program. Both are matching defined contribution programs, with voluntary worker contributions matched by the government.

THE NATIONAL SAVINGS FUND

The purpose of the NSF program is to provide a voluntary pension savings program for the informal sector. The National Savings Fund Act was enacted in May 2011 and was scheduled to go into effect May 8, 2012. This starting date has now been delayed, however, because the government still needs to issue several clarifying regulations. This section describes the structure of the NSF program and outlines the areas of the law that need clarification.

Types of Accounts

The NSF, a new public institution, will maintain three types of accounts—individual accounts, pension accounts, and a central account. The individual account is used to track individual account balances during the participant's working career. At retirement age (age 60), the balance in the individual account is transferred to a pension account. The pension account is used to make pension payments to participants until age 80. The central account belongs to the NSF, not to individual participants. It is used to make pension payments after age 80 and to back investment rate of return guarantees.

Governance Structure

The NSF will be responsible for investment management and all administrative functions for the new pension system. It will also guarantee lifetime pensions for members following their retirement. The governing body of the NSF, the National Savings Fund Committee, is responsible for overseeing fund activities.

The NSF is led by a secretary-general and a director of investments hired by the NSF Committee. The appointment of the secretary-general is subject to the approval of the minister of finance. The committee and its investment subcommittee are responsible for setting investment policy, determining the methods for making contributions and withdrawals, and hiring fund managers.

Eligibility

People age 15–60 who are not covered by any other pension fund that receives mandatory contributions from the state or employers are eligible. The eligible group comprises the informal sector, regardless of income level. At this time, the program supplements the universal Old Age Pension under the Old Age Act.

Contributions

Workers may make contributions whenever they wish; there is no requirement for regular monthly contributions. However, the minimum contribution is B 50, and no more than B 13,200 may be contributed in any one calendar year. Contributions are placed in each participant's individual account.

The government matches workers' contributions. The maximum monthly match increases with the age of the contributor, rising from 50 percent for people age 15–30 (maximum B 600); to 80 percent for people age 30–50 (maximum B 960); to 100 percent for people age 50–60 (maximum B 1,200). The rationale articulated for the increasing match is that people who are older at the time the program begins have less time to save for retirement than people who are younger. This rationale is persuasive for the existing group of older workers at the time the program begins; it may not be as logical for new workforce entrants, who may choose to delay the start of their savings program in order to wait for the higher match. Generally, it is better to encourage workers to start saving as early as possible, as contributions made at younger ages earn interest for a longer period of time.

Investments

The law states that at least 60 percent of the assets must be invested in low-risk securities. The basic structure for the investment process will follow the rules applicable to the Government Pension Fund and the Social Security Office's Old Age Pension program. According to the government pension fund legislation and regulations, low-risk assets include cash, bank deposits, and bank certificates of deposit; government bonds, treasury bills, and Bank of Thailand bonds; debt instruments guaranteed by the Ministry of Finance; bank debt instruments; and highly rated corporate debt.

The other 40 percent can be invested in other permitted instruments, such as equities (maximum 10 percent in any one company and 20 percent of assets in total), overseas investments (maximum 10 percent of assets), real estate, and lower-rated bonds. The government plans to initially use an investment mix of 80 percent low-risk and 20 percent other instruments in order to reduce volatility in rates of return.

There is also an investment rate of return guarantee in the NSF law. If the account balance at retirement is less than it would have been if the rate of return had been equal to the average return on 12-month deposits at the government savings bank, the Bank of Agriculture, agricultural cooperatives, and the five largest commercial banks, the account balance will be topped up using funds from the NSF's central account.

The law states that at least two domestic institutions or people must be hired for domestic investments. It sets no limit on the number of overseas investment managers. All investment managers are required to be properly licensed and supervised in Thailand or their country of domicile. Although not directly stated, the law implies that the NSF itself is not permitted to manage individual or pension account assets.

Payouts

People who retire at age 60 will either receive a monthly pension for life or a living allowance, depending on the size of the account balance at retirement. At age 60, a participant's assets are moved from his or her individual account to a pension account. Assets in the pension account are then converted into a pension payable until age 80.

If the calculated pension is greater than the minimum pension amount specified in ministry regulations, the retiree is eligible for a lifetime annuity. Payments are made from the pension account until age 80. If the participant dies before reaching age 80, the balance in the account is paid to the participant's designated beneficiary. If the participant lives beyond age 80, the remaining payments until death are paid from the central account maintained by the NSF.

If the calculated pension amount is less than the minimum pension, a "living allowance" is paid instead of a lifetime pension. The living allowance is equal to the minimum pension. It is paid from the pension account each month until the account is exhausted. For retirees who receive the living allowance, benefit payments stop when the pension account is exhausted; there is no lifetime pension guarantee. The number of participants who are eligible for a lifetime annuity, therefore, will depend on the procedures adopted by the government for converting the balance in the individual account at retirement into a pension and the level at which the Ministry of Finance sets the minimum pension. These two decisions will have a significant impact on the financial solvency of the NSF.

There are two situations in which payments are made before age 60. If a participant dies before age 60, the balance in the individual account is paid out in a lump sum to the designated beneficiaries. If an individual becomes disabled before age 60, he or she can choose to receive all or part of the balance in the individual account as a lump sum. If any funds remain in the individual account after this distribution, they are paid out as a lifetime pension or living allowance starting at age 60.

In-Service Withdrawals

The law does not make provision for in-service withdrawals by members, except for people who become disabled or die. Members can receive a payout before age 60 only if they opt out of the fund. In this case, they receive a lump sum equal to their own contributions with investment income; they forfeit the government contributions and its investment income in their individual accounts. Given this penalty, there is very limited liquidity in the program to assist members with any type of financial emergency.

Taxation

The NSF is a fully tax-exempt system. Participant contributions are tax deductible, the government's contributions are not taxable income to participants, investment earnings are not taxed when earned, and benefit payouts are not taxed. This type of pension is often referred to as an EEE system, because contributions, investment earnings, and payouts are all exempt from taxation.

Fees

The law indicates that fees of investment managers shall be in accordance with the criteria, methods, and conditions specified by ministerial regulation. All of the costs of NSF operations, marketing, enrollment, and collection of contributions will be paid from the state budget.

Contribution Collection

The NSF is permitted to collect contributions directly or to outsource this function. The community offices of the Ministry of Interior will be responsible for enrolling members in the system and collecting the first contribution at the time of initial enrollment.

Afterward, contributions can be made through the state savings bank, community offices, or the post office.

Members are responsible for visiting these locations to enroll and make contributions. Active marketing by agents is not planned. The government will make trips to each region to educate and promote the new program. However, citizens will be expected to go to appropriate registration centers to enroll in the program and make contributions.

MODIFIED SOCIAL SECURITY ACT PROGRAM FOR INFORMAL SECTOR WORKERS

In addition to creating the NSF, Thailand modified and added another option to an existing but little used program for informal sector workers under Article 40 of the Social Security Act. This change was implemented by the Social Security Office at about the same time as the enactment of the NSF law. The change modifies the insurance benefits available, introduces an option for an old-age savings program, reduces the price, and introduces government cost sharing. The existence of this scheme continues a long history of competition by pension programs established and supervised by the Ministry of Finance and programs established and supervised by the Ministry of Labor. It reflects the lack of a national pension policy in Thailand.

Under the provisions in effect before May 1, 2011, workers who were not eligible for pensions from the Social Security Office or the Government Pension Fund could voluntarily participate in Social Security Office programs that provide death, maternity, and disability benefits at a cost of B 280 a month. Members paid the entire premium. Participation in this program was always minimal. As of December 31, 2010, it had enrolled only 47 participants, compared with 8.8 million mandatory Social Security Office members.

Under the modified program, two benefit packages are offered under Article 40, one of which includes an optional pension savings benefit, and the government now helps finance the cost of the benefits. Option 1 includes insurance but not pension benefits. Workers receive disability, sickness, and death benefits. Workers electing this option contribute B 70, and the government contributes B 30 a month.

Option 2 includes the same insurance benefits as Option 1 plus an old-age savings benefit. For this option, the worker contributes B 100 a month, and the government B 50 a month. The additional B 50 a month goes into the old-age savings program, which pays a lump-sum benefit at age 60.

Only limited information about this program can be given, because details are not included in the Social Security Office law, and the royal decree contains only limited information about the program. Moreover, the benefits, cost, and government match are subject to change at any time.

FISCAL IMPACT OF NEW PROGRAMS

It is difficult to estimate the fiscal impact of the two new voluntary programs. The cost to the government will depend on the number of people who choose to join the programs, the age of the participants who join, the amount they choose to contribute, and the frequency of contributions. Both the NSF and the Social Security Office estimate that only about 10 percent of eligible workers will join their programs and that they will likely be wealthier members of the informal sector.

Under the Article 40 program, people who elect Option 2 will contribute B 100 a month, and the government will contribute B 50 a month. Of this amount, B 50 will go into the pension savings scheme, with workers contributing B 30, and the government contributing B 20; Option 2 provides a 67 percent match. However, in order to get this match, the worker must agree to purchase both insurance and pension benefits; the pension option is not available alone. Option 2 also suffers from legal uncertainty, as the government has not guaranteed to continue the match every year.

The cost to the government for this scheme will depend on the number of participants who choose to join Option 2. The government cost for pensions for each participant will be B 240 a year (B 20 a month for 12 months), assuming participants contribute every month. As of February 2012, about 600,000 people had joined this program. If all of them remain in the program, the cost to the government would be B 144 million a year. If 10 percent of eligible participants join, there would be about 2.4 million members; the cost to the government would be B 576 million.

Estimates for the NSF are more difficult, as the government match varies by age and by the amount the participant chooses to contribute. The maximum match ranges from B 600 to B 1,200 a year, depending on the participant's age.

If 10 percent of eligible participants joined (2.4 million members), the maximum cost to the government would be B 2.9 billion, if all 2.4 million members received the maximum government match of B 1,200 a year. The actual cost to the government would be less, because not everyone will be eligible for a 100 percent match. If the average match is B 800 a month, for example, the cost to the government would be about B 1.9 billion.

Most informal sector workers who want to save for retirement will probably choose the NSF over Article 40 Option 2, because the NSF program provides higher levels of government contributions and has a much stronger legal basis. People who have already joined Option 2 will also be able to switch to the NSF program on January 1, 2013, the first date the switching option will be available.

Program Summary

Tables 14.1 and 14.2 summarize the characteristics and intended coverage of the existing and new Thai pension programs. Table 14.1 shows that Thailand now has seven separate pension programs covering different groups of workers. Of these, only one, the retirement mutual funds, covers both the formal and informal sectors. However, the retirement mutual funds are designed for people who are willing and able to make regular contributions at a minimum level for an extended period of time, effectively excluding most informal sector workers from participation.

Table 14.2 summarizes the basic features of each of the seven retirement programs. The designs of the various programs differ substantially along a number of key characteristics—the eligible group; the program sponsor; whether the programs are mandatory or voluntary; whether programs are defined benefit or defined contribution; how the program costs are allocated among workers, employers, and the government; and the government institution responsible for supervision and control.

TABLE 14.1 **Eligibility of formal and informal sector workers for pension programs in Thailand**

Program	Formal sector	Informal sector
Old Age Pension	✓	
Government Pension Fund	✓	
Voluntary provident funds	✓	
Retirement mutual funds	✓	✓
Old Age Act (social pension)		✓
National Savings Fund		✓
Social Security Act, Article 40		✓

TABLE 14.2 **Features of pension programs in Thailand**

Program	Eligibility	Sponsor	Mandatory or voluntary	Defined benefit/ contribution	Contribution source	Supervisor
Old Age Pension	Formal sector workers	Employer	Mandatory	Defined benefit	Employers, workers, government	Ministry of Labor
Government Pension Fund	Government officials	Employer (government)	Mandatory	Defined benefit/ defined contribution	Government, workers	Ministry of Finance
Voluntary provident funds	Formal sector workers	Employer (occupational pension programs)	Mandatory if employer listed on stock exchange; voluntary otherwise	Defined contribution	Employer, workers	Securities Commission
Retirement mutual funds	All workers	Individual	Voluntary	Defined contribution	Workers	Securities Commission
Old Age Act	Informal sector workers	Individual	Universal	Defined benefit	Government	Ministry of Human Development
National Savings Fund	Informal sector workers	Individual	Voluntary	Defined contribution	Workers, government match	Ministry of Finance
Social Security Act, Article 40, Option 2	Informal sector workers	Individual	Voluntary	Defined contribution	Workers, government match	Ministry of Labor

Analysis and Recommendations

Thailand's pension programs are highly fragmented, at least in part because there is no national pension policy and responsibility for oversight of its pension programs is spread across multiple ministries. The programs sponsored and supervised by the Ministry of Finance openly compete with those sponsored and supervised by the Ministry of Labor. Neither organization is willing to cede control of their programs to the other or to a new national pension supervision agency. Consequently, when the Ministry of Finance created the NSF, the reaction of the Ministry of Labor was to enhance existing but long dormant programs for the informal sector under Article 40. As a result, Thailand now has seven separate pension programs.

It would make sense to try to consolidate the number of pension programs. Selecting one program for each retirement pillar—social pension (Pillar 0), mandatory defined benefit social security (Pillar 1), mandatory defined contribution (Pillar 2), and voluntary defined contribution (Pillar 3)—would reduce the number of programs from seven to four. As part of this process, civil servants and formal sector workers could participate in the same programs. Creating a separate pension supervision agency would help unify and harmonize the rules and regulations governing the various programs.

The new voluntary programs illustrate the problems that arise when programs are fragmented and there is a lack of a strategic vision. For example, the design of the voluntary programs should vary depending on whether the social pension for the informal sector will be universal or targeted and whether it is intended to be permanent or temporary. There is also a lack of clarity about the respective roles of the NSF and Article 40 programs. There has been limited communication about why two programs are needed or what criteria informal sector workers should use in choosing.

The NSF and Article 40 programs are currently designed to attract self-employed professionals and other high-paid members of the informal sector. This strategy may be appropriate if the two programs are intended to supplement, and not replace, the social pension. If the social pension remains universal and is sufficient to prevent poverty, then informal sector workers who want to save more for retirement can use either of these two voluntary pension programs to accumulate additional retirement savings. If, however, the social pension will target only the poor, the remainder of the informal sector will need to use these programs to meet all their pension savings needs. In this case, the amounts that would need to be accumulated would be much higher.

Several changes should be considered if the goal is to have a broader cross-section of the informal sector participate in the voluntary pension programs. The legal structure of the Article 40 programs should be strengthened, and the government match should be codified. The law creates the program, but all important details are found in royal decrees. As a result, there is little assurance that the programs will remain in place in their current form or that the government will continue to contribute.

The pricing of the Article 40 programs might also benefit from additional analysis. The monthly total cost of the insurance programs under Article 40 has been reduced from B 280 to B 100. Although the benefit package under the reformed scheme is less generous, it is not clear that there has been rigorous actuarial analysis to support the reformed pricing scheme.

The NSF law is extensive and carefully outlines the legal structure and benefits of the program. Several provisions could be reexamined, however, to enhance the attractiveness of the program to a wider group of potential participants.

- **Increase withdrawal flexibility before retirement age.** It would be helpful to add more flexibility to withdraw contributions before retirement without severe penalty. Most savings by the informal sector are for consumption smoothing and medium-term needs, such as weddings, funerals, household purchases, and medical expenses. The preferred form of long-term informal sector retirement savings is in the form of hard assets—gold, jewelry, land, and housing. The NSF program requires members to quit in order to withdraw money before retirement, forfeiting all government contributions and the investment income on those contributions.

- **Do more to encourage contributions.** It is questionable whether passive contribution collection methods will be effective for the informal sector. Without more proactive collection mechanisms, it is likely workers will not contribute regularly and there may be many inactive accounts. Many informal sector workers have limited disposable income and often borrow money informally to smooth consumption spending. Long-term savings is likely to have lower priority than other needs, particularly if there is no active encouragement to contribute regularly. For example, microfinance institutions often use weekly community meetings or house-to-house collection of savings to encourage regular participation.

- **Reduce fees.** The NSF law allows the criteria, methods, and conditions for setting fees to be specified by ministerial regulation and the level of fees to be set by the National Savings Fund Committee. The ministerial regulations, when issued, will hopefully offer guidance on the process the committee should follow to establish fees and require that the fees be related to actual administrative expenses and that investment expenses vary with the type of assets under management. Programs for the informal sector that rely on collecting small amounts of money from a large number of participants must have efficient and centralized administration. Processes should be highly automated to keep expenses low, especially as most contributions will be small and contribution payments will likely be irregular. There must also be efficient ways of getting contributions from multiple collection points, sending contributions to a central administrative organization for processing, sending contributions to fund managers, and tracking individual account balances.

- **Develop more effective ways of communicating with potential contributors.** Most low-income workers have only a primary education and may know little or nothing about pensions or finance. The benefits of retirement savings must be carefully explained. Doing so requires a strong ongoing public education effort regarding financial and savings principles and how participation in the government's voluntary pension programs can help reduce the chances of falling into poverty in old age.

- **Anticipate and measure needed NSF pension liabilities.** The NSF will have a substantial liability for payment of lifetime pensions to people who live past age 80. The size of the liability will depend on the assumptions and methods used to calculate the initial pension amount, the manner in which pensions are indexed following retirement (if at all), and the manner in which the rate of return on pension accounts is allocated between the central account and the participant's pension account. It will also heavily depend on the size of the minimum pension and the number of people who qualify for lifetime pensions as opposed to a living allowance. As life expectancy will continue to increase, a substantial number of future pensioners may live beyond age 80. The NSF should hold a central account liability to secure these expected future payments. Sophisticated actuarial projections are needed to determine optimal system design and calculate required reserves.

- **Clarify individual account recordkeeping methodology.** More clarity is needed regarding the method of allocating investment income to participants. It is unclear whether account balances will be updated daily or investment income declared on a periodic basis. The NSF Act requires investment income to be declared at least once a year. International best practice is to allocate investment income daily by marking assets to market, calculating the fund's net asset value and the number of units held by each participant, and updating individual accounts.

Even a well-designed program may not attract the expected level of contributions, for valid reasons. Saving for retirement is usually not the primary concern of informal sector workers, who tend to value short-term savings, microborrowing, health insurance, insurance against natural disasters, and protection against crop failure or livestock loss more than savings for retirement.

For people who are able to save, there may be better investment opportunities than contributing to a voluntary pension program. For example, purchasing land or livestock or using savings for a child's education may produce higher rates of return than investing in market securities. Land and livestock can be used to generate current income and can be liquidated to provide retirement funds. An educated child can increase family income and provide parents with a source of support in retirement.

The pension plans for informal workers should be viewed as one component of an overall program that recognizes their legitimate short- and long-term needs. A better strategy than the one the government has adopted might be to provide such workers with a package of needed benefits rather than establishing free-standing voluntary pension programs.

Note

1.   Currency values in this chapter are given in Thai baht; B 1 = $0.0325.

Bibliography

Jitsuchon, Somchai. 2011. *Thailand Development Report: Protecting Thailand's Aging Population.* Bangkok: Thailand Development Research Institute.

Park, Donghyun, ed. 2011. *Pension Systems and Old-Age Income Support in East and Southeast Asia.* Manila: Asian Development Bank.

Wiener, Mitchell. 2010. "National Savings Fund Draft Law Recommendations." Unpublished, Asian Development Bank, Manila.

PART V

Behavioral and Design Issues

CHAPTER 15

Matching Contributions and Savings Outcomes: A Behavioral Economics Perspective

Brigitte C. Madrian

Including a matching contribution increases savings plan participation and contributions, although the impact is less significant than that of nonfinancial approaches. Conditional on participation, a higher match rate has only a small effect on savings plan contributions. In contrast, the match threshold has a substantial impact, probably because it serves as a natural reference point when individuals are deciding how much to save and may be viewed as advice from the savings program sponsor on how much to save. Other behavioral approaches to changing savings plan outcomes—including automatic enrollment, simplification, planning aids, reminders, and commitment features—potentially have a much greater impact on savings outcomes than do financial incentives, often at a much lower cost.

Acommon feature of schemes designed to increase individual savings is providing a matching contribution to create an incentive for participation in the program and induce higher levels of savings. The vast majority of employer-sponsored savings plans include an employer match, as do many employer-sponsored health savings accounts. The saver's credit, a feature of the U.S. tax code designed to encourage savings by lower-income households, also provides a government match to individual savings. Many field experiments aimed at encouraging savings have also included a match in their experimental design. This rich set of experience informs the understanding of behavioral responses to various matching contribution arrangements.

Traditional economic models point to financial incentives, such as a matching contribution, as the logical mechanism to increase savings plan participation. The first part of the chapter summarizes the literature on the impact of providing a match on savings plan outcomes, including participation, contributions, and net worth. The evidence comes from a variety of sources, including observational data from surveys, natural experiments, and large-scale field experiments. Although the empirical evidence largely supports the predictions of traditional economic models, these models fail to incorporate the many psychological frictions that impede savings, including present bias, complexity, inattention, and temptation, which in many cases exert a much stronger impact on savings outcomes than do financial incentives. Traditional economic models also fail to characterize some significant behavioral aspects of savings outcomes, including inertia and the important role of focal points. The second part of the chapter evaluates the literature on other, nonfinancial approaches to increasing individual savings.

The evidence suggests that matching contributions increase savings plan participation and contributions, although the impact is less significant than that of nonfinancial approaches. Conditional on participation, a higher match rate has only a small effect on savings plan contributions. In contrast, the match threshold has a substantial impact, probably because it serves as a natural reference point when individuals are deciding how much to save and may be viewed as advice from the savings program sponsor on how much to save. Automatic enrollment, simplification, planning aids, reminders, and various commitment devices potentially have a much greater impact on savings plan participation and contributions, often at a much lower cost.

Impact of Matching Contributions on Savings Outcomes: Theory

In traditional models, the impact of a match on savings outcomes depends in part on the structure of the match. The simplest form is a flat match rate on all incremental savings (for example, all new contributions are matched 100 percent). In practice, offering an unlimited match is expensive for the party providing the match; as a consequence, savings schemes typically limit the contributions that are matched (for example, all contributions up to $1,000 are matched 100 percent, and contributions above that level are not matched).

Savings schemes with more complicated match structures are common. For example, the match might be tiered, with contributions up to $500 matched 100 percent, contributions of $501–$1,000 matched 50 percent, and contributions above $1,000 not matched. Alternatively, contributions might be matched only after a certain level of contributions is reached (for example, contributions below $500 are not matched, contributions of $501–$1,000 are matched 100 percent, and contributions above $1,000 are not matched).

In standard economic models of intertemporal decision making, adding a matching contribution or increasing the generosity of a match, whatever its form, should increase participation in a savings scheme through a substitution effect. The match makes consuming income more expensive than saving it, motivating individuals to substitute saving for consumption in response to the match.

The theoretical impact on individuals already contributing to the savings plan, however, is ambiguous. Consider, for example, introducing a scheme in which contributions are matched only up to a certain threshold. Such a scheme would increase contributions for individuals who were not previously participating, as some of these nonparticipants may be induced to start saving by the match. In contrast, individuals who were already contributing in excess of the match threshold are predicted to respond to the new match by reducing their contributions, through an income effect. The match on their existing contributions acts like an additional source of income, some of which individuals use to increase their consumption and correspondingly reduce their savings. Their combined own plus matching contributions, however, should still be higher than before the match.

The impact on individuals previously contributing at or below the match threshold is ambiguous; they are affected by both the income and substitution effects described above. Because they are saving below the match threshold, the match creates an incentive to substitute additional savings, up to the match threshold, for consumption. But the match on contributions already made acts like additional income, some of which will be used to increase consumption and reduce contributions.

The effects would be similar for increasing the match rate while maintaining the same match threshold. The effects of increasing the match threshold while keeping the match rate constant are more complicated. Such a change should have no effect on people contributing below the old threshold. It should increase contributions by people at the old threshold (a substitution effect), have an ambiguous effect on people above the old threshold but at or below the new threshold (opposing income and substitution effects), and decrease contribution rates by people above the new threshold (an income effect).

Impact of Matching Contributions on Savings Outcomes: Evidence

What is the evidence on how people actually respond? Estimating the impact of a matching contribution on savings outcomes requires introducing some variation in the extent or structure of the match. The research has used three sources of match variation: naturally occurring cross-sectional variation (for example, differences in the match rate or match threshold in employer-sponsored savings plans); natural experiments, or changes in the structure of the match, within a savings scheme; and experimental variation generated by researchers, in which some individuals are offered a match, or a more generous match, and others are not.

The advantage of naturally occurring cross-sectional variation is that there can be considerable heterogeneity in the types of matching incentives different individuals face. For example, the match rates in employer-sponsored 401(k) savings plans in the United States range from no match to match rates as high as 200 percent, and the match thresholds range from 1 percent of salary to $17,000 a year.[1] This type of variation can be useful if, for example, one wants to simulate what would happen under a match structure that is very different from what is currently used. A severe limitation of using this type of variation, however, is that it may be difficult to disentangle the impact of differences in the match structure on individual behavior from other factors that might also affect outcomes. For example, individuals who have a strong savings motive may seek employment in firms that offer a savings plan with a generous match, whereas individuals with a weak savings motive may select into firms with a less generous or no match (or no savings plan at all). If this type of sorting occurs, the estimated relationship between the match and savings outcomes will be biased.

The advantage of natural and field experiments is that there are generally fewer concerns about the endogeneity between the generosity of the match and individual savings preferences. In field experiments, individuals are usually randomly assigned to receive different match structures. With natural experiments, concerns about endogeneity can be minimized by focusing on the same group of individuals before and after a policy change, essentially holding savings motives fixed. The limitation of field and natural experiments is that they typically examine a much smaller range of variation in matching schemes, with only two, or perhaps three, different types of match. The generalizability of the results from these studies is limited by the extent of the variation that is actually analyzed. These studies also typically focus on a specific group of individuals (for example, employees at a single firm, customers of a particular financial services provider, or low-income workers), limiting the extent to which the results can be generalized.

Most of the empirical studies on matching and savings outcomes have exploited the naturally occurring variation in the match rates of employer-sponsored savings plans in the United States to examine the impact of matching on savings outcomes. Most of these studies find, consistent with theoretical predictions, that matching increases savings plan participation rates (Andrews 1992; Bassett, Fleming, and Rogrigues 1998; Clark and Schieber 1998; Clark and others 2000; Dworak-Fisher 2008; Even and Macpherson 1997 and 2005; GAO 1997; Huberman, Iyengar, and Jiang 2007; Mitchell, Utkus, and Yang 2007; Papke and Poterba 1995). Some studies, however, find no relationship between matching and savings plan participation (Kusko, Poterba, and Wilcox 1998; Papke 1995).

In evaluating how matching affects savings plan contributions, the empirical evidence is less decisive (as noted above, the theoretical predictions are also not unambiguous). A few studies find a positive relationship between matching and savings plan contributions (Andrews 1992; Even and Macpherson 1997; Kusko, Poterba, and Wilcox 1998; Papke and Poterba 1995). One, Basset, Fleming, and Rodrigues (1998), finds no relationship between matching and savings plan contributions. Several studies estimate that a higher match is associated with lower contributions (Clark and others 2000; Mitchell, Utkus, and Yang 2007; Munnell, Sundén, and Taylor 2001; VanDerhei and Holden 2001). Some studies find heterogeneous effects. Huberman, Iyengar, and Jiang (2007) find that a higher match increases contributions for low-income individuals but decreases contributions for middle- and high-income individuals. Papke (1995) and GAO (1997) find a positive effect of the match rate on contributions when the match rate is low but a negative effect on contributions when the match rate is high.

The most careful and convincing study using naturally occurring variation in match rates is Engelhardt and Kumar (2007). This study has several attractive features:

- It is the only study that appropriately accounts for the nonlinear savings incentives generated by the employer match.

- It uses administrative data on savings plan contributions and earnings (from tax authority records on earnings and savings plan contributions) and on the structure of the employer match (from employer plan documents) to accurately model the incentives that individuals face and to get more accurate measures of their choices than is the case in self-reported survey data.

- It accounts for factors other than the employer match that might also influence savings outcomes, including taxes and alternative savings opportunities that may be equally or more attractive—specifically, individual retirement accounts (IRAs).

The biggest limitation of this study is that the data come from the Health and Retirement Study and thus focus on older individuals (the average age is 55), whose behavior may differ from that of younger people.

Engelhardt and Kumar estimate that increasing the match rate by 25 percentage points (for example, from $0.25 per $1 to $0.50 per $1 contributed) raises savings plan participation by 5 percentage points and increases contributions by plan participants by $365 (in 1991 dollars). They estimate that responsiveness to the employer match increases with the reported education level of respondents. Their overall conclusion is that neither participation nor contributions are very responsive to changes in the employer match and that "matching is a rather poor policy instrument with which to raise retirement saving" (p. 1921).

Duflo and others (2006) report the results of a field experiment on matching and savings outcomes. This study offered clients of the U.S. tax preparation firm H&R Block the opportunity to use their federal tax refund to open an IRA. Some individuals were offered the opportunity to open such an account with no match; others were offered a match of either 20 percent or 50 percent on contributions up to $1,000. Figure 15.1 shows the fraction contributing to an IRA and the amount contributed by those who chose to open an account. Only 3 percent of the study participants in the no-match group elected to open an IRA. With a 20 percent match, 8 percent opened an IRA, and with a 50 percent match, 14 percent opened an IRA.

FIGURE 15.1 **Evidence on the effect of matching and saving from the H&R Block experiment**

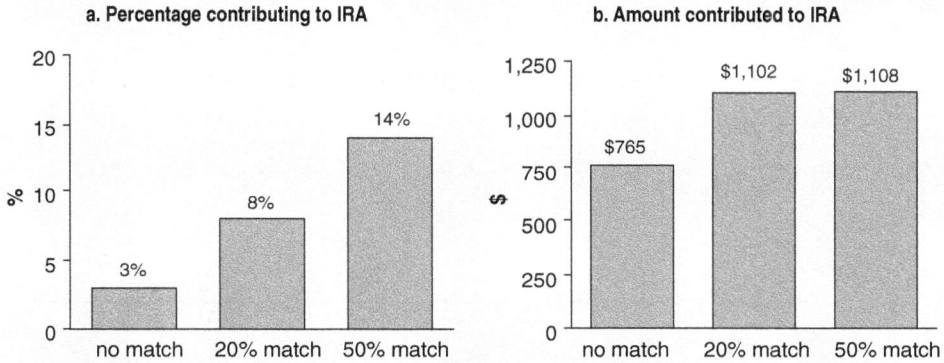

a. Percentage contributing to IRA

b. Amount contributed to IRA

SOURCE: Duflo and others 2006.

The magnitude of the effects estimated by Duflo and others (2006) is strikingly similar to that estimated by Engelhardt and Kumar (2007), even though the two studies examined different mechanisms (saving out of a tax refund versus enrolling in an employer-sponsored savings plan) and different types of individuals (middle-income H&R Block clients versus older Health and Retirement Study survey respondents). Engelhardt and Kumar estimate that increasing the match rate by 25 percent of contributions increases savings plan participation by about 5 percentage points; Duflo and others estimate that increasing the match rate from 0 to 20 percent of contributions increases savings plan participation by 5 percentage points, and increasing the match rate from 20 percent to 50 percent of contributions increases participation by 6 percentage points.

Mills and others (2008) report the results from a different multiyear field experiment on saving in individual development accounts (IDAs) in the United States. Lower-income families (income of less than 150 percent of the poverty level) were randomly assigned to either a treatment or a control group. Members of the treatment group were allowed to open an IDA to which contributions of up to $750 per year were potentially matched. Members of the control group were not allowed to open an IDA. One difference between this program and other savings schemes is that contributions were matched upon withdrawal, with the rate of the match dependent on the purpose of the withdrawal. Contributions withdrawn to purchase a home were matched 200 percent, whereas contributions withdrawn for other qualified purposes, such as education, starting a business, home improvement, or retirement saving, were matched 100 percent. Contributions withdrawn for nonqualified purposes were not matched.

Overall, the results indicate that there is no significant relationship between IDA participation and net worth (figure 15.2). For most of the distribution, the effect is small but negative; in the upper and lower quantiles, the point estimates are positive, and sometimes large, but never statistically significant. These results challenge the effectiveness of match-based savings schemes for increasing the net worth of very low-income families.

FIGURE 15.2 **Impact on Net Worth of Opening and Contributing to an Individual Development Account after Three Years**

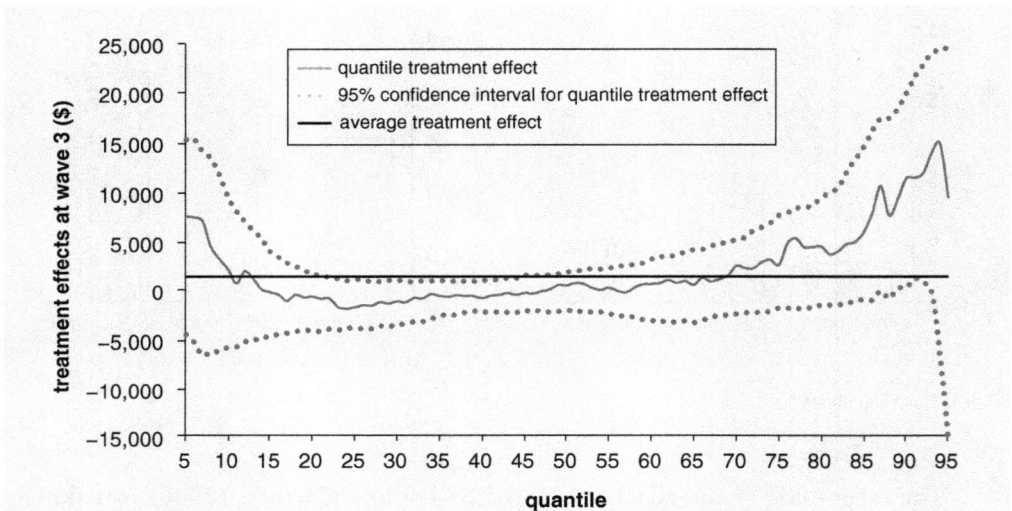

SOURCE: Mills and others 2008.

Choi and others (2002, 2004b, 2006) adopt the natural experiment approach to analyze the impact of matching on savings outcomes. They examine two companies with employer-sponsored savings plans that changed their employer match: one added a match to a plan that did not previously have one, and one increased its match threshold while keeping its match rate constant. This approach uses individual behavior before the changes as a control for employee behavior after the changes in the matching formulas as a way to address concerns about the endogeneity of individual savings preferences with respect to the generosity of the employer match.

The first company (Firm A) introduced a 25 percent match on employee contributions up to 4 percent of income in October 2000; before that date, the plan offered no match. Using data on employees hired up to 26 months before the plan change and up to 14 months after the plan change, Choi and others estimate a hazard model of the time from hire to the date of initial savings plan participation. They find that the introduction of the employer match increased the rate at which employees enrolled in the savings plan by about 25 percent. However, because participation rates at this company were low before the introduction of the match, the absolute magnitude of the estimated participation increase was not large. For example, their model predicts that the 25 percent match adopted by this firm leads to a 4.7 percentage point increase in savings plan participation for 40-year-old men with three years of tenure. This effect is roughly in line with the effect estimated by Engelhardt and Kumar (2007) and Duflo and others (2006).

The second company (Firm B) increased the match threshold in its savings plan in January 1997 while keeping its match rate constant. Before January 1997, unionized employees received a 50 percent match on the first 5 percent of income contributed to the savings plan, and nonunion employees received a 50 percent match on the first 6 percent of income contributed. In January 1997, the match threshold for both groups of employees was increased by 2 percent—from 5 percent to 7 percent of pay for union employees and from 6 percent to 8 percent of pay for nonunion employees. Contributions up to the new threshold were still matched at 50 percent.

Using data on employees hired up to one year before and one year after the plan change, Choi and others estimate a hazard model of the time from hire to the date of initial savings plan participation. They find no significant impact of the increase in the match threshold on savings plan participation. This result is consistent with the theoretical arguments outlined earlier, which posit that an increase in the match threshold does not affect the marginal incentives to participate in the savings plan. As expected, Choi and others find no effect on participation of such a plan change.

The more interesting results in Choi and others (2002, 2004b, 2006) address the impact of the match threshold on savings plan contributions. Figure 15.3 shows the distribution of contribution rates in the savings plan at Firm A for participants who joined the plan when it had no match and for participants who joined the plan after it introduced a 25 percent match on employee contributions up to 4 percent of income. With no match, the most frequently chosen contribution rates were 5 percent, 10 percent, and 15 percent of income—numbers that are multiples of 5. After the employer match, many participants also chose contribution rates that were multiples of 5. In addition, there was a large increase in the fraction of participants who made a 4 percent contribution, the new match threshold. In the absence of an employer match, very few employees chose to participate in the savings plan at a 4 percent contribution rate; with the employer match, the 4 percent match threshold became the modal contribution rate.

The distribution of contribution rates at Firm B, which increased its match threshold, exhibits a similar pattern. Figure 15.4 shows the distribution of contribution rates to the savings plan for two groups of participants: those who joined the plan in the nine months before the increase in the match threshold, and those who joined the plan over a similar period of time after the increase in the match threshold. As in figure 15.3, there are clear spikes in the distribution of contribution rates both before and after the change in the match threshold at multiples of 5 (5 percent, 10 percent, 15 percent, 20 percent, and 25 percent of pay). And, as in figure 15.3, the modal contribution rate under both distributions is at the match threshold: 5 percent or 6 percent of pay before the change in the match threshold and 7 percent or 8 percent of pay after the match threshold.

Figure 15.5 examines the impact of the increase in the match threshold of the Firm B savings plan for individuals participating in the plan before the match threshold changed. It shows how the contribution rates of these participants evolved over time after the plan change. The sample in figure 15.5 is restricted to employees contributing to the Firm B savings plan nine months before the increase in the match threshold. As in figure 15.4, a large proportion of participants (more than 45 percent) start with a contribution rate of 5 percent or 6 percent of pay. The switch from the old threshold to the new threshold is clearly apparent: there is an immediate shift from the old threshold (5 percent or 6 percent of pay) to the new threshold (7 percent or 8 percent of pay) when the match threshold change occurred, in January 1997, and a slower adjustment over the next three years, as more and more participants shifted from the old to the new threshold. In contrast, the fraction of participants at the other contribution rates remained fairly stable over the entire time period.

The patterns in figures 15.3, 15.4, and 15.5 reveal the behavioral nature of savings plan participation. The fact that the contribution rates spike at multiples of 5 suggests an important role for focal points in savings choices. When individuals face complicated decisions, such as deciding how much to save, they adopt heuristics to simplify the decision-making process. This pattern of contribution rate outcomes suggests that one such heuristic is to winnow the set of potential contribution rates to a subset of the possible options—in this case, those that are multiples of 5. The predominance of the match threshold in the distribution of contribution rates suggests that it also serves as a focal point in participants' considerations about how much to save. The kink in the budget set generated by the match threshold would be expected to result in bunching at the match threshold, absent any behavioral considerations. But it is likely that the match threshold gets additional consideration as participants evaluate how much to save because it serves as a natural focal point (precisely because it is where the financial incentives to save change); individuals may also view the match threshold as carrying an implicit recommendation about how much they should save; this endorsement effect would further reinforce the focal nature of the match threshold. Finally, the slow movement of existing participants away from the old match threshold and toward the new match threshold in figure 15.5 suggests inertia on the part of savings plan participants. Such inertia in savings plan outcomes has been well documented (see Beshears and others 2008 for a review of this literature). It is also consistent with participants' anchoring on the original match threshold.

Perhaps the most surprising finding in the literature on matching and savings plan outcomes is that even with a match, participation rates are often surprisingly low (Choi, Laibson, and Madrian 2011). Collectively, the research on matching and savings outcomes suggests that at best, increasing the match rate on savings leads to small increases in participation and contributions conditional on participation. The more important match-related tool is the match threshold, which serves as a strong focal point as individuals decide how much to save. A lower match rate with a higher match threshold may be a more effective way to increase individual contributions than a higher match rate with a lower match threshold—that is, providing a match of 25 percent on contributions up to 10 percent of pay will induce individuals to save more than a match of 50 percent up to 5 percent of pay at a similar (or lower) cost to the organization providing the match.

FIGURE 15.3 **Distribution of contribution rates at a firm that added an employer match: Firm A**

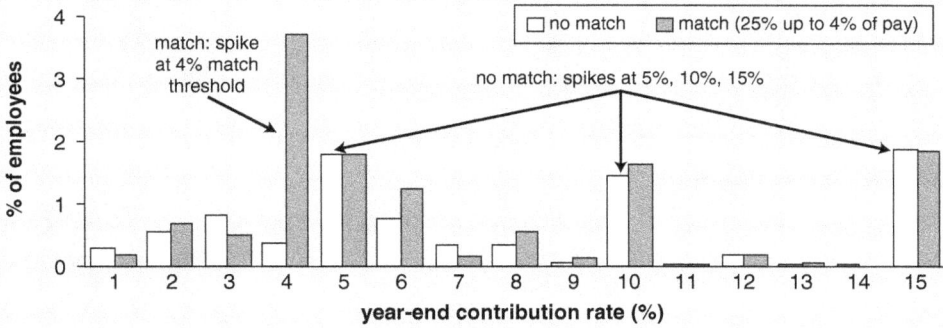

SOURCE: Choi and others 2006.

FIGURE 15.4 **Distribution of initial contribution rates at a firm that changed its match threshold: Firm B**

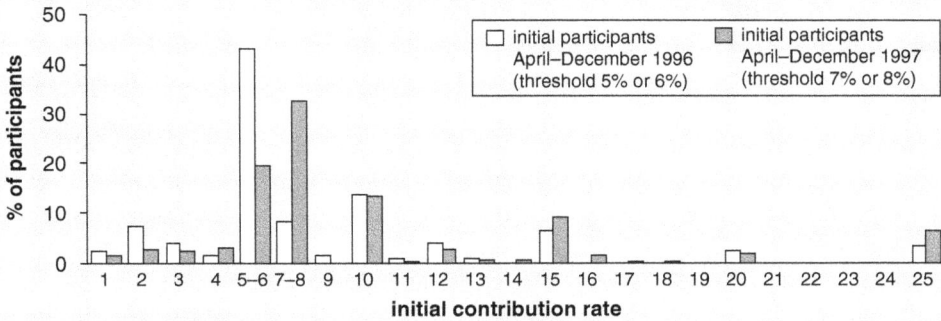

SOURCE: Choi and others 2004b.

FIGURE 15.5 **Evolution of contribution rates over time: Firm B**

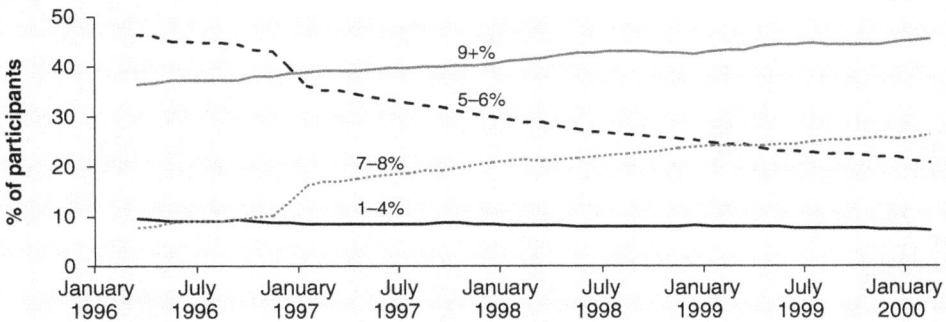

SOURCES: Choi and others 2002, 2006.

Complementary and Alternative Approaches to Increasing Saving

The literature on behavioral economics and savings plan outcomes suggests several alternative, and potentially more cost-effective, strategies to increase individual saving. This section reviews some of these approaches.

AUTOMATIC ENROLLMENT

By far the most effective method to increase participation in defined contribution savings schemes is automatic enrollment. The research on participation in employer-sponsored savings plans in the United States shows that participation rates are substantially higher when the default is enrollment in the savings plan (that is, individuals must opt out if they prefer not to save) than it is when individuals must take action to participate in the savings plan. The impact of automatic enrollment on participation rates can be sizable. In the first study of the impact of automatic enrollment on savings outcomes, Madrian and Shea (2001) document a 50 percentage point increase in savings plan participation for newly hired employees (less than 15 months of tenure) at a large employer that switched from an opt-in to an opt-out automatic enrollment regime. Other studies also document significant increases in participation as a result of automatic enrollment (see Beshears and others 2008; Choi and others 2002, 2004a, 2004b; Nessmith and others 2007). The impact of automatic enrollment is greatest for groups with the lowest saving rates initially: younger, lower-income workers.

Matching is not completely irrelevant in plans that have automatic enrollment. A more generous match is associated with higher participation rates, with effects that are roughly in line with those discussed earlier in the context of savings schemes without automatic enrollment.

Beshears and others (2010) take two different approaches to evaluating the importance of the match in employer-sponsored savings plans that have automatic enrollment. First, they examine a firm that replaced its employer match of 25 percent on the first 4 percent of pay contributed to the plan with a noncontingent employer contribution (that is, the firm made a savings plan contribution on behalf of all employees, regardless of whether employees made any contributions of their own to the savings plan). They estimate that eliminating the employer match reduced participation by at most 5–6 percentage points, an effect very similar to that estimated by Engelhardt and Kumar (2007), Duflo and others (2006), and Choi and others (2002, 2004b, 2006) for similar changes in the match rate in savings plans without automatic enrollment.

The second approach taken by Beshears and others (2010) in evaluating the impact of matching in savings plans with automatic enrollment is to exploit variation in the match structure both within (for firms that changed their matching policy) and across a sample of nine firms with employer-sponsored savings plans with automatic enrollment. This analysis is potentially confounded by endogeneity between the generosity of the match and employee saving preferences; in addition, the sample of firms included in the analysis is small. With these caveats in mind, Beshears and others find that a 1 percentage point increase in the maximum potential match as a fraction of salary is associated with a 2–4 percentage point increase in savings plan participation (figure 15.6). Based on these

estimates, decreasing the match rate from the modal match in employer-sponsored savings plans in the United States of 50 percent on the first 6 percent of pay to 25 percent on
the first 6 percent of pay (a reduction in the match rate of 25 percentage points) is predicted to reduce savings plan participation under automatic enrollment by 3–6 percentage
points. This estimate aligns with that from the single firm case study discussed in Beshears
and others (2010); it is also consistent with the studies of similar match changes in savings
plans without automatic enrollment discussed earlier.

FIGURE 15.6 **Matching contributions and savings plan participation in firms with automatic
enrollment**

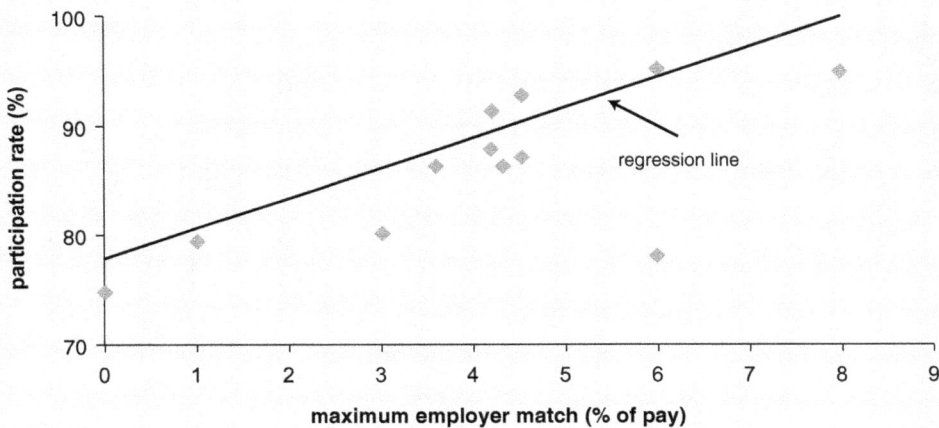

SOURCE: Beshears and others 2010.

These results confirm the earlier conclusion: increasing the match rate on savings
leads to small increases in savings plan participation. This conclusion holds for schemes
with and without automatic enrollment.

Although automatic enrollment leads to unambiguous increases in savings plan participation, its effects on savings plan contributions conditional on participation depend
very much on the default contribution rate at which individuals are automatically enrolled.
Just as the match threshold for savings plan contributions attracts the largest share of savings plan participants when there is a match, so too does the automatic enrollment default
contribution rate when there is automatic enrollment. Contributions are higher with a
higher default contribution rate under automatic enrollment than with a lower default
contribution rate. The distribution of contribution rates for employees at a U.S. company
that increased the default contribution rate in its savings plan from 3 percent of pay to
6 percent of pay is shown in figure 15.7. With a default contribution rate of 3 percent,
28 percent of plan participants contribute 3 percent of pay to the plan; another 24 percent contribute 6 percent to the plan, the match threshold; and 41 percent contribute at
a rate above 6 percent, primarily either 10 percent or 15 percent of pay (although these

two contribution rates are aggregated with other contribution rates in the figure). With a default contribution rate of 6 percent of pay, which coincides with the match threshold, almost half of employees contribute 6 percent of pay to the plan, twice the fraction observed with a default contribution rate of 3 percent; the fraction of employees contributing 3 percent of pay to the plan is an almost negligible 4 percent.

FIGURE 15.7 **Automatic enrollment for new hires and the distribution of savings plan contribution rates**

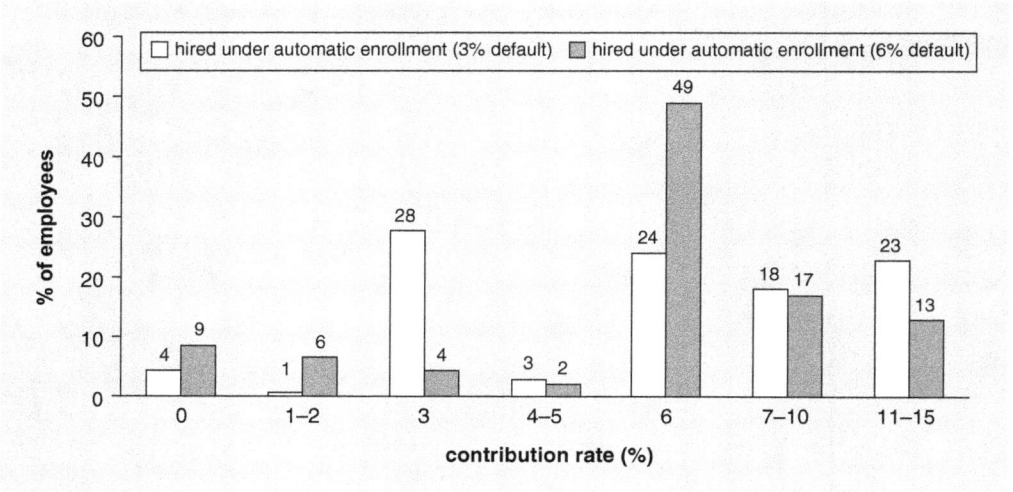

SOURCE: Beshears and others 2008.

A more extreme form of automatic enrollment is mandatory enrollment: individuals are automatically enrolled without the option of subsequently opting out. Most of the literature on defined contribution savings plans has focused on employer-sponsored 401(k)–type plans in the United States, where voluntary participation is standard. In other contexts, participation in defined contribution savings schemes is mandatory. For example, public sector entities in the United States that have a defined contribution scheme as their primary retirement savings plan (or one of their primary plans if participants have a choice of plans) tend to have mandatory enrollment with no option to opt out (Beshears and others 2011). Countries with defined contribution social security systems typically have automatic and mandatory participation, at least for workers in the formal sector. Whether to make participation voluntary or mandatory is an important policy question for defined contribution savings plans.

SIMPLIFICATION

One limitation of automatic and mandatory savings plan enrollment schemes is that these approaches work only in formal sector labor markets with developed financial institutions that can facilitate payroll deduction. In informal labor markets, these approaches are more difficult to implement. Lessons from the effect of automatic enrollment on increasing participation rates in these contexts can inform the structuring of savings schemes in other contexts.

The success of automatic enrollment in employer-sponsored savings plans in the United States is predicated on two factors: (1) that most people recognize the need for retirement income above and beyond what they will get from social security and therefore want to save and (2) that automatic enrollment simplifies what individuals already want to do. Several pieces of evidence support the notion that people generally want to save. First, when asked, individuals typically state a desire to save.[2]

Second, when asked to actively make a choice about whether and how much to save, most people choose to save. Carroll and others (2009) compare the savings outcomes in an employer-sponsored savings plan before and after employees were compelled to make an active choice about whether to participate in the savings plan. They find that when not required to make a choice, only 41 percent of newly hired employees enrolled in the savings plan. In contrast, when required to make an active choice about savings plan participation (which could include not participating), 69 percent enrolled. They conclude that most employees want to save but that an opt-in enrollment regime does not accurately reflect these preferences, because nonparticipation is consistent with both a preference not to save as well as with a preference to save accompanied by a delay in execution.

Third, very few people opt out of savings plan participation when they are automatically enrolled. Choi and others (2002, 2006) show that savings plan participation is very persistent regardless of whether employees are automatically enrolled. In particular, only 2–3 percent of automatically enrolled employees opt out of savings plan participation in a 12-month period. That savings rates are high and persistent under automatic enrollment is further evidence that most people generally want to save.

An important caveat to these findings is that they yield evidence on saving preferences for a specific set of individuals in a very specific context: employees in U.S. firms with access to employer-sponsored savings plans. These findings say nothing about saving preferences outside the United States (although one would surmise that many individuals throughout the world also want to save; see for example, Soman and Cheema 2011) or about saving preferences in other types of savings vehicles. Most employer-sponsored savings plans in the United States offer an employer match, which may induce some otherwise reluctant individuals to save. The evidence suggests that the effect of a match on savings plan participation is not large; nonetheless, a financial inducement is one way to shape saving preferences.

A potentially more important contextual factor is the level of trust individuals have that their savings will be secure. Guiso, Sapienza, and Zingales (2008) show that differences in the level of trust across countries explain a sizable share of the cross-country variation in individual stock holding: in countries with higher levels of trust, citizens are more willing to invest in equities. Adopting a regulatory framework that increases trust in financial institutions and the financial system may be a prerequisite to successfully increasing saving with any savings scheme.[3]

The second factor accounting for the success of automatic enrollment is that it simplifies the execution of what individuals already want to do—save. Indeed, automatic enrollment is an extreme form of simplification; individuals who want to save need not do anything. Psychologists have long recognized that choice complexity can affect decision-making outcomes. One result is procrastination—individuals put off decision making as choices become more complicated (Dhar and Nowlis 1999; Iyengar and Lepper 2000; Shafir, Simonson, and Tversky 1993; Tversky and Shafir 1992).

Iyengar, Huberman, and Jiang (2004) show that in the United States, enrollment in employer-sponsored savings plan is negatively correlated with the number of investment options in the savings plans: having 10 additional options in the investment menu led to a 1.5–2.0 percentage point decline in participation.[4] They hypothesize that having more investment options increases the complexity of choosing an asset allocation. Automatic enrollment decouples the choice about whether to save from the choice about how much to save or which asset allocation to select. The initial participation decision is simplified from one that involves evaluating myriad options to a simple comparison of two alternatives: nonparticipation (consumption or saving outside of the savings plan) versus participating at a prespecified contribution rate with a prespecified asset allocation. Madrian and Shea (2001) and Choi and others (2004a) find that automatic enrollment has its largest impact on participation for workers who are least financially sophisticated—the young and people with lower levels of income. These are the individuals for whom the complexity of the participation decision under an opt-in savings regime poses the greatest deterrent to participation (Beshears and others 2008).

If complexity is a deterrent to participation in a savings plan, then simplifying the task of savings plan enrollment, even if less extreme than automatic enrollment, should increase participation. Choi, Laibson, and Madrian (2009) and Beshears and others (2012) study the impact of a simplified enrollment process on outcomes in employer-sponsored savings plans. The intervention they evaluate, Quick Enrollment, gives employees a way to enroll in their employer-sponsored savings plan at a contribution rate and with an asset allocation preselected by their employer. Like automatic enrollment, this approach allows individuals to evaluate savings plan participation (at the preselected contribution rate and asset allocation) as a simple binary choice, without having to confront the multidimensional challenge of choosing a contribution rate or an asset allocation. At the two firms studied, Quick Enrollment increased savings plan participation by 10–20 percentage points relative to a standard opt-in enrollment regime (figure 15.8). This finding suggests that complexity can be a significant deterrent to savings plan participation and that other measures to simplify the process of saving in this or other contexts could materially affect savings outcomes.[5] Although the participation increases from this simplified approach to savings plan enrollment are not nearly as large as the estimated effects of automatic enrollment, they are sizable and much larger than the estimated effects of matching contributions. Simplifying and streamlining the saving process can have a sizable impact on outcomes and may be a much more cost-effective approach to changing behavior than financial incentives.

Merely providing access to a simple and straightforward way to save may increase saving. Dupas and Robinson (2010) in rural Kenya and Aportela (1999) in rural Mexico find that increasing access to the formal saving sector leads to higher levels of saving. In the case of the field experiment evaluated in Dupas and Robinson (2010), the newly available savings account offered no interest and charged withdrawal fees, yet demand for the account was still high.

FIGURE 15.8 **Quick Enrollment and savings plan participation: Firms C and D**

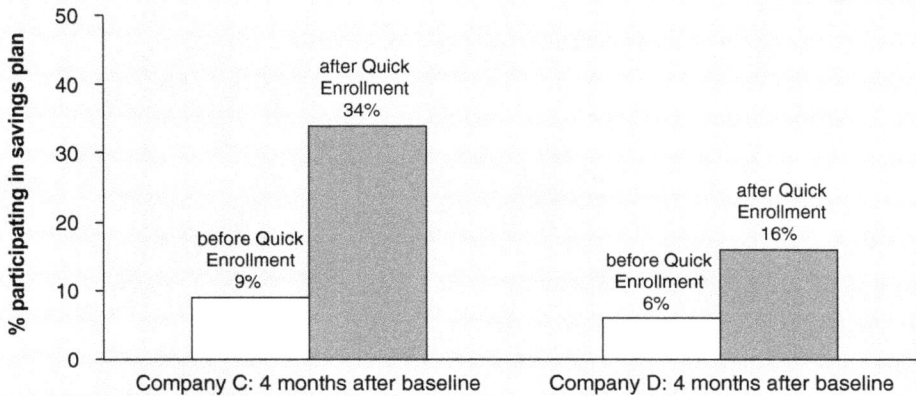

SOURCE: Beshears and others 2012.

EXECUTION AIDS

Even if individuals want to save, forgetfulness and procrastination may prevent execution of even the best-laid plans. Many strategies have been adopted to help individuals follow through on their savings goals. Research has identified a lack of planning as a primary reason why individuals fail to achieve their goals (Gollwitzer 1999; Gollwitzer and Sheeran 2006).

Lusardi, Keller, and Keller (2009) study the impact of helping individuals form and implement a savings plan on savings outcomes. The intervention they study—a planning aid for savings plan enrollment at a U.S. employer—encourages individuals to set aside a specific time for enrolling in their savings plan, outlines the steps involved in enrolling in a savings plan (for example, choosing a contribution rate and an asset allocation), gives an approximation of the time each step will take, and provides tips on what to do if individuals get stuck. Provision of this planning aid increased enrollment in an employer-sponsored savings plan by 12–21 percentage points for newly hired employees (figure 15.9). This effect is two to three times the estimated impact of matching contributions on savings plan participation. Like simplifying the saving process, providing execution aids is extremely cost-effective.

In a series of field experiments conducted in cooperation with banks in Bolivia, Peru, and the Philippines, Karlan and others (2010) evaluate the impact of providing savings reminders (text messages or letters) on savings outcomes in bank savings accounts. They find that people who received reminders were 3 percent more likely to achieve a pre-specified savings goal and saved 6 percent more in the bank sending the reminders than did people who did not receive reminders. They also find that reminders that highlighted individuals' savings goals were twice as effective as generic reminders.

FIGURE 15.9 **Impact of planning aids on savings plan participation**

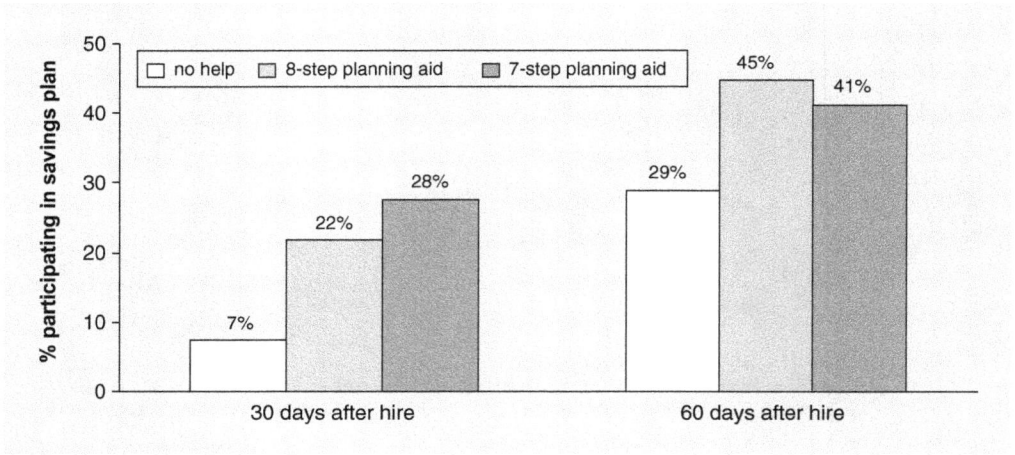

SOURCE: Lusardi, Keller, and Keller 2009.

Kast, Meier, and Pomeranz (2012) evaluate the impact of providing text message reminders on bank savings outcomes in Chile. They also find that individuals who received text message reminders saved substantially more than individuals who did not.

For the populations in the developing countries targeted in the field experiments of these two studies, ongoing saving requires ongoing action—automatic enrollment and direct deposit are not relevant alternatives. These results suggest that limited attention can be an important impediment to saving in such contexts. Text messages are a cost-effective and scalable way to create attention shocks that motivate people to take action and follow through on prespecified savings goals.

The field experiments discussed in Karlan and others (2010) and Kast, Meier, and Pomeranz (2012) included treatment arms that offered individuals higher than market interest rates as an inducement to save. Neither study finds any statistically significant impact of a higher interest rate on savings outcomes. The higher interest rates were admittedly much lower than the match rates that typically characterize matched savings schemes (in Kast, Meier, and Pomeranz 2012, for example, the high interest rate treatment group was offered an interest rate of 5 percent as compared to a then-prevailing interest rate of 0.3 percent). Although these studies are not directly comparable to the studies discussed earlier on the impact of matching contributions on savings outcomes, the results support the general qualitative conclusion that financial incentives have at best modest effects on outcomes.

A growing body of literature examines a broad class of execution aids known as commitment savings products. In the most influential paper in this literature, Ashraf, Karlan, and Yin (2006) evaluate a field experiment in the Philippines that offered one such product to current or former clients of a local bank. In this field experiment, participating bank clients who opted for the commitment savings product voluntarily restricted the right to withdraw their savings until reaching either an individually chosen goal date or an individually chosen goal amount. They show that there is a demand for commitment: among people who were offered the option to open a commitment savings account, 28 percent did so, even though it offered reduced flexibility and no higher interest than a standard bank account. Commitment products can have a sizable impact on savings. Relative to a control group not offered the commitment savings product, people offered a commitment account had bank balances that were 82 percent higher 12 months later. Corroborating work on commitment savings products in other countries includes Gugerty (2007), Ashraf and others (2011), Brune and others (2011), and Dupas and Robinson (2011). The reasons why commitment savings products are so effective at increasing saving are both internal (reducing the temptation to spend) and external (credibly telling others, primarily friends and family, that one's savings are inaccessible).

Soman and Cheema (2011) evaluate one interesting variant of a commitment savings technology in a field experiment targeted at unbanked construction laborers in rural India who are paid cash wages. In this experiment, individuals earmarked a certain amount of their weekly wages as savings. A social worker visited participating households every pay day to set aside the earmarked savings amount into either one (nonpartitioned) or two (partitioned) sealed envelopes. The challenge in this field experiment was not to motivate individuals to set aside money for savings but to prevent them from raiding their savings. The authors show that partitioning earmarked savings into multiple "accounts" increased realized savings by 39–216 percent. They hypothesize that opening a savings envelope, or violating the partition, induces guilt. Having multiple accounts, or partitions, increases the psychological cost of spending money that has been set aside for a specific purpose. This simple, low-cost execution aid has obvious extensions to other contexts. For example, having multiple retirement savings accounts may be more effective than relying on one type of savings account (for example, having both a retirement income account and a retirement health account may induce higher savings than a single generic retirement account).

Collectively, the research on execution aids suggests that many psychological impediments stand in the way of carrying out even the best-laid plans to save. Financial incentives do little in the face of such barriers. A more effective strategy is to directly address the barriers themselves.

Conclusions

A large body of literature has examined a wide variety of approaches to encouraging individuals to increase their savings. Traditional economic models point to financial incentives, such as a matching contribution, as the logical mechanism for increasing savings plan participation. The research on matching contributions and savings plan participation is largely consistent with traditional economic models: a matching contribution does increase participation. But the quantitative impact of matching contributions on savings plan participation is small. The studies using the most credible empirical methods find strikingly similar results in a variety of different contexts using a variety of different data sources: a matching contribution of 25 percent increases savings plan participation by roughly 5 percentage points.

The theoretical impact of matching contributions on the level of savings in traditional models depends on how much an individual would save in the absence of a match. The empirical results on this question finds results are inconsistent, although the most credible empirical work corroborates the predictions of traditional economic models.

Traditional economic models fail to characterize the most interesting features of the savings choices that individuals make. Savings rates cluster heavily around focal points, including the match threshold (as traditional economic theory would predict) and numbers that are multiples of five (something traditional economic theory would not predict). This finding suggests that the match threshold may be a much more important parameter in a matching scheme than the match rate.

Traditional economic models also fail to incorporate the many psychological frictions that impede saving, including present bias, complexity, inattention, and temptation. In many cases, countering these frictions leads to increases in savings plan participation and asset accumulation that surpass the effects of a typical matching contribution, potentially at a lower cost.

Notes

1. Individuals 50 and older may also be allowed to make additional "catch-up" contributions of up to $5,000 a year.

2. For example, Choi and others (2002 and 2006) report the results of a survey on retirement savings adequacy conducted by a large U.S. employer. Two-thirds of the responding employees stated a desire to save more than they were currently saving; one-third reported that they were saving about the right amount; and less than 1 percent responded that they were saving too much.

3. There is no evidence on how financial incentives interact with the level of trust to affect saving. If financial incentives substitute for trust, the small impact of financial incentives on saving in the United States may reflect a high level of trust in the United States but might not rule out a larger effect of financial incentives in countries with lower levels of trust. Alternatively, trust may be a precondition for financial incentives to have any impact at all.

4. This correlation is documented only among plans that do not have automatic enrollment.

5. Research has documented sizable impacts of simplification in contexts other than saving, including school choice (Hastings and Weinstein 2008); health plan choice (Kling and others 2008); mutual fund selection (Choi, Laibson, and Madrian 2010); and both college financial aid applications and college attendance (Bettinger and others 2009).

References

Andrews, Emily. 1992. "The Growth and Distribution of 401(k) Plans." In *Trends in Pensions 1992,* ed. John Turner and Daniel Beller, 149–76. Washington, DC: U.S. Government Printing Office.

Aportela, Fernando. 1999. "Effects of Financial Access on Savings by Low-Income People." Banco de México Working Paper.

Ashraf, Nava, Diego Aycinena, Claudia Martínez, and Dean Yang. 2011. "Remittances and the Problem of Control: A Field Experiment among Migrants from El Salvador." Universidad de Chile Working Paper SDT 341.

Ashraf, Nava, Dean Karlan, and Wesley Yin. 2006. "Tying Odysseus to the Mast: Evidence from a Commitment Savings Product in the Philippines." *Quarterly Journal of Economics* 121 (2): 635–72.

Bassett, William F., Michael J. Fleming, and Anthony P. Rodrigues. 1998. "How Workers Use 401(k) Plans: The Participation, Contribution, and Withdrawal Decisions." *National Tax Journal* 51 (2): 263–89.

Beshears, John, James J. Choi, David Laibson, and Brigitte C. Madrian. 2008. "The Importance of Default Options for Retirement Savings Outcomes: Evidence from the United States." In *Lessons from Pension Reform in the Americas*, ed. Stephen J. Kay and Tapen Sinha, 59–87. New York: Oxford University Press.

———. 2010. "The Impact of Employer Matching on Savings Plan Participation under Automatic Enrollment." In *Research Findings in the Economics of Aging*, ed. David A. Wise, 311–27. Chicago: University of Chicago Press.

———. 2011. "Behavioral Economics Perspectives on Public Sector Pension Plans." *Journal of Pension Economics and Finance* 10 (2): 315–36.

———. 2012. "Simplification and Saving." *Journal of Economic Behavior and Organizations*.

Bettinger, Eric P., Bridget Terry Long, Philip Oreopolous, and Lisa Sanbonmatsu, 2009. "The Role of Simplification and Information in College Decisions: Results from the H&R Block FAFSA Experiment." NBER Working Paper 15361, National Bureau of Economic Research, Cambridge, MA.

Brune, Lasse, Xavier Giné, Jessica Goldberg, and Dean Yang. 2011. "Commitments to Save: A Field Experiment in Rural Malawi." Policy Research Working Paper 5748, World Bank, Washington, DC.

Carroll, Gabriel D., James J. Choi, David Laibson, Brigitte C. Madrian, and Andrew Metrick. 2009. "Optimal Defaults and Active Decisions: Theory and Evidence from 401(k) Saving." *Quarterly Journal of Economics* 124 (4): 1639–74.

Choi, James J., David Laibson, and Brigitte C. Madrian. 2009. "Reducing the Complexity Costs of 401(k) Participation through Quick Enrollment™." In *Developments in the Economics of Aging*, ed. David A. Wise, 57–82. Chicago: University of Chicago Press.

———. 2011. "$100 Bills on the Sidewalk: Violations of No-Arbitrage in 401(k) Accounts." *Review of Economics and Statistics* 113 (3): 748–63.

Choi, James J., David Laibson, Brigitte C. Madrian, and Andrew Metrick. 2002. "Defined Contribution Pensions: Plan Rules, Participant Decisions, and the Path of Least Resistance." In *Tax Policy and the Economy*, vol. 16, ed. James M. Poterba, 67–113. Cambridge, MA: MIT Press.

———. 2004a. "For Better or for Worse: Default Effects and 401(k) Savings Behavior." In *Perspectives on the Economics of Aging*, ed. David A. Wise, 81–121. Chicago: University of Chicago Press.

———. 2004b. "Plan Design and 401(k) Savings Outcomes." *National Tax Journal* 57 (2): 275–98.

———. 2006. "Saving for Retirement on the Path of Least Resistance." In *Behavioral Public Finance: Toward a New Agenda*, ed. Edward J. McCaffrey and Joel Slemrod, 304–51. New York: Russell Sage Foundation.

Clark, Robert L., Gordon Goodfellow, Sylvester Schieber, and Drew Warwick. 2000. "Making the Most of 401(k) Plans: Who's Choosing What and Why." In *Forecasting Retirement Needs and Retirement Wealth*, ed. Olivia Mitchell, Brett Hammond, and Anna Rappaport, 95–138. Philadelphia: University of Pennsylvania Press.

Clark, Robert L., and Sylvester Schieber. 1998. "Factors Affecting Participation Levels in 401(k) Plans." In *Living with Defined Contribution Plans: Remaking Responsibility for Retirement,* ed. Olivia Mitchell and Sylvester J. Schieber, 69–97. Philadelphia: University of Pennsylvania Press.

Dhar, Ravi, and Stephen M. Nowlis. 1999. "The Effect of Time Pressure on Consumer Choice Deferral." *Journal of Consumer Research* 25 (4): 369–84.

Duflo, Esther, William Gale, Jeffrey Liebman, Peter Orszag, and Emmanuel Saez. 2006. "Saving Incentives for Low- and Middle-Income Families: Evidence from a Field Experiment with H&R Block." *Quarterly Journal of Economics* 121 (4): 1311–46.

Dupas, Pascaline, and Jonathan Robinson. 2010. "Savings Constraints and Microenterprise Development: Evidence from a Field Experiment in Kenya." International Policy Center Working Paper 111.

———. 2011. "Why Don't the Poor Save More? Evidence from Health Savings Experiments." NBER Working Paper 17255, National Bureau of Economic Research, Cambridge, MA.

Dworak-Fisher, Keenan. 2008. "Encouraging Participation in 401(k) Plans: Reconsidering the Employer Match." U.S. Bureau of Labor Statistics Working Paper 420.

Engelhardt, Gary V., and Anil Kumar. 2007. "Employer Matching and 401(k) Saving: Evidence from the Health and Retirement Study." *Journal of Public Economics* 91(10): 1920–443.

Even, William E., and David A. Macpherson. 1997. "Factors Influencing Participation and Contribution Levels in 401(k) Plans." Florida State University Working Paper.

———. 2005. "The Effects of Employer Matching in 401(k) Plans." *Industrial Relations* 44 (3): 525–49.

GAO (General Accounting Office). 1997. "401(k) Pension Plans: Loan Provisions Enhance Participation But May Affect Income Security for Some." Report to the Chairman, Special Committee on Aging, and the Honorable Judd Gregg, U.S. Senate, GAO, Washington, DC.

Gollwitzer, Peter M. 1999. "Implementation Intentions: Strong Effects of Simple Plans." *American Psychologist* 54 (7): 493–503.

Gollwitzer, Peter M., and Paschal Sheeran. 2006. "Implementation Intentions and Goal Achievement: A Meta-Analysis of Effects and Processes." *Advances in Experimental Social Psychology* 38: 69–119.

Gugerty, Mary Kay. 2007. "You Can't Save Alone: Commitment in Rotating Savings and Credit Associations in Kenya." *Economic Development and Cultural Change* 55 (2): 251–82.

Guiso, Luigi, Paola Sapienza, and Luigi Zingales. 2008. "Trusting the Stock Market." *Journal of Finance* 63 (6): 2557–600.

Hastings, Justine S., and Jeffrey M. Weinstein. 2008. "Information, School Choice, and Academic Achievement: Evidence from Two Experiments." *Quarterly Journal of Economics* 123 (4): 1373–414.

Huberman, Gur, Sheena S. Iyengar, and Wei Jiang. 2007. "Defined Contribution Pension Plans: Determinants of Participation and Contribution Rates." *Journal of Financial Services Research* 31(1): 1–32.

Iyengar, Sheena S., Gur Huberman, and Wei Jiang. 2004. "How Much Choice Is Too Much? Contributions to 401(k) Retirement Plans." In *Pension Design and Structure: New Lessons from Behavioral Finance*, ed. Olivia Mitchell and Stephen Utkus, 83–95. Oxford: Oxford University Press.

Iyengar, Sheena S., and Mark R. Lepper. 2000. "When Choice Is Demotivating: Can One Desire Too Much of a Good Thing?" *Journal of Personality and Social Psychology* 79 (6): 995–1006.

Karlan, Dean, Margaret McConnell, Sendhil Mullainathan, and Jonathan Zinman. 2010. "Getting to the Top of Mind: How Reminders Increase Saving." NBER Working Paper 16205, National Bureau of Economic Research, Cambridge, MA.

Kast, Felipe, Stephan Meier, and Dina Pomeranz. 2012. "Under-Savers Anonymous: Evidence on Self-Help Groups and Peer Pressure as a Savings Commitment Device." IZA Discussion Paper 6311, Institute for the Study of Labor, Bonn.

Kling, Jeffrey R., Sendhil Mullainathan, Eldar Shafir, Lee Vermeulen, and Marian Wrobel, 2008. "Misperception in Choosing Medicare Drug Plans." Harvard University working paper, Cambridge, MA.

Kusko, Andrea, James Poterba, and David Wilcox. 1998. "Employee Decisions with Respect to 401(k) Plans." In *Living with Defined Contribution Pensions: Remaking Responsibility for Retirement*, ed. Olivia Mitchell and Sylvester Schieber, 98–112. Philadelphia: University of Pennsylvania Press.

Lusardi, Annamaria, Punam Anand Keller, and Adam M. Keller. 2008. "New Ways to Make People Save: A Social Marketing Approach." In *Overcoming the Saving Slump: How to Increase the Effectiveness of Financial Education and Saving Programs*, ed. Annamaria Lusardi, 209–36. Chicago: University of Chicago Press.

Madrian, Brigitte C., and Dennis F. Shea. 2001. "The Power of Suggestion: Inertia in 401(k) Participation and Savings Behavior." *Quarterly Journal of Economics* 116 (4): 1149–87.

Mills, Gregory, William G. Gale, Rhiannon Patterson, Gary V. Engelhardt, Michael D. Eriksen, and Emil Apolstolov. 2008. "Effects of Individual Development Accounts on Asset Purchases and Saving Behavior: Evidence from a Controlled Experiment." *Journal of Public Economics* 92 (5–6): 1509–30.

Mitchell, Olivia S., Stephen P. Utkus, and Tongxuan Yang. 2007. "Turning Workers into Savers? Incentives, Liquidity, and Choice in 401(k) Plan Design." *National Tax Journal* 60 (3): 469–89.

Munnell, Alicia H., Annika Sundén, and Catherine Taylor. 2001. "What Determines 401(k) Participation and Contributions?" *Social Security Bulletin* 64 (3): 64–75.

Nessmith, William E., Stephen P. Utkus, and Jean A. Young. 2007. "Measuring the Effectiveness of Automatic Enrollment." Vanguard Center for Retirement Research, Malvern, PA.

Papke, Leslie E. 1995. "Participation in and Contributions to 401(k) Pension Plans." *Journal of Human Resources* 30(2): 311–25.

Papke, Leslie E., and James M. Poterba. 1995. "Survey Evidence on Employer Match Rates and Employee Saving Behavior in 401(k) Plans." *Economics Letters* 49 (3): 313–17.

Shafir, Eldar, Itamar Simonson, and Amos Tversky. 1993. "Reason-Based Choice." *Cognition* 49(1–2): 11–36.

Soman, Dilip, and Amar Cheema. 2011. "Earmarking and Partitioning: Increasing Saving by Low-Income Households." *Journal of Marketing Research* 48 (S1): S14–S22.

Tversky, Amos, and Eldar Shafir. 1992. "Choice under Conflict: The Dynamics of Deferred Decision." *Psychological Science* 3 (6): 358–61.

VanDerhei, Jack, and Sarah Holden. 2001. "Contribution Behavior of 401(k) Plan Participants." *Investment Company Institute Perspective* 7 (4):1–19.

CHAPTER 16

Implementation Issues in Low- and Middle-Income Countries

Robert Palacios and Mike Orszag

Experience in a number of countries indicates that matching contribution schemes can potentially increase pension coverage and the level of retirement savings. However, this hopeful assessment is derived mainly from outcomes observed in a relatively small number of high-income settings with relatively small programs supplementing extensive and long-established national pension systems. These schemes have been set up in environments characterized by high levels of public and private institutional development and benefit from well-established and sophisticated financial and information management systems. Implementing matching contribution pension schemes in other settings requires careful consideration of the necessary enabling conditions and system parameters that will ensure viability. Enabling conditions include the legal, institutional, and information systems required to maintain and control individual accounts; the capacity to invest accumulated assets efficiently; and the ability to exercise oversight and control to ensure the integrity of the matching payments. Design parameters include the target benefit level, the total contribution required to achieve the benefit level, the extent of the match itself, the age of withdrawal, and the rules for accumulation and withdrawal. These parameters will need to be adjusted as incomes grow, the size of the formal sector expands, and the population ages.

In response to persistently low coverage rates, a growing number of low- and middle-income countries have been exploring alternatives to traditional social insurance models that link retirement benefits to payroll tax payments. Targeted or universal cash transfers to the elderly are one response to the coverage gap, especially in countries where broader social assistance programs do not already exist. Another approach is to increase incentives to participate in contributory programs, especially for the self-employed and informal sector workers.

These programs can be seen as a subset of a broader category of voluntary contribution-based pensions. In richer countries, the incentive to sacrifice current consumption or liquidity in order to save for retirement typically takes the form of tax incentives that exclude or defer income taxes on earnings that are saved in designated retirement savings vehicles or through the provision of tax credits that effectively subsidize contributions. The tax incentives result in foregone revenues and are therefore often characterized as "tax expenditure." Tax-deductible contributions are common in Organisation for Economic Co-operation and Development (OECD) countries, although tax credits are limited to a few countries (for example, Turkey). Participation in voluntary private pensions is correlated with these incentives although not to the extent that is typically expected (see chapter 2).

The use of tax expenditures to encourage pension savings is premised on the public policy objective of generating adequate retirement income for some portion of the population. This premise implicitly assumes that this type of incentive increases the net level of retirement savings. As discussed in earlier chapters, however, the empirical evidence is mixed. Some studies show a positive savings impact, while others find that only the composition of savings is affected. At the same time, progressive income tax schedules combined with deductions that take place at higher marginal rates for the rich often lead to a regressive subsidy, especially when there is a significant substitution of tax-preferred savings for savings that would otherwise have occurred.

In countries with very low or zero marginal tax rates for low-income individuals, this preferential treatment provides no meaningful incentive for pension-related saving. In poorer countries, tax incentives are less relevant, because only a small share of the population actually pays income taxes. The rationale for a tax-based subsidy that could be expected to accrue only to the highest quintile of the income distribution is therefore even weaker than in richer countries.

An alternative approach that equalizes the incentive regardless of income tax status is to provide the subsidy directly, in the form of matching pension contributions. This approach is being implemented in several low- and middle-income countries, including Colombia, Mexico, and Peru; China; and India (see chapters 10, 11, and 12, respectively). Others have passed laws to create matching programs which are in the very early stages of implementation. There is little evidence yet of the likelihood of success or the outcomes to be achieved by these initiatives.

To some degree, these new programs are motivated by the positive results in expanding voluntary pension coverage in several high-income countries, notably the United States, Germany, and New Zealand (see chapters 3, 4, and 5, respectively). These results have been achieved under very different circumstances. The schemes have all been conceived as complements to long-established national pension systems that have already achieved very high rates of coverage and participation and that provide basic levels of guaranteed old-age income support for the vast majority of people. Most have been introduced as complements to occupational pension systems that benefit from a well-developed legal, financial, and institutional infrastructure that either predates the pension system or has been developed to support it. This infrastructure includes reasonable, functioning markets for financial services and products and a vibrant, competitive industry that provides recordkeeping and asset management for pensions and other savings and investment institutions. Further, these pension systems have arisen in countries where property rights and reliable third-party management of financial assets are relatively effective. They also have social security and tax administration institutions with information systems that can issue and control individual identification numbers and maintain data to track transactions to ensure the reliability and integrity of contributions and payments.

Although matching contributions are not restricted to defined contribution schemes, these are the most common variant found in developing countries, largely due to the difficulty of applying a defined benefit or quasi–defined benefit approach to informal sector workers where it is extremely difficult to track earnings that tend to be highly variable. For this reason, this chapter focuses on the case of matching defined contributions (MDCs). Specifically, it reviews the key challenges, minimum enabling conditions, and some of the key parameters to be determined when designing a matching scheme in low-income countries—keeping in mind that, like other pension policies, design choices should anticipate an evolution of conditions over the long run and be designed accordingly.

Challenges

There is a vast literature on the determinants of informal economic activity (see, for example, Loayza 1997). The very definition of this term poses a challenge (Godfrey 2011). The challenge of formalizing the labor force and economic activity is generally multidimensional and requires a comprehensive approach. It is a subject well beyond the scope of social insurance policy. Nevertheless, changes to contribution- or payroll tax–based social programs can be important in influencing participation in the formal sector. Some analysis shows that the incentives that these programs create can matter, especially at the margin (see Auerbach, Genoni, and Pagés 2007).

For decades, governments and their social insurance agencies attempted to expand coverage of pensions through the traditional social insurance model. This model relied on the imposition of participation mandates and payroll tax collection in economies dominated by agriculture and microbusinesses. In many cases, the legal mandate did not apply to large segments of the workforce—and, even where it did apply, evasion ensured that coverage levels remained low. Pension coverage in the social insurance sense was determined by the size of the formal sector, which itself was a function of many other factors outside the purview of the relevant agencies.

In low-income countries, roughly 1 in 10 workers contributes to a pension scheme; the figure is about 1 in 3 in middle-income countries, depending on the definition applied. Transition economies have higher coverage, thanks largely to the legacy of the old systems, in which the state was the main employer, although coverage is falling in many of these countries as the role of the state is reduced and the labor force becomes increasing informal.[1]

TRANSACTION COSTS

By definition, informal sector workers are not captured by traditional social insurance or pension mandates. The new MDC initiatives in low-income countries recognize that participation will necessarily be voluntary, which has several implications. Notably, the transaction cost of participating in a voluntary system becomes very important. Solutions that reduce these costs must be explored wherever possible; a design that allows for flexibility in contribution levels for workers with volatile income sources is preferable.

Recent experience in India demonstrates two possible ways of reducing transaction costs. The first is to harness the infrastructure set up for the formal sector as much as possible. This includes systems of recordkeeping and account maintenance as well as management of funds. Regulation and supervision, where they overlap, can also be utilized. In the case of India, discussed in chapter 12, the defined contribution scheme established for civil servants provided much of the infrastructure for the system later opened up to informal sector workers. Use of this infrastructure reduced the marginal cost of expanding coverage (some elements specific to the informal sector scheme—in particular, a contribution collection system accessible by these workers—did have to be added).

The volume-oriented approach can also be used with government programs, particularly those that have targeted a population deemed to merit subsidy. In Mexico in 2006, a proposal by former president Vicente Fox to match the contributions of working-age members of households covered by the Oportunidades program was conceived but never implemented. The idea had the advantage of harnessing the existing recordkeeping and payments infrastructure. Using a targeted program can also help constrain the fiscal cost and, in principle, increase the progressivity of the subsidy, as discussed below.

Another cost reduction strategy used in India has been to harness the existing infrastructure of various groups, ranging from dairy worker associations to microfinance agencies. These groups tend to have registries and periodic interactions with their members to which an additional transaction can be added at relatively low cost. By plugging in the group records and contribution flows to the central system, costs can be drastically reduced.

PORTABILITY AND ACCESS TO FORMAL FINANCIAL SECTOR

Many informal sector workers have variable career and earnings paths. Farmers may migrate to urban areas and take up informal sector employment; people remaining in rural areas may have seasonal incomes, migrate during the course of the year, or both. The self-employed may become informal or formal sector employees. The transient nature of informal sector work makes ensuring that pension contributions are portable even more important than for formal sector pension schemes.

Informal sector workers also tend to have low exposure to the formal financial sector. Thus, using traditional venues such as banks or insurance companies to collect contributions may not be an effective mechanism in this regard. In many settings, initiatives such as village-level banking correspondents or outreach to certain groups of workers have been put in place to improve financial inclusion. Technology that leapfrogs traditional modalities may also be useful in connecting people with little knowledge of or interaction with formal financial institutions. For example, the Kenyan Mbao pension scheme combines technology and financial inclusion (using mobile phones for contribution collection and account balance checking) with efforts to harness existing groups (members of the informal workers association). The same scheme allows for extremely small contributions to be made cheaply (ISSA 2011).

OUTREACH

In addition to technology, which requires up-front investments from government or the private sector, outreach to remote areas and illiterate populations involves information and education campaigns and direct contact with communities that may not have access to mainstream forms of communication. Whether implemented by the public or private sector, this outreach costs money. In China, local governments tasked with implementing the rural pension scheme bear this cost. In India, nongovernmental organizations and other entities licensed as "aggregators" implement the program (see chapter 12).

FINANCIAL NEEDS AND RESOURCES

Most low-income workers have low saving capacity and a high preference and need for liquidity and precautionary savings. In low-income countries where the informal sector is the largest, there will be significant variation in the potential for long-term saving across the income distribution. Nevertheless, at the bottom of the distribution, many households will be operating at, or just above, subsistence; it is not practical to expect them to forgo access to their savings in the face of income uncertainty. In contrast, in middle-income countries, even programs targeting the poor may include households with some saving capacity; this was the assumption of the Mexican proposal cited above.

Other characteristics that affect take-up include coverage of other insurance programs. Unlike formal sector workers, few informal sector workers have health or other kinds of insurance. The fact that they must self-insure against these risks reduces their ability to save for the long run. The potential link between attempts to expand pension coverage and health insurance coverage is not often exploited.

INCENTIVES

The last challenge implies the need for robust incentives to offset high discount rates. The key question for policy makers is the elasticity of participation for the target population. One study in Peru asked individuals about their willingness to contribute if contributions were subsidized. The results, shown in figure 16.1, are intuitive. Workers at all income levels were more willing to contribute when offered larger subsidies, but the marginal impact of doubling the subsidy level was less than proportional. If behavior were to follow these stated intentions, the impact of the subsidies on participation would be huge, increasing coverage in the bottom 40 percent of the income distribution from about 10 percent to more than 60 percent with a 1:1 match. Unfortunately, answers to questions about willingness are not necessarily good predictors of actual outcomes, and there does not appear to be empirical evidence on the actual take-up elasticity in developing countries.[2]

FIGURE 16.1 **Effect of subsidy on likelihood of participating in pension scheme in Peru, by income quintile**

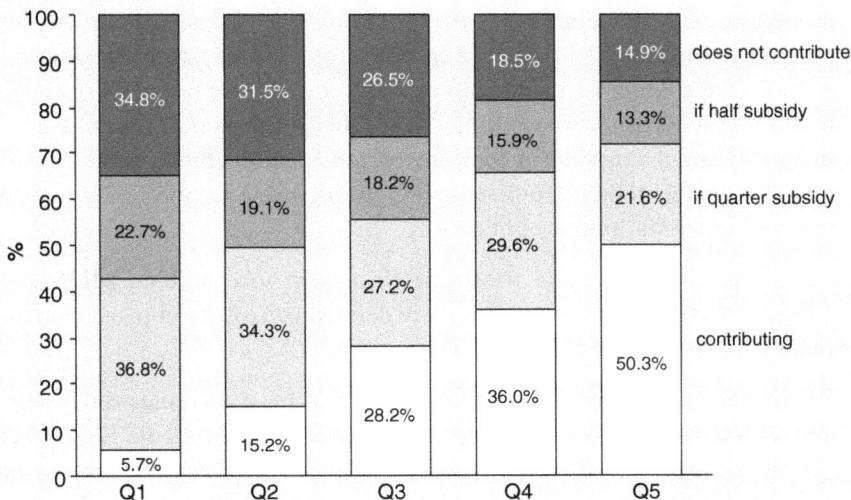

SOURCE: Pagés 2012.

NOTE: Q1 is the lowest income quintile, and Q5 is the highest.

Enabling Conditions

There are at least four key enabling conditions that are necessary to make MDC plans work:

- **Capacity for informed choice within the target population.** If individuals cannot understand the implications of the matching provisions and make choices in an effective and consistent manner in response to the incentives, the flexibility of defined contribution is potentially a problem rather than a benefit.

- **Administrative systems.** Administrative systems consistent with the requirements for tracking individual contributions, maintaining records of account balances, and responding to individual choices are essential. If systems cannot handle the complexity of choice or can only implement additional choices and matching programs expensively, the benefits of defined contribution and matching programs will be significantly diluted.

- **Reliable governance.** Reliable governance is needed to ensure appropriately designed contribution choices and investment options and to provide system oversight. If the choices are not appropriate, individuals are not likely to respond to the incentives in the manner intended. If management systems and processes are inadequate, confidence in the system will be impossible to sustain. Both of these conditions will require a well-functioning and reliable governance structure, including ongoing oversight and evaluation to adapt the system to changing conditions. As with any pension system, the governance process will need to be sufficiently insulated from political pressures to ensure that assets are protected and incentives are not manipulated to achieve short-term political objectives.

- **Sustainable commitment.** A sustainable commitment to the system requires a reasonably stable political environment and design features that produce consistent and predictable outcomes over time. This latter is particularly important, as pension arrangements involves long lead times between contributions and benefits. In the absence of sustainability, a system will not be able to deliver secure retirement income. Any matching system that achieves meaningful coverage will inevitably entail a significant fiscal investment if public funds or tax incentives are included in the design. Consistency of governance and political support will be required to sustain public confidence.

Several structural conditions also must be present to enable an MDC system to function. These conditions are required for any defined contribution pension system, but are essential to the operation of an MDC-type system:

- **Long-term asset classes consistent with the needs of pension investments.** The membership of any successful matching system will be highly heterogeneous with regard to their investment requirements. The target groups will typically be diverse in age and have higher levels of volatility in earnings, liquidity preferences, and other risk management attributes. Addressing these needs will require underlying assets that range from short-term, highly liquid instruments to longer-term asset classes that can exploit time-related risk premiums. While matching provisions can induce short-term contributions, achieving the long-term outcome of secure retirement savings requires the same range of longer-term financial products as in any pension system. Inducing contributions without the underlying investment products would likely result in an expensive system that produces little advantage in terms of retirement savings.

- **Well-supervised financial markets and institutions.** A perception of reliability and long-term confidence in the financial system will be essential to the success of any matching system. This perception can only be achieved with the appropriate products and effective regulation and supervision—especially in developing and transitional economies. Without long-term confidence, members are likely to make contributions in response to incentives and then withdraw them as quickly as possible, severely diminishing the capacity of the system to achieve long-term objectives and threatening the continuity of political support. The financial system in the country needs to be sufficiently developed to handle the funds flowing into the defined contribution system, and needs to be thought of much more broadly than just in terms of asset management infrastructure. Intermediaries such as financial advisers can play a critical role in improving and facilitating appropriate choice. The presence of reliable third-party oversight to undertake audits and a system of information disclosure and individual account statements are essential for a system to succeed.

- **Instruments and policy framework to convert accumulated savings into reliable income.** Establishing a matching contribution arrangement as a pension system rather than simply as an inducement to increase savings in general will require a means of converting account balances to a stream of retirement income. Ideally, this would take the form of an efficient annuity market that would enable members to manage mortality risk while continuing to accrue some benefits from their accumulated savings. However, this ideal is extremely difficult to attain in many settings; alternatives include a policy framework and related instruments for programmed withdrawals or mandates for minimal or deferred annuity purchases where markets are less efficient. The essential condition is that there be an explicit framework to ensure that a significant portion of the savings induced by the matching arrangement be translated into old-age income of some sort.

Finally, certain elements are important for implementation of the MDC system. These may be listed as the "seven Cs":

- **Communications.** Without appropriate communications, individuals are not going to make effective decisions and will not normally develop their capabilities to make future decisions.

- **Complexity.** Individuals are typically able to make simpler decisions but often have difficulty with more complex decisions.

- **Community.** Friends and family are often a critical part of decision making and an important socioeconomic enabling factor behind the success of matching programs.

- **Credibility.** The system needs to be credible in order to be sustainable and to function.

- **Complements.** The system needs to work in tandem with other vehicles that will produce retirement income.

- **Culture**. The system needs to be consistent with social norms and the historical development of other social protection arrangements.

- **Connection.** Intermediaries play an important role in connecting an individual with products and in aiding his or her decisions.

All of the above-mentioned elements are important to defined contribution plans in general, not just to matching programs. It is therefore helpful to focus attention on what is special about matching programs in terms of the difficulties and issues likely to be encountered.

- Matching programs that are publicly sponsored involve the credibility of the government in visible ways; hence, the expectations of the populace are higher. In particular, as matching systems aim to increase participation in the system, any failures will be particularly poorly received. The pressure to get people to participate is likely to be very intense.

- Matching can introduce complexity. If individuals have difficulty making decisions without matching, they may have even more difficulty factoring in the extra challenges of calculating incentives from matching programs. This complexity increases the administrative load and makes governance arrangements that much harder to get right.

- Matching is more vulnerable to agency issues than systems without matching. Any time the government or another party is paying for something, there is likely to be some part of the benefit that accrues to parties other than the consumer. For example, intermediaries might charge more, or employers may constrain wage increases or cut benefit programs in response to the provision of contribution matches.

Matching therefore imposes additional implementation challenges and makes the enabling environment that much more significant. The issues outlined above are of greater importance within this environment; the capacity for choice, administrative systems, and effective governance are discussed in more depth below along with general issues of implementing defined contribution plans.

INFORMED CHOICE

Consider the problem of getting an individual to make an informed choice about matching contributions when individuals seem to have difficulty making any sort of complex decision about retirement saving. In 2005, Watson Wyatt conducted a survey of U.K. individuals in which half were presented with a graph of annuity payouts as a function of age and given a choice between a level annuity and an indexed annuity. The other group was presented with the same choice in tabular form. Figure 16.2 and table 16.1 present the choices given to individuals.

FIGURE 16.2 **Graphical presentation of annuity choices**

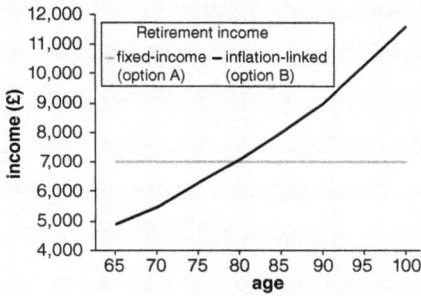

SOURCE: Watson Wyatt Limited 2006.

TABLE 16.1 **Tabular presentation of annuity choices**

Age	Annuity (£)	Inflation-linked annuity (£)
65	7,000	4,900
70	7,000	5,500
75	7,000	6,300
80	7,000	7,100
85	7,000	8,000
90	7,000	9,000
95	7,000	10,300
100	7,000	11,600

SOURCE: Watson Wyatt Limited 2006.

The results are shown in figure 16.3. Sixty-five percent of those shown the table picked a level annuity, whereas only 48 percent of those shown the graph picked a level annuity. Clearly, the form of presentation of options matters.

One could infer a similar dichotomy to choice on contribution levels with matching contributions. The impact of a decision of an individual's choice of contribution level on the flow of funds into an account can be illustrated either graphically or as a table. Although the numbers in a graph and table could be the same, individuals could draw different conclusions.

FIGURE 16.3 Choice between annuities

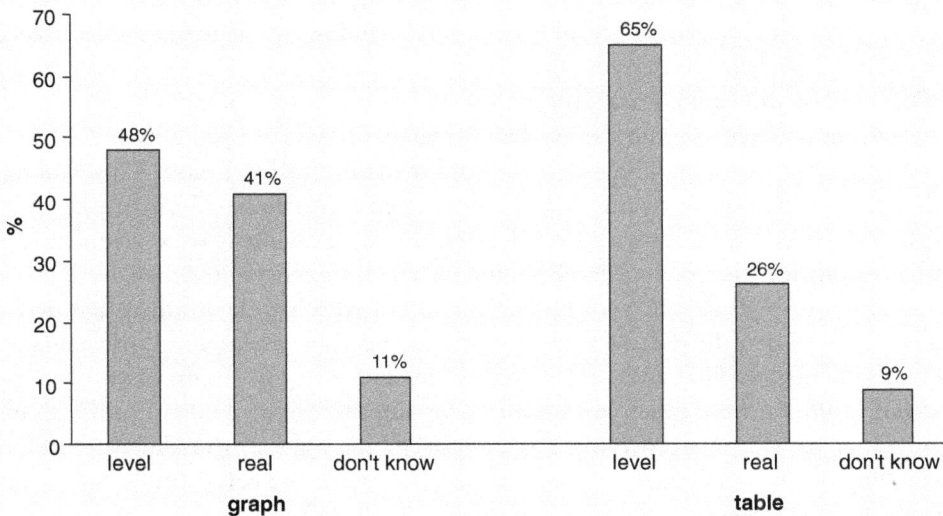

SOURCE: Watson Wyatt Limited 2006.

The importance of communication in decision making is illustrated by work Towers Watson has done with employee/employer data over time. This research found that communication plans often have more impact on decisions than matching programs. An analysis of individual-level data for more than 306,000 workers at 48 firms indicates that communication has a significant impact on contribution and participation rates. In general, high levels of communication increase participation quite significantly over a baseline case of low communication, although low communication will clearly be better than no communication. There does not appear to be a significant age gradient in how communication affects participation rates in defined contribution plans. In the context of matching plans, there is little evidence to suggest that the effectiveness of communication will be age specific, which in turn implies that communication issues are pervasive across all age groups instead of specific to one age segment (Towers Watson 2011). The likely cause of this outcome is that without meaningful assistance individuals typically get the answers to complex questions wrong. For example, when in 2003 Towers Watson asked individuals which investment offered the best protection against inflation, only 19 percent were able to correctly identify an index bond as that vehicle; this result was in the United Kingdom, where indexed bonds had been in place for two decades.

There is clear evidence across many markets that individuals have difficulty making highly technical decisions, and matching is inherently technical particularly if the matching structure is nonlinear. While individuals cannot make technical decisions very well, there is a fair amount of evidence that individuals do a better job with intuitive decisions. Evidence of this can be found in a three-country study in which individuals in Germany, Holland, and the United Kingdom were able to adjust their retirement choices using a dashboard. The survey format was unique in that it started with a set of standard questions on desired income, retirement age, and risk tolerance, and used these to populate a dashboard with which individuals could explore trade-offs involving risk and levels of benefits. All decisions were tracked, and individuals were subsequently asked why they had made the changes they did. In the three countries, the percentages of respondents who rated the survey as good or average on these parameters of length, understanding, relevance, and interface were 99 percent, 83 percent, 96 percent, and 96 percent, respectively. The decisions emerging from the exercise were quite reasonable, and indicated that individuals did have reasonably heterogeneous preferences, with a heavy bias for safety (Towers Watson 2009).

The social context in which decisions are made is also important. This finding is indicated by a quasi-experimental survey undertaken in Australia, Germany, the Netherlands, the United Kingdom, and the United States. Individuals were given different default options for their savings levels. Some were given no default; others were given a low, medium, or high default with no explanation of who had determined that default. Others were told that the default level was recommended by an employer, friends/family, or a financial advisor. The results were striking. In contrast to the findings of other studies, defaults did not have much impact on saving rates (mean or median) in the absence of context as to who was providing the choice. For example, in the United States, the mean saving rate was 6.3 percent in the absence of a default and 6.1, 5.6, and 6.7 percent, respectively in the presence of low, medium, and high defaults with no default context provided. In no country was the difference between default results and decisions without defaults significant. However, the difference became very significant in the presence of context—for instance, when the individual was told that an employer had recommended the default. Interestingly, outcomes varied considerably by country setting, possibly reflecting differing levels of credibility and trust. In some countries, financial advisers are highly trusted; in others, recommendations of high saving rates from financial advisers are viewed with considerable doubt.

In general, where individuals are searching for credible information in a sea of confusing choices, a trusted party providing implicit guidance though a default or the provision of a matching contribution becomes an effective reference point that can have a powerful influence on outcomes. In the context of matching programs, this suggests that the entity providing the match is particularly important. For example, if employers provide matching contributions and are trusted, the impact on saving may be considerably greater than provision of contributions by a government that is mistrusted. A reasonable precondition for implementing matching contributions would be a credible party to design the matching provisions and other choices to be made by participants.

If individuals were proficient at making informed choices, there would of course be little need for matching contributions. Therefore, the condition that individuals have the ability to make informed choices will never be satisfied fully, but will always be a matter of degree. It is important to keep in mind that a key advantage of matching contributions over strategies such as default options is that the former aim to engage the individual in active decision making and to help the individual learn. In this sense, an important implementation requirement is the capacity to monitor and evaluate choice behavior to ensure progress is being made. It is also important to allow the system to evolve over time.

ADMINISTRATION

Matching contributions impose significant challenges for recordkeeping and administration. The additional payments into the system must be carefully tracked, effectively accumulated into individual accounts, and invested properly; and information about contributions and account balances communicated accurately to participants. Any errors will reduce confidence in the system. If systems cannot handle the complexity of the choices required to be made or can only implement these expensively, the benefits of defined contribution and matching programs will be significantly diluted.

Administration costs are a significant component of the total costs of running a defined contribution system. While much literature and thinking have focused on how to minimize investment costs through index funds and other approaches, in practice a large share of costs arise from administration, recordkeeping, and marketing. Consequently, minimizing administration costs is a key element of the enabling environment for matching defined contribution scheme implementation.

One common approach to reducing administrative costs is reliance on the information technology platform. However, individuals consistently exhibit a strong preference for receiving paper rather than electronic statements, and in all but a few environments electronic communication is not feasible for the relevant populations. In higher-income settings, customers consistently refuse to buy packaged financial products that are long term in nature—such as pensions and insurance—through the Internet. Thus any attempt to mitigate the administrative cost issue by establishing information technology as the sole mechanism for administration is doomed to experience significant problems.

Individuals clearly want direct service: they want to be able to call someone up who understands their questions and can help them sort through complex issues and decisions. The presence of credible institutions with experience in handling these sorts of issues for long-term financial products is thus very helpful for successfully implementing a matched defined contribution system. Where customer service is outsourced or "off-shored," individuals will be particularly critical when things go wrong. The cost-benefit of outsourcing and off-shoring thus needs to be weighed against the risk that a perception of poor or remotely provided service could undermine the system.

While it would be a mistake to look only at the information technology system in developing a matched defined contribution system, the quality of that system is extremely important. Misallocated or missing transactions and payments are a major source of participant anxiety and stress. The integrity of contribution records is particularly an issue with matching systems, as changes in contributions need to be linked to any changes in the matching contributions. Matching contribution payments need to be calculated accurately and tracked, and any error has the possibility of resulting in adverse publicity—especially if the customer service arrangements are not up to an appropriate standard.

GOVERNANCE

A high-quality governance system is required to deliver good choices and decent management systems. If choices are not well aligned with the preferences and behavior of target groups and do not evolve in response to changes in these, the system will not be sustainable. If management systems and processes are unreliable, confidence will be undermined. When a matching defined contribution system is first put in place in a country with some significant experience with defined contribution systems in general, the governance issues may be relatively incremental. Still, matching contributions pose unique governance issues that non-MDC systems do not. First, with matching contributions, there is a need for adequate oversight and strategy on the matching contribution rate. There is also a need to continuously monitor take-up of matching contributions and the overall effectiveness of the strategy, communicate the matching contribution design, oversee administration arrangements, and monitor costs. It is especially important to ensure the extra contributions are not being appropriated by intermediaries or service providers such as fund managers through higher charges.

Addressing these challenges requires resources and significant data, system-specific regulations, and the collaboration of many parties whose incentives may be limited. There are several ways to help address these governance challenges:

- Define in advance success metrics (such as coverage) that can be tracked and evaluated over time in an appropriate way
- Establish human capital metrics for the development of management and governance expertise around matching contribution programs
- Define appropriate service standards for components of provision such as administration
- Set up appropriate mechanisms for comparing/measuring best practice from other markets

- Create mechanisms for participant feedback on a regular basis
- Define in advance a planning and review cycle to discuss issues that may arise.

The common thread in this regard is advance planning; thus, there should be significant discussion of governance issues in the run-up to implementing a MDC program.

Governance of a defined contribution pension system requires many specific types of expertise that are often underappreciated. First, there needs to be an understanding of investment options, determining options for individuals to select from, and expertise in selecting and evaluating the performance of fund managers. Second, there needs to be a good understanding of how the advisory process works and monitoring to ensure individuals are making informed choices and intermediaries are acting in accordance with good market practice. Third, there needs to be a good understanding of administrative systems and how to make them work well for defined contribution plans. In general, the provision of choice that is inherent in the matching design makes administration of defined contribution plans more complex. This complexity is exacerbated by the fact that individuals have much less clarity than in traditional pension plans regarding the anticipated nature of their benefits.

Initial Parameters

The relevant initial conditions that affect the best design choice for an MDC scheme vary by country. Table 16.2 shows three stylized cases that can be helpful in thinking about these conditions. The first group of countries is low-income countries with young populations and low coverage rates. The second group is middle-income countries with older populations and higher coverage in which, nonetheless, a significant and persistent gap still exists. The last group is transition socialist economies in Eastern Europe and the former Soviet Union. These countries are at an advanced stage in their demographic transition and have coverage rates higher than would be expected given their income levels. In many transition economies, coverage rates are still declining, as state employment levels fall and the informal sector grows.

These conditions have implications for the short- and long-run prospects of MDCs. One concern is that the matching contribution incentive may lead workers to move from

TABLE 16.2 **Initial conditions affecting the design choice of a matching defined contribution scheme**

Country type	Purchasing power–adjusted income per capita, 2008 ($)	Coverage ratio (%)	Ratio of age 20–59/60+ population (%)
Low income	> 4,500	17	7.6
Middle income	4,500–15,000	51	6.3
Transition economy	2,000–20,000	66	3.7

SOURCE: Author's calculations, based on *World Development Report* tables (http://data.worldbank.org/data-catalog/world-development-indicators).

the formal to the informal sector. This threat is greater in middle-income countries than in low-income countries, especially when the MDC is targeted to the lower end of the income distribution. In middle-income countries and transition economies, the potential to move in and out of the formal sector and game the system tends to be greater, as coverage rates extend well into the bottom half of the distribution. In fact, special attention must be given to the potential for a transition from MDC status to traditional contributory status, as there may be frequent shifts in status and "graduation" out of the targeted population. In low-income countries, in contrast, there is little interaction between the labor force in the bottom deciles and the top deciles where most of the pension coverage occurs, much of it in the public sector (see chapter 12).

Along similar lines, the match that is fixed in a low-income country environment may be set much lower relative to the average wages covered in the contributory scheme for formal sector workers. The MDC plan in Colombia has this feature.[3] In China, too, rural pension levels are not at all comparable to formal sector pensions in urban areas.

In middle-income countries, the match should not be set in such a manner as to influence the decision at the margin as to whether to move to the informal sector. Such a situation could emerge among self-employed workers or through collusion between workers and employers in small firms. One way to address this potential problem is to target occupations that are either de jure or de facto excluded from the contributory scheme. Farmers are one such category in many countries. Another approach is to target households covered by cash transfer programs, where eligibility has already been determined and a recordkeeping infrastructure exists. This option may be particularly attractive for programs that graduate households after a certain number of years or after they reach a certain level of income. In these cases, the subsidy period is finite, and workers can continue to contribute to the scheme after they leave the program, hopefully having become accustomed to the contribution process.

Initial conditions such as the current poverty line and life expectancy also affect key parameters of the MDC scheme, including the target benefit level, the contribution level, the age of withdrawal, the rules for the accumulation phase, and indexation. Each of these parameters is discussed below.

TARGET BENEFIT LEVEL

The target benefit level is the starting point for determining the parameters of the scheme, as the MDC is, by definition, fully funded through its contributions, including the match. The contribution level will therefore depend on the target benefit.

From a public policy viewpoint, a reasonable target would be that someone who participated for most of his or her working life would accrue a benefit sufficient to provide old-age income above the poverty level.[4] How poverty is defined varies across countries. An important distinction is absolute versus relative poverty. In low-income countries, it may be more reasonable to target absolute poverty; in richer countries, relative poverty is often the metric of interest. In either case, the target benefit could allow for other sources of income or could place the entire burden of achieving the target on the MDC scheme. It may be useful to take into account the different needs of the elderly as well as intrahousehold dynamics.

It is good practice to set the target benefit level using objective criteria such as income per capita or an empirically based poverty line (as opposed to politically determined criteria such as the minimum wage). So doing allows for a coherent pension system design, as the parameters can be set to be consistent with both existing contributory and noncontributory schemes or social assistance programs (see discussion below). The absence of a clear and objective rationale for target benefit levels opens the program to arbitrary changes, political manipulation, or both, undermining the original goals of the scheme, including its sustainability, and reducing its credibility in the long run.

CONTRIBUTIONS

Contributions of informal sector workers cannot be easily linked to income, which is not easily verifiable. Instead, a flat amount or several levels of flat contributions would be specified. The match would apply only to these flat amounts up to a ceiling consistent with the target benefits of the scheme. Indexation of contributions is discussed below along with benefit indexation.

The total contribution required to achieve this benefit level—which includes the contributions of both the worker and the government—must be calculated. This calculation is somewhat complicated, as it requires a set of assumptions about the rate of return on investments and the annuity factor. (Even if an annuity is not required, a calculation that translates the projected value of accumulations in an account to a target benefit stream is useful.) Returns (specifically, net returns after fees) depend on what contributors are charged for administering their accounts and the performance of the assets in which they are able to invest. This calculation is necessarily an estimate with a fairly large dispersion of possible outcomes. Shah (2005) presents a good example of how this calculation could be made using historical asset prices and a Monte Carlo simulation approach. In each country, this set of calculations will be different and will result in a different contribution level according to local circumstances.[5] Budget constraints will also have to be taken into account in setting matching levels, determining the target population, or both (as discussed below).

AGE OF WITHDRAWAL

The term *age of withdrawal*, as opposed to *retirement age*, recognizes the fact that many if not most participants in MDC schemes are likely to continue working in one form or another. Typically, however, their ability to maintain their income level is limited. MDC funds can supplement their partial retirement and may eventually provide their only source of income. *Age of withdrawal* is also a more appropriate term to use with regard to people who were never employed outside the home.

In low-income countries, there may be substantial differences between the life expectancy and health status of people covered by formal pension schemes and people covered by an MDC scheme, particularly targeted programs. Restricting withdrawals until the formal system retirement age may not make sense for informal sector workers who are likely to need their savings earlier, as their productivity and therefore their incomes decline. In middle-income countries, where there is greater overlap between people in and outside the formal sector, these differences may not justify different age restrictions.

RULES FOR ACCUMULATION

The main set of rules for the accumulation phase relate to investment options. Low financial literacy is common even in rich countries; a paternalistic view may be even more justified for informal sector workers. As discussed in chapter 15 and elsewhere in this volume, default options are highly influential; limited investment choice with simple portfolio choices that do not require significant financial literacy are preferable. Low-risk alternatives such as government bonds are preferable to government guarantees. At the same time, low risk implies relatively low returns. A possible alternative would be life-cycle defaults, which gradually reduce risk automatically as workers approach retirement age.

RULES FOR WITHDRAWAL

A number of policy choices in addition to age must be made regarding withdrawal of the MDC accumulation upon death or during old age. Funds could be withdrawn in a lump sum, after full or partial annuitization, or in some other form, such as a phased withdrawal (which mimics an annuity but does not pool longevity risk across the group). The choice should take into account the qualification criteria for other programs, such as social assistance. There may be practical reasons for withdrawing as a lump sum, such as balances that are too small to annuitize to consider. An innovative option would be universal pooling of mortality risk to avoid problems of adverse selection in annuity conversions. A simple solution is for the government to offer an actuarially fair annuity based on the mortality rates of the group in question. The annuity could be managed directly or contracted out on a competitive basis.

Allowing at least partial withdrawals for unpredictable expenditures, such as health shocks, would make the program more attractive. These contingencies are difficult and expensive to monitor and enforce, and may inevitably be based on subjective criteria related to needs. The potential need for liquidity suggests that a holistic approach should consider the overall set of risks faced by workers and to use complementary programs, such as health and other types of insurance (for example, crop or cattle insurance), wherever possible.

INDEXATION

In a growing economy with inflation, the initial parameters of the system will soon become inadequate without some form of indexation. Even the absolute poverty line will require adjustment for inflation, even if not for relative income or expenditure. The target benefit level should thus increase over time, at least in nominal terms. As in the case of the initial value, it is important to avoid arbitrary, intercohort variation of the level of the target benefit by indexing it to an objective indicator. The most obvious indicator may be inflation, but other measures that reflect changes in the definition of absolute poverty in a particular country or take into account structural changes (such as the extension of health insurance coverage) can be used.

Any change in the target benefit level implies a change to the contribution level. In order to maintain the initial target in real terms, the contribution could be gradually increased as accumulated price inflation leads to a discrete increase (for example,

10 percent). Alternatively, the contribution may be indexed to changes in per capita income levels, particularly in fast-growth environments, so that it does not become irrelevant to large portions of the contributor population over a few decades. Indexation is the bridge between current and future policy and the role of the MDC in the overall system.

INSTITUTIONAL FACTORS

It is not possible to discuss parameters without considering institutions and other relevant local conditions, especially with regard to the financial sector. Some countries may have specialized providers and regulatory capacity that could make MDC schemes more viable and less costly to establish. In others, local conditions may not be conducive to the MDC approach. This discussion is beyond the scope of this chapter, but has been covered in the broader policy debate over the potential role of defined contribution schemes (see Rocha and Rudolph 2009).

Planning for the Long Run and Internal Consistency

By its nature, pension policy has to be formulated for the long term. The conditions discussed above change as incomes grow, the size of the formal sector expands, and the population ages. These changes mean that the role of the MDC should evolve. Ideally, contributors to the MDC scheme should be seamlessly joined with contributors to the formal contributory scheme. Doing so requires careful planning of the transition path and the portability of benefits. For example, administrative recordkeeping could be harmonized and common identifiers used to allow for portability. In some cases, the same delivery infrastructure and information systems could be used from the outset, reducing set-up costs, as was done in Colombia and India and proposed in Mexico.

Perhaps the most important intersection of policy for MDC schemes is with noncontributory or social pensions. A growing number of countries have introduced or expanded cash transfer programs aimed at the elderly. In some cases, they are targeted to discrete populations or means tested; in other cases, they feature universal age-based categorical benefits. Bolivia, Botswana, Brazil (rural areas), Kosovo, Maldives, and New Zealand provide universal age-based benefits. They provide a floor for old-age income support and a short-term, simple solution to an important policy challenge—the coverage gap. As the population ages, these programs may become expensive, especially if their role goes beyond providing solely a poverty alleviation benefit.[6]

Viewing pension policy in a dynamic manner, MDC schemes (and contributory schemes in general) do little or nothing to address the coverage gap in the near term, because pension income is generated only after decades of accumulation followed by a payout. For people currently reaching old age or who are already old, only a social pension can address the gap in pension coverage. For younger cohorts, expansion of MDC and contributory schemes generally can help address the gap.

In the example in figure 16.4, the changing role of social pensions over time for a hypothetical low-income country is shown. For simplicity, the initial period has zero coverage for the contributory scheme. The figure shows the case of a universal social pension worth 40 percent of income per capita in its first year. Figure 16.4a shows the replacement rate of the social pension value to people with one-third to three times income per capita.

Figure 16.4b shows that, as a share of income per capita, the benefit is equivalent for all recipients across the income spectrum.

FIGURE 16.4 **Replacement rates from universal flat pension for hypothetical worker by income level**

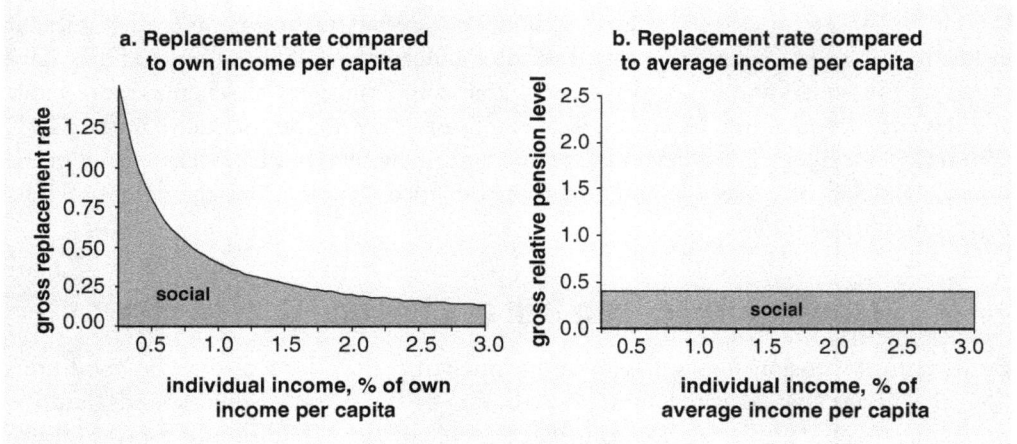

Figure 16.5 shows the situation after 40 years. The simplified example shows what would happen if the initial social pension value was linked to a real absolute poverty line and indexed accordingly. Under reasonable assumptions of real wage growth, the social pension provides a much lower replacement rate of only about 10 percent of income per capita. People who participated in the contributory scheme (partly financed through matching contributions) have earned sufficient pension incomes to make up the difference.

FIGURE 16.5 **Role of social pension after maturation of contributory scheme**

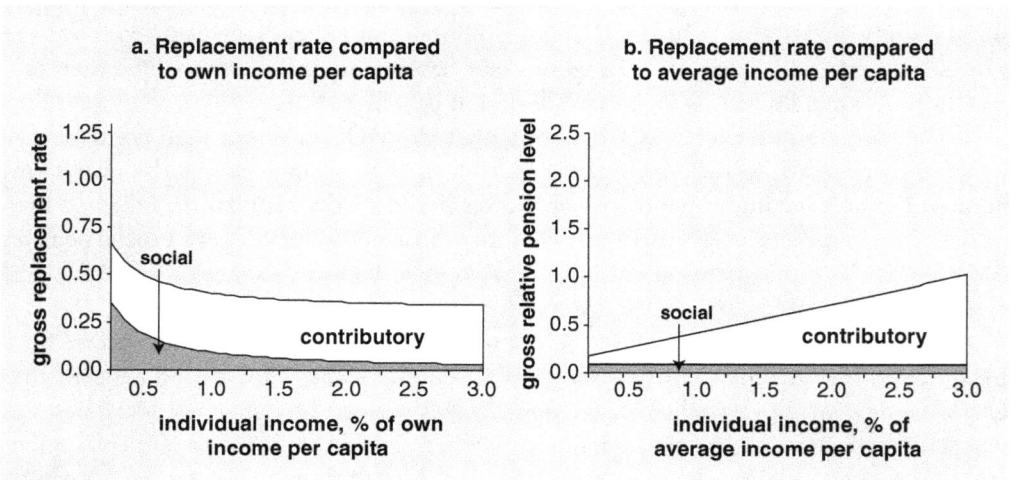

In this case, the contribution is assumed to be 10 percent of income per capita during the entire period (that is, effectively indexed to income growth). Taking into account the net rate of return and annuity factors for the stylized low-income country case, the result is a replacement rate of 40 percent for the average-income person and about 60 percent for the lowest income category.

This microlevel view can be translated into a set of long-run fiscal projections for the cost of the MDC scheme. The starting point is the initial year. Assuming a target benefit level of 40 percent replacement rate and an informal sector that makes up 80 percent of the labor force, half of the 10 percent of income per capita contribution would require 0.8 percent of gross domestic product (GDP), assuming that the match would result in complete take-up. Relaxing this unrealistic assumption and aiming for take-up rates that are more in line with those shown in figure 16.1, about half the informal sector population would receive a match, at a cost of 0.4 percent of GDP. This level of spending could also be achieved by targeting the subsidy.[7] Other variants would involve different matching rates. As discussed earlier, however, there is almost no evidence as to the elasticity of take-up of MDC schemes, especially in developing countries.

The path of these costs would depend on the interaction of the MDC with the other components of the pension system. If, for example, the formal contributory scheme were able to absorb a growing share of the labor force as incomes rose and formalization spread, costs could be gradually reduced without sacrificing the overall objective in terms of pension adequacy. A design that allowed for an offset to the social pension—such as the scheme recently implemented in Chile—could further reduce the total cost to government. In this case, the MDC subsidy reduces future social pension costs.

Conclusions

Coverage in formal pension systems has failed to expand (and in some cases has contracted) in low- and middle-income countries for decades. In many cases, lack of coverage is linked to increasing levels of informal labor or the failure to formalize much of the economy as it develops. Financial incentives linked to income taxes imposed on earnings are associated with higher participation rates in voluntary pensions in high-income countries—although experience in a variety of high-income settings indicates that the relationship between the value of tax preferences and supplemental savings for retirement is not particularly strong. Such incentives are largely irrelevant and may even be regressive in their distributional outcomes in developing countries. In these settings, matching contributions may provide a greater incentive that is more effective in drawing low-income and informal sector workers into the pension system.

Implementation of an MDC pension system in any setting, but especially in the low- and middle-income environments where it has increasingly being presented as an option, should only be considered after careful review of enabling conditions. These include a reasonable capacity of individuals to make informed choices to respond to incentives, administrative capacity to deal with the complexity and challenges of processing contributions and maintaining individual accounts, a reliable governance mechanism, and a sustainable commitment that includes a political environment that will support the system over the decades required for it to mature and pay benefits. Operating a system requires a developed and well-supervised financial system with the appropriate long-term products to reliably accumulate savings and convert these into secure retirement income.

Establishing an MDC pension scheme in a low- or middle-income country will also require effective choices to be made regarding basic parameters so as to align the system with individual needs and objectives. Key factors that should be taken into account in designing an MDC scheme include anticipated contribution flows and individual levels, the size of the match, (although the empirical evidence on how much coverage could be increased through different levels of matching does not yet exist[8]), targets for benefit levels, and rules for withdrawals. In settings in which MDCs are viewed as a useful policy instrument for addressing the coverage gap (taking into account the opportunity cost of the resources required), policy makers must also consider the effect of MDCs on existing contributory and noncontributory pension schemes over the long run. MDCs could otherwise encourage evasion of contributory schemes, and the cost of social pensions could be greater than required to meet public policy objectives as contributory schemes mature.

The combination of all these factors makes the decision to pursue a matching contribution scheme and its design a complex process that will require considerable analysis before it can be effectively implemented.

Notes

1. In fact, in the countries in which public employment has been reduced least, such as Belarus, coverage remains much higher than would be predicted by the level of income per capita (see Pallares-Miralles, Romero, and Whitehouse 2011).

2. The study cited most often, by Duflo and others (2005), is for low-income workers in the United States.

3. The Colombian scheme is called Beneficios Económicos Periódicos (Periodic Economic Benefits), as it could not legally be termed a pension, which according to the country's constitution cannot be lower than the minimum wage.

4. In practice, there will be contribution gaps (contribution density will be less than 100 percent), which will vary widely across workers. Allowing some flexibility in the timing of the match may be warranted. For example, matching could be cumulative over a multiyear period rather than annual. Such a feature would add to the complexity of system administration, however, and has limitations.

5. See chapter 12 for a discussion of India.

6. The second key objective for pension policy is consumption smoothing. Most countries use contribution-based schemes to achieve this objective. New Zealand is one of the few countries that provided only a universal pension until recently, when it made efforts to increase voluntary contributory pensions to address the consumption-smoothing objective. See chapter 5 for a detailed description.

7. Alternatively, a budget envelope could be established and take-up rationed on a first-come, first-served basis.

8. See Palacios and Robalino (2009) for simulations of different take-up elasticities.

References

Duflo, E., W. Gale, J. Liebman, P. Orszag, and E. Saez. 2005. "Savings Incentives for Low- and Middle-Income Families: Evidence from a Field Experiment with H&R Block." NBER Working Paper 11680, National Bureau of Economic Research, Cambridge, MA.

Godfrey, P. C. 2011. "Toward a Theory of the Informal Economy." *Academy of Management Annals* 5 (1): 231–77.

ISSA (International Social Security Administration). 2011. *MBAO Pension Plan.* Good Practices in Social Security Series, ISSA, Geneva.

Loayza, N. 1997. "The Economics of the Informal Sector." Policy Research Working Paper 1727, World Bank, Washington, DC.

Palacios, R., and D. A. Robalino. 2009. "Matching Defined Contributions: A Way to Increase Pension Coverage." In *Closing the Coverage Gap: The Role of Social Pensions and Other Retirement Income Transfers*, ed. R. Holzmann, D. A. Robalino, and N. Takayama, 187–202. Washington, DC: World Bank.

Pallares-Miralles, M., C. Romero, and E. Whitehouse. 2011. "International Patterns of Pension Provision II: Worldwide Overview of Facts and Figures." Draft, World Bank, Washington, DC.

Rocha, R., and H. Rudolf. 2009. "Enabling Conditions for Second Pillars of Pension Systems." Policy Research Working Paper 4890, World Bank, Washington, DC.

Shah, A. 2005. "Pension Outcomes Associated with Alternative Asset Allocation Under the New Pension System." Unpublished.

———. 2009. *Directions: A New Lens on Retirement Preferences.* http://www.watsonwyatt.com/pubs/directions/.

———. 2011. "Clear Direction in a Complex World: How Top Companies Create Clarity, Confidence and Community to Build Sustainable Performance. 2011–2012." http://www.towerswatson.com/united-kingdom/research/6639.

Watson Wyatt Limited. 2006. "The Pension Research Forum Research Results: DC Investment Choice—Can Employees Make Appropriate Investment Decisions?" Watson Wyatt Limited, London.